ENVISIONING REFORM

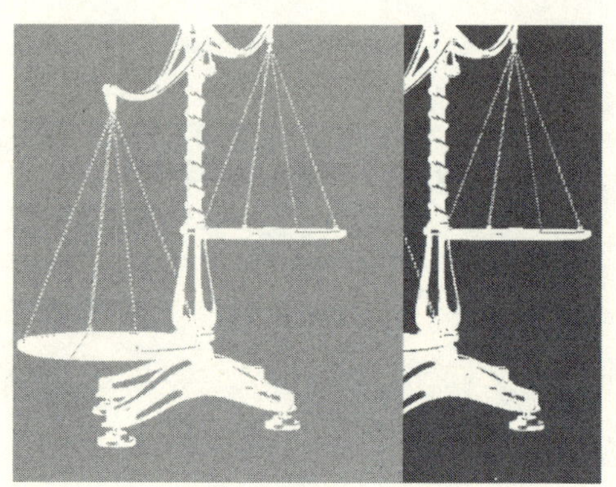

ENVISIONING REFORM

IMPROVING JUDICIAL PERFORMANCE IN LATIN AMERICA

LINN HAMMERGREN

THE PENNSYLVANIA STATE UNIVERSITY PRESS
UNIVERSITY PARK, PENNSYLVANIA

Library of Congress Cataloging-in-Publication Data

Hammergren, Linn A.
    Envisioning reform : improving judicial performance in
    Latin America / Linn Hammergren.
        p.   cm.
Includes bibliographical references and index.
ISBN-13: 987-0-271-02933-5 (cloth : alk. paper)
ISBN-10: 0-271-02933-1 (cloth : alk. paper)
1. Judicial reform—Latin America.
2. Justice, Administration of—Latin America.
I. Title.

KG86.H36 2007
347.8—dc22
2006032378

The Pennsylvania State University Press is a member of
the Association of American University Presses.

CONTENTS

ACKNOWLEDGMENTS

This book is the product of twenty years of working on and thinking about judicial reform in Latin America and occasionally elsewhere. As the author, I owe an enormous debt to a list of individuals so long it would constitute a chapter in itself. They are the people who have taught me; worked with me and sometimes for me; shared their experiences and opinions; offered their data, documents, and written thoughts for my consideration; apprised me of other work relevant to my own ponderings; opened their courts and offices so I could make my own observations; invited me to conferences and workshops as a participant or speaker; encouraged me to write; reviewed and criticized this and other manuscripts; tolerated my interviews and occasionally impertinent questions; and sometimes frustrated me to the point of having to get my ideas down on paper. The present book in fact was inspired by a series of debates among friends. Our inability to reach agreement on a few fine points of reform produced the first and second chapters, and from there it grew. Thus, to Juan Enrique and Alberto I owe a debt of which they may have been completely unaware.

For the rest, a list would not suffice and in any event, would inevitably run the risk of significant exclusions. Those who have put their own ideas on paper or into Internet exchanges are recognized in the references and footnotes. For the numerous others, both advocates and opponents of the reforms, I apologize for the absence of a more explicit acknowledgment, but it was just not humanly possible. As for my two principal employers, the U.S. Agency for International Development and the World Bank, I should recognize that, wittingly or not, they provided the opportunity for a twenty-year education on the theme but that they are not responsible for what I made of it or what is written here. I thank Sandy Thatcher of Penn State University Press for having taken the trouble to review this project; Joseph Parsons, who did the massive copyediting; Michael Dodson and Keith Rosenn for providing useful critiques; and Anne Pillay for typing up the final manuscript.

INTRODUCTION: TWENTY YEARS OF REFORMS AND NOT A CONSENSUS IN SIGHT

OVERVIEW

Judicial reform remains a growth industry in Latin American, for both practitioners and, increasingly, their critics. Nearly twenty years of experience in promoting change in the region's judiciaries seems hardly to have tapped the potential or dampened the enthusiasm for arming new programs. Courts, which once regarded the reforms with utmost suspicion, now have become proponents in their own right. They have been joined by a wide variety of domestic and international players who also want a part in defining what will be done and providing assistance in carrying it out. The reform agenda has expanded well beyond the judiciary, including police, prosecution, public defense, the private bar, and law schools and extending into legal and regulatory areas where courts often have little relevance. Although the present discussion will focus on judicial reform, it is worth noting that the judiciary is no longer the sole target and thus that the substitution of such titles as legal and judicial, justice, or rule of law reform is more than a semantic exercise.

Despite near-universal consensus on its importance, the reform movement has been subjected to external questioning almost since its inception. As its practitioners often complained, much of this was based on little if any knowledge of the situation on the ground. The critics often got their facts wrong;[1] slighted over the

---

1. Where this was most obvious was in the descriptions of donor programs. Differences between grants (used by bilateral donors) and loans (by the multilateral banks) seem to escape many of the early critics. The World Bank is still charged with having supported a large judicial reform project in Peru under the Fujimori government despite, to its credit, having pulled out at the last minute (as documented in Lawyers Committee for Human Rights 2000). Critics often speak of the U.S. government as a single agency, overlooking the different, and often conflicting roles of USAID, the Department of Justice, the State Department, and the Drug Enforcement Agency, to name just a few of the many players. (See Salas 2001 for one of the few written discussions of the differences.) There are also frequent errors in describing national practices or the contents of reforms. An additional problem for anyone writing about the region is the rapid pace at which legally mandated procedures and organizational structures change or the fact that so many legal changes remain paper transformations at best. Still, critics seem reluctant to credit any advances, often relying on outdated descriptions of vices and weaknesses that are gradually being eliminated. For a discussion of some of these problems as encountered in an otherwise excellent overview (Méndez et al. 1999) of the region's systems, see Hammergren (2000b).

political and practical impediments to rapid change; confused poor planning, inadequate information, or simple incompetence with lack of will and hidden agendas; called for more donor intervention where it appeared inadvisable; and criticized it when it occurred.

In this regard, the past decade has seen a dramatic change. There has been a proliferation of books and articles describing reforms in a number of the region's countries, many of them written by observers with substantial experience both with local judiciaries and with the reform programs.[2] Despite their insider's view, or better-documented outsider's perspective, the authors have been no less harsh in their assessments of the movement's achievements or of its chances of eventual success. They almost inevitably find major shortcomings in a series of design and implementation flaws or in participants' failure to tackle the fundamental causes of poor performance. In the majority view, most reforms are still on the wrong track and thus, if they get anywhere, will likely arrive at the wrong destination.

What remains unclear is whether their comments are having any impact on current reform trends or, in fact, whether the reform practitioners are learning much from one another. One emerging criticism on which many observers agree is that participants are constantly reinventing the wheel, when not attempting to produce one with square edges.[3] A twenty-year-old reform movement in which the major actors simply forge ahead without engaging in constructive dialogue or building on each others experience is unusual to say the least. The situation is both perplexing and symptomatic of some basic weaknesses in the overall effort. The goal of the present work is to explore the problem, explain its causes, and suggest some remedies that might improve both the impact of ongoing programs and the theoretical and empirical foundations underlying the design of new ones.

Judicial reform is still very much an advocate's art. Its practitioners generally prefer axiomatic principles to testable hypotheses and action to contemplative evaluation. Their external critics are no less susceptible to these leanings. Ideology and subjective preferences continue to shape their understandings of what has been attempted, what is possible, and what was accomplished. In recent years, another, less noticed development has aggravated the traditional gap between those who act and those who critique—the fact that between and within each group the definitions of reform and of the objectives it pursues have also diverged. It is no longer clear that we are talking about the same phenomenon and, thus, that the criteria applied for assessing its achievements are universally relevant.

2. Binder and Obando (2004), articles in Carbonell (n.d.), Castelar, ed. (2003), Correa (1999), articles in Domingo and Sieder (2001), Dezalay and Garth (2002), articles in González Compeán and Bauer (2002), Fix Fierro (1995 and 1999), Hammergren (1998e), articles in Jensen and Heller (2003), chapters in Pásara, ed., 2004, Popkin (2000), Prillaman (2000), Sadek (2004), Thome (1998), and Ungar (2002).

3. See Carothers (2003) for one of the strongest statements of this point and one that has aroused extremely negative reactions from practitioners. For other discussions, see articles in Jensen and Heller (2003).

When Latin America's current round of judicial reforms began in the early 1980s, the task looked daunting but fairly straightforward. Following decades of neglect so pronounced they were commonly termed the "orphan branch of government," frequent political interference, and consequent internal disorder, the region's judiciaries were widely regarded as incapable of performing their basic functions in a fair and competent manner.[4] Whether couched as an effort to improve an essential public service or raise the missing pillar of democratic governance,[5] the aim was to strengthen the courts and other sector institutions to make them more efficient, effective, and accessible while enhancing their role in checking illegal actions by governmental and private actors.[6] "Strengthening," a favorite word of reformers, meant increasing judicial independence, updating laws and internal processes, professionalizing judges and other judicial employees, adding modern technology, improving administrative systems, and educating the private bar and the public in general to make them better users of judicial services. As for why this needed to be done, the answer was equally simple: courts existed to resolve conflicts by applying and, where required, interpreting established legal norms. In the process, they reinforced the legal framework itself. To the extent courts were not performing these roles in accord with social expectations, they needed to be reformed. There are certainly more elegant and sophisticated means of reaching this conclusion and more complex understandings of what courts do and how they do it. It should be emphasized, however, that the reformers' vision did not derive from weighty theoretical arguments about the judiciary's place, but rather from concrete complaints about court performance and their own observations as to what appeared not to be working.[7] In societies less influenced by Western juridical traditions, they might have been accused of applying an ethnocentric model, but, at a general level, local expectations were fairly congruent with their own.

More than twenty years into the process, the initial simplicity appears disingenuous. On the one hand, the justifications for the reforms have become more complex. Reform is no longer a question of making an institution of government carry out its official role, but rather of enhancing its contribution to a number of

4. A detailed discussion of this "internal disorder" and its impact on basic services is provided in the following five chapters, each of which deals with one aspect of the situation.

5. The third pillar metaphor comes from the President's National Bipartisan Commission on Central America (1984) reviewing the prospects for democratic governance in Central America.

6. See Alvarez (1992) for a good statement of early USAID objectives. See Blair and Hansen (1994) for an official agency statement, heralding the shift to access goals and a downgrading of institutional strengthening (called "capacity building").

7. A series of country studies conducted by Florida International University summarize the initial situation as perceived by foreign and local reformers. Several of the reports were later published independently. See Chinchilla and Stodt (1993); Florida International University (1987); Gamarra (1991); and Rico et al. (1993). Thome (1992) is also relevant. Although this work was commissioned by USAID, the findings influenced other donors as well.

broader social projects. Well-functioning judicial systems are supposed to control government abuses and protect basic human and civil rights; create an environment that fosters the development of market-based economies; deter crime and civil violence; reduce levels of societal conflict; support the development of legitimate democratic governance; and reduce social inequities by helping spread the benefits of development to marginalized groups. However one feels about the validity of each of these arguments, they collectively reinforce the importance of the entire undertaking.

On the other hand, the number of activities included in justice (no longer judicial) reforms also continues to increase, now including

- Creation, strengthening of judicial governance bodies,
- Legal and other measures to enhance judicial independence (for example, higher budgets, tenured careers),
- Improved selection systems for judges and support personnel,
- Courtroom administration,
- Judicial (system) administration,
- Information and communication technology,
- Training programs,
- Introduction of monitoring, evaluation systems,
- Judicial disciplinary systems,
- Judicial ethics codes and citizen complaint services,
- Strengthening of auxiliary institutions (police, prosecution, and public defense) in all the above areas,
- Modernization of legal framework to regulate new economic and social practices,
- Simplification of procedural codes,
- Modification of legal codes and procedures to strengthen human, civil, and due process rights,
- Legal-assistance programs,
- Reforms of professional associations,
- Popular legal education,
- Strengthening of legally oriented nongovernmental organizations (NGOs),
- Court annexed and freestanding alternative dispute resolution (ADR),
- Recognition/strengthening of traditional (indigenous) dispute-resolution systems,
- Constitutional courts and judicial review powers for supreme courts,
- Promotion of public-interest law and means of protecting collective and diffuse interests,
- Creation of specialized courts,
- Creation of small claims and other courts for poor populations,
- Integration of administrative court systems into the ordinary judiciary,

- Creation of independent regulatory agencies with adjudicative powers, outside of the ordinary court system, and
- Dejudicialization of some issues traditionally seen by the courts.

This is only a partial, illustrative list, but it should be evident that it contains internal contradictions. Although individual reforms often mix and match several objectives and activities, and a few appear in virtually every large program, a case can be made for the gradual emergence of a series of reforms or reform strategies.[8] Each of them incorporates a different vision of the judiciary's essential role in and impact on broader societal development and thus implies different objectives and means to reach them. Moreover, although a truly "holistic" project often works on several fronts at once, the compatibility of the aims, visions of the judicial role, use of the necessary components, and financial implications are not at all apparent. The parallel tracks do help explain some of the external criticisms. A reform intended to increase courts' efficiency in processing cases may introduce elements not completely in line with an access-enhancement strategy or one augmenting the judiciary's ability to check governmental abuses. Sometimes this is just a matter of priorities. The efforts to improve criminal justice proceedings do consider efficiency, but only on a secondary plane. In other cases, the ends pursued really are different, and both the external critics and the reform designers either fail to see the conflict or choose not to take it into account.

These different definitions of reform, with their corresponding objectives and strategies, could be seen as mutually exclusive alternatives. The divergences, however, seem more a consequence of varying emphasis. Like the fable of the blind sages attempting to describe an elephant, each is capturing only a part of the whole. The underlying challenge is how to combine the partial appreciations into a single definition and model. If the model cannot reconcile the differences, it can recognize them as explicit political choices, which at some point in its development may produce divergent designs. Proceeding obliviously on parallel tracks has its disadvantages not only in terms of tactical inconsistencies and unrealized synergies, but also because, in the long run, each works to maximize a different set of values and define a different end point. Contemporary reformers in the industrialized nations have begun to note the inherent contradictions and thus necessary trade-offs in the various values defining good judicial performance—goals relating to costs, access, efficiency, efficacy, and basic fairness at some point come into conflict with

8. If this was ever a unique conclusion, it by now is shared with several other observers. Kleinfeld (2005), while attributing the problem to competing definitions of the rule of law, makes a similar argument. Alvaro Santos has shared with the author several versions of a still unpublished article on how groups within the World Bank complicate that organization's work with their varying approaches to the role of law and thus to judicial reform.

each other, and thus require fundamental political choices.[9] These same and other observers have also begun to question the historical model of the judiciary's role and operations, which suggests that it may itself require modification.[10] The various Latin American approaches to reform in some sense arise as extrapolations from this traditional model and, to the extent they do, may be incorporating its logical inconsistencies.

These comments focus on emerging problems. They should not divert attention from what two decades of efforts have achieved, the substantial changes produced in the sector's resources, composition, and activities. The appearance of Latin American judiciaries and other sector organizations has changed a great deal in twenty years, and they operate differently as well. Many of the partial goals have indeed been advanced—as witnessed by higher budgets; better salaries and career status for judges and other personnel; new organizations and substantial restructuring of traditional ones; a greater penetration of the national territory with services now delivered in more areas and to more of the population; changes in internal procedures; reduction of some traditional ills; and greater political presence.[11] Nonetheless, as a whole, Latin American judicial systems seem no closer to meeting citizen expectations. Changes in internal structures and practices are not reflected in changes in outputs, or at least not sufficiently to meet increased and more discriminating demands. Over time, public opinion polls show no great improvement in citizen appreciations of the quantity or quality of services or of the organizations' dedication to achieving them.[12]

9. See chapters in Zuckerman (1999) for a good discussion. See also Jolowicz (2000). For an early discussion of some contradictions emerging in the constitutional area, see Tate and Vallinder (1995).

10. From the reformers' standpoint, many of these questions relate to the expectation that courts will resolve all conflicts in societies where that seems increasingly impossible. See chapters in Zuckerman (1999). On this point Komesar (1994) offers an approach based on the strengths and weaknesses of different institutional alternatives for resolving societal disputes. Shapiro (1981) provides another line of argument, drawing on comparative examples to question basic assumptions about the characteristics of courts. See Burbank and Friedman (2002) for contrasting views on the role and nature of judicial independence.

11. Although observers tend to focus on weaknesses, they have generally been willing to concede these points. See works cited in note 2 above. Correa (1999) offers an explicit discussion of changes in criminal justice, though with questions as to their impact, especially for the poor.

12. As a rule, no Latin American judiciary scores any higher than 40 percent in terms of citizen approval, and many have approval rates ranging between 10 and 30 percent. See Martínez (1997, 21). The high scorers are Costa Rica and Uruguay. Peru's experience may be more typical. When Alberto Fujimori staged his auto-golpe in 1992, more than 90 percent of citizens supported his closure of the courts because of rampant corruption and incompetence. After some slight improvements during the early 1990s, a recent poll (December 2002) in Lima asking respondents to name the institution in which they had least trust, found the courts being mentioned, spontaneously, by 43 percent. Although Latin Americans usually complain about corruption and incompetence, it should be recognized that satisfaction with court performance is not all that high (and less than commonly believed) in the developed world as well. Toharia (2003, 29) reports citizens' belief in court efficiency is only 33 percent in the United Kingdom, 14 percent in France, and 8 percent in Italy. Still, citizens in Finland, Denmark, and Austria have a largely positive view of their judiciaries. Unlike most Latin American polls, Toharia's work distinguished among several dimensions of criticism, finding in some cases that it is the "system" not the judges that gets most of the blame.

Moreover, the changes have brought new complaints. More-independent supreme and constitutional courts routinely engage in conflicts with other branches of government, declaring the illegality of high-priority programs or insisting on larger investments in nonpriority areas. For the first time in the region, there are criticisms of policymaking by unaccountable judges.[13] Judicial councils and other new governance mechanisms demonstrate no marked improvement in the quality of budgetary or human resource management and often have entered into confrontations with the organizations they are supposed to oversee.[14] The introduction of judicial careers and secure tenure has brought complaints that "bad" judges now enjoy considerable immunity and that judicial leadership has been lax in monitoring performance and removing the ethically unfit.[15] Higher budgets seem only to produce demands for more funding and a notable disinclination to subject its use to ordinary accountability mechanisms.[16] For many courts, budgetary independence seems to mean they should get what they want and spend it as they see fit. Access-enhancement programs have increased budgetary outlays without necessarily improving service delivery to target groups; moreover, there are indications of a negative impact on juridical security. With more cases and more diverse issues being adjudicated, outcomes have become less predictable, both at the trial and appeal levels. Efficiency-enhancement mechanisms have in some cases posed new barriers to poor users, as demonstrated by a marked reduction in annual filings in several countries.[17] The list goes on, but the more general point is that the once-orphan branch of government is now attracting more attention, much of it critical. Enhanced powers and resources have increased the judiciary's impact so that how they use them has become much more important.

13. See Wilson et al. (2004) on Costa Rica and Fuentes and Amaya (2001) on Colombia. Three other countries where court interference with government policy is a complaint are Brazil, Argentina, and Peru. For Brazil, see Ballard (1999) and Santiso (2003). Argentina's experience has recently received attention because of difficulties it posed in reaching an agreement with the IMF in January, 2002. When judges at all levels consistently overruled the government's emergency economic measures, the fund expressed concern about the lack of control over the judiciary. Peru's experience is also very recent, but the post-Fujimori constitutional tribunal has begun to overturn some decisions of the prior administration on the basis of their violation of constitutional rights. Terrorist cases and dismissals of government workers are prime targets.

14. See Hammergren (2002a).

15. The most dramatic example was the threatened impeachment of the entire Argentine Supreme Court in 2002 and 2003. Although politically motivated, it was based on the large number of uninvestigated complaints lodged against every one of the justices. In post-Fujimori Peru, much criticism has been directed against the judicial council for its failure to remove judges believed to be corrupt, and especially those remaining from or being reinstated after the end of the Fujimori government.

16. The Mexican federal judiciary, which currently receives about 1.4 percent of the federal budget is campaigning for a constitutional earmark. It originally aimed at 6 percent, but later reduced its demands to 2.4.

17. This is often connected to the introduction of court fees, in part to discourage frivolous litigation. A study done in Ecuador (Simon et al. 2002) shows an immediate decline in filings following the fees' instatement.

Reform programs had not anticipated these problems and have yet to develop a means for addressing them. For many reformers, they do not exist, at least not in terms of the objectives they are promoting. For virtually every development occasioning alarm on the part of some observers, there are backers arguing that it has not gone far enough. On the one hand, budgets should be still higher, courts more activist, users afforded more due process guarantees, judges better protected from removal, and services further expanded. On the other, judicial councils should have more control over appointments and promotions, discipline and accountability should be increased, dispositions expedited, conflicts dejudicialized, and costs cut or passed on to the users. The goals are all admirable, but in conjunction anything but consistent. As the contradictions are only now becoming apparent, the task ahead is for the reforming countries to decide how to deal with them. The present volume does not assume to do that for them. Its ambitions are more modest—to highlight the inherent dilemmas, explore the alternatives for resolving them, and so encourage the interested parties' collective reexamination of what they are attempting to create. This treatment should also help external observers understand why such discussions are increasingly necessary and what the arguments represent.

A BRIEF HISTORY OF THE CONTEMPORARY LATIN AMERICAN
JUDICIAL REFORMS

As must be apparent from the discussion so far, one initial problem is defining judicial reform. The best we can do is tie the definition to the targeted entities. Judicial or justice-sector reforms are thus programs that attempt to improve the performance and impact of court or sector operations. *Sector* is itself a vague term, but it is usually taken to encompass those institutions most closely related to the courts—police, prosecution, public defense, and the private bar. How reformers define *improvement*, what means they use to achieve it, and how they measure success vary. The first section of this work looks in greater detail at a series of the most common approximations. Whereas some authors attempt to summarize the goals in terms of a short list of common goals—access, efficiency, and independence—these have not figured in all reforms, and, even where they do, they receive different definitions and different emphases.[18] As several observers have noted, we may all agree on the desirability of these three general goals, but additional clarification is needed before they can guide action. As just a start, several further questions loom large: access to what,[19] efficiency of what,[20] and independence from

18. Most notably Prillaman (2000), but others have also used these categories or other, similar ones.

19. As has been repeatedly noted, access to justice is not the same as access to the courts; it could be both more and less.

whom?[21] As we will see, even those pursuing an apparently similar end often appear to answer those basic questions quite differently. They also are quite capable of ignoring the other elements of the short list. A first point then is that all judicial reforms are not the same and that, evaluated in their own terms, they require different criteria for assessing success. A second is that there really is no universal consensus on the aims and content of reforms, whether in Latin America or worldwide. Behind this is a lack of agreement on the contemporary judicial role. Although both points will be elaborated at length in the following chapters, a brief historical treatment of the movement's evolution in Latin America provides us with a start.

Judicial reform became a part of the Third World development agenda at the beginning of the 1980s.[22] Three events were instrumental to its emergence: first, the redemocratization of Latin America, where the movement really initiated;[23] second, the move to create or strengthen market economies (first in the former Soviet Bloc) and its connection to judicial performance; and third, the discovery, by development theorists, of second-generation (institutional) reforms.[24] The different timing and content of these three events, as well as the addition of other elements (the rise in crime rates following the creation of more open political systems, the impact of economic globalization, and an increasing reliance on the judiciary to resolve political conflicts, once handled by fiat or simply nonexistent under prior regimes) have generated considerable confusion concerning the ultimate objectives of the reform movement both in Latin America and elsewhere. That confusion has its positive side. It has helped attract broader support for what otherwise might be perceived as a dull, thoroughly esoteric set of programs. At the same time, however, it has also discouraged and complicated the evaluation of their underlying premises and eventual achievements.

In Latin America, the first round of reforms, in the early 1980s, focused largely on criminal justice from the standpoint of containing human rights abuses and ending the impunity of abusers. On the Latin American side, the reforms drew on

---

20. Jolowicz (2000, 319).

21. Here there is also a tendency to conflate independence with other values such as impartiality, honesty, and competence, though independent courts and judges are quite capable of being biased, corrupt, and incompetent. See USAID (2002b) and Burbank and Friedman (2002), for a more nuanced approach.

22. It was of course preceded by the law and development movement of the 1960s and 1970s. Although the two share many characteristics, law and development (see Gardner 1980; Alvarez 1992; Salas 2001) had already declared itself over, and in terms of scope, objectives, and participation the post-1980 reforms are quantitatively and qualitatively different.

23. Correa (1999) is particularly eloquent on the renewed importance of the courts with the democratic opening. See also President's Bipartisan National Commission on Central America (1984), with its contention that the judiciary is the forgotten pillar of democratic governance.

24. The World Bank has been the most prominent promoter of this connection, drawing on the work of North (1990) and others. See Burki and Perry (1998), Webb (1996), and World Bank Institute (1997, 2002).

a longer-standing interest in adopting more accusatory procedures, which the proponents believed were more respectful of due process rights than the existing inquisitorial systems.[25] Allowing for variations of detail, the traditional Latin American system featured the investigation of a purported crime by an instructional (or investigative) judge and its presentation to the trial judge (in some cases the same person) in the form of a written dossier (*expediente*). The process lent itself to a series of abuses, many of which were arguably not a necessary consequence of the basic structure.[26] Nonetheless, to overcome these problems, the reformers had proposed the transition to an accusatory proceedings, featuring investigation by an independent prosecutor (rather than a judge), provision of defense counsel who would conduct his own investigation, oral trials in which both the prosecution and defense presented their own evidence and arguments, and a decision by a judge or jury who would hear the arguments for the first time and so be able to assess them more objectively.

The reforms received financial backing and additional impetus from foreign donors, especially the United States. The latter added an interest in prosecuting state agents who had perpetrated abuses.[27] In the short run, this additional interest occupied another parallel track. The main thrust of the reforms was the drafting and enactment of new procedural codes. Donor concerns often were realized in funding of special investigative units or diplomatic pressures to resolve certain cases. When the opening to democracy brought with it an increase in ordinary criminality (either as a result of the end of dictatorial control or, in the case of post-conflict countries, the release into civilian life of former combatants), the two interests were reunited and the code reforms were presented as a means of both guaranteeing due process rights and more effectively combating crime.[28] As developed in the next chapter, this semantic sleight of hand overlooked some real problems in the codes themselves and the potentially contradictory ends they were supposed to pursue.

25. This movement goes back to the 1960s and the Latin American model codes movement. See Llobet Rodríguez (1993). A group of Argentine jurists have been especially active in promoting the change throughout the region. See Maier et al. (1993) and Davis and Lillo (1996).

26. These include the delegation of judicial functions to untrained courtroom staff, the complete failure of the police to cooperate with the judicial investigation, the investigating judge's dual role as sentencing judge, as well as delays, bias, impunity, and, of course, various forms of corruption.

27. U.S. support began in Central America at the end of the various civil conflicts in that region. The first project was in El Salvador, where the murder of four U.S. religious workers was a special interest for the U.S. Government. See Popkin (2000), Prillaman (2000, 39–73), Spence and Vickers (1994), Spence et al. (1995), and Hammergren (1998e, 206–19), for discussions.

28. To my knowledge, this have never been documented in writing, but those, like the author, who were in the region in the early 1990s are well aware that the shift in purposes involved no immediate change in the draft codes. In fact, USAID workers used to joke that, when a congressional or other U.S. delegation visited, it was well to determine whether they were human rights advocates or crime fighters so as to know which message to push.

While the Latin American reformers were most interested in new laws, it soon became apparent that absent other changes they would have little impact on either of the objectives. Thus, the subsequent history of the criminal justice reforms demonstrates a growing recognition and incorporation of additional elements to turn legal theory into practice. These included training programs, the creation of new organizations (public defense and prosecution), restructuring and reorientation of existing ones (the courts, police, and, where they already were present, public ministries responsible for prosecution),[29] provision of new equipment and infrastructure more compatible with the new procedural requirements, education of private lawyers and law students, and public information campaigns.[30]

Greater familiarity with the sector's weaknesses in general and as they affected the transition to the new systems eventually turned attention to some other elements: measures to strengthen judicial independence, reduce politicization of the appointment process, and increase the professional quality of judges and other officials and staff and to augment the general efficiency of courtroom and system-wide administration.[31] Local reformers were particularly active in promoting the first elements. Their interest, like the code reforms, had earlier origins, but it took new significance with the realization that incompetent, corrupt, politically dependent judiciaries and judges were unlikely to apply the new codes in the spirit in which they were written. Throughout the region, countries adopted judicial councils, representative bodies usually located outside the judiciary and intended to manage the selection and promotions of judges and sometimes court staff. The move was usually linked to the creation of permanent judicial careers, increases in salary levels and budgets, which sometimes were also under the control of councils, and the development of training programs. Donors usually collaborated in setting up judicial schools but provided little more than moral support to the other measures. The Spanish assistance agency is one notable exception. Because Spain has a council system, the Spaniards offered their own experience as a model.[32]

Donors were instrumental in introducing efficiency measures, because these were concerns in their own countries and elements they thus associated with

29. See Chapter 1 for a discussion of these institutions and their peculiar development in Latin America.

30. Many of these activities are discussed in Hammergren (1998a, 1998b, 1998c, and 1998d). For a lengthy and very discursive reflection on these issues (and many others), see Binder and Obando (2004).

31. Although many donors are not quite as much on the cutting edge as they like to believe, a review of the contents of conferences and summary publications they finance is a good indication of the state of the contemporary art. For the USAID and IDB view in the early to mid-1990s, see topics and articles in Crohn and Davis (1996).

32. Although several Latin American councils drew on the Spanish model, they often copied poorly and also overlooked some of Spain's problems with the innovation. See Rico (1993); Hammergren (2002a), for a general discussion of councils; and López Guerra (2001), for a sympathetic explanation (by the council's vice president) of the Spanish model. Renoux (1999) provides extensive descriptive background on the use of councils throughout Europe.

judicial reform. The U.S. Agency for International Development (USAID) was especially important here, because the U.S courts were the most advanced in court administration,[33] and the United States at the time still dominated the field in donor assistance. As U.S. courts were themselves entering the computer age, it was not long before automation became a standard element in donor-assisted programs and one that many Latin American judiciaries also promoted on their own. Resource constraints meant that most of this early work focused on the criminal courts where delays were seen as damaging to both human rights goals and the interest of combating crime.

When the multilateral development banks (MDBs) entered the scene in the early 1990s, they did so over considerable internal resistance because the judiciary was considered "political." Hence, judicial programs were seen by many as violating the MDBs' articles of agreement (which emphasized a role in promoting economic growth and explicitly prohibited political involvement). The initial response was to focus on civil and commercial law, which was believed most relevant to the economic mandate.[34] Timing was also critical. Donors had extended their programs to the former Soviet Union and Eastern Europe, where market development was accorded the highest priority. The earlier arriving donors were still involved in Latin America's criminal justice reforms, which left the way open for the banks to work on noncriminal law.

It should be emphasized that the connection between market-based growth and civil and commercial law was a purely deductive conclusion. There was little empirical evidence that the judiciary, in these or any other areas, had an impact on economic development. It just seemed logical that, if it did, it would be channeled through commercial and civil cases. MDB programs first emphasized law revision but quickly moved into court and system administration, trying so far as was possible to limit their actions to the "civil half" of the courts. Needless to say, auxiliary organizations, like the public ministry, public defense, or police were completely beyond the pale. Over time, they have gradually lessened the strictures, and the Inter-American Development Bank (IDB) in particular soon moved into support for criminal justice and some of these other institution as well.[35]

The court and judicial administration element has been especially favored by

33. The United States had gone through its own court administrative reform a few decades earlier. See Tobin (1999) for a discussion. The U.S. NGO most involved in the reforming the U.S. state courts, the National Center for State Courts (NCSC), and a few of its Spanish-speaking consultants carried the program forward.

34. Ibrahim Shihata (1991), then the World Bank's chief counsel, made the determination that governance and some aspects of judicial reform were within the Bank's mandate because of their relevance for economic growth. He is also credited with the decision that criminal justice would be excluded because it is more "political."

35. See Biebesheimer (2001) and Biebesheimer and Payne (2001) for a review of the IDB's portfolio. Biebesheimer and Cordovez (1999) provides an overview of themes the IDB has found important.

the MDBs because it is seen as highly technical and, to the extent it requires major investments, it is a logical candidate for loan programs. Bilateral donors, the United Nations, and the number of foundations already working on reform programs could at best finance pilot court administration programs. Because they work with grants, none had the funds to support systemwide replication. The MDBs could also finance infrastructure, something both ideologically and financially outside the limits for the other donors. Although a negative NGO report on the World Bank's first project in Venezuela brought a cutback in these investments, the IDB was never affected, and the World Bank eventually returned to financing infrastructure.[36]

The MDBs also found stronger support for their judicial reform ventures in the post–Washington Consensus discovery of neoliberal institutional economics. The argument that "institutions matter," drawing on the theoretical framework developed by fellow economists such as Douglass North, provided both an explanation for the failure of the Consensus formula of macroeconomic discipline and a real impetus to work with governmental organizations.[37] Of course, North's interest was in the way informal rules and incentive systems shaped behavior. His discussion of institutions was not directed toward encouraging investments in computers and buildings, but absent arguments to the contrary, reforming judicial and other institutions quickly became conflated with large loan programs to benefit these same organizations. As long as money was spent on the judiciary, it was advancing institutional reform.

A second source of support came from a series of macroeconomic analyses correlating "judicial development" with economic growth.[38] The positive findings provided further justification for the programs, though, as critics continually note, the nature of their guidance was fairly ambiguous and the methodologies themselves

36. See Lawyers Committee for Human Rights and the Venezuelan Program for Human Rights Education and Action (1996) for the report. The World Bank still attempts to limit loan financing of construction, leaving that for counterpart (that is, country) funding; however, a newly approved judicial reform loan in El Salvador looks much like the initial Venezuela model. Most funds go to a construction program and secondarily to computer purchases, although the major justification is delay reduction. Another program with an Argentine provincial court is also financing a new courthouse. In that case, it was used to leverage other changes. Still, $16 million is a fairly large lever.

37. The term "Washington Consensus" was popularized, and possibly coined, by John Williamson in an article (Williamson, 1990) describing the economic policy reforms promoted by the international financial institutions (the International Monetary Fund and the multilateral development banks, or MDBs) and others during the 1980s and 1990s. Williamson describes the consensus in terms of ten policy instruments aiming at fiscal discipline, trade and investment liberalization, market deregulation, and privatization of public enterprises. Although proponents of the consensus still hold that the measures (also called "first-generation reforms") paid off in Latin America by reactivating economic growth, they generally admit that implementation has been imperfect and that the impact on reducing poverty and inequality has been far less than promised. (Burki and Perry, 1998; 3). Among their suggested solutions was increased attention to improving the quality of institutions (also called "second-generation reforms), including those of the justice sector.

38. See Kaufmann et al. (1999, 2002), LaPorta and López-de-Silanes (1998), World Bank Institute (1997, 2002), and Djankov et al. (2002).

were not above question. First there was the issue of defining "judicial development." Absent a structural (what a developed judiciary looks like) or functional (how it operates) definition, the researchers relied on public opinion surveys or expert assessments, asking panels of local or international informants to rank the performance of national court systems.[39] Where local experts ranked their own courts, there was the issue of cross-national comparability. Standards vary, and a good court system facing demanding experts might get a far lower rating than one whose local panel figured that a certain measure of corruption and exclusionary practices was inevitable.[40] Because international experts often tended to be businessmen, theirs was a one-sided view and measure. Singapore, for example, ranks at the top of many ratings. Reviewers more aware of or concerned about protection of human rights or treatment of political opposition might contest this placement.[41] Shifting to another source of foreign expertise—say, human rights advocates— alters the perspective but still keeps the view narrow.

More complex methodologies, featuring questions as to how much a local entrepreneur would be willing to pay for or invest in a "well-functioning" judicial system are still in the end opinion polls.[42] And in this case, with the aggravating factor of relying on what people say they will do in a completely hypothetical situation. Nonetheless, the banks, as well as many other donors, took heart from the findings as an indication that they were doing the right thing. One potentially positive result was that many countries also took heed of the studies and decided that an investment in improving justice might indeed produce economic growth and attract foreign investment. Not all were quite as disingenuous as an extraregional example, Cambodia, which in 1996 was proposing to rewrite its entire legal framework on the assumption that modern laws would bring in a flood of foreign

39. Even the best-known researchers in this area are beginning to have doubts about the adequacy of their ability to measure the quality of institutions. See the *Economist*, August 7, 2004, 63, for a brief discussion.

40. José Juan Toharia (above) has a wonderful story to illustrate this problem as recounted in a speech to a World Bank group. In conducting survey research on attitudes toward citizen security, his team found that inhabitants of London felt more threatened by crime than those in Caracas. As the researchers knew both cities, they found the results odd. On investigating further, their conclusions were as follows: those living in Caracas were more tolerant of the kinds of petty crime (purse snatching, car theft, and the like) that Londonites found threatening. Thus, what the latter regarded as a dangerous situation was viewed as normal by the former. Slight changes in how questions are posed can also make a big difference. Where courts are so corrupt that no one uses them, they will be "less of an impediment to business transactions" than others that are more honest but highly bureaucratized.

41. For example, Freedom House's survey for 2005, gives Singapore a ranking of 5 (7 is worst) and 4 on political rights and civil rights, respectively (Piano and Puddington 2005, 123). Two of the World Bank's tools for measuring judicial performance demonstrate a similar point. The World Bank Institute's rule of law indicator (Kaufman et al. 1999, 2002) highlights the level of judicial corruption, thus explaining why some of the country's it ranks lowest (for example, Nicaragua and Paraguay) come out significantly better on the Doing Business (World Bank 2005b) scale measuring speed and complexity of case processing.

42. See Sherwood et al. (1994) and Castelar (1998).

investors. Nevertheless, many countries have revised codes or introduced new bank-ruptcy, secured collateral, or corporate governance laws on just such reasoning.[43]

Even assuming that the rankings approximated some measure of judicial devel-opment, the second problem is how to translate them into reform programming. At most, the rankings provide opinions about overall timeliness, honesty, and cost. They do not indicate which kinds of courts, which proceedings, or which laws pose problems. Perhaps it is administrative not commercial law, or appellate not trial courts, that create impediments. Perhaps it is rampant crime and not slow debt col-lection that most deters investors. These issues will be revisited in subsequent chap-ters. The point for now is that the arguments about economic impacts behind the MDBs' and other actors' entrance into judicial reform in general and in areas such as delay reduction and commercial law are only partly supported by the evidence and, whether supported or not, provide insufficient detail to guide program design.

In the second decade of the reform movement, two other themes joined the institutional strengthening repertoire. The first of these is the issue of access or the provision of judicial services to groups traditionally excluded from their benefits. Rather surprisingly, this had not come up earlier except in efforts to provide legal assistance to indigent criminal defendants. Probably, it took a turn to noncriminal justice to create an interest in the positive service aspects of judicial output and the fact that for many citizens they were beyond reach. Both judiciaries and donors encountered additional reasons for advancing in this area.

On the judges' side, there was a sincere or calculated interest in improving their image and overcoming the impression that they served only the elites. Judiciaries in many countries began programs to expand the number and distribution of trial courts and to add still lower-level justice of the peace or small claims courts intended to serve the small users. Brazil began such a program under the military government of the 1980s, formally recognizing it in its 1988 constitution.[44] Its small claims courts with special expedited procedures have since spread at both the state and federal level. They have become so popular that they are experiencing their own problems of congestion. Peru's justice of the peace courts, while traditionally only tolerated by the regular judiciary (because they use lay judges), were also given a push in that country and now represent another regional model.[45] Other coun-tries have followed suit, if on a less expansive scale. Except in Brazil's small claims courts, the creation of simplified procedures has not been a pattern, but courts did make other efforts to remove additional barriers—introducing court interpreters, information kiosks, and similar devices to orient first-time users and public edu-cation campaigns to help those unfamiliar with judicial proceedings.

The donor impetus had a similar source—criticism from within and outside their

43. For a discussion of the Eastern European experience, see Gupta et al. (2002).
44. For discussions, see Rodycz (2001), Sadek (2001a), Watanabe (1986), Pinheiro Carneiro (2000).
45. See Brandt (1987, 1990), Instituto de Defensa Legal (1999), Lovatón et al. (1999).

organizations that their programs benefited principally state and elite actors, but were not contributing to the new battle on poverty.[46] Thus, in the early 1990s, they also began to expand their activities to include support to general legal assistance, often channeled through NGOs, an emphasis on lower-level courts, popular legal education, and public forums for discussing reforms.[47]

For both donors and judiciaries, the entrance into access programs coincided with the emergence of a new reform mechanism: ADR or the creation of arbitration, mediation, and conciliation services within or outside the courts. ADR was introduced both as a means of expanding access to nontraditional users and decongesting court dockets (an efficiency-enhancement measure that was also supposed to make room for more cases). As a reform tool, ADR thus extends across several objectives. In some countries it has even been suggested as a mechanism for resolving human rights cases.

Although first strongly resisted by judicial and legal actors, ADR has gained dramatically in popularity in the past ten years.[48] Many judiciaries have introduced their own programs. Ministries of justice and other executive agencies have done so as well. Alongside these public-sector programs, NGOs, professional associations, and for-profit entities have also been active in promoting the programs and introducing their own services. Among the donors, the IDB has taken a special interest in ADR and also added its own twist to the goals—the reduction of civil violence. Whereas donors began by funding extrajudicial programs, often with NGOs, court interest in having their own ADR facilities has also led to their inclusion in donor projects. In some sense, the ADR movement has a life of its own, independent of judicial reform. Its most fervent proponents present it as a direct and more effective means of resolving any number of societal problems—ranging from communal violence to weakened family ties. ADR's attachment to the judicial reform movement is a result of historical and tactical considerations. It was often introduced by advisors working on other judicial areas (often court administration or human rights), and, because it had no more logical place in other ongoing programs, it was easiest to promote it through those with the judiciary.

A related theme, the recognition or reactivation of traditional dispute-resolution mechanisms (indigenous law), entered at about the same time, although advances in this area have been minimal.[49] Several Latin American constitutions now incorporate such practices as an alternative source of law but leave numerous unresolved

46. See, for example, Golub (2003), and Golub and McClymont (2000).

47. For a discussion of the World Bank view, see Dakolias (2001) and World Bank, Legal Vice Presidency (2002, 2003a, 2003b). Blair and Hansen (1994) mark a shift to access in USAID programs. Their strategic framework demotes institution building (called capacity building) to a lower position. See USAID (2000, 2002a) for the agency's self-assessment of the results.

48. See Álvarez and Highton (2000) for a review of programs throughout the region.

49. Both Faundez (2005b) and Golub (2003) offer discussions on the potential for incorporating these mechanisms in overall strategies, but this is as far as the literature has gone.

questions as to how this will operate in fact. In some cases, progress here would appear to conflict with efforts to promote ADR or to provide special or small claims courts for the rural poor.

A second area also receiving more attention in recent years is that of constitutional and legal controls, or the judiciary's checks and balance function. This has been largely an internal initiative and has received little funding from or promotion by donors.[50] This is understandable in that the major activity has been constitutional change to create constitutional courts or enhance the judicial review powers of supreme courts. The initiative is linked to concerns about judicial independence, but, unlike the earlier stage, is no longer limited to curbing external interventions in the resolution of ordinary cases. Instead, the call was for the judiciary to assume its role as a check on the other branches of government, controlling abuses of power, nonrecognition of constitutional guarantees, and other illegal actions.[51] Although several courts in the region historically had these powers, they used them rarely and with extreme deference to governmental preferences. Constitutional changes combined with demands from legal activists and the courts' greater political autonomy produced a surge in judicial involvement. Costa Rica's Sala Constitutional (constitutional chamber), created in 1989, was soon receiving and deciding 2,000 and then 10,000 cases annually, over a ten-year period. Colombia's Constitutional Court quickly accumulated more than 100,000 requests for a final review of *tutelas* (alleged rights violations, comparable to *amparo*, a legal protest of violation of a constitutionally guaranteed right), including those arising from lower court judgments on other issues, and also entered into a series of decisions curbing government programs. Even where sheer numbers were not that high, decisions were often of great consequence. Filings were also encouraged by the development of new mechanisms for making complaints, the creation of specialized bodies (human rights ombudsmen, or, as in Brazil, special prosecutors[52]) that could represent citizen claims, and a growing interest among legal NGOs in public-interest law.

While often supporting changes in other areas (guarantees of rights in criminal justice, enhanced access), judicial activism also introduced its own contradictions with the broader program.[53] It frequently had negative impacts on efficiency; more

50. One significant exception was a USAID project undertaken in Costa Rica in the early 1990s. As the new Constitutional Chamber of the Supreme Court was in danger of being overcome by its burgeoning workload, USAID provided a $100,000 grant to hire law clerks and set up a computerized case management system for the chamber.

51. See, for example, articles in Werneck (2002).

52. For a discussion of the role of Brazil's public ministry in protecting constitutional rights, see Bastos Arantes (2002) and Sadek and Batista Calvalcanti (2003).

53. This appears to be less the case in Eastern Europe, possibly because of lower litigation levels and the absence of a longer tradition of constitutional checks and balances. See Schwartz (2000) for a discussion of trends there. Trochev (2004) offers a critical look at the lack of impact in Russia.

opportunities to protest due process violations also enhanced the chances for creating more delay. In addition, some measures to improve criminal justice procedures (the use of abbreviated trials or plea bargaining) or enhance access (via alternative mechanisms) would face their own constitutional challenges. Finally, once the genii was out of the bottle, there were many who questioned the desirability of giving so much power to courts that still had not undergone other more basic reforms. Constitutional courts and chambers were often politicized, they did not always have the most eminent jurists as their members, and their decisions, especially on judicial matters, were often seen as undercutting the independence of ordinary courts or as posing their own conflicts of interest. One example is the expansion of the *amparo* in Mexico's federal courts.[54] A Supreme Court decision in the mid-nineteenth century allowed the use of the *amparo* (as a due process guarantee) to question the judgments of state courts. This has given the federal courts an enormous and much-resented power over state judiciaries, created delays in reaching firm decisions, and has arguably added to the public and private costs of justice. Moreover, because the majority of *amparo*s against state judgments do not overturn the latter, there is a real question as to the value added of the procedure.[55] As currently constituted, the process for placing an *amparo* also raises access issues. Lawyers specialized in this proceeding are very costly, and even the state finds its own attorneys unable to prevail against them.

A SCHEMATIC OVERVIEW OF THE LATIN AMERICAN APPROACHES

As contrasted with judicial reform movements elsewhere in the world, Latin Americans continue to have their own distinctive approach to the issues. The regional linkage of democracy building, human rights, and an end to political impunity has been joined to an emphasis on economic impacts, but judicial reform (as the creation of a strong, politically independent judiciary) has tended to be seen as more of an end in itself. In fact, attempts to emphasize its instrumental nature, especially in terms of the consequences for economic growth, have often been resisted as somehow denigrating the judiciary's own importance.[56] Attempts to equate reform with improving the courts' public service delivery (for example, by reducing delays, expanding access, and introducing ADR) have received somewhat more acceptance, but there are still holdouts on the bench and in the wider legal community

54. This is discussed in greater detail in Chapter 5. For a brief overview of the proceeding, see Fix-Zamudio (1979).

55. Magaloni and Negrete (n.d.).

56. Members of Brazil's national bar (Organização de Advogados do Brasil, OAB) and largest judicial (Associação dos Magistrados do Brasil, AMB) associations have in fact protested this linkage as a proglobalization plot, promoted by the World Bank among others. See Calvalcanti Melo Filho (2003).

who interpret this as an unhealthy commoditization of justice and a violation of its status as a universal, indivisible right. Strengthening the judiciary's role (and that of other sector institutions—the police, public prosecution, and so forth) in combating crime has been less resisted, because of both the growing public demand and the threats to the courts themselves—via attacks on judges, corruption, and the emergence of extrajudicial mechanisms, ranging from vigilante justice to special tribunals outside the ordinary court system.[57]

In Eastern Europe and the former Soviet Union, the situation has been much the reverse. Reforms started with an emphasis on economic impacts.[58] It was somewhat later that democratizing themes and the judiciary's political role began to receive attention. Furthermore, whereas in Latin America, a usually abysmal public image has not affected an escalating demand for court services, in the former Soviet region the problem has more often been convincing people to use the courts, which are still seen as instruments of state control of citizen behavior. In other regions, it is more difficult to generalize about the justifying themes and interests.[59] On a case-by-case basis, much depends on who initiates the reform, the extent of voiced, nonjudicial discontent with the sector's performance, and the political role currently played by the judiciary. Not surprisingly, judicially initiated reforms tend to be least instrumental in nature, focusing more on enhancing the courts' status and powers. Those promoted by governments often point to efficiency and modernity, downplaying power enhancement, though not necessarily independence or status. Many governments do not welcome a court system that can effectively oppose their actions, but they increasingly see the value of enhancing the authority accorded judicial decisions.[60] More instrumental reforms (those seeking extrajudicial impacts) are usually favored by outside groups, either national stakeholders or international allies.

Table 1 lays out some of the most common goals and related activities. In descending order, they are presented from the least to most instrumental in focus.

The objectives are presented with their logical activities and results. It should be noted that many reforms are not designed or implemented quite so rationally. Although the objectives are not mutually exclusive, it is difficult to pursue them simultaneously. This has not impeded a move to "holistic" or comprehensive

57. Noteworthy here are the "faceless judges" used in Peru and Colombia for terrorism and drug cases.

58. Here general overviews of trends and programs are only beginning to appear. See Frydman et al. (1996), Gupta et al. (2002), Hendley et al. (1999), Kryshtalowych and Smith (2000), Ramasastry et al. (2000), Sachs and Pistor (1997), Schwartz (2000), Smith (1996), Solomon (2004).

59. See articles in Jensen and Heller (2003) and Faundez et al. (2000), for a sample of overviews from other regions, especially Asia and Africa.

60. This might be called the Singapore ideal—a well-run, extremely efficient system that only does "telephone" (directed) justice when cases are of extreme importance for political elites.

Table 1 Reform goals and activities

Objectives	Common Activities	Indicators of Success	Major Promoters
Building a strong, professional judiciary as an independent political institution	Merit appointments, new forms of judicial governance, budgetary autonomy and higher budgets, professionalization of staff, training, monitoring, and evaluation	Better public image. Over longer run, fewer complaints; over shorter run, more judges disciplined, dismissed for cause	Judges, civic interest groups, donors, and international NGOs
Judicial modernization as a goal in itself or to meet rising demands for greater quantity, different quality of services	New technologies, organization, administrative techniques	More efficient service, more cases resolved, backlog reduction, fewer delays in resolving cases	Government, donors, the judiciary (but more for the inputs than the results)
Strengthening the judiciary's role as an independent check on abuses by other governmental actors, branches of government	Enhanced powers of judicial/constitutional review (legal change), creation of constitutional courts, chambers, protected appointments and tenure	More rulings against government agencies, at least over the short run; greater tendency to take legal actions against political leaders.	Civic action groups, sometimes elements of local bar or judiciary
Increased accessibility to wider range of social groups, for rights protection, equitable treatment, and effective conflict resolution	More courts and judges, simplified and alternative procedures, rights-oriented training, subsidized legal services, popular legal education	Change in socio-economic identity of users, decisions upholding constitutional rights	Political parties, civic groups, external actors
Improved criminal justice system to decrease human rights violations and improve citizen security	New procedures, strengthening of other sector institutions (police, prosecution), judicial training and protection	Higher clearance rate for criminal cases, decline in crime rate, fewer human rights abuses, including those by judicial actors	Government, public, some foreign donors
Enhancing the judiciary's ability to deal with economically relevant disputes	Law modernization, training, specialized commercial courts, delay reduction, ADR for business groups	More economic cases to courts or formal alternative forums, faster resolution, economic growth?	Economic groups, government, donors

reforms that often work unselfconsciously on parallel tracks.[61] Moreover the choice of activities often seems to operate separately from their most logical placement. Multiple goals may be associated with a narrower range of means (some of them not even logically related) or means may be completely disassociated from their ends. Certain activities the judiciary favors (training, buildings, equipment) may be introduced or justified for reasons having little apparent relationship to their likely impact, especially in the form they take. Training, for example, can be quite effective in producing behavioral change, but only when designed to do so and paired with complementary organizational and procedural modifications. Absent these conditions, it becomes simply a way of absorbing resources (often supplied externally), symbolically attacking problems, and keeping judges happy. Activities have also been designed or subverted to produce results quite contrary to their assumed purpose. Modifications in appointment and tenure systems provide means of stacking the bench with friends of government, removing overly independent judges, or holding off more fundamental change. Special courts are used to facilitate directed justice or conflicts reassigned to the judiciary to postpone their effective resolution.

The reasons for this disarticulation of means and ends are further explored below. The explanation begins with the multiple and not always compatible objectives pursued and the various origins of and interests behind them. Judicial reform as a now fairly standard set of activities has in its short life almost transcended the need for justification. It has also become an assumed solution for an increasing number of extrajudicial problems—poverty and inequality, democratic instability, and inadequate economic growth and investment. Anyone wishing to contest or simply explore some of those connections thus risks attacking numerous sacred cows as well as their associated lobbies. As is often the case with programs serving multiple interests and ends, it is usually easier to leave conventional wisdom unchallenged. The firemen's syndrome ("don't step on the hose") is the safest course, allowing each faction to pursue its own projects, however much it may doubt the validity of those of its allies. External critics have viewed the results less sympathetically, but their relative insensitivity to the politics of program definition has reduced the impact of their commentaries.

READER'S GUIDE TO THE SUBSEQUENT DISCUSSION

Figure 1 is the point of departure for the following discussion. In the next section, the five chapters address the origins and evolution of the strategies outlined above

---

61. One wonders, for example, when the MDBs will recognize that their new emphasis on access and public interest law may soon have the courts (as in Argentina, Brazil, Colombia, and Peru) overruling neoliberal economic policies. A few outside observers have begun to ask that question (Wilson et al. 2004; Santiso 2003).

in the Latin American context. Two of the objectives, modernization and economic goals, are combined because of their use of many of the same activities and justifications. These individual treatments also discuss effects and problems arising from the compartmentalized pursuit of goals. The sequencing varies from that of the chart, instead based on an approximation of the chronological order in which the different approaches emerged in the region. To avoid repetition, activities that are common to several approaches (for example, ADR, training, legal change) are discussed in detail only in the approach in which they appear most central.

Following the courtroom tactic of anticipating obvious criticism, I will note that the five chapters on reform strategies may well overstate the strategic content of many reform interventions. The treatments represent ideal types, based on what certain general categories of efforts appear to be attempting, explicitly or implicitly. Admittedly, some complex and many unidimensional reform programs seem to have very little strategic vision behind them. They simply imitate actions that have been taken elsewhere, at best justifying their presence by a vague reference to "lessons of experience." Some of the most common activities—training, ADR, and automation—are the worst offenders, where any organization with some experience in their adoption in any other setting, seems to feel this makes it a reform expert. In the second part of this volume, discussing the routes and impediments to a real comprehensive reform, these "solutions in search of a problem" will be discussed in more detail. Even if those responsible do not seem to know where they are heading, however, they usually benefit from the protection of one of the principal strategic umbrellas.

The second section raises issues related to the failure to develop a truly comprehensive approach and recommends ways in which this might be remedied. It discusses both the incentive structure supporting the current situation and the steps needed to change it. A good deal of emphasis is placed on what the donors now call "knowledge management," the use of past experience and lessons learned, as well as external criticisms, to improve an ongoing program. Rather ironically, the invention of the term "knowledge management" seems to have coincided with a lesser interest in actually effecting it. Although a volume of this size can hardly cover all the pertinent lessons and findings accumulated in twenty years, it is hoped that by calling attention to some of them and to the issues they raise, individually and collectively, it can encourage the knowledge managers to take their responsibilities more seriously. Academics writing on the topic have made the effort, despite the still enormous obstacles to accessing information from judiciaries or donors; however, many of the donors have a long way to go in this regard. They frequently do a poor job of collecting and disseminating the information they produce, even among their own employees, sponsor research that is not incorporated in their projects, and have tended to do few evaluations of their work. A final question is thus how the various reform participants can overcome less helpful past practices and the incentive systems underlying them and so adopt a more collaborative approach to identifying what they collectively know and using it to improve their common efforts.

PART I FIVE APPROACHES TO JUDICIAL REFORM

ONE CRIMINAL JUSTICE REFORM: HUMAN RIGHTS, CRIME CONTROL, AND OTHER UNLIKELY BEDFELLOWS

Criminal justice was the target for the first Latin American judicial reforms, and for many it remains the main act. Implementation of the reforms that began in the mid-1980s continues to this day. Their early emergence is explained by the conjunction of several factors. First was the longer-term interest among Latin American jurists in effecting a change to more accusatory criminal justice proceedings, following trends in Europe and some earlier initiatives in Latin America itself.[1] Second was the region's emergence from a period of authoritarian governments during which its judicial systems had generally deteriorated in quality because of political interference and chronic underfunding.[2] Finally, there was the interest on the part of donors and local and international nongovernmental organizations (NGOs) in the human rights implications of criminal justice and in the presumed role of the judiciaries in strengthening democratic governance.[3]

Judicial weaknesses clearly extended beyond the criminal justice area, but this was where external manipulation, political dependence, and a series of traditional vices had the most visible impact on citizen well-being. Political intervention could hardly be blamed on the legal tradition. Local reformers, however, believed this and many other flaws were closely tied to procedural requirements. The claims are debatable. That made little difference to their effect on policy. It may have had considerable impact on the subsequent outcomes of the programs.

Criminal justice may not seem the most logical place to initiate a review of Latin American judicial reform efforts. Its placement here follows its historical lead. In this chapter, we review the situation prior to the reforms and its impact on shaping them, the evolution of the programs over time, their achievements, and the variety of preferences and prejudices (mental models or strategic paradigms) that have tended to impede progress in reaching the presumed goals. I say "presumed" because aside from the uncomfortable juxtaposition of the two principal objectives

---

1. See Llobet (1993), Maier et al. (1993), Baytelman (2002), Correa (1999). The province of Córdoba, Argentina, enacted a criminal procedures code in 1939, which is regarded as the first step in the regional reform process.

2. Correa (1999) gives a good overview. See also Hammergren (1998a, 1998e), Popkin (2000), Spence and Vickers (1994), Spence et al. (1995), and Washington Office on Latin America (1990).

3. Alvarez (1992) and Bipartisan National Commission on Central America (1984).

(reducing human rights abuses and enhancing crime control), the reforms demonstrate a certain substitution of means for ends. Rather than being equated with the production of these downstream impacts, success is often measured by the extent to which new procedures are adopted. Criminal justice is not the only partial reform where such strategic shortcuts have confused the issue of what would constitute success. It is, however, a very good example of these characteristics, for which reason they are discussed in more depth in this section.

THE STATUS QUO ANTE AND ITS INFLUENCE
ON REFORM GOALS AND DESIGN

Reform is often a reactive undertaking. Its proponents are attempting to eliminate weaknesses in existing practices, often with far less clarity as to what they will substitute. Much of the Latin American judicial reform movement can be interpreted in this fashion. Reactive reform is not necessarily a bad approach; the few examples of proactive reform (for example, modernization) in which proponents were clearer about the solutions than about the problems have faced their own setbacks. Nonetheless, it is virtually impossible to understand Latin America's criminal justice programs without taking the status quo ante into account—for which reason the following brief summary is provided.

There can be little debate as to the largely unsatisfactory nature of the region's criminal justice systems over time, and especially from the mid-twentieth century. Although the situation has been attributed to their inquisitorial nature, other special circumstances may be more important. Latin America's inquisitorial criminal procedures had been inherited from Spain and Portugal during the colonial period. Early independence (in the 1820s[4]) meant that their subsequent development continued on its own track, largely unaffected by new trends in continental Europe. This, combined with the socioeconomic environment, led to a certain distortion of the basic model. The criminal justice systems found throughout Latin America in the late twentieth century demonstrated a variety of flaws. Many of their characteristic practices, however, would have looked odd by twentieth- or even nineteenth-century European standards. In fact, some scholars argue that they did not even successfully imitate the changes introduced in Napoleonic France, but retained many elements of the prior Luso-Iberian system.[5]

4. Brazil's independence experience was unique, first passing through a constitutional monarchy, headed by members of the Portuguese royal family, and only reaching republican status in 1889. This gradual evolution may account for several special characteristics of the Brazilian justice system as a whole, including the higher level of institutionalization among its various organizations and, closely tied to this, the equally high level of procedural formalism.

5. See Duce (1999) on the Latin American public ministry's different evolution.

In the classical and modern inquisitorial proceedings as developed in Europe, the formal investigation of a purported crime is conducted by an instructional (investigative) judge, working with and directing the efforts of the police investigators.[6] The judge collects all relevant evidence in a written dossier (*expediente*) that becomes the basis on which another judge or panel of judges will decide the case. Although the trial judge or judges have access to the dossier once it is completed, the instructional judge has no further participation in their deliberations. As a rule, European trial judges take a much more active part in the proceedings than do their common-law counterparts.[7] This is also true in terms of their participation in juries, which are usually mixed—a group of citizens with one or more judges.

Although the investigation lies largely with one individual, both the prosecutor, a member of the public ministry, and defense counsel have access to the findings and can make their own suggestions as to lines of inquiry. The instructional judge is charged with "finding the truth of the matter" and may, as a result of these efforts, recommend dropping charges against the suspect. If the case goes to trial, it usually involves an oral hearing in which witnesses and evidence are presented to the judge, judges, or jury, if used. Parties may not introduce evidence not in the dossier (though, in some cases, the trial judge or judges may request further investigation), but instead focus on its interpretation, the implications as to the legal responsibility of the suspect, and recommendation on the verdict and sentencing. As the French like to say, the process is contradictory but not adversarial. When carried out by serious professionals, it hardly constitutes a fait accompli, in term of either a guilty verdict or an automatic acceptance of the state's recommendations.[8]

The European system has been in flux for centuries, and even these generalizations are not universally applicable. In some countries the investigative judge has disappeared, replaced by a prosecutor who plays much the same role and thus is expected to do an objective investigation. In France, instructional judges are now used only for serious crimes. For others, the prosecutor works directly on the basis of investigation done by the police. Whereas the European system does not use plea bargaining, there is a tendency to adopt similar practices in the interest of procedural economy.[9] Caseload has been reduced by decriminalizing some actions and

6. For an overview of the European variants, see Damaska (1997), Fennell et al. (1995), Fionda (1995), Freccero (1994), Jacob et al. (1996), Stepán (1994), and West et al. (1992). Merryman (1985) is the classic source, but his work is marred by a very visible anticontinental bias.

7. It is unclear how much of this is legally based as opposed to a matter of practice and custom. The U.S. Federal Rules of Evidence (Pub. L. 93-595, § 1, Jan. 2, 1975, 88 Stat. 1937) allow judges to call and interrogate witnesses (Rule 614), but, as Richard Messick, who brought this to my attention, notes, they are less likely to do so "for a variety of reasons" Messick (personal communication) adds that there are indications this may be changing, but no hard evidence to support that belief.

8. In fact, in recent years, a number of common law jurists have begun to suggest the advantages of certain elements of the inquisitorial system. See Strier (1996).

9. See Langer (2004) for a discussion of the variations. He finds the Italian practice most similar to that of the United States.

leaving others to administrative officials. Police and prosecutors often have the ability to impose fines or work out agreements with alleged violators.

In its most common Latin American versions,[10] a certain short-circuiting of the early nineteenth-century European model, several additional legal details, and a general lack of professionalism on the part of many of the actors led to very different results. First, in many countries, the process was less complex and enjoyed fewer safeguards than in the continental system. The duties of the prosecution (public ministry), instructional and sentencing judges tended to be handled by a single judicial actor. The public ministry, where it even existed, often played a highly symbolic role in the proceedings, and much of the real investigation fell to a single judge.[11] This individual, the instructional judge, having concluded his study of the case, often changed hats and became the sentencing judge; only in more complex cases might his findings be sent to a separate judicial panel. Obviously, this worked against a neutral consideration of the evidence in any eventual hearing, which often was not even held.[12]

Second, Latin American instructional judges have commonly delegated responsibilities for interviewing witnesses and collecting evidence to courtroom staff. The practice is disappearing, but it has not been eliminated. It is reported that in Peru, following the shift to a more accusatory system, the investigating judges are again having their assistants depose witnesses. In a recent visit to a Mexican state court, I interviewed the presiding judge in his chambers, while other court personnel conducted the oral "hearing."

Third, in both criminal and civil trials, many Latin American countries still required that prosecution and defense counsel provide written lists of the questions they would ask of witnesses to the judge for his determination as to whether they would be allowed. Then, either the counsel or the judge asked the questions

10. Here Brazil constitutes an exception to patterns in the rest of the region. Although its criminal justice system is roundly criticized for the usual reasons (excessive formalism, impunity, corruption, and a tendency to fall most heavily on the poor), many of its specific characteristics are quite different from those in Spanish-speaking Latin American. For example, a police official (the *delegado*, usually a lawyer) conducts the equivalent of the *instrucción*, in Brazil called the *inquérito*. This is used by the prosecutor (*procurador* or *promotor*) as the basis for the indictment. As compared to Spanish-speaking Latin America, Brazilian judges, prosecutors, and even police tend to be better trained, equipped and paid. This has not eliminated complaints about corruption and abusive treatment. A more common criticism is that members of the different organizations seem more hostile than cooperative toward each other. Brazilian jurists do consider their system "overly inquisitorial" and have been exploring the adoption of more accusatory proceedings. Most public criticism is directed at the aspects of the procedural codes that allow a skillful lawyer to avoid a final verdict for years, possibly until the statute of limitations runs out for his client.

11. In Guatemala, prior to the enactment of the new codes, it was reported (Mudge 1997) that when the *fiscales* (prosecutors) appeared in court, the judges often asked who they were. In several countries (for example, Peru during the 1970s, Colombia, Uruguay, Bolivia), the public ministry completely disappeared.

12. Although these were written proceedings, most traditional codes made room for hearings where the parties met before the judge. These hearings were frequently ignored, or reduced to depositions conducted by low-level courtroom staff.

with no deviations allowed from the approved script. In another version (seen in El Salvador prior to its reforms of the late 1990s), prosecution and defense tended to limit their courtroom arguments to reading sections of the *expediente* to the jury and/or judge. El Salvador was one of a minority of countries with jury trials for some offenses. It was not uncommon for judges to fall asleep during the presentations or step out of the courtroom to relieve their boredom. In short, the usual Latin American practices deviated from the continental model in the quality of judicial investigation, the neutrality of the trial judge, and the spontaneity of the trial itself.[13]

In many countries, additional details of the criminal and criminal procedures codes posed significant problems. Rules concerning compulsory pretrial detention (often for any crime with a penalty in excess of three years) and their exaggerated application produced a high proportion of unsentenced prisoners. As many as 90 percent of those held in prison might still be awaiting trial.[14] The problem was and is aggravated by a near absence of public defenders, who might have contested the detentions or at least worked to speed up the pretrial period.[15] Prison statistics are not reliable, an indication of a series of other problems of prison management. Still, there are endless examples of individuals being left in pretrial detention for years, often far longer than the maximum sentence had they been found guilty. Most of these detainees are poor, have never seen a lawyer, and are probably the victims of police who were just looking for someone to take the blame.

Legal difficulties were compounded by the shortcomings of human resources. Years of political intervention in judicial appointments often produced judges who were inadequately trained in legal principles and disinclined to apply them accurately in any event.[16] Public ministries, where they had not been entirely eliminated (another Latin American anomaly), were equally susceptible to manipulation of appointments and usually even more severely underfunded than the courts themselves. In the scheme of things, lawyers interviewed in Peru and several other countries frequently commented that an attorney who could not survive as an

---

13. Stepán (1994, 187) reports, however, that depositions taken by a judge may still be entered as evidence in Germany.

14. Carranza et al. (1988). Although the statistics on which the study is based are highly suspect, it was a path-breaking work in calling attention to this problem.

15. Although many countries have improved their public defense services, the number of defenders remains inadequate. As of late 2005, Peru had fewer than 300 state-financed defenders for its population of 24 million (interviews, Ministry of Justice). In 2003, Ecuador had fifty-five (Hernández Breña 2003, 65). While Colombia, for its population of 43 million has 1,200, they work part time and, as far as can be determined, carry an annual caseload of fifty each. Some countries still retain the traditional *defensor de oficio*, a lawyer appointed by the judiciary or ministry of justice to attend to all indigent defendants in a given district. Pro bono defense supplied by private lawyers is highly underdeveloped, and often is as subject to abuses as the *defensor de oficio* system. Such counsel either neglect their clients or charge illegal fees.

16. These problems are discussed in detail in Chapter 3.

independent practitioner or get a job as legal counsel in a government office or state enterprise would try for a judicial position. If that failed, an attorney then sought a position as a prosecutor or state-appointed defense counsel. Because salaries for public-sector jobs tended to be low, it was not uncommon for those holding them to have outside activities, despite the legal prohibitions on doing so.[17]

Because most Latin American police forces are themselves in need of reform, the quality of investigation, and thus their ability to identify the real perpetrator, is itself questionable.[18] Police are usually paid very poorly. For these reasons, corruption is a nearly universal problem, meaning that those with money to pay bribes can avoid any involvement while those without funds become the scapegoats. An antiquated tradition of weighted evidence (*prueba tasada*)[19] gave most importance to a confession. The police thus used any and all means at hand to extract one.

Supervision of the police by investigative judges, or where they existed, prosecutors, was usually minimal. Prosecutors or instructional judges were often called the "secretaries of the police," meaning that they simply signed off on whatever the police presented as findings. The police generally operated as they wished, routinely violating whatever rules existed on treatment of suspects and the collection of evidence. Where prosecutors and investigating judges bothered to gather their own evidence, they usually did "desk investigations," relying heavily on the contents of the police charge sheet (*expediente policial*) to guide them.[20] These practices were encouraged by their institutions' modest operating budgets. Even if they wished to do field investigations they usually lacked funds for transportation or access to vehicles. Forensics laboratories and other facilities to process physical evidence were near absent, and personnel lacked training in its handling and interpretation.

The resulting situation was characterized by high levels of inefficiency in identifying and processing the guilty and extremely abusive treatment of those who were pulled in as suspects. Guilt or innocence was ultimately determined by the police — who commonly fingered the "usual suspects" as perpetrators, regardless of whether they were actually responsible for the crime in question. Individuals with resources to hire a capable attorney could either buy their way out of the charges or easily defeat them in court. Those without representation or dependent on state subsidized counsel either languished in jail without trial or were quickly found guilty if their cases got that far. Even in the best of situations, the arrangements were suited only to dealing with conventional crimes. With the rise of organized criminality,

17. During the early 1990s in El Salvador, donor staff soon recognized the impossibility of scheduling meetings with members of the *Procuraduría General* (legal and related services for the poor) after 4:00 in the afternoon, because that was when they left for their other jobs.

18. See chapters in Méndez et al. (1999).

19. Many codes literally assigned weights to different types of evidence, creating a mindset that the new codes had problems breaking.

20. See Hammergren (1998e, 120–25) for a discussion of these practices in Peru.

drug trafficking, terrorism, and rampant corruption in the closing decades of the twentieth century, the existing system only generated more abuses and fewer completed cases. The law, existing practices, and the criminal justice personnel were rarely up to the new challenges. It is thus not surprising that critics sought solutions in altering the basic system. The question is whether they focused on enough of the contributing factors.

ORIGINS AND EVOLUTION OF THE CRIMINAL JUSTICE REFORM MOVEMENT

The reform movement started with an emphasis on human rights and due process protections. This was a logical result of the widespread abusive practices under the region's de facto regimes of the 1970s and 1980s. Governments used the already dysfunctional justice system to punish political opponents and repress individuals and groups seen as threatening to the prevailing social order. It was only with the rise in criminality and the emergence of new forms of crime following the democratic opening that the reformers amended the objectives to include more effective crime control. The principal strategy for both goals, however, has remained the same—the introduction of an accusatory, oral criminal justice proceeding in which the judge no longer conducts the investigation but instead oversees and adjudicates the conflicting arguments put forth by the prosecutor and defense counsel. Had crime control entered as a concern earlier, other strategies might have been adopted. By the time it came to the fore, the strategic die was already cast.

"Orality" is often presented as the crux of the new procedures.[21] Reformers argue that with public, oral trials there will be fewer opportunities for manipulating outcomes, defendants will get fair hearings, and decisions will be based on an immediate appreciation of the evidence, not on a written dossier prepared by a biased state official. Due process protections are emphasized at all stages of the proceedings.[22] Detained suspects must be provided with a lawyer, prosecutors and police generally require judicial permission to conduct searches and seizures or to hold a suspect beyond a minimal initial period, forced confessions are forbidden, and any evidence collected as a result of prohibited practices is automatically excluded. Some codes have been revised to retract a few protections.[23] Others never included them. Under Colombia's first new criminal procedures code (1991), prosecutors

---

21. See Maier et al. (1993), Davis and Lillo (1996), and Baytelman (2002).

22. Most new criminal procedures codes feature an introductory section (*Parte General*) listing the due process guarantees. Many of these have in turn been placed in the respective constitutions.

23. El Salvador is one notable example. What came to be regarded as an overly permissive code ("designed for Switzerland, not for Latin America") was subsequently amended to strengthen its law and order elements. See Popkin (2000, 218–41).

could order pretrial detention, searches, and seizures without judicial approval.[24] Prosecutors and police in other countries appear to do so routinely, relying on the exception provided for criminals apprehended in flagranti. A few countries (Peru until the turn of the century, Argentina at the federal level and in many provinces) retain an investigative judge as well as a prosecutor. As they have introduced oral trials, they are considered to have a "modern-mixed," rather than an accusatory system.

With the exception of these reactive amendments, the codes have not been further modified to reflect the addition of the crime control objectives. Instead, backers of the codes simply tacked on this second goal, claiming that the accusatory system is also more effective in investigating crimes and bringing the guilty to justice. As will be argued below, this strategic sleight of hand has created some serious problems. Codes written from a due process perspective sometimes interfere with effective investigation and prosecution. The conflicts are not inevitable. The problem is that the additional needs were never taken into account in any more specific fashion.

Over time the code-driven strategy has become more sophisticated and complex. The earliest reformers simply attempted to draft and enact a new law. As they were fond of saying, the rest would be worked out later. The earliest attempts with that approach, notably Guatemala in 1992, Colombia in1991, and Argentina in 1994, quickly demonstrated that nothing would be so automatic. Since that time the strategy has been amplified to include

- A period of preparation before the enacted law takes effect, often about two years;
- Gradual implementation, either by region or by including only cases commencing after the law's entrance into force;
- A staged training program (more than the initial short, mass instruction in the new codes), including orientation, general instruction, and specialized skills for different judicial officials;
- Creation or strengthening of public prosecution and defense prior to the code's introduction, with continued attention afterward;
- Police reform, especially, but not wholly, in the investigative areas and relations with prosecutors;
- Measures to simplify and rationalize courtroom procedures;

24. As has been noted by students of the Colombian reforms, as the first new code was being drafted, the law and order interests took over, giving the new prosecutors "judicial powers," or an ability to order detentions and conduct searches and seizures without judicial permission (Gómez Albarello 1996). In fact, in Colombia, unless a defendant objected to such practices, he might never see a judge until the case was transferred to the courts for trial. The code has been rewritten twice. The third version, approved in 2004 and beginning incremental implementation in 2005, has reduced some of the prosecutors' special, "judicial" powers.

- Infrastructure and equipment to support the new proceedings;
- Public education campaigns and programs for private attorneys and law students;
- Measures to evaluate progress and detect problems; and
- A variety of general institutional strengthening measures to combat traditional weaknesses and vices that would also impede the code's effective enactment.

Not all programs have included all of these measures. Even those included show enormous variations in the attention given to them and thus the results. One recurring question is the extent to which new codes can be effectively implanted absent broader changes in the courts and other implementing institutions. This is the last item on the list, but it is the one the criminal justice reformers have given least attention. It is obvious that implementing the greater reform first would put off criminal justice for some time. The reformers may also be counting on the more targeted changes leveraging the bigger ones. Nonetheless, the strategy does raise some doubts. Can an investigative police function without a broader police reform? Can a corrupt, disorganized, politicized, incompetent judiciary, or, still worse, public prosecution successfully carry out its new role? Without an adequate number of trained defenders how well will the system work?

These are not idle questions. Most reforms seem to be betting on making progress without broader institutional change. Most countries introducing the new codes have not reformed the police. Many have very weak, underfunded prosecutorial offices and near-nonexistent public defense services. Many have court systems that still lack autonomy from political forces and that, though they may enjoy more resources, have so far shown no ability to manage them well. Where codes have added further complexities—some form of plea bargaining, mediation of some types of cases, or the use of juries—observers have also questioned their wisdom, suggesting that such details might have been left for a later stage, when the basics of the new procedures were already in place.[25] Others have argued, before or after the fact, for a still-more-gradual phasing in of the entire procedures—perhaps starting with only major felonies and leaving the minor crimes to the old inquisitorial system.[26] As with the questions about the desirability of working systemwide improvements first, however, the reformers have preferred to bet on mandating the entire package as quickly as possible, probably fearing that a more incremental approach would give the opposition too much opportunity to water down the reform's aims.

25. Soon after its enactment in the mid-1990s, El Salvador made a rapid modification of its new juvenile justice code (considered a minicriminal procedures code as it dealt with crimes committed by juveniles) when it developed that the open-ended use of conciliation with the victim had unanticipated negative results. Commonly, friends of the suspect would visit the victim to encourage conciliation, or else.

26. This was a suggestion offered by one of the promoters of the Colombian reforms, after he saw how the code worked in fact.

RESULTS AND IMPACT

By now the majority of the region's countries have introduced some sort of modified code.[27] Most are in the early stages of implementation. Chile, for example, only put the new procedures into effect in two of its regions in 2001, planning to continue by adding regions, ending with the capital, Santiago, in 2005. Although it kept to the timetable, procedural adjustments are still being made. Some countries (Ecuador) have implemented nationally, but only for cases entering after the code went into effect. Cases entering before that time continue to be processed under the old system. The courts viewing them will be converted to the new system gradually as the old cases are resolved. Other countries (Costa Rica, for example) have enacted across the board, for all cases and for all courts. This clearly is the most difficult approach, and it is not surprising that Costa Rica's statistics indicate a median time for case disposition far longer than the period for which the code has been in effect.

Regardless of the code's details, the level of preparation, or the implementation strategy, the process has been difficult. As the most concerted effort to introduce change in judicial operations, it has still not been even moderately successful anywhere in just getting the various actors to carry out their functions according to the new legal mandate. The inquisitorial habits, along with numerous traditional vices, were difficult to eliminate. Observers note that prosecutors still attempt to document an entire investigation before asking for an indictment, that they are struggling with their new role in "leading the police investigation," that judges take too active a role in the oral trials, and that evidence continues to be collected and presented in written form. If anyone thought oral trials would eliminate the possibility of manipulation of evidence, they have only to look at the first such event held in Guatemala in 1994. There were charges of bribes being paid to everyone, from the witnesses, to the judge and the prosecutor.[28] Whether true or not, the accusations do suggest the enormous challenges of introducing a new proceeding in a still-unreformed environment.

Nevertheless, the effective implantation of the new proceeding was the goal only for the reformers. The expectations of the rest of the population, and the larger objective, were an improvement in the overall handling of criminal cases. A reduction in the frequency of traditional abuses (excessive use of pretrial detention,

27. The most significant exception remains Brazil. Mexico is also a slow starter, and it was only in 2004 that several states adopted new, accusatory codes. Mexico, however, eliminated the instructional judge in the early twentieth century. Local critics complain that its *procuradurías* (prosecution) then adopted "inquisitorial" habits.

28. Interviews by the author, Costa Rica and Guatemala, 1994. It was also evident that the trial was highly politicized both because of the context and the identity of the parties. A foreign prosecutor serving as a consultant in Guatemala suggested that despite the dubious quality of the evidence, the state needed and thus got a conviction to prove the new system worked.

forced confessions, and unrepresented defendants) was of interest to some, but most citizens will assess the success of the reform in terms of its efficacy in processing cases, identifying the guilty, and bringing them to justice. Until recently, any effort to evaluate those areas depended only on anecdotal evidence. Recently the Latin American Center for Judicial Studies (CEJA, Centro de Estudios Judiciales de las Américas) began a series of evaluations of progress in various countries.[29] The first evaluations were done in Paraguay, Costa Rica, Córdoba (Argentina), and Chile. A second series was later completed in Ecuador, El Salvador, Guatemala, and Venezuela. In addition, several Argentine NGOs have conducted evaluations of the new criminal procedures adopted in the Argentine province of Buenos Aires.[30] Some donors (notably the U.S. Agency for International Development [USAID]) have evaluated their own programs, but generally stop short of impact, instead focusing on success in implanting the new systems.

The results of the studies are not entirely negative, but they do indicate the enormous amount of work that remains to be done. One of the NGOs, FORES (Foro de Estudios Sobre la Administracion de Justicia [Forum for Studies on the Administration of Justice]), in its study of Buenos Aires Province, in fact concluded that the government was paying 50 percent more for its criminal justice system and resolving 20 percent fewer cases.[31] The CEJA study is most positive about the Chilean results but as of 2002 indicated that an enormous number of cases were stuck in the system.[32] Few came to oral trial, the alternative abbreviated proceedings were hardly used, and the most serious cases were still "under investigation." As the majority of the evaluators were most fixated on the conduct of the oral trials, the others did not provide figures on the rest of the cases. Judging by the number of oral trials held, however, it is clear that there were bottlenecks in all the other countries covered in the first and second rounds of evaluations.[33]

There is no disputing the need for criminal justice reforms in Latin America or the significance and achievements of the movement to produce them. Since their beginnings, in the early 1980s, the regionwide efforts have managed to make important changes both in how criminal justice is administered and with what results.

29. See Riego (2002) for a summary of the findings in the first four evaluations. J. E. Vargas (2005) provides an up-to-date but less detailed summary of the entire evaluation effort.

30. FORES (For de Estudios de la Administración de Justia), CELS (Centro de Estudios Legales y Sociales), and PENT. PENT's study (Herrero 2005) only reviews the criminal justice system in passing, but the others focus on it specifically.

31. Information on FORES's study comes from interviews with the authors, as it remains unpublished. CELS (2004), however, provides figures suggestive of the same conclusion.

32. Baytelman (2002); J. E. Vargas (2005). Vargas in a presentation at the Inter-American Bank on January 20, 2006, did note some improvements in Chile's use of abbreviated procedures.

33. See Cóppola (2002) and Rivas (2002), for Argentina and Paraguay, respectively. Baytelman's study summarizes the Costa Rican findings, but information on trials held (and times to disposition) is taken from an oral presentation given in a meeting of the research team (Rio de Janeiro, August, 2002). J. E. Vargas (2005) reviews both rounds of evaluations and gives some figures.

Still, as the recent evaluations suggest, they are far from achieving all they promised, and there is clearly room for improvement. Some of the disappointments only reflect the need for more time, but others may indicate more fundamental problems. In the remainder of this chapter, I address the source and nature of these problems, which affect not only criminal justice, but also many of the other reforms.

SOURCES OF UNDERACHIEVEMENT: STRATEGIC PARADIGMS AND TACTICAL SHORTCUTS

On the basis of my own observations, donor assessments of their own projects,[34] and what the CEJA evaluations uncovered, I would suggest that a series of initial assumptions weakened the process of planning and implementing the new reforms. Some have now been corrected; others have neither been recognized nor caught in the evaluation process. The latter in particular are probably the most controversial but, as argued below, will eventually require either midcourse adjustments or further choices on the part of the reformers. They refer in particular to the more detailed definition of the model each country is trying to adopt. With some effort to place the most fundamental first, the following summarizes how these strategic and theoretical oversights impeded program implementation.

The Reformers' Excessive Faith in the Power of Law to Induce Behavioral Change

This lesson has been absorbed by long-term participants, but the initial belief explains many problems.[35] Moreover, there are always newcomers ready to enact a law to change the world. Drafting law is easy and even enactment is far less difficult than other aspects of reform. It is often argued that once a law is in force, the rest of the changes can be worked out. That may be true, but it also runs the risk, as happened repeatedly with earlier code reforms in the region, that the impetus for change will expire long before much behavior has actually been altered.[36] This reinforces a certain cynicism about the law and can also leave room for subsequent modifications that undercut the initial intent.

Faith in legally induced change has been called a Latin American vice, but it is hardly limited to that region. Both bilateral and multilateral donors have made

---

34. The best sources are the evaluations done by USAID of its support to criminal justice reforms. See Checchi and Company Consulting (1991), Mudge (1997), Mudge et al. (1988, 1995), and Leeth et al. (1997). A more positive view is found in USAID (2002a). See also Hammergren (1998a) for a summary drawn from several USAID evaluations.

35. See Riego (2002, 5).

36. Latin America has a long tradition of importing "modern" codes. See Hurtado Pozo (1979). For Peru's experience with earlier criminal codes, see Hammergren (1998e, 116–17).

and continue to make their own errors in this area.[37] Human rights groups also seem to see legal change as a sine qua non in effecting reforms. Clearly, when pursuing procedural change, a new law could be a first or early step. In addition to defining the new procedures, it sets out the objectives of the change and can also indicate the key elements for producing it. Few laws are self-executing, however, and expecting them to be so is an invitation to disappointment. Even when supported by public education campaigns and judicial training, they are unlikely to alter much behavior. As we have learned, far more attention is required to creating and strengthening critical organizations, changing internal incentive systems, overcoming external opposition and customary practices, building new forms of interaction among key actors, and monitoring for results and emerging problems. Of course, as further discussed below, the quality of the new laws is also important, but the central point is that law indicates an intent to produce change. It does not in itself effect it.

The Reforms' Excessive Reliance on the "Inherent" Superiority of the Accusatorial Proceeding and on a Series of "Axiomatic Principles" to Justify It

The reform process was also driven by a series of testable, but largely untested, propositions. These comprise the "principles" justifying the reforms: that in contrast with inquisitorial proceedings, the accusatory system is less abusive of human rights, less expensive, more likely to get at the truth of the matter, more effective in bringing the guilty to justice, more transparent, more timely, and so on. These propositions, heavily influenced by European and especially German legal scholarship, were presented as "axiomatic truths."[38] They are actually verifiable hypotheses. To the extent they have been subjected to testing, the results are hardly clear-cut.

Much depends, however, on where one looks for examples and how one situates the results within the larger context. On the one hand, oral trials are far less expensive and far more rapidly conducted in Europe than in the United States, but in the latter country most cases do not go to trial, and, if they are included in the calculations, the results could be different. On the other hand, although the highly adversarial U.S. trials may take transparency to its maximum, the bulk of cases that are pleaded out are conducted far less transparently. Abuses of human rights depend on what is counted. Compared to Europe, the United States has a far higher prison population and, surprisingly, following a series of recent European

---

37. Certainly USAID's reliance on support to code-driven reforms is an example. In the commercial area, all donors have sponsored the overhaul of legal frameworks in the former Eastern Bloc countries, only to discover that old practices continue despite the new laws. See Gupta et al. (2002).

38. Most of them are still kicking around. See the chapters in Davis and Lillo (1996) for an example. Some of the authors now cite scientific studies, but are conspicuously short on footnotes identifying them.

reforms, puts more prisoners into pretrial detention.[39] Still, French instructional judges and prosecutors have more freedom to detain those "cooperating" with the police in the early days of the investigation. Police and prosecutorial abuse is rarely life-threatening in the United States, but there is ample evidence of other abuses, for example, dodges to get detainees to waive their rights to an attorney or psychological ruses to elicit confessions.

There is a tendency in Latin America to define everything that is bad as inquisitorial and all desirable outcomes as accusatorial. Mexicans, who in 1917 adopted a system structurally similar to that in the United States, now contend they have the most inquisitorial of all Latin American criminal justice processes. In fact, some local critics have suggested reinstating the instructional judge to introduce more accusatorial elements! Colombians characterize the extraordinary powers accorded to their prosecutors (*fiscales*) as an inquisitorial holdover. The determination of what is inquisitorial or accusatorial becomes so slippery as to resemble the arguments of neoliberal economists about the ubiquity of market mechanisms. Just as the economists support their position by monetizing all values, so judicial reformers find inquisitorial elements in everything that does not work. If the debate is ever to be resolved, participants will first have to be much clearer as to the basic characteristics of each model. Arguably the critical differences do not lie in the presence or absence of oral trials, representation of the parties, or the presentation of exculpatory and incriminating evidence—and probably are not found in the relative proactivity of the judge.[40] A more systematic examination might conceivably find that one or the other system tends to be more susceptible to certain vices. In the real world, however, systems that are usually classified into one or the other category seem equally vulnerable to similar problems, and their resolution appears to be independent of the specific legal tradition. Many due process rights were in fact added relatively recently to the U.S. criminal proceedings and thus cannot be seen as inherent to its basic structure.

The real problem with the axiomatic principles is that they presume a solution as a consequence of formal structural change. As suggested by the examples given above (and a host of others), this is a risky strategy. Leaving aside the accusatorial-inquisitorial debate, it might be wiser to separate structure from outcome and focus directly on the improvements in performance being pursued. Because most reforms

39. Kagan (2001, 65–66) thus notes that "American police are more likely than their French or German counterparts to arrest and lock up crime suspects rather than simply issuing a summons, and American defendants are more likely to be held in jail until both their first court appearance and the final decision." His contention is based on research cited in the text. Stepán (1994) makes the same point.

40. Damaska's (1997) assertion that the real difference lies in the view of how the truth is best derived (by competing parties or by a "neutral," expert investigation) may be most accurate—as the cynical version has it, "two lies" as opposed to one biased investigator. The U.S. model adds other elements—a distrust of authority of any kind and a highly aggressive bar. These are less characteristics of an accusatory system than of a national institutional environment. See Kagan (2001) for an elaboration.

are still engaged in structural transformation, this issue has not yet emerged. Still, before the structures are perfected, reformers would be well advised to proceed on this parallel track, pursuing adequate transparency, efficiency, and efficacy as goals in their own right.[41] This after all is the objective of the exercise of improving criminal justice. The basic models may condition the acceptable remedies but do not ensure that the best of them will be selected.

Academic Code Drafting in an Empirical Vacuum

By now, not even the drafters would disagree that the codes had some shortcomings and that some of these originate in their own oversights and ambiguities. Moreover, many codes experienced critical changes during their review by the legislature, and, in at least some cases, they were for the worse, not for the better. Two dramatic examples are the "judicial" powers awarded to the public ministry (ability to order preventive detention, searches, and seizures without judicial supervision) in both Colombia and Córdoba, Argentina. Some codes have suffered subsequent amendments—for example, the anticrime elements added to El Salvador's initial law. It should also be recognized that for the most part code drafting was done by academics, many of whom had negligible experience in litigating cases under any system. They were very knowledgeable about the content of a variety of existing codes but had never participated in the practices ordered by any of them. Hence, their ability to determine what "worked" and why was severely constrained, and they tended to adopt elements from among their catalog of codes on an often arbitrary basis or because of their presumed consistency with the overarching principles.

In consequence, many codes suffered from two kinds of failings: the errors of commission that led to the functional equivalents of building staircases into walls and the errors of omission that just did not change enough of the former system and thus left practical (not principled) inconsistencies. Many of the first set have already been detected and rectified. For example, there is the frequent stipulation that the suspect be notified within ten days of the start of an investigation. This is reasonable for petty crimes but not very practical for more complex ones. Other examples include arbitrarily set deadlines, which subsequently proved inappropriate for many types of cases; phrases like "the immediate provision of a public defender," which in their strictest interpretation proved impossible to realize; or discussions of the relationships between the prosecutors and police, which again lent themselves to inconvenient interpretations. Apprised of their new role, Salvadoran prosecutors asked for guns and finger-printing kits so that they could go

41. The Centro de Estudios de Justicia de las Américas (CEJA) evaluations do make some attempt to do this, but it is very narrow. Costs are measured only in terms of budgetary allocations, and transparency seems restricted to attendance at oral hearings.

to the crime scenes and collect their own evidence. Police also complained that prosecutors' efforts to be at every crime scene tended to obstruct routine investigations.[42] Salvadoran police could use more supervision, but the prosecutors seemed unable to distinguish those cases where it was really necessary.

Those charged with implementing reforms have also begun to adopt practices to catch these problems earlier rather than later. These include consultations with representatives of key institutions, simulated trials, and, in Bolivia, the use of computerized flowcharts as a means of feasibility testing.[43] In Costa Rica, consultations with prison staff inspired a change in the new requirement that prisoners not be transferred between penal facilities without judicial permission. As the officials noted, this is fine for ordinary transfers but would not be appropriate under emergency conditions—a threatened riot or an actual outbreak of violence. Many of the oversights are at this level of detail and are easily understandable in that the drafters could not be expected to comprehend all the needs of those who would be bound by the code. Although it is the grand principles that shape the codes, these mundane details determine their workability. When the drafters get them wrong, as they often do, one of two undesirable effects is likely: either the new procedures do not work at all, or those expected to follow them find ways to circumvent the law.

The errors of omission still persist in many cases. They often represent aspects of the process the drafters had not thought out and where they thus either said nothing or simply left the former elements in place. Some codes have descriptions of the trial based on the outlines of the old *expediente*. Evidence is to be presented in a set order, not according to how counsel wants to develop the theory of the case.[44] Although due process guarantees are often set out in considerable detail, the other routine aspects of normal operations are given short shrift or not covered at all. In some sense, this may be better than an innovative but uninformed effort to describe them, but, in light of the human tendency to follow past habits until forced to change, it also is an invitation to business as usual. The common observation that newly empowered prosecutors still operate much like investigating judges (in some instances, because that is where they came from) is a case in point. The Salvadoran enthusiasts are an exception but not a better alternative. Few code drafters had any experience with investigation, under any system, and thus could not be expected to understand how it might have to change both to reflect the new principles and to become more effective. Another area getting little attention was

---

42. As Stepán (1994) notes, and most practitioners will agree, investigation is always done by the police. They are organized to carry it out. Prosecutorial oversight means ensuring the police do not violate evidentiary rules and that what they collect is useful in building a case.

43. Interviews with Joseph Caldwell, chief of party for the USAID project, November, 1998, La Paz.

44. This is admittedly more in line with current European practices, but the drafters apparently thought they were moving beyond them.

the issue of police-prosecutorial coordination. The common phrasing that the *"fiscal would direct the police investigation"* has received any number of practical interpretations, many of them not very helpful in terms of improving real performance.

Had reformers expected less of their laws as a source of change, the code's oversights and errors of detail might have been easily remedied by sheer common sense and organizational innovation. Their law-based approach only compounded a longer tradition of formalistic legalism. Lacking other guidance and practical preparation, even judges and other officials convinced of the need to change often worked to the letter and not the spirit of the law. For those less convinced of that need, the law's details frequently provided a protective cover, letting them do what they wanted or what appeared to be required rather than what really made sense.

*Delays in Drafting Complementary Legislation and
Insufficient Attention to Its Content*

To be effective, the new procedures required more than oral trials or different treatment of the suspect, though this was where most focused. One problem with the new procedural codes in general is that they tend to be very court and judge centered. Whereas drafters envisioned a different role for the prosecutor, police, and defense, they clearly had not given as much thought to the organization and operations of these auxiliary institutions.

Often the laws that would shape these details were delayed in their appearance. When they were written, it was sometimes by experts whose vision differed considerably from those writing the basic codes. Thus, we might find a Germanic criminal procedures code combined with a Costa Rican prosecutorial law and a Spanish influenced police organization.[45] Where external experts assisting the drafters actually came from the respective agencies, the laws might faithfully reflect their national processes but did not exactly complement each other. They also tended to overlook local capacities and other factors that might make a familiar organization operate differently in a new setting. Although charged with creating new entities, they were, like the code drafters, more likely to be experts in laws than in operations. Alternatively, they might be very capable operational staff that had never given a thought to the organizational requirements that made their work possible.

In some cases, the new procedures simply had to go into effect without new complementary laws, either because local vested interests opposed their enactment or because by then the impetus for change had partially dissipated. In others, the tendency for congressional redrafting was still more pronounced and accounts for the lack of compatibility. In any event, because the codes and complementary

---

45. This appears to be the case in Guatemala, judging by the experts involved in each stage.

laws were rarely enacted as a package, the coalition of forces behind the later legislation was often quite different from that backing the basic codes. By then the code drafters had moved on to another country and their local allies were engaged in basic preparation and had less time to spend shepherding the other laws through the legislature.

Unfortunately, this secondary legislation is often quite critical to the code's full implementation. In fact, one could argue that the police and prosecution are far more important than the judge in making the new systems work. The principles for their operations were usually included in the procedural code, but, absent considerable internal reorganization and reassignment of power, they were unlikely to shape real behavior. Even assuming the validity of a more judge-centered model, as the evaluations indicate, the poor performance of the police and prosecutors has been an initial and very important bottleneck to implementation.

Excessive Optimism About the Time Needed to Produce Change

Things have definitely improved from the early days, when proponents appeared to envision an immediate implementation on passage of the procedural code. For this we can thank Guatemala and a few other countries that attempted the impossible and failed on the first round.[46] Even with an emerging recognition of the need for a preparatory phase (and more than a new law and a little training), the time frames still seem too short. Moreover, there appears to be a notion that the remedies consist in just lengthening the preparations by a few months or a year or, as in Chile, by a staggered implementation. In fact, one of the major lessons to be drawn from the recent evaluations is that implementation is iterative. No matter how much time is given for preparation (and two to three years appear to be an absolute minimum), no one is going to get it right on the first attempt. Thus, after the first try, additional readjustments are virtually inevitable.

Reformers should be prepared and organized to undertake these midcourse evaluations and corrections. They also need to find a way to maintain citizen, organizational, and political interest in reform. The danger of a lengthy and imperfect implementation is that support for change will lessen, as allies find other causes to occupy their time. Providing reports on progress and successes, and admitting and discussing problems may be useful. Creating organizational working groups and inviting citizen participation might also help. We have no clear lessons on the ways to maintain and broaden support over the longer run. We do know that without

---

46. In Guatemala, the new procedural code was enacted in 1992, and went into effect two years later. There had been virtually no preparation for the change, however, and, as a result, the post-1994 years were highly chaotic. In Nicaragua in the early 1990s, an adjustment to the criminal procedures code, requiring the use of juries, was also ignored until the day it was to go into effect. It took the country several more years to make any dent in the usual practices.

efforts in these areas, reforms inevitably lose impetus and can eventually grind to a halt without realizing a significant portion of their goals. A half-implemented criminal justice reform may be better than nothing, but it also risks considerable backsliding as sector actors return to the vices of the past.

The Failure to Recognize That There is No Single "Accusatorial" Model or to Realize That the Reforms Were Borrowing Pieces from Different Systems

There was no reason for the Latin American systems to copy those of the United States, Great Britain, Germany, or any other country. In fact, experience indicates that faithful imitation often does not work because of the many contextual factors shaping organizational and societal behavior. Certainly, Latin America's earlier efforts to imitate "advanced" criminal or civil justice proceedings or other practices (judicial review, council governance, constitutional courts), whether from Europe or the United States, suggest just that point.

Experience also demonstrates the dangers of pure innovation or the undiscriminating adoption of practices from a variety of legal systems. Innovation is a leap off the deep end and, if it is to work, requires an understanding both of the internal logic of the invention and of the setting in which it will operate. Logical and theoretical arguments may be a good place to start, but an innovator must also come to grips with the messiness of reality. More eclectic approaches to reform design, borrowing bits and pieces from individual systems, also have their dangers. First, the success of the borrowed mechanisms in its country of origin is often overstated. Judicial councils had already encountered considerable criticism among the European adopters before the Latin Americans decided they were a magic bullet. Juries in both criminal and civil cases are widely questioned in the United States as the best means of reaching good decisions.[47] Nonetheless they have been proposed and sometimes adopted in Latin American reforms as a way of "democratizing justice."

Second, even if the mechanism does work in its country of origin, its performance there depends on a broader institutional environment—and its organizational and purely cultural components. Mirjan Damaska (1997) thus notes in his comparative study of inquisitorial and accusatorial criminal justice systems that selective imitation is often not successful because practices are imbedded in a larger procedural whole. The French notion of the "criminal chain" (*la chaine pénale*) is relevant here—and might have been more usefully heeded by the code drafters and other reformers.

It is impossible to say whether the reform proponents believed they were imitating or innovating. I suspect the answer is that they were not of one mind either

47. See Sunstein et al. (2002).

on the basic approach or, if the answer was imitation, which model they were following. And even where they had a model in mind, they or their followers often left the way open for subsequent contributors who worked off a different script. One example is the role of U.S. lawyers in providing assistance on oral trial techniques in many countries in the region. As elaborated in the next section, the U.S. approach to oral trials is highly adversarial and makes certain implicit assumptions about how many cases will actually go to trial, how evidence will be collected, and the role of the judge in overseeing its presentation. In Bolivia, where a U.S. and a German judge collaborated in holding practice trials, they found they held very different views of what a judge does in the courtroom and consequently of how the prosecution and defense would themselves operate.[48]

Another example is the introduction of a rule or principle on judicial impartiality holding that this is best guaranteed by not letting judges who have participated in pretrial hearings be involved in later procedural stages. As applied to the new criminal procedures, it results in as many as four different judges being required to process a case at the trial level—a *juez de garantías* (responsible for overseeing the investigative stage and ensuring due process rights are respected), a judge for the intermediate stage (deciding whether the case will proceed to trial), a trial judge or panel of judges, and still a fourth judge who oversees the execution of the judgment. The principle is definitely not part of the U.S tradition, and U.S judges tend to see it as an affront to their ability to maintain impartiality. It does shape German practices and also accounts for Germany's having a near-world-record judge-to-population ratio. For Latin America, it may be a questionable choice, and not only for the cost implications. In the regional context, it appears to create delays (as each judge familiarizes himself with the particulars of the case in which he or she must intervene), encourage additional bureaucratization and formalism (by cutting the case into parts with no one responsible for the whole), and so provide further opportunities for a miscarriage of justice. As often happens with imitations, the adopters appear to have carried the principle to extremes not seen even in Germany—adding layers of judges not existing in the former country and insisting on introducing them even in jurisdictions where the level of demand might not fill the docket of a single judge.

The larger point is that the accusatorial system, like all other major legal traditions, takes a variety of forms, and its operation in the United States or Great Britain or, in its modified form, in Germany and Italy is hardly uniform. The differences lie in the details of each proceeding but, more important, in the underlying logic of the system itself. Latin Americans are apparently moving toward their

---

48. The German judge expected to have a more active role in the trial; when the American played the part of the prosecutor, he found himself frustrated by the "judge's" interventions. Interviews with the participants, Bolivia, 1999.

own variation, but it is not evident that all of them recognize this. There appear to be many who assume they are in conformity either with some generic model or with the system as practiced in some other country. Unfortunately, this may lull them into a sense that the only challenge is to ensure conformity with the basic paradigm. Because there does not appear to be one, their complacency is misplaced. For better or worse, Latin Americans appear to be forging their own, distinctive criminal justice systems, borrowing from a number of existing systems and also innovating freely. This is a legitimate approach as long as (1) it is recognized for what it is and (2) there is far more attention to the results (as getting the model right is not itself a guarantee they will be achieved). For several of the reasons outlined above, it may also be the only practical solution, but it does require far more effort and far more critical examination than does simple imitation.

An Excessive Emphasis on the Oral Trial

The oral trial lies at the center of the new procedures, as the principle means for guaranteeing immediacy and thus determination of the factual truth, public accountability, and a protection of various due process rights.[49] Fully adversarial, oral trials (as conducted in the United States) and especially those with juries are extraordinary costly. Figures from the United States suggest that each such event can easily cost the state upwards of $80,000.[50] As is well known, the only thing standing between these costs and judicial bankruptcy is the fact that so few criminal cases go to oral trial—anywhere from 10 to 2 percent of those initially filed. Most of the rest are pleaded out. The defendant confesses to a lesser crime in return for a lesser penalty. Many Latin Americans and many U.S. citizens consider that practice unsatisfactory, for reasons ranging from its lack of transparency to the dangers of convicting an innocent, but more timid defendant, one who succumbs to prosecutorial threats.[51] In fact, U.S. prosecutors often ask for higher penalties for defendants unwilling to negotiate a plea, and many U.S. judges take a similar tack in their sentences.[52] Juries are less predictable than judges. This is another problem. As studies of jury verdicts in both criminal and civil cases demonstrate, they are highly dependent on such presumably irrelevant factors as race (of the victim or defendant), public or private counsel, or even the location of the trial

49. This is certainly clear from the CEJA evaluations, most of which see this as the central aim of the reforms. In evaluating case disposition, the only element they consider in any detail is the oral trial.

50. Kagan (2001, 82). This does not include lawyers' fees paid by defendants. The substantial sums paid by an O. J Simpson are unusual but not unique; an ordinary defendant with his own lawyer can still expect to pay thousands if not hundreds of thousands of dollars.

51. See both Kagan (2001) and Strier (1996) for two very critical views. Both favor a less adversarial system and the adoption of some European practices.

52. Jacob (1996, 43) and Kagan (2001, 85).

itself (rural versus urban, small versus large city, and region of the country).[53] Press coverage of major trials in the United States is remarkable for its emphasis on counsel's strategy, the composition of the jury, and even the clothes chosen by the parties as clues to predicting the verdict. The law and the apparent facts of the matter are often only secondary considerations.

Many European systems, including some that have moved toward more accusatorial proceedings, have resolved the inherent dilemma by adopting a less adversarial approach to the trial process.[54] They hold oral trials but rely on an initial agreement over the facts of the case, as usually established by the prosecutor or investigative judge's findings. France in fact, as the inquisitorial hold out, brings roughly 95 percent of its cases to some kind of oral hearing.[55] In Great Britain, there is a tendency to assign most cases to magistrates' courts, which assign lower penalties and use a less adversarial process. In some of the Nordic countries, Germany, and the Netherlands, the need for oral hearings is reduced by giving the police or prosecutor the right to dismiss less serious offenses or resolve them by levying fines or alternative penalties.[56] Judges in these countries also have a more prominent role in the courtroom, commonly questioning witnesses or requesting additional evidence.[57] Similar judicial engagement in the United States, while possible, is less common and could be grounds for a retrial. Thus, the European transition to more accusatorial proceedings still retains many inquisitorial elements, as does the traditional English version—a more proactive judge, reliance on prosecutorial investigation, which may or may not reach the judge as a written case file, a far less adversarial exchange between prosecution and defense counsel, and the prosecution's ability to negotiate a lesser penalty with the offender, albeit not one involving a confession or judicial acquiescence.

One could treat the different approaches as a question of degree, but the basic issue is more radical than that. It appears to require a fundamental choice on the part of the Latin American reformers.[58] If they adopt the highly adversarial U.S.-style accusatorial system, they will either have to pay substantially, probably impossibly, more for every case to go to trial, tolerate lengthy delays, or accept the necessity of something like the plea bargaining system, to which there is still considerable

53. See Kagan (2001, 91–93). For one of the most thorough discussions of empirical research on jury performance, albeit largely in civil cases, see Sunstein et al. (2002).

54. For comparative discussions see chapters in Jacob et al. (1996), Fennell et al. (1995), Fionda (1995), Kagan (2001), and Strier (1996).

55. As reported by Judge Christine, Capitaine of the Tribunal de Grande Instance de Meaux, France, in a World Bank discussion, April 30, 2002.

56. See Fionda (1995), for a comparative treatment of prosecutorial powers. Fennell et al. (1995), Jacob et al. (1996), and Kagan (2001) also cover these.

57. Blankenburg (1996, 289). See also chapters in Fennell et al. (1995).

58. In discussing the possible convergence of the two systems, Jörg et al. (1995, 41) reach a similar conclusion, holding "that there is a critical limit at which each system would start to risk disintegration."

principled resistance.[59] They will also adopt a system that is able to offer dramatic attacks on abuses by authority but also routinely tolerates considerable unpredictability and a highly unequal treatment of similar cases. Judges will have preliminary hearings with the defendant, but these will be extremely brief, and only to ascertain that the accused understands the charges, is not being subject to undue pressures, and has representation.

If they adopt the more consensual European variation (contradictory, but not adversarial), they can give each case its day in court, but it will be a short day because of a greater faith placed in the prosecutor's collection of the facts (albeit with the participation of the defense), court-appointed experts, and possibly the retention of the written case file as the common script for all parties.[60] Outcomes will be more predictable, and less dependent on how defense counsels style their hair. They will also be more in line with establishment preferences. In any case, if Latin Americans adopt the European version, they would be well advised to stop using U.S. experts to teach trial practices. Aggressive examination and cross-examination, prepping of witnesses, lengthy debates over jury selection, competing experts, and manipulation of discovery (the exchange of information on evidence collected) are inherent to the U.S. system but have little if any place in the European inquisitorial or quasi-accusatorial one.

U.S.-style oral trials are demonstrably more expensive, both for the parties and the public treasury, but that is only one selection criterion. The more fundamental questions have to do with less quantifiable values—beliefs as to how the truth is best achieved, how basic rights are best protected, and how equal treatment is best realized. All of these questions are susceptible to empirical investigation, but even the sources cited here hardly provide definitive answers. They have marshaled their evidence in a legal, not scientific sense, intending to demonstrate, not test, their arguments. Hence, over the short to medium run, the choice is normative, but it appears to be inevitable and, unfortunately, has yet to be faced adequately by those shaping the region's reforms.

A Court-Centered Approach That Discouraged Sufficient Preparation of Other Organizations

This is another area where the reforms are making progress but still underestimate the real needs. The problem starts, as noted above, with the absence of an adequate

---

59. The problem here is that many Latin American constitutionalists believe this violates the defendant's right to a trial before a "natural" judge. Even alternatives short of full plea bargaining (for example, the mediation of claims between the defendant and his or her victim) have been protested for this reason.

60. I would emphasize here that the written case file does not disappear from the accusatory proceedings. It is less likely to be given to the judge; however, written records of investigations are especially important in any system (inquisitorial or accusatory) that proposes to protect due process rights.

legal framework. One suspects that this is a consequence of a lower interest in these other entities. Latin American reformers have focused on the judge and the trial. Here they might take a lesson from a U.S. prosecutor's version of the accusatory system: "What's the problem? The judge just listens to the evidence and decides." Clearly the prosecutor underestimated the judicial role. He did have a point, in that the crux of the new proceedings, in fact of any criminal proceedings, really rest on how evidence is collected and what use the parties make of it.

The fact that so many of the problems encountered with the new proceedings tend to lie in the investigative stage supports this view. There is an obvious temporal aspect to this problem. Investigation comes first, and, until it is well done, we cannot begin to appreciate any judicial shortcomings. Still, even in their most conservative interpretation, the findings do indicate the need for more attention to the investigative stage and thus to the prosecution and police. These are highly politicized institutions with far less independence than the judiciary and thus their ability to oppose change is often quite strong. Moreover, their reform is more costly then that of the courts. This is partly because of new needs, partly because of longstanding neglect and partly because, at least in the case of the police, their investigative function cannot be improved without a more broadly based reform. No matter what kind of internal or external specialized investigators are added, the ordinary administrative police will still be involved in the investigation. So long as they are left unreformed, there will be problems.

Although public defense is a less expensive undertaking, it is usually in as bad, if not worse, shape and likewise must be improved if the new system is to work. Defense requires a less complex organization than the police or prosecution, but it does require one, with rules, policies, supervision, and training. Just naming and orienting an army of *defensores de oficio* (court-appointed lawyers) is demonstrably insufficient.[61] Finally, the private bar has received still less attention though it usually accounts for at least 50 percent of counsel provided for defendants (and still more if it is also doing pro bono work). Remedial work with lawyers already in practice and more basic orientation in the law schools are also part of the reform plan.[62]

There are two aspects to the neglect of these auxiliary organizations. One regards the operational requirements for their new role. These are often areas where even the basic codes fall short, either by requiring the impossible or not mentioning the

61. These are discussed in greater detail in the chapter on access.

62. Despite long-standing complaints about the quality of contemporary legal education, it is only recently that attention has turned here. Criticisms tend to be similar throughout the region—an excessive reliance on lectures and memorization of the law, little opportunity for practical clinics, an absence of attention to ethics and client relations, and a proliferation of schools of dubious quality in the last quarter of the twentieth century. See Binder (2005), Boehmer (2005), Burridge (2000), Pásara (2005a, 2005b), Pérez-Perdomo (2005). Chapter 3 also reviews the topic in more detail.

necessary. The other is sheer organization—and here the code drafters, who usually were anything but institutional development experts, generally erred by omission. In terms of the first area, codes have often been long on restrictions as to what the prosecution and police may not do and very short on positive guidance as to how they should behave individually or in cooperation. Conceivably, most of this is not something the codes should define, but, because the conventional outlook relies on the codes for guidance, what was not said is often not done. Thus, once the general outlines of the code are written, a good deal more time must be spent within the organizations determining how they will alter their standard practices to comply with the new outlooks. This is an enormous task, composed of myriad details, which in combination should drastically alter how officials spend their time and what they produce. It means defining new procedures, training officials in their performance, providing them with the necessary skills and equipment, and overseeing their actual behavior. This, it should be stressed, means more than just changing individual routines—the most difficult part is undoubtedly modifying their interactions with each other, within organizations and among them.

It is a conventional and probably accurate truth that, absent any instructions to the contrary, prosecutors have tended to operate like investigating judges and police have simply continued as they always did. In the case of prosecutors, this has meant an emphasis on the written *expediente,* a tendency to let police define the nature of the investigation with the prosecutors only signing off on the results, an arguably excessive individual independence and thus a failure to follow organizational policies or even to create them, and finally a tendency (more compatible with the European version of the accusatorial process than with the U.S. model) to require that initial investigation be conclusive rather than simply indicating probable cause. This last trend, is should be noted, is also supported by the judges, but it probably arises in prosecutorial uncertainty. The prosecutors simply do not understand the less exhaustive requirements for bringing a case to trial or even, for that matter, for requesting a search warrant.

For the police, the situation is still worse. Absent an overall reform as in El Salvador, or the existence or creation of a special body attached to the public ministry (Colombia, Mexico, Panama, Costa Rica),[63] police investigators are usually part of an underpaid, undermotivated, underprepared, and largely unreformed organization. A hyperactive judiciary can curb some of their traditional abuses, but it cannot in and of itself improve the quality of investigation. To do so is an enormous undertaking with high financial and political costs. Most countries have

---

63. This is not always an advantage. In Mexico, it is generally recognized that the judicial police, attached to the public ministry (*Procuraduría General*) are responsible for much of the corruption in that institution, at both the federal and state levels.

simply been unable to realize this challenge, and thus the police remain the weakest element of the criminal chain.

Overly Conservative Estimates of the Costs of Reform

As with the question of time, reformers seem overly optimistic as to the savings represented in the new systems. In light of the underfinancing of all elements prior to the reforms, it seems highly unlikely that however measured (costs per case, overall expenditures, or some more sophisticated form of cost-benefit analysis) the new system will cost less. Nonetheless, this has been the promise in various countries. In Peru, for example, it was reported that a "Chilean expert" had determined that the new procedures would not only be more cost effective; they would also cost less. Although the Chileans claim never to have reached such conclusions, their estimates for their own system also seem low. After the fact, they can blame the unrealistic productivity estimates provided by still other experts. They might, however, have been slightly less disingenuous in adopting them for their own calculations.

Without benefit of anything more sophisticated than a seat-of-the-pants estimate, I would hazard a guess that the new systems will cost considerably more everywhere. This is a logical deduction from how little was spent before and how badly staffed and equipped the previous system was. Better justice, whether inquisitorial or accusatorial, will cost more, in term of not only initial investments, but also operating budgets. Possibly in the longer run, there will be improvements in cost per conviction or in estimated losses from crime (presumably deterred under the new arrangements), but by every other standard the public and private contributors will pay more for the service. This is especially true when one considers the vast investments required to improve police performance or create an adequate public ministry. No one is going to get good police performance paying the average cop on the street $50 to $100 per month or the average investigator even five or six times that amount. Moreover, in light of the constant temptations, a good monitoring and disciplinary system will be a constant need, and those staffing it will have to be paid accordingly. Prisons that rehabilitate rather than train criminals are another pressing need everywhere in the region, and they will require large up-front investments and significantly higher operating costs.[64] Prosecution may be in slightly better shape than either of these other elements, but both prosecution and defense will require higher operating budgets and initial investments.

Possibly the overly optimistic financial estimates were based on the judiciary, the institution that in many countries needs only to use its resources more efficiently,

---

64. Only Chile has included prisons in its reform program. The Ministry of Justice is currently advancing a proposal to privatize a part of prison services, a move it claims will cut costs and eliminate problems of abusive staff.

not to have them enhanced. For the rest of the *chaîne pénale*, however, better performance will cost more over the short, medium, and long run. Presumably the benefits (in terms of reduction in crime and its impact on society) might move the equation into the black, but this cannot eliminate the need for higher real budgets and those are what citizens first consider.

CONCLUSIONS

The Latin American judicial reforms started with criminal justice, and, although they have moved into other areas, it remains a major focus of their efforts. We began our examination of the various strategies here, not only to respect the historical order, but also because the longer experience allows more time to test the results and mistakes along the way. Many of the (mis)guiding assumptions also operate in other programs—the reliance on legal change or a few other single inputs (automation, to name one), lack of attention to the surrounding environment and the obstacles it will create, overly optimistic estimates of time and resources required, and so on.

The goals pursued by criminal justice reformers also pose certain conflicts with those sought in later programs, and many of the latter also contain their own inconsistencies and contradictions. The reasons for the persistence of these tendencies are themselves worth exploration. In the last section of this volume, they will also be examined. One evident problem, already suggested here, is a failure to evaluate progress or present programs in manners facilitating evaluation. When benchmarks are ignored and overarching objectives are not converted into measurable terms, it becomes very difficult to determine whether we are indeed advancing. Unlike other types of reforms, criminal justice actually has some advantages here. Although its two objectives present some internal conflicts, they do lend themselves to operationalization and thus measurement. In other areas, the objectives are often far vaguer and there is less agreement on what could be used to indicate their achievement. There is also far less consensus among the reform group as to their relative merits. No one argues that crime control is undesirable, though there may be questions about the trade-offs with full realization of due process rights. Reducing delays, increasing the courts' powers to check other branches of government, and expanding access to marginalized groups, however, more quickly run into opposition because of the other values they may compromise and the groups that stand to lose from their realization.

Nonetheless, judicial reform obviously involves more than criminal justice, and it has therefore been necessary to move beyond these programs into other areas. In the following chapters, we examine four other types of programs, their evolution over time, their effects, and the obstacles they have faced. All, like criminal justice reform, are termed "partial" reforms because they consciously or unconsciously limit their aims to a single dimension. This may be because proponents believe it is the most important, think it is the most likely to leverage further change, or just do not find the other dimensions all that significant. As we shall see, this single-mindedness has costs, not only for what it ignores, but also in advancing what it deems most worthy of attention.

 JUDICIAL MODERNIZATION: INCREASING THE EFFICIENCY
AND EFFICACY OF COURT ACTIONS

The discussion in this chapter focuses on two versions of judicial modernization strategy: that seeking modernization "for its own sake," a frequent goal of judiciaries, and efforts to augment the efficiency and efficacy of court actions, largely through the rationalization of internal processes and the addition of modern technologies. A final note reviews a related strategic objective, improving the courts' impact on economic transactions and investment. It is included here because it also emphasizes efficiency, albeit with a few additional activities—modernization of laws and the creation of special courts. In light of the frequent argument that a well-functioning, modern judiciary is essential to the creation of market-based economies, this appears to be the best place for addressing how that axiom has been operationalized.[1]

When outsiders talk about judicial reforms and especially those with donor financing, they often focus on court administration, automation, and related activities introduced to reduce backlogs and delays and otherwise make court services more efficient. For many external critics, this is the sum total of donor support, what they frequently describe as "buildings and computers" or "equipment drops."[2] Because these are often the most costly items in assistance packages (both loans and grants) they get a good share of the attention in documents explaining and justifying donor actions. The attention is not only a result of the financial investment. These elements are most easily explained to and understood by those not familiar with judicial issues, and it is these nonexperts who usually have to approve the programs. These technical packages have also become increasingly popular with judicial counterparts for reasons discussed below. Finally, along with the criminal procedures reforms, the use of judicial modernization to enhance efficiency constitutes one of the best-defined strategic approaches to reforming judicial operations. Its objectives are clear, its impacts at least theoretically measurable, and there is a straightforward, logical, and empirical linkage between the

1. This expression has become almost a mantra with the donor community. See World Bank, Legal Vice Presidency (2002, 13); Biebesheimer (2001, 99); USAID (2000, 55).
2. This term is used by USAID's first evaluators of its overall programs. See Blair and Hansen (1994).

activities included and the ends sought.[3] As discussed below, the linkages are often short-circuited in practice, and there are further questions about the relative importance of the aims in the Latin American milieu. Nonetheless, when they choose to do so, proponents of this approach stand on far firmer strategic ground than many of their colleagues pursuing other definitions of reform.

Most reform programs, whether donor or locally driven, do include additional objectives, but, at least on the donor side, the critics may be correct in contending that "efficiency" receives excessive attention.[4] No matter what the other components and goals, success is frequently defined in terms of backlog and delay reduction or increases in the number of cases resolved. It is not only the donors who do this. Peru's very controversial executive-led judicial reform of the 1990s had "zero carga laboral," or zero retained workload, as its official goal.[5] This was taken to mean that judges would keep abreast of their caseloads, absolutely eliminating any backlog. The economic analysis done by the Peruvians for a World Bank loan under preparation in the early 2000s also highlights the impact on caseloads and delays—what they would be with and without the project and the imputed financial savings.[6] The loan has many higher priority objectives, but, as the example illustrates, the emphasis on results indicators and economic justifications often pushes project design into a fixation on efficiency—because of the ease with which it can be measured and understood by other disciplines.

Thus, for many outsiders, and some insiders, judicial reform has come to be equated with augmented efficiency in processing the caseload. This is undeniably important. As will be argued, however, this perspective ignores other aspects of change and incorporates a very limited understanding of what judiciaries actually do. It uses a model of the judiciary that equates it with an ordinary provider of public (or private) services and consequently overlooks the courts' political role, their ability to shape demand, their deterrent function, and thus the importance of distinguishing between the sheer number of rulings and the differential impact they can have.[7] These additional considerations make efficiency enhancement a partial

3. Much of this draws on experience in more developed regions, and especially the United States. See, for example, Infante (2002) and Solomon and Somerlot (1987). Stand (2003) offers a European view. Although these sources are enthusiastic about the benefits of better caseload management, others have questioned impact on decreasing delays or increasing output. The caveats never reached Latin America.

4. See Tshuma (2000, 23).

5. Hammergren (1998e, chap. 6; 2000a). In 2005, President Alvaro Uribe of Colombia took a similar stance, insisting that the elimination of judicial backlog become a priority and instructing the judicial council and the Ministry of Interior and Justice to take steps to bring it about.

6. Peru, Poder Judicial (2002). The analysis was prepared to pass muster with the Ministry of Economy and Finance, which had insisted on a cost-benefit analysis.

7. In effect, many conventional public services should also be assessed in these broader terms. No one seriously considers evaluating health programs only in terms of the number of sick treated or defense as a question of the number of wars fought and won.

approach. They also undermine its success on its own terms. The big picture is essential to achieving smaller goals as well.

Latin American judges are usually less enamored of the accent on efficiency. They commonly argue that they are already overburdened with work and that the only solution is more judges and more courtrooms. This presupposes that, whatever number of cases they normally handle, they are working to their maximum capacity and thus that increases in productivity (a term they rarely use) are impossible. They have, however, gradually become fans of automation and other modern technologies because they see them as freeing up time for them and their staffs and because they are the mark of a modern judiciary. As one colleague has noted, the judiciary has an unusually inflexible production structure.[8] As anyone who has debated with Latin American judges about time-saving shotcuts can attest, most suggestions are stopped short by such arguments as "the law doesn't allow it," "it is in conflict with some basic right," or "it is not our responsibility to suggest changes; that is up to the legislature." The standard technical recommendation that computers be introduced only after procedures have been rationalized is extremely difficult to realize in these circumstances.

Most judiciaries seem to see technological innovations as at best a way of speeding up things as usual, not as a means to facilitate more radical changes in current practices. Electronic case files (*expedientes*) may be created, but the paper ones are still assembled and retained. Filings by Internet or fax must be followed by the paper copy before they assume legal weight. Use of standardized forms for the entry of information accompanying filings or subsequent motions is resisted; the computers simply speed up the entry of pages of documentation, much of it irrelevant or reiterative of what has already been recorded. Automation is rarely seen as a means of reducing the armies of courtroom staff required to draft responses or just move paper around. In fact, most proposals feature a computer for just about everyone except the coffee servers and clean-up crew.[9] The result tends to be a judiciary with modern equipment using the same antiquated procedures as before. Courts increasingly demand automation as a major part of any reform but rarely understand its potential for resolving performance problems or in fact recognize that the latter exist. As one Argentine provincial court succinctly put it, "We want computers because we want to be modern." This should come as no surprise in a region where updating of laws traditionally followed the same logic: "We need them to be modern," not to improve services or alter our most deeply ingrained practices.[10]

8. I thank Fernando Rojas of the World Bank for this insight.

9. Vargas and Correa (1995, 102) report a still odder phenomenon. In Chile in 1992, the 15 percent of the courtrooms with automation equipment had 31 percent of the total personnel and only 25 percent of the workload.

10. The criminal code reforms transcended this barrier, but most other legal reforms (of the basic substantive and procedural codes) seem more focused on modernity and less on behavioral change. This is one of the reasons they have so often produced few results, or even achieved full implementation.

HISTORY

The early Latin American reformers had been most concerned about the failure of courts to control human rights abuses and impunity, their inability to fight corruption within their ranks and in the wider polity, and their dependence on outdated substantive and procedural legislation. It was generally external collaborators, and especially those from the United States, who first focused on the inefficiency of judicial processes. This was an obvious consequence of concerns about growing backlogs and delays in the U.S. court system and the use of consultants who had worked on reforms of U.S. state and federal courts.[11] For many of these consultants, delay and overload were the fundamental problems and the crux of any reform. Over a period of just a few years, they also appeared on the local reform agenda, in some cases replacing many of the initial complaints.

There are several reasons for this transformation. First, delay and backlogs were also a Latin American phenomenon, just not one that had received particular notice. Second, although the eminent jurists shaping reform had paid little attention to them, they were a complaint of many traditional court users.[12] Third, in light of the nature of the analysis and the remedies offered, these programs were less threatening to the judiciaries. Delay and related problems were often attributed to external causes—inadequate funding, outdated procedures, lack of equipment, or the inadequacy of courtroom staff. The implied solutions—higher budgets, more equipment, courtroom reorganizations and staff replacement or training—were either welcomed by judicial leadership or accepted because they did not seem to imply any radical change in their own positions and operations. It is one thing to be accused of corruption and incompetence, but it is another to be told one cannot work efficiently for lack of the necessary tools.

On the donor side, the programs were also convenient. They involved less intrusion into political issues, instead focusing on technical and technological change. Although begun by bilaterals (and especially USAID), they were picked up as a major element in the IDB and World Bank programs because of their seemingly apolitical character and higher funding requirements. Technological modernization is

11. Many of these consultants were affiliated with the National Center for State Courts, which had supported massive court administration reforms in the U.S. state courts a few decades earlier. Descriptions of the situation in the states (see Tobin 1999) sound much like that encountered throughout Latin America, extending beyond inefficiency to corruption, politicization, and other abuses. The court administrators, possibly because of a disciplinary bias, focused largely on courtroom procedures alone when taking their experience to Latin America.

12. Whereas polls of court users in Latin America often place corruption as a prime complaint, delay is another major category. See Ledesma (1999, 155) for the Peruvian situation during the Fujimori reforms, when, for a time, delay actually surpassed corruption as a criticism. Surveys of business users in Mexico (ITAM and Morailia, 1999; Moody's 2002) and in Brazil (Castelar 1998; Castelar, org., 2000) also indicate a greater concern with delay.

an inherently expensive undertaking and thus well suited for large loan programs. Moreover, because neither bank first believed its mandate allowed entrance into criminal justice reforms, this gave them an area in which to work without political impediments.

Over time, additional arguments were added, linking pure efficiency strategies to the attainment of other goals. Proponents of the new programs contended that better management of cases would increase the supply of judicial services and thus broaden access to new users. They also found links between efficiency and an attack on corruption, arguing that judicial corruption was a consequence of delays.[13] More usually, improved courtroom processing of cases was presented as a way to eliminate opportunities for bribe taking.[14] All these additional benefits, like the implied more basic changes in judicial attitudes, were either not taken seriously or simply ignored by many judicial leaders. Their immediate goals were higher budgets and more equipment, often because they assumed they would resolve any problem of themselves and, unfortunately, in some instances, because controlling large purchases offered new opportunities for private gains.[15]

PROGRAM COMPONENTS

The Setting

Had critics of the efficiency approach spent more time in Latin American courtrooms, they might have been more sympathetic to its objectives—perhaps not those tied to total automation or "e-justice," but simply the attempt to bring some order to the reigning chaos. In the early 1980s, most Latin American courtrooms not only lacked computers, photocopiers, and faxes. At best, they had manual typewriters, and usually not enough for all staff; made copies by hand or with hoarded, ragged carbon paper; entered filings manually in large ledgers; stored documents on a few inadequate shelves or on the floor; and kept evidence in the judges' chambers or in disorganized common storerooms. Of all the public sector, the courts were undisputedly the most backward in their internal organization and practices.

13. Buscaglia and Dakolias (1999).

14. John Blackton, a former USAID employee and contractor, has argued that this is the only measurable impact of improved court administration.

15. In Bolivia in the late 1990s, one member of the new judicial council was widely known to have links to a computer hardware and software business and to be lobbying, not exactly discretely, for its contracting through several donor projects. Irregularities in the purchase of hardware and software for Peru's judicial reforms of the 1990s are still being investigated—though in this case, if anyone profited, it is more likely to be the executive-appointed administrators. In the early 1990s, El Salvador's supreme court canceled a proposed, government-funded purchase, suspecting its administrative staff was rigging the bids. A later IDB project in El Salvador was plagued by problems with contracting, especially for infrastructure.

Even the term "courtroom" conveys an erroneous impression, given its meaning elsewhere. The typical Latin American "courtroom" (*juzgado*) is a multipurpose judicial office in which considerable numbers of support staff (usually eight to fifteen, but sometimes as many as thirty) labor in very cramped quarters, drafting and processing the written documents on which the judicial proceeding is based, taking depositions from witnesses, and even holding what constitute any hearings. Usually composed of one large common office, the *juzgado* often has an adjoining room in which the judge works and another room for archiving. In more sophisticated versions, the judge's chambers may be glass walled so that he or she can oversee the rest of the staff. Where space and budgets are limited, the judge may work in the same room as his staff. Only in countries using oral trials (Panama, Costa Rica, El Salvador) were there separate facilities in which to hold these and other hearings.

Written documents connected to a case were inevitably collected in a large file, the pages of which were sewn into place to prevent their intentional or unintentional loss. These files (the *expedientes*) might number fifty pages for a very simple matter and comprise multiple volumes of hundreds of pages each for a more complex one. There was typically no systematic way for keeping track of files, which in some cases might be loaned to lawyers, kept in the desks of individual court staff, or accumulate in piles in the archive room. It was thus not uncommon for files to go missing, on purpose or out of sheer carelessness. It was rare to find a courtroom with any sense of modern filing techniques—such simple measures as storing case files vertically rather than in horizontal piles, or using cards or markers to indicate when a file had been removed from the archive and by whom. It was also rare to find a case retirement policy. Cases remained in judicial offices until they were completed, even if years had passed without action from the parties. In a recent visit to an Argentine federal court, in the city of Buenos Aires, we saw an estimated 13,000 civil case files piled on every available flat surface in the courtroom. Not surprisingly, most of the courtroom staff was occupied in moving them around or locating any that the judge might require.

When case purging exercises have been conducted in courtrooms, it commonly results that half to three-quarters of the cases can be closed and sent to the permanent archive, in civil matters for simple inactivity, in criminal matters because the statute of limitations expired long before. Thus, a 2,000-case backlog may suddenly be reduced to 600, as occurred in one trial court in San Salvador, El Salvador in the early 1990s.[16] Transfer to permanent or common archives had its own disadvantages if there was any chance an *expediente* might be needed later. They were usually no better run, containing endless stacks of bundled *expedientes*,

---

16. Subsequent backlog reduction exercises in El Salvador, Peru, and Argentina have produced similar results.

arranged on teetering shelves and held together by twine that inevitably cut into the papers. Further damage by water seepage, rodents and insects, or the occasional fire or flood was all too common.

The usual methods for registering case filings also complicated matters. Traditionally, cases arriving at a *juzgado* (either directly or, in more modern versions, from a central reception desk) were recorded in a *libro de registros* (registry book), essentially a large ledger in which court staff added hand-drawn columns to insert the data required by law or that they found convenient. Cases were sometimes assigned numbers to aid in their retrieval, but more commonly they were identified by the name of the parties, which might be recorded in a separate book. In theory, major events in the processing of the case were entered in this or one of several additional registry books, but the system allowed ample opportunity for mistakes and omissions. To this day, determining the status or location of a case filed in a busy *juzgado* can be an exercise in frustration. Registries from prior years sometimes disappear, entries are incomplete, or *expedientes* are misfiled.[17]

Although courtroom staff rarely received any training for their tasks, simply learning on the job, they were critical to maintaining whatever order existed. It was staff's memories and personalized systems that allowed documents to be located and kept the courtroom running. This explains why staff often enjoyed more permanence than the judges and why even those suspected of bribe taking or other irregular actions might be kept on. Sacking the old crook would have resulted in still more chaos. Staff also frequently invented routines and practices that had no legal basis but became more important than the formal rules in determining how things would be done in each courtroom. Judges were often unaware of these measures, which sometimes added delays or additional difficulties for lawyers. Needless to say, a lawyer who wanted reasonable service found it important to cultivate good relations with staff and avoid complaints about treatment.[18]

System administration (that for the entire judiciary), whether managed by a ministry of justice or, more frequently, by the supreme court, was in similar shape. With few exceptions (Costa Rica, for example), judges saw this as at best a necessary evil and so were unwilling to spend funds to attract good employees or equip them adequately. In the mid-1980s, Peru's administrative offices were located in a ramshackle building a few blocks from the supreme court. Passages between offices

17. In a recent exercise in case file analysis conducted in Peru (Gonzales et al. 2002), the team had to do their own inventory of all 1998 filings in Lima's sixty-nine *juzgados de paz*, after discovering that several of the *libros de registro* had simply disappeared.

18. A variation on the system, in place in Peru until the mid-1980s and still existing in some Brazilian state courts, gives some pretrial clerical work to private lawyers with offices outside the courts. This is a holdover from historical tradition, and its modification faces strong resistance from the private staff. Though often better trained than their courtroom equivalents, these individuals work without direct judicial supervision. They are thus suspected of many irregularities, including charging illegal fees and retaining some legally established tariffs they are supposed to forward to the judiciary.

were often uncovered—at least, it never rains in Lima—and employees had only the most rudimentary equipment with which to conduct their work. They were often tardy in submitting budgets or in requesting funds from the treasury. For what statistics they used, they had to depend on the goodwill of the district courts, because they had no power to demand them. Planning and forecasting were unknown, and budgeting was strictly on a cash-flow basis. The major interest of the supreme court, on whose every whim the administrators depended, was to ensure that the various special privileges and allowances accorded to the justices continued to be provided. The court's priorities remain very much in that line; when the Peruvian government cut the judiciary's budget in 2002, the justices campaigned successfully for higher salaries for the judges, but not for the administrators. Among the prominent casualties of this policy were the judicial school and the judicial archives. The archives, one of the major achievements of the reforms conducted under the Fujimori government (1990–2000), immediately lost ground. The situation threatens to undo several million dollars invested in making it a state-of-the-art model for the region.[19]

The situation described had changed little over the better part of the twentieth century and in many cases remains in place today. For *juzgados* with a light workload and not very demanding clients, it was adequate. As caseloads increased, it posed obvious difficulties. Except for the opportunities for corruption, Latin Americans had paid little attention to the shortcomings of conventional practices, assuming this was just how things had to be done. Thus, foreign advisors accustomed to working with courts that had moved beyond the nineteenth-century practices found a fertile ground for practical changes and zeroed in on courtroom (and system) administration as the key to improvements in overall performance.

Working Around Assumed Constraints

Introduced in the days when donors were still reluctant to suggest revising local laws and continuing after they saw how difficult that was to effect anyway, most of the efficiency-enhancement programs have attempted to work within the existing legal framework. This meant specific provisions—included in procedural codes, organic (organizational) laws, and at times the constitutions—defining such details as the number of courtroom staff, their responsibilities, and how paperwork would be processed. Laws might stipulate the use of paper registries (*libros de registro*) to record filings, of physical (and not electronic) *expedientes*, or even the way the latter would be assembled (sewn, not clipped together). Even when such details

---

19. As discussed in greater detail below, and in several separate studies, the Fujimori reforms get a low grade for their impact on judicial independence and judicial integrity and are an excellent cautionary tale as to the dangers of executive-imposed reforms. See Hammergren (1998e, 2000a); Lawyers Committee for Human Rights (2000); De Belaunde (1998); Ledesma (1999).

were not legally formalized, efforts to establish alternative practices were usually so strongly resisted by judges and their staff that a new law might be required to change them.

In light of these problems, most programs leave room for subsequent legal change but assume it cannot be the crux of their strategies. They also tended not to recommend alterations in the number or identity of courtroom staff, once more working with what is there already on the assumption that attempting radical changes might generate considerable opposition. Courts, like other public-sector entities in Latin America, have served as public employment agencies. Although some are overstaffed to the point of counterproductivity, court leadership is rarely willing to brook the resistance that would result from changing things. Judges never go on strike. Their staff is often well organized and unionized and not at all averse to striking. The few exceptions have always been local decisions.[20] No donor or foreign consultant has been willing to risk an abrupt end to their programs by making the obvious suggestions on their own.

Procedural Rationalization and Technological Innovation

Programs have worked on two main tracks: (1) reorganizing, rearranging, and rationalizing the use and deployment of human and physical resources and (2) adding modern technology. The latter is usually computer and communications equipment, but it may also be something as simple as file cabinets, file covers, or Rolodexes. For the most part, foreign consultants have never claimed that the equipment will produce changes on its own. They have, however, often soft-peddled the other elements to avoid immediate rejection of their efforts. Like the code-driven criminal justice reformers, they seem to work on the assumption that what can be changed easily will leverage the more difficult transformations. Unfortunately, in most cases, we are still waiting for the other shoe to drop.

Most programs, and certainly the best of them, require considerable preliminary changes in manual practices, reassignment of job functions, and physical reorganization of the courtroom layout before bringing in the computers.[21] In reality, advisors have had to work many compromises in the proposed preparatory steps and sometimes have simply stopped pushing when resistance began to emerge. If the courts insist on keeping their paper registries or maintaining paper flow as it has always been done, they are allowed to exist alongside the automated systems.

20. It is interesting to note that governments and courts have had more luck replacing judges than staff. The Dominican supreme court, which recently forced all judges to compete for their jobs (replacing a substantial number with outsiders), has yet to tackle the staff question. Although Peru's executive-led reforms replaced both judges and staff, the post-Fujimori program is still focusing only on the judges.

21. See USAID (2001), which makes it abundantly clear that computers are the very last step in an entire process of rationalizing and improving court information management strategies—including both judicial statistics and case-tracking systems.

Staff may be retrained and given different functions, but they generally are left more or less where they are found. Advisors have had more luck in promoting the adoption of pooled staff and services (for example, centralized notification offices as opposed to the traditional assignment of process servers to individual courtrooms, court clerks responsible for managing dockets for a group of judges, shared archives). This is especially true when the changes are backed by construction or remodeling of facilities and when they do not imply staff reductions. Nonetheless, resistance is often overwhelming. Most Mexican state courts still give judges their own process servers and bailiffs, arguing that this is the only way to provide adequate oversight. A review of court practices indicates that judges actually have little means of controlling these individuals, who are consequently a focus for corruption.[22] States that have successfully adopted pooled systems, however, have been reluctant to promote this model, arguing that their success was based on special circumstances.

Unassisted equipment purchases have not worked even that well. When the Costa Ricans added automation to their modernization efforts in the early 1990s, a common practice was to assign computers to staff members so that they could do their usual work faster. Staff occupied the same locations, did the same jobs, and for the most part simply used the new machines for word processing. Since then, the Costa Ricans have gone to the other extreme, creating "megaoffices" of as many as fifty judges with shared facilities and staff. The reaction from judges and clients is mixed, with many complaining of excessive bureaucratization. The Mexican federal courts appear to have followed the first Costa Rican approach. Despite a hefty investment in automation equipment, their courtrooms retain the same vast army of support staff needed when everything was done manually.[23]

In the early years, similar developments were not uncommon in donors' programs, often because purchasing and technical assistance were done out of sync, donor project managers did not understand the basic principles, or contractors providing technical assistance were not up to the task. Occasionally, and more frequently with MDB projects, the software and hardware providers were supposed to do the preliminary reorganizational work but gave this short shrift. Whatever their terms of reference said, they interpreted "implementing a new system" as installing the computers and software and training staff to use it. Because local counterparts let and supervised these contracts, the oversights usually went unnoticed. This has not lessened the judiciary's enthusiasm about new technology. It has fortified the skepticism of those describing the investments as equipment dumps.

This skepticism could be combated if judiciaries made an effort to track and document improvements. Most have failed to do so, in part, one suspects because collecting and releasing such information would give outsiders the ability to monitor

---

22. World Bank (2002b).
23. Individual trial judges commonly average thirty staff members.

the performance of individual judges and of entire court systems.[24] Although the region's judiciaries increasingly support citizens' right to information from the rest of the public sector, they frequently exclude themselves from these mandatory practices.[25] Judicial independence or the parties' right to privacy (in the case of publication of judgments) is often used to justify this exclusion.[26] Not all judiciaries are opposed to improving service provision or even to monitoring internal performance. Nonetheless, they prefer to do this on their own terms, and publicly setting new standards and publishing results does threaten to take this out of their hands.

Thus, despite the relatively simple concepts underlying the strategy, there was ample room for imperfect execution. First, there was the failure of many courts to understand or adopt the goal of improving and speeding up their handling of cases. For these judiciaries, the means were the end. Even those recognizing the potential for improving service have generally preferred to speak in general terms, without setting quantitative benchmarks. A second contributing factor was the assumption by many donors that the new technologies would leverage other change. If on a somewhat more sophisticated level, this was the functional equivalent of the same inversion of means and ends. In addition, donor project managers, under pressure to demonstrate results, had strong incentives to take this shortcut. It is thus not uncommon to find, in the logical frameworks used in project documentation, that the performance indicators are the successful installation of the new hardware and software, rather than any further transformation of court outputs. Where practices such as USAID's introduction of results indicators forced movement to measures of impact, no one apparently kept track after the fact.[27]

More complex program design provided other opportunities for slippage. Because neither local nor external reformers were knowledgeable about the judicial applications of administrative and technological reform, they might set impossible requirements, choose their contractors poorly, decide to let in-house experts design the systems (usually a bad idea), over- or underbudget drastically, work on several parallel and uncoordinated tracks (with different donors funding separate automation efforts[28]), adopt already-outmoded or otherwise inappropriate equipment, and

24. This is hardly unique to Latin American courts. A review of experience with the U.S court delay-reduction programs of the 1970s concludes that evidence offered as to results was largely anecdotal, qualitative, and highly selective. The evaluation did find impacts worth reporting but had to collect its own data to do so. The courts were not keeping track. See Neubauer, et al. (1981).

25. See Motta (2001) for a discussion of the Argentine supreme court's rulings and practices in this area.

26. The Mexican federal and state courts are only now beginning to reconsider this policy. In 2002, the federal chief justice, Góngora Pimental, promised that from then on judgments will be published. Two years later, state courts had yet to take a position, and the federal courts' implementation remains only partial.

27. As USAID has stopped doing compulsory project evaluations and decided to place results indicators at an agency level, it is not clear they will have to do so anyway.

28. USAID and the World Bank faced several years of difficult relations over just this practice in Bolivia. USAID had funded a locally developed automated system for criminal courts; the bank financed

omit the necessary consultations with users as to what they need in a system.[29] These operational problems were not the only weaknesses of the strategy, but they obstructed the achievement of even their partial goals.

Pilot and Demonstration Programs

For donors with limited funds, and even for the MDBs, a further problem was the reliance on pilot projects. Some of these projects did demonstrate improvements in disposition rates and backlogs. This is not uncommon in experimental efforts because participants are often selected for their willingness to try new methods and receive special attention from the project directors and consultants. The expectation that these demonstration efforts would inspire nationwide replication has rarely been met. Some countries, usually with additional donor funding, have attempted to expand the models, but it appears without duplicating the initial successes. So far no country in the region has been able to adopt the new models across the board.[30]

Peru's self-financed experiment with corporate courtrooms (*juzgados corporativos*) is illustrative of the problems.[31] Like the Costa Rican "mega-courtrooms," it featured pooled resources, automated case-tracking systems, and a single administrator to direct the work of a number of judges. In contrast with Costa Rica, the groups were smaller, and the judges kept their own offices (in which they held hearings and did their own work), though in the beginning they shared all staff. Initial results in the first pilots (in the criminal trial courts of the town of Chiclayo) indicated considerable success in reducing backlogs and delays.[32] Over time, the improvements were reversed, and there were reports of increasing corruption (orchestrated in part by the administrators). According to some observers, the early success was largely due to the salary bonuses paid to judges and staff who met quotas. Once the bonuses disappeared, so did the improvements.

The experiments have been expanded to civil trial and some appellate courts

---

a separate system for civil courts. As of 2004, the two systems remained partially implemented and completely separated, and arguments continue about which one "really works."

29. Although, as in Bolivia, there were political and other interests at work, the Ecuadorian court continues to complain that the system financed under a World Bank loan is incomplete and inadequate. A major problem is that the judges and court staff find it difficult to use. A USAID-funded project to establish an automated system for Colombia's *fiscalía* (Prosecutor's Office) encountered problems since its inception more than a decade ago. Local experts report that the initial vision was overly ambitious and that, as a result, the system is too heavy, has a slow response time, and is prone to crashes. It is also interesting that both the bank and USAID have faced similar problems with their own integrated management systems—with complaints in the first case that the results are not user-friendly and in the second that the system was too large to be supported by the agency's hardware.

30. In the context of a much broader program, including legal reform, addition of many more judges, infrastructure, and some courtroom reorganization, Uruguay has apparently reduced the time to judgment for civil cases. See Gregorio (1996).

31. See Hammergren (2000a) and Ledesma (1999).

32. See Dakolias (1999).

in Lima and other major cities. Once the judges got their own assistants back, they became more positive about the experience — perhaps not surprising, because most of the written work is done by staff, with the judges at the end of a sort of assembly line, waiting for papers to cross their desks or to hold an occasional hearing. In fact, visits to several such corporate courts in Lima and Chiclayo in 2002 suggest the judges are relatively underused and have finally been able to legalize a long-criticized practice, the delegation of most work to nonprofessional personnel. Because no one seems to be keeping statistics on delays any longer, it is impossible to tell whether the replication has met with success in that area. A study of 1998 filings in Lima's trial and justice of the peace courts indicates that both had a much better record (time to resolution and percentage of cases disposed) in resolving debt collection cases despite the peace courts' not having benefited from either automation or reorganizations.[33]

Quite apart from any impact on delay, the experiment also suggests the dangers of an exclusive focus on its reduction. First, the study also noted a tendency of trial court staff to reject initial filings to reduce their own workload (and possibly to double their disposition rate). This type of reaction has been recorded elsewhere.[34] Second, the judges apparently sacrificed any supervision of their own caseload and, thus, the ability to counter delay-creation tactics or other abuses on the part of the litigants. Third, and as a consequence, questions have been raised about the quality of the decisions eventually delivered by overly bureaucratized judges. This may be less of a concern with simple debt collection (*juicios ejecutivos*), which is theoretically fairly straightforward, especially, as was frequently the case, when the debtor does not even appear in court. It does, however, raise questions about inadequate notification or a failure to detect abusive credit policies. The corporate model, introduced by engineers and court administrators, does look very much like an assembly line, possibly not the best choice for a judiciary.[35]

Infrastructure

Although new infrastructure is not a necessary part of this approach, a few words are warranted on its addition. To the extent the courts showed any interest in expanding services, their traditional solution had been, as noted above, the addition of judges and courtrooms. They also obviously wanted better housing, contending

33. See Gonzales et al. (2002). Improvements must be interpreted with caution as there is really no baseline data against which to assess the rates; however, the median of less than three months to adjudicate debt cases stands up very well against other countries in the region.

34. See Magaloni and Negrete (n.d.), for Mexican federal courts.

35. There are two further aspects that probably never occurred to the engineers. Many of these rulings were against absent defendants because court fees and the required legal representation keep many parties (including civil defendants) out of court. In addition, the researchers found indications that many judgments were never enforced — the plaintiffs (often banks and pension funds) won but did not collect.

that their current courthouses did not enhance the institutional image. This latter argument frequently led to funds (almost always from MDB loans[36]) being used to build new palaces of justice rather than lower-level courts in far-removed areas. The World Bank's first Latin American project, in Venezuela, received extensive criticism for the massive investments intended for construction and consequently was redesigned to pass most of these activities to the counterpart's contribution.[37] Since that time, the willingness to fund buildings has gradually returned. On the one hand, this increases the size of the loan (a primary internal measure of success) and, on the other, makes the courts' more enthusiastic allies in the loan negotiations. The Inter-American Bank has been less wary of construction. Most of its projects have a large infrastructure component though often, as in Peru, to finance buildings intended to take services to the poor.[38]

The final argument for new infrastructure is more closely related to the efficiency goals. If automation equipment is to be installed, or if courtrooms are to be reorganized, the existing buildings may not be suitable. Many courts rent their installations and have argued that the costs of cabling alone merit moving to more permanent quarters.[39] Similar arguments cite the need for new layouts or more room for archives and for the common services often recommended as a part of rationalization programs. It is clear that there are less costly alternatives, but, where both donor and recipient have a common interest in increasing the size of the loan, they are easily ignored. In loan programs, the courts are the direct beneficiaries, but to date the loans have always been backed and repaid by the central government. Hence, for the judiciary, this is free money and there is little incentive to economize on its uses.

In Mexico, during the 1990s, a similar effect is seen in the use of a special fund (derived from interest paid on escrow accounts managed by the courts). The

36. One exception is USAID's financing of a new palace of justice for Panama's supreme court. This was done because the former building had been a casualty of the U.S invasion in 1989. Limited funds and agency policy precluded other construction projects and restricted work to remodeling some dilapidated buildings or the provision of far simpler structures in areas without court services.

37. See Lawyers Committee for Human Rights and Venezuelan Program for Human Rights (1996). Both loan- and grant-funded programs usually require an additional contribution from the recipient government, calculated as a percentage of the total program's value. Where donors' policies or other restrictions do not allow the financing of certain items, these may be passed to the counterpart element.

38. Inter-American Development Bank (1997). The initial project design is virtually all buildings and computers. The only additional funds are for training judges in gender sensitivity. The project hit predictable problems when it developed that the Peruvian agencies expected to staff the courts did not have the resources to do so.

39. Donors seem to have bought into the courts' prejudices against using rented facilities, so much so that project documents often cite rented buildings as a problem in their own right. No one has ever conducted an analysis of the financial and other advantages of one system or the other. One could argue that, in light of pending changes in procedural systems, deployment of personnel, and the like, longer-term rental might be wiser.

extremely high interest rates of the mid-1990s considerably augmented the monies available to the state courts, and many went on a construction spree, building courthouses and buying equipment that still remain underused. With a windfall like this, Mexico's state courts had no need to worry about efficiency. Now that interest rates have fallen, their expansion plans have come to a near halt. The state courts are looking to a solution in a proposed budgetary earmark of 3 percent—which would triple their current ordinary budgets—or in the attraction of donor funding. One can hardly begrudge them their better quarters, but the entire experience seems to have entrenched the notion that the principal route to better service is higher budgets, more judges, and more courthouses.

RESULTS AND IMPACTS

Despite starting later, the modernization strategies have produced almost as much change as have the criminal justice reforms.[40] As with the latter, most of this is restricted to internal conditions and practices. The presumed downstream benefits—delay and backlog reduction, greater user satisfaction, more control over "irregular" behavior, and overall enhanced productivity, production, and quality—have been limited to pilot ventures, and in no case, produced permanent, system-wide impacts. The projects have been most successful in converting courts to new technologies. They have been least successful in leveraging additional attitudinal and behavioral change.

With respect to the first version of the objectives, modernization for its own sake, this can probably be counted as a success. The transformation is an important one. Unlike the days when judges viewed computers, e-mail, and bar codes (to identify *expedientes*) with enormous skepticism, these now figure at the top of their wish lists. They even have begun to appreciate the importance of more mundane innovations—improved filing systems and centralized services. Moreover, the new technologies are used, if not always to the many ends for which they were intended. One should also not discount the potential for subsequent impacts on behavior. Many of the changes courts will have to make to augment their service production and productivity will be greatly facilitated by the new equipment. It is true that they could make them without computers, but by removing practical barriers technological modernization may facilitate adoption. This puts the strategic

---

40. This is a point worth emphasizing as many critics assume all donor programs began with court administration. In fact, USAID, the first to enter the latter area, did not begin to emphasize it until the late 1980s, after several years of criminal justice reforms. The confusion may originate because of the title "administration of justice," used for the early programs. It was a direct translation from the Spanish and did not in any sense imply a focus on "administration," as understood in English.

cart before the horse and conceivably could discourage any sense of urgency. Nevertheless, computer-generated statistics now give judicial leaders a better view of how their judges are doing, help pinpoint bottlenecks and problem areas, and have occasionally made them more aware of the need to improve services. Despite the general resistance to standardized documents, some judges are introducing them on their own, and the practice is gradually spreading. Some forms of corruption have become more difficult to continue, and record keeping on a whole is generally better. Much of the new equipment and many of the new buildings are severely underutilized, but the installed capacity will help meet new demands and benefits users as well as judicial staff. Any improvements to the courts' image could also have further positive impacts, in terms of both better attention to the public and the judiciary's own sense of the importance of further improvements in what it delivers (as well as how it is housed).

Nonetheless, the critics are correct in that the societal payoffs have so far not justified the investment. The most direct benefits still stop at the courtroom door or, at most, in the attorney's office (for those who now can file claims and receive notifications by Internet or fax). Ordinary clients who already send their conflicts to courts, or those who might do so were they not so skeptical about the results, will notice little difference in delays, costs, or quality of judgments. There are some important exceptions. The judiciaries in this category adopted the modernization efforts as means to other ends, not as ends in themselves. Even here, documentation of progress is slight, and one has to take the advances of judiciaries like that of Costa Rica largely on faith. Because it, like other courts in the region, is undergoing a continuing reform process and experiencing a growing demand for services, improvements in internal processing of cases, introduction of abbreviated proceedings, and related changes may make little dent in the ever larger workload.[41] There are also concerns, as discussed in the next section, that the administrative improvements do not touch many underlying causes of inefficiency—and, in some instances, may aggravate them. Costa Rica's highly automated civil courtrooms now allow lawyers to file even longer briefs and pleadings, which are in turn answered by legal staff using their own computer equipment. The temporal and monetary economies allowed by Internet exchanges and cut-and-paste documents may further string out the preparatory stage as lawyers introduce still more issues for pretrial resolution. Faster notification and distribution of case files hardly compensate for the persisting incremental approach to deciding what will be presented to the judge.

41. On curious aspect of current statistics from the region's courts (CEJA 2005; World Bank 2005c) is that recent increases in clearance rates have not reduced backlogs. Courts claiming clearance rates in excess of 100 percent still seem to accumulate work. This raises suspicions of statistical manipulation as well as questions of what is not being processed.

THE EFFICIENCY MODEL AND ITS STRATEGIC OVERSIGHTS

As the Costa Ricans have discovered, a certain amount of success may only lead to greater demand and a sense that they have to run faster to stay in the same place. Significantly, after years of accepting their current workload as a given, the Costa Rican judiciary initiated a radical change—dejudicializing the more than 50 percent composed of traffic cases in the realization that the automatic chance to contest a parking fine or moving violation does not necessarily protect any basic right.[42] In fact, many of those affected would probably prefer to pay the fine and miss their day in court. The suggestion, made by a few critics of the approach, that enhanced efficiency may contain the roots of its future failings, may be less significant over the short run than the secondary lesson, that courts' current workloads should themselves be reexamined. This leads us to some more basic concerns about the efficiency approach, introduced below as three "strategic oversights."

Strategic Oversight 1: Some Questionable Assumptions on the Incidence, Causes, and Importance of Delay

The Costa Rican case raises several issues, some of which are treated in the following sections. The issue addressed here is that the efficiency-enhancement strategies usually were introduced without any basic data on the nature of the caseload and how it was being processed. Courts universally believe they are overburdened with cases and just as universally blame this on excessive demand and inadequate resources. They are far less inclined to believe the problem could be treated by changes in the production function—how they handle what they get—or, as in Costa Rica, by diverting some demand. Comparative statistics on Latin American caseloads, to the extent they are even available, suggest a very different picture. Because these statistics either did not exist or were not consulted by those designing programs, the assumptions about the nature of the problem, and thus the optimal solutions, were often simply in error. Table 2 provides the basis for elaboration on these points.

As suggested by the above, few Latin American judiciaries can claim an absolute excess of caseload. In much of the region, litigation rates (cases per 100,000 inhabitants) tend to be modest as compared to industrialized nations. They are lowest throughout Central America (with the exception of Costa Rica and Panama), in the poorer states of Mexico and Brazil, and in the less developed South American countries. Although countries with higher rates tend to have more judges to take

---

42. Mora Mora (2001) states the general argument, but the measure was not approved by the congress until 2005 and still excludes accidents covered by the state insurance agency.

Table 2 Comparative statistics on judicial workloads[1]

Country	Filings (dispositions) per 100,000 Population	Judges per 100,000 Population	Filings (dispositions) per Judge
Honduras[2]	1,200	8.8	136
Venezuela[3]	2,375	6.3	377
El Salvador[4]	2,454	11.8	208
México, Federal District only[5]	2,600	4.0	650
Brazil[6] (federal, labor, and state only— military, electoral and *juizados especiais* not included)	7,171	5.3	1,357
Argentina[7]	9,459	10.9	875
Colombia[8]	3,298	7.7	430
Costa Rica[9]	21,000	15.9	1,320
England and Wales (disposed)	(9,800)[10]	11[11]	(891)
France (disposed)	(6,200)[12]	13[13]	(477)
Italy (disposed)	(14,000)[14]	20[15]	(700)
Germany (disposed)	(15,600)[16]	23[17]	(678)
U.S., District of Columbia (civil only)[18]	20,321	10.21	1,992
U.S., Maine (civil only)[19]	2,821	1.29	2,187

Notes:

1. Dates for figures vary as indicated. Workloads are calculated by dividing the number of first-instance filings or dispositions by the number of judges. This may slightly understate the first-instance workload, as the number of judges also includes those in higher instances. However, the bias can be assumed to be consistent, and is necessary because some information on the total number of judges does not offer breakdowns by instance.

2. World Bank figures, from project preparation documents, corresponding to 2002.

3. World Bank figures, from project preparation documents, corresponding to 2002.

4. World Bank figures, from project preparation documents, corresponding to 2001.

5. Litigation rates elsewhere in Mexico are usually lower—for example, the State of Mexico, the Federal District's neighbor, showed figures of about 1,600 per 100,000 inhabitants, World Bank (2002b).

6. For 2002, from *Supremo Tribunal Federal* data bank; http:/www.stf.gov.br/bndp/stf/ As figures on *juizados especiais* (small claims courts) are incomplete, as is the information on their judges, neither is included.

7. Argentina, *Ministerio de Justicia y Derechos Humanos* (2002; 16).

8. Fuentes (2004; 150 and 152). Figures are for 2001 and cover only ordinary courts, not the administrative or constitutional systems.

9. Mora Mora (2001).

10. Blank et al. (2004; 93). Figures are for 2001. Dispositions per judge are calculated by dividing the number of judgments per 100,000 inhabitants by the number of judges per 100,000 inhabitants. Although this is one of the more up-to-date compilations of European statistics, it does not include total filings, and it mixes administrative, criminal, and civil judgments. In a further breakdown (p. 93) of judgments by jurisdiction, Germany shows the greatest differences—192 judgments in criminal courts, 1,116 in civil, and 150 in administrative. The authors do not indicate whether the latter figures were calculated against all judges or only those handling the specific type of case.

11. Blank et al. (2004; 93).

12. Blank et al. (2004; 93).

13. Blank et al. (2004; 93).

14. Blank et al. (2004; 93).

15. Blank et al. (2004; 93).

16. Blank et al. (2004; 93).

17. Blank et al. (2004; 93).

18. Marcus (1999; 112), for early 1990s. Judges may get more filings if they are also receiving criminal cases (general jurisdiction).

19. Loc cit.

up the slack, some of the least litigious have a relatively high number of judges, meaning that caseloads per judge are frequently minimal.

In a majority of the region's countries, average filings per judge, to the extent that can be determined, rarely work out to more than 700 annually and sometimes drop to as low as 200 (El Salvador) or 136 (Honduras). Latin American judges, however, tend to estimate their own capacity even lower—frequently noting that 250 to 300 filings annually are the optimum amount.[43] When filings increase and judicial leaders begin to take notice of backlogs, one unfortunate consequence is a tendency to increase formalism—judges lower the quality of the decisions to keep up with the augmented workload,[44] cherry picking the easy cases and leaving the rest in what the Brazilians call the *"deus me livre"* (god forefend) pile, or indulge in tactics to increase artificially the apparent number of dispositions.[45]

Admittedly, the distribution of the workload is often highly unequal, but that implies finding ways to reassign it, not the addition of judges. In both Paraguay and Honduras, well over half the judges are justices of the peace residing in rural areas, where, for various reasons, the caseload is near nonexistent.[46] Many judges in the urban centers of these nations do look overburdened when only the number of filings is considered; however, much of their workload is only apparent. It includes many cases filed and abandoned by the parties—requiring only that the judge admit the demand and possibly take a few further steps –as well as a large proportion of relatively simple disputes, usually debt collection based on the presentation of documentary evidence of the debt, repetitive consumer and administrative complaints, uncontested divorces, requests for child support, and a variety of documents only requiring judicial validation.

Even these simple cases may require less work than it appears. A recent study reviewing a random sample of debt collection cases (*juicio ejecutivo mercantil*, or JEM) in Mexico's Federal District courts found that 60 percent never advanced

43. This is true even of jurisdictions like that of São Paulo, Brazil, where state judges average more than 2,000 dispositions annually. Nonetheless, the president of the state tribunal recently noted that according to the state's judicial organic law, once average filings reached 300, more judges should be placed to take up the excess. See A *Folha de São Paulo*, June 24, 2004, p. A-4.

44. See Magaloni and Negrete (n.d.), for a study of the situation in Mexico's federal courts and their description of what they call "deciding without resolving," the disposition of cases on the basis of minor technical errors, not substance. Anecdotal evidence suggests similar practices in other countries.

45. Sudden increases in caseloads registered in come countries (for example, Ecuador) in CEJA's 2004–2005 review of the state of the region's justice arouse such suspicions. A World Bank study (2005b) on judicial statistics found evidence of intentional or unintentional caseload inflation in Brazil arising from the separate counting of attachment proceedings and similar peripheral actions. The authors and others have observed similar practices in other countries, for example, the Paraguayan courts' tendency to count "*autos*" (any decision by a judge, including on interlocutory motions) rather than cases.

46. Aside from a tendency for rural areas to generate less litigation (because of poverty, attitudes toward courts, or lack of access to lawyers), in both countries the justices of the peace are limited as to the types of cases they can hear—often in terms of amounts, but also, in Paraguay, because serious crimes require an investigation by a prosecutor, and these officials are often not present in the outlying districts.

beyond the stage of admission and that only 20 percent reached judgment.[47] Thus, courts reporting annual filings of more than a thousand cases were actually processing a much lower number. (The debt collection cases represent 30 percent of the filings in civil courts and 70 percent in peace justice courts). Mexico's results are extreme, but in these and more complex civil cases, the *principio dispositivo* (only the parties move the case ahead) not only creates delays (which will not be remedied by speeding up administrative processing), but also reduces the judges' work. Similar studies in Buenos Aires (Argentina), Quito (Ecuador), Lima (Peru), and São Paulo (Brazil) found comparable practices[48] — filings which are never followed through because the plaintiff had other reasons for taking the action (declaring a tax loss, maintaining a right to future action), because he sees no point in continuing (can identify no assets the defendant could use to pay the claim) or because the parties have settled out of court. Out-of-court settlements are usually not recorded in Mexico. Elsewhere parties are more likely to register them with judges, but this is still far less work for the courts than the full-blown trial process.

The *juicio ejecutivo* is theoretically extremely simple, requiring only judicial validation of the supporting document, an order to pay, and, if that fails, the seizure of the debtor's assets. In much of Latin America, it takes a more complex form, requiring, as in Mexico, a judgment in addition to validation when payment is not spontaneous, providing the defendant separate opportunities to protest both the validity of the debt and the attachment, and including a postjudgment phase establishing the value of the assets and of any fines and interest, as well as a judicially supervised auction of seized properties. Trial court decisions are subject to appeal and even to constitutional protests. Although these additional steps can be used by a defendant to create delays, judges often allow time for them even in the absence of an active defense.

Figure 1 offers a schematic representation of these practices, showing the trajectory of debt collection cases (JEM) filed in the Mexico City courts. Cases not proceeding to judgment or not going through the formal enforcement process are considered to have exited, formally or informally. Formal exits are those recorded with the courts. It is worth noting that, despite the required judicial auction for seized assets, few judgments are enforced in this fashion, and there is in fact no record of whether the majority result in payment. Thus, informal exits are still more common after than before judgment. Prior to judgment, a majority of cases exit before notification and *embargo* (attachment or seizure of assets). Here lawyers offered two explanations: payment or refinancing of the debt was negotiated by the parties, or the plaintiff gave up because no attachable assets could be found.

47. World Bank (2002b, 2003a).

48. See World Bank (2003a, 2003b); Simon et al. (2002); Gonzales et al. (2002); Centro Brasileiro de Estudos e Pesquisas Judicias (CEBEPEJ; 2003). These studies also reviewed ordinary proceedings, where longer delays, lower closure rates, and more active defendants were often more frequent.

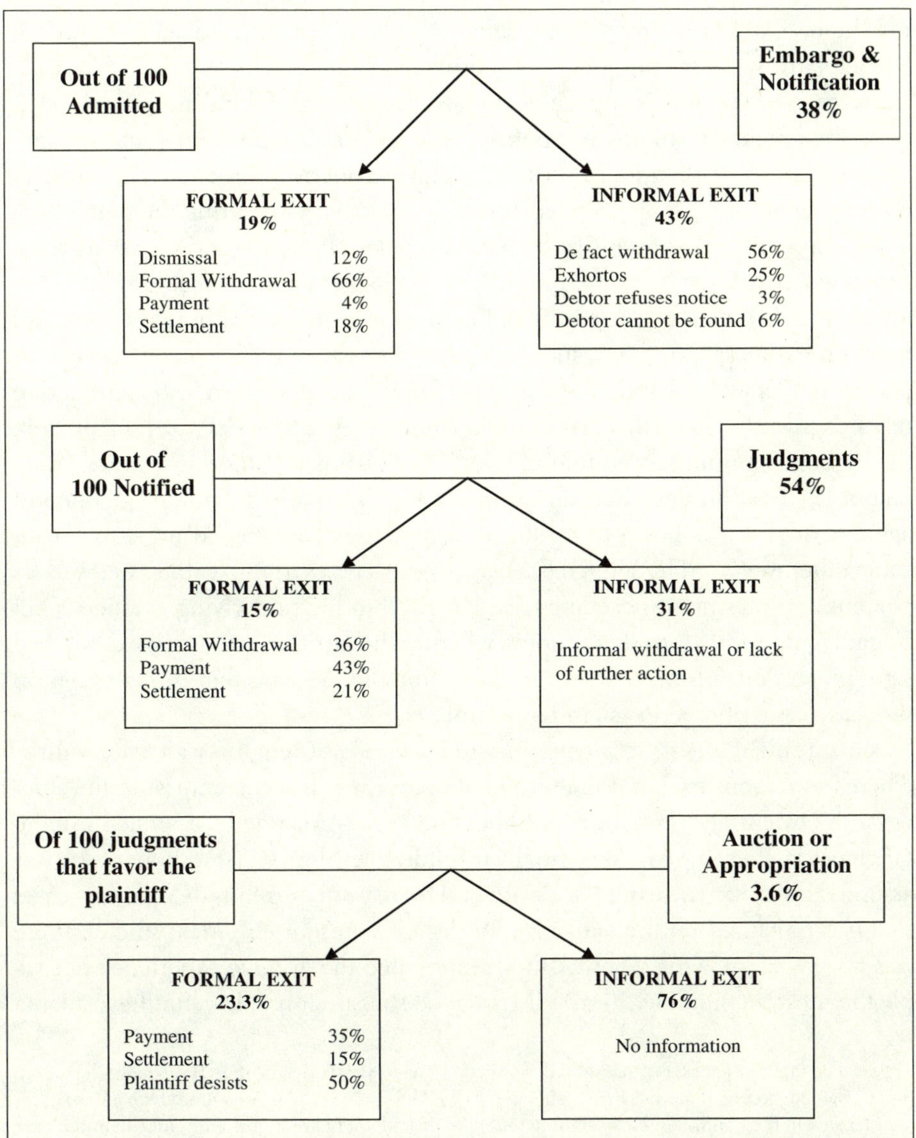

Fig. 1. Mexico JEM: formal and informal exits in three moments of the proceedings. *Embargo* refers to the attachment or seizure of assets. *Exhorto* is the request that a judge in a different jurisdiction take an action needed to proceed with the trial. From World Bank (2002b).

An *exhorto,* or request, that a judge in another jurisdiction take an action needed to proceed with the trial, while far less common, usually precipitates another informal exit. Apparently such requests are accorded low priority by those receiving them, a fact probably used by defense counsel. An active defense, however, was a relatively rarity and not closely correlated with delay.

As the above examples and tables demonstrate, several of the assumptions underlying the efficiency-enhancing strategies have not held up to subsequent examination. Latin American judiciaries in general are not overburdened with work, in terms of either the filings they receive or those actually requiring their attention. Thus, the notion that excessive demand impedes efficiency and causes extreme delays in reaching rulings does not ring true. If judges are not capable of handling an average workload of a few hundred new cases a year, something is wrong, but it does not originate in the quantity of filings. Moreover, the Mexican findings on parties' tendency to abandon cases short of judgment, a pattern also identified in other countries, suggest this may be a more critical issue than delay. In and of itself, the high attrition rate is not unusual. Universally, it is common for parties to initiate a legal action and then desist, because they have reached an out-of-court agreement (for which the initiation of legal action serves as an impetus) or for some other motive. The United States is an extreme example, with as many as 98 percent of filings not proceeding to judgment, but the underlying practice is not unique to its courts.[49] In determining whether the attrition rate is a good or a bad sign, much depends on why parties desist from action, and that is a question no one has ever bothered to ask in Latin America.

Parties might desist, it is true, in anticipation of a lengthy wait for a ruling. There are reasons to doubt that explanation, raising an issue central to the strategy—the extent of delay under present conditions. Amazingly, proponents of the efficiency strategy have made virtually no effort to explore this question. Delay was assumed but never measured.[50] Critics said there was enormous delay, citing cases that had remained on the active list for decades. Absent empirical studies, there was no way of knowing whether they represented the average experience or simply the most memorable.[51] We still lack good statistics on delay, but the available

49. The rate of out-of-court settlement, however, remains under debate. See Barr (1999), for a contrarian view suggesting it has been overestimated in the U.S. and Canada. See Doriat-Duban (2001), for another side to the contrarian view, arguing that rates of settlement are higher in France than the classic juridical doctrine would allow.

50. Delay is actually very difficult to measure and usually is inferred from clearance rates (cases out, over cases in). This, however, is only a rough approximation because, among other things, we do not know how old the "cases out" really are. See Gregorio (1995), for an early attempt to cope with the problem.

51. Researchers in the United States and other countries have long recognized the dangers of relying on what the "experts" say about things like delay and clearance rates. See Kritzer (1983), for a discussion of why the experts tend to guess wrong. Unfortunately, much of the macroeconomic analysis of court performance depends on just such data. One example (Djankov et al. 2002) uses estimates provided by one lawyer per country and, to aggravate the problems, selected elite attorneys unlikely to have

few studies suggest that, among cases reaching judgment, many are processed in reasonable time, in light of the procedural rules and the dispositive principle—the requirement that in most noncriminal cases the parties not the judge determine the forward movement.[52] Where delay does occur, aggressive defendants taking advantage of every opportunity for dilatory practices are often a factor, but in many instances it is the plaintiff or the plaintiff's counsel who is at fault. Various steps in the movement forward require a request from the plaintiff, and it is not always forthcoming. In a study of all civil proceedings in Buenos Aires, there was an average delay of 100 days between the filing of the complaint and the request, from the plaintiff, that the defendant be notified.[53] Although *juicios ejecutivos* were not separated out, they constituted 60 percent of civil filings. Under the current procedural system, there is little a judge can do about this—and all the computers in the world will not make a difference.

The situation varies widely by country and type of case, but real delays, as well as prodefendant biases, are commonly exaggerated by critics. The Mexican study found that the 20 percent of debt cases reaching judgment do so in a median time of 223 days, lengthy but less so than the Mexican bankers' estimates of three to four years. In Buenos Aires, the median time for cases to reach judgment (60 percent of all filings) or other type of closure (10 percent) was 300 days. It was the same for all civil cases, and median times for labor and criminal cases were 200 and 100 days, with closure rates of 60, 85, and 50 percent, respectively. In Peru, more than 98 percent of debt collection cases sampled in Lima civil and justice of the peace courts (from 1998 filings) were closed (70 percent by judgment) in less than three months.[54] The contribution of court automation might be cited as a factor here, except that the justice of the peace courts were not automated and still decided a high number of cases (roughly twice those seen in the average civil court) in record time.[55] In Brazil, a different approach to the debt collection proceedings (cases require judgments only when contested by the defendant) saw lengthier times (478 days) for the 7 percent so affected. The rest reached closure far earlier,

---

much experience with the types of cases covered (bounced checks and evictions). The Moody's (2002) study of Mexican courts and Castelar's work on Brazil (1998, 2000) use a similar methodology to rank state judiciaries.

52. See World Bank (2002b); Gonzales et al. (2003); and Garavano et al. (2000).

53. See Garavano et al. (2000). The interpretation offered by the Argentine consultants was that the plaintiff used the additional time to try to reach an out-of-court agreement with the defendant.

54. Gonzales et al. (2000).

55. Peru's justice of the peace and ordinary civil courts showed more disparity in their handling of other civil cases. In the justice of the peace courts only 5.4 percent of all civil cases reached judgment in more than a year. Assuming those lasting longer are largely ordinary proceedings, this is an estimated 18 percent of the latter. In the civil courts, 39 percent of the cases not involving debt collection had not reached judgment in the four years covered by the study and the median time for those that had was 566 days. See Gonzales et al. (2002).

though fully 48 percent had no recorded action, or payment, after admission.[56] In Ecuador, on the other hand, for the 31 percent of debt cases disposed within the four-year period covered, median times were 442 days for cases filed by individuals and 369 for organizational plaintiffs with little if any evidence that judgments were enforced. Moreover, the bulk of unresolved cases showed no signs of moving further, with most of them still in the initial stages of admission, summons, or response by the defendant.

Even the Peruvian ninety-day record might be considered excessive for simple debt collection, especially in light of the frequent nonappearance of the defendant and the plaintiffs' nearly 100 percent win rate. In fact only in Argentina and Brazil were defendants markedly more successful, favored by 37 and 46 percent of the judgments, respectively.[57] Nevertheless, the lack of evidence of pre- or postjudgment payment in all debt cases, and, except in Peru, the high numbers abandoned or stalled at very early stages of the proceedings are causes for greater concern.

In short, efficiency-enhancement strategies have rested on three questionable assumptions: first, that excessive delay in reaching judgments is the primary problem presented by the courts; second, that judges face an overwhelming workload; and third, that the sheer difficulty of managing this workload is the principal explanation for delay and backlog. If these assumptions are correct, the mechanisms adopted—improved courtroom administration and automation—might be expected to produce positive results. Where they are not, the mechanisms' impact is also in doubt, and reformers might be advised to consider the additional causes of delay and the other problems identified.

Strategic Oversight 2: The Limits of Technically Induced Change

In light of the lack of good statistics from around the region, it would be premature to suggest that backlog and delay really are not problems in their own right and thus that better courtroom management and automation might not have a place in resolving them. The examples given do suggest that, when cases do not move forward in a reasonable time, there are other factors at work. Some of these factors also contribute to the frequently more common outcome, the tendency of cases to go inactive far short of judgment. Here first mention goes to the actions required or allowed under existing civil procedures codes that may string out cases that could be disposed more rapidly. Although most commonly abused by parties to more complex ordinary proceedings, they have turned the theoretically straightforward *juicio ejecutivo* into a minitrial even when little or no resistance is offered by the defendant.

---

56. CEBEPEJ (2003).
57. The rate drops to 15 percent in Brazil if split judgments are counted.

Second is the potential for entering multiple appeals, again a function of procedural rules and how parties and judges use them. Even if handled individually in a reasonable time, they contribute to congestion in higher level courts and postpone definitive decisions. A lengthy appeals process also undermines the benefits of a relatively rapid disposition at the trial level and can discourage parties with limited resources from pursuing their complaints. Final and interlocutory appeals rates for debt collection are lower than for other types of cases, but they are often high enough to suggest abusive use. In the debt cases sampled, they ranged from o in Ecuador to 88 percent in Brazil. Judgments by Peru's speedy civil and justice of the peace courts were appealed 17 and 6 percent of the time, respectively, while the combined rate for the Mexican judgments was 30 percent for ordinary appeals and 12 percent for *amparos* (constitutional appeals).

Third, the dispositive principle does not allow the judge to manage his or her caseload proactively. Thus, party-initiated delay will not be much affected by improved information on case status. Fourth, many judges are reluctant to use even those possibilities they have for pushing cases along. They often allow parties to exceed deadlines for filing pleadings or permit repeated continuances, sometimes because they fear a complaint from the affected actors. Finally, much backlog could be retired for expiration of time limits but instead remains in the active files. Where parties have lost interest in the cases, or have reached extrajudicial solutions, these abandoned cases artificially inflate the backlog. Despite a 1996 amendment to the procedural code requiring Mexican judges to close debt cases after six months of inactivity, judges continue to leave the cases open. The reason usually given is the fear of complaints from the affected party. Interviews in Paraguay where a similar rule is in effect found judges reluctant to make this determination for similar reasons. In Colombia, judicial closure for inactivity was actually eliminated because of pressure from the banking system. The banks use the existence of outstanding debt cases sitting in judicial offices, a major part of the civil backlog, to reduce their tax payments and inflate the assets they report to the banking regulatory agency.[58]

Better courtroom management and automation might call attention to these problems, but it will not resolve them.[59] To do so requires a different understanding among judges, judicial leadership, and the parties as to the rules and purpose of the game. For all the parties' complaints about delay, it appears that they are often a primary cause and that they object to efforts to change anything when their

---

58. Interviews, Bogotá, February 2006. Apparently the Peruvian banks use a similar system. In the two countries and possibly in others, if the tax and regulatory agencies ever compared the financial reports they receive from the banks, much judicial backlog might have no reason to exist.

59. Better information on case status can be used to other ends—for example, combating corruption or standardizing outcomes—especially if the results are publicized. See Highton et al. (2000), for one experiment in Argentina.

own actions are the target.[60] This is as true of plaintiffs' counsel as of those defending the debtors. Attorneys specializing in debt cases often have their own priorities, pushing along the most promising cases and letting the others rest.[61] Judges share part of the blame in their failure to use their existing powers to overcome party-initiated delays or indeed to recognize delay-reduction as one of their responsibilities. Active or passive resistance is a well-recognized tactic in Mexico's debt cases. The debtor knows he will lose but counts on the judge's admitting his defense or in the face of his failure to respond to a summons, simply postponing a decision.

There are some additional problems having to do with the nature of the demand, which are addressed in the next section. Those of concern here revolve around internal practices mandated by law or dictated by custom. These elements are a missing factor in the efficiency enhancing strategy. Courts that use computers to facilitate and possibly expedite what they have always done will not make much of a dent in delay or backlog. Those using automation to take the burden off staff are unlikely to effect any change at all. Automation makes case management easier, but in many countries and in many courtrooms it would be hard to argue that manual control was not up to the task. When cases accumulated or went years without a ruling, it was demonstrably not because the judges were overwhelmed with work.

In its more sophisticated versions, the modernization strategy recognized this, by insisting that courtroom practices be rationalized prior to automation or placing its faith in the power of automation to produce an attitudinal sea change. Unfortunately, the insistence often disappeared in the interests of gaining judicial acceptance of the programs, and the sea change has still not occurred. Moreover, expedited paper flow within a courtroom has little or no effect on procedural rules, those defining the basic steps in how a case will be handled. Where rules allow or require parties to raise each issue separately, stop forward action for interlocutory appeals, or provide other opportunities to increase delay, and where judges have no ability or incentive to discourage this, cases will move slowly, regardless of the level of organization of courtroom staff. If Latin American judiciaries have not been able to meet the efficiency goals, this is because they have not internalized them and they still see procedural rules and conventional practice as something for someone else to decide, and thus beyond their control.

To the extent that increasing the efficiency of ordinary operations is a valid goal

60. As banks are frequent critics, arguing that high interest rates are a direct result of drawn-out judicial collections, it is interesting that as defendants they appear to take full advantage of available dilatory practices. A study (Brazil, Poder Judiciário, 2004) performed in the Rio de Janeiro state courts showed their dockets filled with cases brought by clients alleging various kinds of poor service. Like debt collection, these cases should be disposed quickly. Instead, they reach resolution, often against the bank, after nearly three years of legal conflicts. The banks do not give up without a struggle.

61. Interviews with elite law firms specializing in debt collection in Paraguay revealed that they, unlike the courts, kept statistics on the cases enabling them to determine which ones had the most chance of success. See World Bank (2005a).

of reform, there are important questions as to how effective simple technical and technological change can be in producing it. Automation, improved courtroom administration, and infrastructure can provide a means for reducing delay and backlogs when these problems are a consequence of disorganization or excessive workloads. They cannot provide the institutional will, nor can they do much about bad-faith litigation protected by law. Much the same can be said of the other attributed impacts—increased access, decreased corruption, or a better public image. If the criminal code reforms put excessive faith in the power of laws to change behavior, the efficiency-enhancement programs may have erred in their dependence on the impact of technology.

Strategic Oversight 3: The Judiciary Is Not a Widget Factory

Having once announced to a reform-planning group that tracking cases in a courtroom is no different from tracking beer bottles in a brewery, I find myself especially suited to addressing this topic. In the most limited sense (related to developing a case-tracking system) the comment was probably accurate, but arguments like this have only served to distort the potential benefits from an efficiency-enhancing strategy. They tend to equate judicial success with getting cases through the system, entirely overlooking content, quality, and whether they should be there in the first place. The brewery analogy could be extended to cover these problems—at least insofar as content and quality. Breweries, unlike courts, however, do have a more flexible production structure. Tradition is important, as one of their ads used to say, but if there are faster and more economical ways of producing beer, the arguments that "we have always done it this way" or "the law doesn't allow alternatives" are unlikely to stand in the way of adopting them. The final issue is more complicated. In an era when courts can hardly pretend to address all societal conflicts, at least not on a one-by-one basis or unless they absorb the entire national budget, there is a real need for asking which they ought to handle. Perhaps the analogy here is a buggy whip factory, which could be made very efficient, but still would not be relevant to modern needs and demands. Unfortunately, the economic forces that would cause the buggy whip factory to go out of business or change its product line do not work on courts.

Efficiency-enhancement programs tend to operate at the lowest level of the strategic pyramid, adding means to speed up the handling of the normal caseload in the normal fashion. They rarely address the higher-order questions as to the courts' overall contribution to reaching societal goals, their comparative advantage in doing so, and the alternative judicial and extrajudicial means for achieving these ends. Recent studies on the normal caseload, and our suspicions concerning what never gets added to it, suggest that it would be better, and more efficient, to ask these questions first. For example, in most Latin American countries a majority of civil complaints involve debt collection; these cases are commonly decided in favor of the creditor, after a certain amount of delay.[62] There are, however, additional problems in collecting on the judgment through a second judicial enforcement process. Most delay-reduction programs have focused on the time to judgment and ignored the time to payment, or the possibility that it will never occur.

Because the existence of the debt (the subject of the pre-judgment proceeding) is rarely in question, the initial trial can become a time-buying device for the debtor. Latin American judges and attorneys are very frank about this—and cite cases of debtors who use the proceedings as a means to live rent free in their apartments for the year or more it takes to reach judgment and/or enforcement. This can hardly be considered a good use of judicial resources or an economically beneficial outcome. Thus, many European countries, which had similar proceedings, have taken steps to shorten them still further.[63] These include default judgments (as an insolvent debtor frequently does not answer the demand), an immediate ruling on the presentation of a valid document establishing the debt (and thus eliminating the entire trial phase unless the debtor can provide evidence of the invalidity of the claim),[64] and, in the Netherlands, the elimination of the abbreviated debt collection proceedings itself.[65] Here, private bailiffs conduct the enforcement proceedings on the basis of the documented claim; debtors who wish to protest the debt have to go to court under a more complicated ordinary proceeding.

Suggesting these remedies to a Latin American judicial audience brings immediate protests of due process violations, procreditor biases, and their impracticality in the local environment. There may be some truth to the latter argument. One would hardly trust most Latin American bailiffs with unsupervised debt collection. Some of the other protests, however, are questionable. The example of Costa Rica's traffic cases is worth noting here. Apparently most of the beneficiaries of these due process protections were willing to have them eliminated. Another example comes from the province of Salta in Argentina. Here the civil judges have been experimenting with changes to the civil procedures code, which they have negotiated with the provincial legislature.[66] One very successful innovation involves an expedited, oral proceeding for landlord-tenant disputes. The proceeding eliminates many of the tenant's former opportunities for creating delays by giving the judge the power to convoke both parties to a single oral hearing and threatening a default judgment if they do not appear. The change faced considerable opposition and dire warnings about the homeless population it would create. The judges report

62. See World Bank (2002b); Gonzales et al. (2002); Simon et al. (2002); and Garavano et al. (2000).
63. See chapters in Jacob et al. (1996) and Zuckerman (1999).
64. This practice was already adopted by Brazil and is under consideration in several other countries. It has reduced some delays in Brazil, but its impact on the incidence of payment remains uncertain. See World Bank (2003b).
65. See Blankenburg (1999, 446–47).
66. Interviews in Salta, August 2002.

that rather than increasing the number of homeless citizens it has made more rental properties available—because landlords no longer fear that they will never rid themselves of a tenant who decides he will not pay his rent. It is clear that more serious study is required before declaring this example an unmitigated success. It does illustrate that, once judges decide they have the power to change things and the responsibility for facilitating conflict resolution, they can do a great deal.

The Argentine judges needed legislative cooperation to introduce the abbreviated proceeding, but the rest of the innovation rested on their preexisting, legally recognized powers to interfere with the pure dispositive principle. Judges from other countries report that, even under existing codes, they could operate more proactively. They have been unwilling to do so, even to counteract the most abusive dilatory practices and frivolous litigation. Further legal changes might enhance these abilities, but the underlying problem appears to be attitudinal, fortified by the existing judicial incentive structure. Latin American judges are usually not interested in antagonizing lawyers. Whereas once this was for fear of political repercussions, the change to greater institutional independence has shifted the fear to a complaint to the judicial council or disciplinary boards. Until the incentives change, and judges perceive that those overseeing their careers will back and encourage their efforts to prevent bad-faith litigation, they are unlikely to change their behavior. Party initiated delays will continue unabated, and increased efficiency will remain an unrealized dream.

Dejudicialization is another option. Much of the courts' workload in many countries consists of conflicts that might be resolved by executive agencies or by a single governmental decision. Both inertia and the judges' belief that they are protecting social values work against this transfer. This swells the demand and displaces conflicts of potentially greater importance. For example, in both Argentina and Brazil, conflicts over governmental policies affected by devaluations (social security benefits and frozen bank accounts) have been sent to the courts for resolution. The advantages to the government are substantial. The judgments are handled individually, though their content is virtually identical, thus creating delays in the need to make good on them.[67] Moreover, some of those affected do not bother to go to court, thus letting the government off the hook. In the Dominican Republic, divorces by mutual consent get full judicial treatment and represent a substantial portion of cases heard by civil courts.[68] As with Costa Rica's traffic cases, the potential beneficiaries may be less than happy with the protection of this right.

Courts have not been adverse to transferring cases to other jurisdictions. The

67. Brazil's federal small claims courts (discussed in more detail in Chapter 4) constitute the judiciary's response to this problem. Although delays in processing the demands remain, the courts have cut them considerably through investments in automation—allowing quicker filing, batch processing of similar demands, and template rulings, often signed digitally.

68. See Pastor and Vargas (2001a).

Mexican state courts continue to lobby for the return of debt collection cases to the federal judiciary, because it is federal legislation that governs their treatment. State judges like the idea because it would reduce their own workload. They tend to overlook the inconveniences for the clients facing a lesser number of federal courts, or the potentially reduced need for state judges, in light of the substantial cut in the cases they would see. Judiciaries have been less inclined to opt for dejudicialization. In fact, the current often runs in the other direction, as with demands that separate administrative tribunals be incorporated into the ordinary court system.[69] Because this move would presumably include the transfer of their budgets, personnel, and infrastructure, the ordinary judges do not envision this as a swelling of their workload, but rather heightened protections for users of these services and a significant increment in institutional powers. Some of these reincorporations seem to make sense. When executive tribunals handle all administrative disputes, there are reasons to doubt their objectivity. Still, there are many factors to consider before loading the judicial dockets with more responsibilities, and among them is the question of how well they do with what they already have.[70]

Another area of great resistance, but with potentially great impact on overall efficiency is the introduction of binding precedent, expanding the impact of higher court judgments on those of lower-level tribunals. Many of the repetitive cases mentioned above could be quickly resolved or eliminated if this practice were introduced. Some courts have taken steps in this direction, but it continues to be regarded as a violation of judicial independence—the individual judge's right to come to his or her own decision based on an understanding of the law and the facts of the case. Brazil may offer one of the most extreme cases. Here decisions of the constitutional court (Supremo Tribunal Federal) have broadly binding effects only in the case of the finding that a law is constitutional.[71] Findings of unconstitutionality are not binding on the rest of the judiciary, though where a law is involved, the relevant government body is instructed to rescind it. Efforts to introduce binding precedent (*súmula vinculante*) have been attacked as enhancing the powers of upper-level judges and reducing the protections lower-level courts afford to the poor.[72] They have also been interpreted as a plot by international actors (including the World Bank) to further the impact of globalization.

69. This was done for some administrative tribunals in Ecuador and Bolivia during the 1990s, without much apparent success in improving performance. Mexico and Peru are now considering similar moves, in the former because of the judiciary's interest in a "unified jurisdiction" and in the latter because the remaining administrative tribunals are associated with abuses under the Fujimori regime.

70. When the Peruvians incorporated the separate agrarian courts into the ordinary court system, their former efficiency declined notably, as did their tendency to lean over backwards to support the small claimant. Latin American administrative courts are generally not known for greater efficiency and user friendliness (except when the friend is the government), but there are always exceptions.

71. See Rosenn (1998); Sadek (1995); Sadek, ed. (2001a, 2001b); Ballard (1999); and Bermudes (1999).

72. See Sadek (2001b). The battle was lost in 2004 when a constitutional amendment introduced the *súmula vinculante*.

Of course, the most favorable, propoor judgment by a lower-level court can be appealed to and overturned by the presumably more elitist higher tribunals, thus making the poor clients' victory entirely pyrrhic. Even without binding precedent, higher court decisions are apparently taken into account by Brazil's lower-level judges and potential litigators, the former because the judiciary controls the career system, the latter because, unless they are interested in buying time, they may not want to fight a foregone conclusion. This has less impact on governmental lawyers who are under instructions to appeal all but the most inconsequential decisions against the state. Much of the Brazilian courts' workload, and especially that of appellate tribunals, can be blamed directly on such practices.[73] They seem especially pointless in the case of complaints about administrative violation of basic rights (*mandados de segurança*) where the initial decision holds unless overturned on appeal, a relatively rare occurrence.

In summary, as with the criminal justice approach, greater familiarity with court operations tends to put in question some of the assumptions underlying court modernization efforts. On the basis of the discussion above, table 3 is provided to indicate where alterations in our understanding might argue for a new set of assumptions to guide these reforms. Several of these revised assumptions are pursued further in later chapters.

THE BOTTOM LINE: DO WE NEED A DIFFERENT MODEL?

As all this indicates, the efficiency-enhancement strategy, even when well implemented, places far too much attention on making things as usual work better, and far too little on examining what the courts are actually deciding and with what effect. Courts in industrialized nations, having already adopted the normal efficiency measures, are finding the impacts fall short of resolving their problems. They thus have begun to consider more drastic steps in altering how they do business and finally, in restructuring demand.[74] More proactive judging has become the order of the day. In both civil and common-law countries, it has become apparent that decisions as to what issues will be litigated and how the proceedings will move ahead can no longer be left entirely to the parties and their lawyers. There is always at least one side, and sometimes both, who find reasons to add complications, string out timing, and ask for rescheduling to meet their own convenience. Obviously there are some basic values in conflict here, but the courts are increasingly opting for limiting the parties' freedom to determine the course of

---

73. A random sample of case files from the São Paulo courts hearing *mandados de segurança* found that every one of them was appealed by state agents. See World Bank (2003b).

74. See Zuckerman (1999) and Jolowicz (2000), for discussions. See also Woolf (2000), for the most famous effort to introduce these changes.

Table 3 A second look at the foundations for modernization reforms

Original Assumption	Revised Assumption Revised
LAC courts are overloaded	Aggregate statistics and case file analysis indicate most trial courts do not receive unmanageable numbers of filings, and that what they do receive often represents little work
Excessive delays are the principal problem of court performance	Case file analysis again indicates that delays are often less than believed, especially at the trial court level, and that inconclusiveness or nonenforcement of judgments may be more critical
Automation and changes in courtroom processing will reduce delays	Most delays seem to derive from procedural and attitudinal factors—excessive opportunities for dilatory practices and judges' reluctance to curb them
Speed and number of judgments are the best indicators of court efficacy	Latin American courts may render too many judgments—more attention is required to enforcement (does the winner collect?), out-of-court settlement, and broadening impact of judgments rendered
Augmenting courts' processing capability will make room for new users	Growth in caseload largely more of the same (debt collection against individuals, many of whom can't afford a legal defense); one exception is the increasing role of the state as party—most notably in repetitive conflicts that might be handled administratively
Commercial justice is the key to a market-enabling environment (discussed in annex)	Within Latin America, criminal and administrative law has more impact on business operations and decisions to invest. For their own disputes, businesses often prefer ADR or still less formal mechanisms, universally
Law and justice problems are best resolved by improving court performance	Sometimes the solutions lie outside the courts, or outside the sector—with auxiliary institutions ranging from police and prosecutors to property registries and credit bureaus
Capacity building will lead to performance improvement	Absent changes in judicial culture and incentive systems, capacity building may only produce a very expensive but still mediocre justice system

events in favor of their own ability to decide how they will distribute their efforts. Further procedural simplification or targeted code reform is also part of this approach as is the addition of stronger disincentives—fines for counsel not meeting deadlines or persisting in abusive practices, filing fees, and so on. Finally, these judiciaries have also adopted practices to encourage out of court settlement, or the use of alternative forums, seeing themselves as the instance of last resort when the parties cannot reach a satisfactory resolution elsewhere.

The practices are not limited to civil cases. Many European countries hold down the number of criminal cases coming to court by granting police and prosecutors the ability to resolve minor infractions through the application of fines or warnings.[75] In light of the quality of the police and prosecution services in most of Latin American, it may be premature to suggest such remedies. Nevertheless, many countries, in their new criminal procedural codes have adopted similar outlets. For some reason, judges seem to find this less objectionable than efforts to channel civil cases elsewhere.

All of this stems from what can be considered a paradigm shift as regards the courts' functions and how they carry them out. The longstanding model of a court that resolved all societal conflicts and in the process strengthened the legal framework is increasingly regarded as neither a practical possibility nor a desirable goal. One part of the change is the recognition that many conflicts would benefit from diversion to other forums and that sending them to the judiciary may actually undermine the latter's rule-strengthening role. Many conflicts are only marginally over legal matters, and might be resolved more satisfactorily by something other than the win-lose judicial outcome. This is especially true of those where the parties seek to continue a relationship and thus need to remain on good terms. The outcomes of these conflicts do not affect the legal framework, though they should certainly take it into account. Decisions like these, in the shadow of the law, however, need not be made by a judge.

The paradigm shift also incorporates a separation of the judicial product into its public and private good elements.[76] All judgments have some impact on the legal framework; the nth decision upholding the creditor's claim will marginally strengthen the general principal that debts must be paid. Nevertheless, some decisions are more transcendental in this regard and can be seen as having a higher public good element—by underlining and thus reinforcing legal principles society wants strengthened. Those conflicts, like disputes over debt payments, with a lesser legal significance, involve predominantly private goods. Economists have gone so far as to describe judicial services as private goods (because their benefits

---

75. See Fionda (1995); Kagan (2000); and Stepán (1994).

76. See Shavell (1997). Among the Latin Americans, this theme has also been picked up by Chilean reformers. See J. E. Vargas et al. (1998, 2001).

accrue to individuals) with public good externalities and to recommend that users be charged accordingly.[77] Here they find a strong analogy to health services. It is the individual who most directly benefits; the public good or externality is a healthier population that will spread fewer diseases to others, require less curative treatment, and presumably be more economically productive and socially responsible. The public as a whole can benefit from the justice or health externalities without directly using the service, but when the service is free there may be a strong temptation to overuse. The same, it should be noted, could also be said about any alternative mechanism that decides conflicts on a one-by-one basis. Shifting to mediation or arbitration does not eliminate the public and private goods division. It may have other advantages in terms of the types of resolutions or greater efficiency. Whether countries can or wish to subsidize these individualized services is a political decision. They do need to recognize that provision of a public service does not necessarily imply public financing.[78]

Even for publicly provided and financed services, there are other ways of making demand more manageable. Using courts as a substitute for administrative or political decisions is increasingly regarded as a very expensive alternative. The former often involve a large number of similar cases and, except where the administrative decision is arbitrary or irregular, need never be seen by a judge. What is needed here is a uniform policy, applied equitably. As note above, government often benefits from a judicial treatment, though one wonders whether the monies spent on paying judicial salaries and state lawyers might not eat up a good share of the profits coming from delayed payments to plaintiffs. Using the courts to make policy is another questionable practice. It relieves politicians of handling controversial subjects but in the end may produce less than optimal outcomes. In the meantime, it unnecessarily increases the courts' workload. While that workload may be less than many judges believe, courts reviewing repetitive administrative and political issues are often the most overburdened. When Argentina froze bank accounts in 2002 and converted dollar amounts to devalued pesos, its courts were flooded with *amparos* requesting relief. Because *amparos* get precedence over other cases, this added to delays in hearing the latter. The earlier decision to transfer disputes over pension payments to the courts created so great a workload that additional courts had to be created.

The new paradigm is hardly well established in the industrialized countries. Its conceptual elegance belies some serious operational problems.[79] It also invites

77. Some lawyers have picked this up as well. See J. E. Vargas et al. (2001).

78. As Juan Enrique Vargas et al. (2001) note, there are two decisions here—who will provide the service and who will pay for it. A privately provided service may be publicly subsidized or a publicly provided one may be user financed.

79. The results are not in on the Woolf reforms in Great Britain, but some observers contend the only beneficiaries are the lawyers, who now get paid earlier. See also Leubsdorf (1999), Kritzer (1996), and Marcus (1999), for a discussion of the difficulties of change.

considerable resistance from judges and parties who find the notion of prioritizing cases according to their "public good element" potentially risky and markedly inegalitarian. There is the question of how such standards will be set and by whom. A recent German decision to remove the lower monetary limit for access to appeals and to instead use a standard of legal importance is a case in point.[80] The decision is theoretically attractive, but the removal of the former bright-line rule opens the door to all manner of manipulation. In the Latin American environment, the new ideas are only beginning to be introduced. Their further acceptance will hinge on considerable change in judicial and public attitudes. Where justice as a basic right has been equated with full access to court services, and justice itself is seen as an immeasurable quality, the idea of explicit, policy-based rationing, as opposed to the present implicit system, has a long way to go.

CONCLUSIONS: THE PLACE OF EFFICIENCY IN A REFORM PROGRAM

Whether under the traditional or new paradigm, increased efficiency is an important goal and should be compatible with other reform objectives. In fact, the earliest application was in criminal justice programs, by donors who were already working in this area. It quickly met criticism from within the donor groups, however, and the exchange of their own axiomatic principles: "justice delayed is justice denied" versus arguments that a too speedy trial was likely to deny due process rights. As usual, most of this discussion occurred in an empirical vacuum, relying on anecdotes and apocryphal examples rather than an examination of how cases were actually being processed. Many of the criminal justice reformers have been more flexible with respect to the efforts to reduce delays in criminal proceedings. They have not opposed the programs but have seen them as secondary to their promotion of accusatory proceedings, making criminal justice less abusive of legal and human rights and more effective in dealing with alleged criminals.

Those on the human rights side seem of two minds about efficiency. They have been critical of trials that occur too rapidly and verdicts that are reached too quickly but also worry about delays in investigations with detained suspects. Their answer to this dilemma has usually been enforcing legal deadlines—not an examination of where and why delays might occur. Unfortunately, the deadlines have largely benefited well-off defendants with lawyers skilled in dilatory maneuvers and have created further public criticisms of due process rights and the codes that protect them.

On the more effective crime-control side, efficiency also gets short shrift. Most of the foreign advisors brought in to assist code implementation are judges, public

80. Germany, Bundestag (2002).

defenders, and prosecutors, not administrators, economists, or public policy analysts. They usually opt for more resources for whichever group they are advising and consider efficiency in the context only of improving the quality of output. Thus, they might favor unified data bases on criminal cases, not for the cost implications, but because they will give investigators access to more information. Unlike the Ministry of Economy, which usually focuses only on the cost element of a cost-benefit analysis, their tendency is to emphasize benefits and forget costs.

As discussed later, efficiency has also been a secondary if not ignored element in the other strategic approaches. The sole exception is access enhancement, where it frequently appears as an argument in favor of alternative dispute resolution (ADR). Notwithstanding its utility as a justification, efforts to make ADR more efficient are remarkable for their absence and findings that it is sometimes neither faster nor less costly than the judicial route are routinely ignored.[81] Thus, efficiency stands somewhat by itself, a recipient of considerable funding, and a promised indicator of success, but otherwise running on its own parallel track. Better integration might have advantages on all sides. If the efficiency gurus were more plugged into the other issues being raised, they might broaden their notion of their task. And, in the more substantive areas, more focus on efficiency might be the common denominator for working out their potential contradictions. This is especially true with regard to budgetary implications. Everyone wants more funds for their particular objectives but, at some point, probably approaching rapidly, more will not be available. At that stage, both costs and benefits will have to be considered, and the possibility of increasing productivity and not just production may provide part of the way out of the emerging dilemma. That is, of course, assuming that agreement can be reached on the fundamental question—efficiency of what?

ANNEX: MAKING THE JUDICIARY MORE BUSINESS FRIENDLY

The donors are not bereft of axiomatic principles. One of the most popular is the argument that "a well-functioning judiciary is essential for the furthering of market-based growth." As mentioned in the introduction, the empirical evidence for this statement is indirect at best, and the assumption that the most economically relevant judicial functions lie in the commercial and civil areas rests on still-less-certain ground. None of this has prevented governments and donors from moving ahead with reform programs specifically aimed at enhancing the courts' influence on economic activities.

81. See Hensler (1994), for a brief summary of some preliminary findings, suggesting that, whatever its merits, ADR is often neither less mostly nor faster than court proceedings. The topic is addressed further in Chapter 4.

Increased efficiency, in the sense of moving cases more rapidly through the system, is obviously a major consideration. For businesses, time increasingly is money and waiting years for a decision is a luxury few can afford. Businesses in Latin America, like businesses everywhere, generally try to stay out of the courts. It is significant that, in the studies of debt cases cited above, most pitted a firm or individual plaintiff against an individual debtor. Large amounts and firm-to-firm disputes were quite rare. Even in the best of systems, judicial processes are slow and often reach decisions that are less than helpful. For this reason, many businesses look to other means to resolve their conflicts. Private arbitration and mediation are one common solution. There are also many less formal means for moving beyond the initial dispute and returning to business as usual. A company, unlike an individual, can factor any additional costs into its price structure—and this is what commonly happens to bribes, speed money, and negotiated agreements. Businesses resolve their credit problems by recourse to supplier credit (a euphemism for not paying your bills on time). They trade favors, work with known parties, and rely heavily on the weight of reputation.[82] Where they need new laws, they lobby to get them, but they are less confident in the advantages of a business-friendly legal framework than are many of the politicians and donors working to produce one.

In a recent article, written for the Carnegie Endowment, a lawyer specializing in commercial cases argues that academic and theoretical attempts to make countries more business friendly are relatively superfluous.[83] Business goes where the profits look promising and figures out how to deal with the legal system later. In fact, well-meaning reformers can create their own obstacles, changing a legal framework within which businesses worked comfortably, introducing new laws with serious imperfections, and otherwise altering the predictable, if less than ideal, environment within which entrepreneurs have learned to operate. This is not an argument against any legal change, it should be stressed, but rather against that introduced by those without a concrete stake in the system and an adequate understanding of how it really works.

Nonetheless, the power of the axiomatic principle carries weight, and both donors and governments have taken it to heart, creating programs to reduce the courts' presumed negative impact on economic activities. Aside from efficiency, three other activities have been key: modernization of laws to bring them into compliance with contemporary business practices; creation of special court to hear business cases; and introduction of arbitration and other forms of ADR.

Businesses themselves have often lobbied for these changes independently. The difference is the reformers' efforts to second-guess their needs, based on their belief

---

82. See Stone et al. (1996), who argue that Brazilian entrepreneurs' greater reliance on informal mechanisms stands them in as good stead as their Chilean counterparts' reliance on the law.

83. See Hewko (2002).

that the laws can accelerate economic transformation, rather than economic development forcing legal change. Legal modernization has been the most important of the additions, though less so in Latin America than in the former Soviet Bloc.[84] The results in the latter region do give pause for thought. A massive effort to modernize the legal framework has caused far less change in real practices than had been anticipated and has sometimes produced its own perverse applications and undesirable outcomes. Latin American reformers, here as in other strategic areas, have paid little attention to events elsewhere and have forged ahead with efforts to introduce new banking, secured credit, and bankruptcy laws as well as incorporating specific references to modern business practices (for example, leasing, franchises, corporate governance) in their civil codes. They are also beginning efforts to revise their civil and civil procedures codes, frequently on as grand a scale as the earlier efforts with criminal procedures.[85]

Because these efforts are recent, any evaluation of their success is premature. Nonetheless, Mexico's experience with a new bankruptcy law, introduced in April 2000, is not positive. Two years later, only two insolvency cases (from a total of four) had ended in liquidation and only thirteen more were moving through the courts. None constituted the kind of complex bankruptcy case the law was intended to improve.[86] Things are not necessarily worse than before. They just are no better. The law also moved the bankruptcy proceedings out of the state and into the federal courts. The transfer was supported by the national business and banking elites because of a fear that the state courts were too sympathetic to local interests. Federal judges, however, show considerable resistance to the principle underlying the law: that economic efficiency, rather than the survival of the firm and the jobs it represents, is the ultimate goal. In addition, the transfer required the creation of a new institute with specialized personnel to oversee reorganization and assessment of the worth of corporate holdings. The goal of thus dejudicializing the process has been subverted by the novelty of the arrangement, the judges' own prejudices, and the tendency of the parties to raise legal issues to bring the arguments back into the courts.

A related effort, again in Mexico, to introduce secured lending as a way of facilitating debt collection proceedings is likely to meet similar obstacles. Although it

---

84. See Sachs and Pistor (1997); Frydman et al. (1996); Gupta et al. (2002). The World Bank and other donors have been particularly concerned about "contract enforcement," especially in terms of debt collection. See Siebrasse (1997) and Walsh (1997), for World Bank sponsored studies on secured credit arrangements.

85. For one set of recommendations, atypically based on more empirical evidence and with more targeted suggestions, see Cantuarias Salaverry (2001). The authors are also unusual in their law and economics perspective, still a relative novelty for a region where doctrine has played a much larger part in code redesign.

86. *Latin Finance*, April 2002, 48. One reason for the slow progress is that companies anticipating the change rushed to get their cases into court before the new proceedings went into effect.

will eliminate the challenge of identifying goods to back up a loan after the fact, it will not reduce problems of contested ownership or multiple claims (because of poorly run registries), the delays incurred in the judicial enforcement proceedings, or the questionable behavior of the bailiff (responsible for serving notice and seizing or attaching goods). Mexico's current foreclosure proceedings (by definition with their own secured collateral) are generally acknowledged to run fairly rapidly through the judgment. The real delays and problems begin afterward and should be a lesson to those believing secured lending is a panacea.[87] It will resolve only one of a series of institutional obstacles, all of which lessen the creditors' chance of satisfaction.

Shifting jurisdictional responsibilities (as with Mexico's bankruptcy proceedings) or the creation of special commercial courts is another common addition. It is often supported by bankers and business elites because of their probably justified belief that a change of venue could produce more sympathetic hearings of their complaints. The reverse is likely to be true for local businesses and others without equivalent political contacts. Such procedural changes are never neutral, and the parties oppose or support them in accord with their own anticipation of the impact on their bargaining positions.

In federally organized judiciaries (Argentina, Brazil, and Mexico), subnational courts can be expected to be more influenced by local politics. Bankers and other national groups may be right in guessing they will get less favorable treatment there. As with Mexico's bankruptcy proceedings, they may also be underestimating the additional institutional obstacles. Federal courts can also play to the crowds, as witnessed by the Argentine judiciary's efforts to counter the De la Rúa government's freezing of bank accounts in 2001. Although a majority of observers believe the judges took the correct position, it is their motives for doing so that remain in question.[88] In an era where courts are again under attack for excessive privileges, inefficiency, and possible corruption, we can probably expect to see more instances of judicial populism—the tailoring of decisions to garner public support for the institution. It is clear that an antibusiness line would lend itself to this tactic.

The suggestion as to the creation of separate commercial courts is another

87. See World Bank (2002b), for a general discussion. Additional information supplied by Mexican lawyers interviewed indicated that foreclosing on a home was often made difficult because of the activities of debtors' unions (like the *Barzón*). These unions discourage potential bidders on the confiscated properties. In addition, poorly run, and often corrupt property registries mean that at the last moment it may develop the debtor never had clear title.

88. This was the famous *corralito* (little corral) imposed by the De la Rúa government in late 2001 to prevent a bank run. Individual federal judges ruled in favor of many individual account holders, leading to a hefty outflow of monies. It was, however, a subsequent supreme court ruling, later negotiated with the government, which threatened to overturn the entire scheme. The court's motives were transparent. With several of its members under threat of impeachment, and having placed itself above the economic crisis by refusing to cut its budget and in fact demanding higher salaries, this appeared to be a last-ditch move to show it was on the side of the people.

matter. Though often supported, sometimes suggested, by business groups, it is not entirely clear how or whether this would further their own interests.[89] They may be anticipating more friendly judges, less congestion, fewer delays, and greater understanding of the issues. To the extent we have data on the parties, businesses and banks tend to be minority users of the courts, enough so that one can ask whether their current level of engagement justifies the creation of special tribunals.[90] The one exception is their use of courts for debt collection, but here most defendants are individuals. This is less a matter for commercial courts than the far less common disputes between enterprises.

A more interesting venture, for reasons of efficiency and specialization, might be the Argentine suggestion of a special *fuero* (set of courts) to handle debt collection, whether between individuals, individuals, and banks or businesses or just among the latter. This could be a first step to simplifying and dejudicializing many of these cases, and given the percentage of total filings they usually represent, would guarantee a sufficient workload. It would also give the normal civil courts time to concentrate on the usually more complex additional cases they also handle, including those of a commercial nature. If the new *fuero* is to work, it will also require changes to the procedural rules for debt collection and to some traditional, if not legally mandated, practices.

The lesser use of courts by businesses in many countries is partly explained by their recourse to other forums, either informal negotiations or private arbitration and mediation. Their willingness to pay for the latter services, which do not come cheap, suggests they find them a more satisfactory means of resolving conflicts. (Of course, in some cases they may have no choice, as the stronger party to a contract insists on a clause mandating arbitration.) Governments and donors have financed the creation of such forums. Many have also arisen spontaneously among chambers of commerce and professional associations. A major obstacle to their further spread is the frequent lack of legislation giving their decisions official weight, and thus discouraging the losing party's taking the case to court after the fact. Because ADR has begun to receive more acceptance among judges and private lawyers, this problem, which may remain even in the face of legislation to the contrary, is disappearing, but it persists in several countries. Judges still see ADR as the much-feared privatization of justice and, although the parties are usually on a more or less even footing, warn that it may lead to abuses of basic rights.

Curiously, the one angle not pursued by those seeking a more business-friendly environment is the improvement of the situation in administrative and criminal

---

89. For a discussion of the brief U.S. experience with a separate commercial court, raising many of the issues suggested here, see Geyh (2002, 178–82).

90. A case from outside the region, in Tanzania, is an interesting argument to the contrary. Businesses supported the creation of courts, but a year after the fact, their caseload remained very small. See Finnegan (2001). See also Cazelet (2001), on the use of commercial and other types of specialized courts.

law. As regards the former, the usual problem is the lack of control over agency rule-making powers and of standardized, easily managed procedures to protest unnecessary regulations and other arbitrary acts by government agencies.[91] Although arbitrary issuance of regulations and rules does not reach the heights in Latin America it does in other regions, efforts to enforce more order have so far failed for the most part. There is an additional, possibly more widespread problem of arbitrary interpretations of rules that are made in a regular fashion.

What remedies exist, Mexico's *amparo* and the like, are generally accessible only to those who can afford lawyers specialized in their use.[92] Moreover, the Brazilian government's alleged instructions to its lawyers to appeal every negative decision are apparently not unique. Thus, a company or individual seeking redress from arbitrary or unfair treatment may have a long legal road ahead. In addition, governments have sometimes closed certain doors—denying judicial recourse for certain types of action; as in Brazil, stipulating that only individuals (and not collectivities) have standing in certain cases; limiting the deadlines for registering judicial complaints; or requiring a convoluted administrative procedure before the judiciary can be accessed. Judges frequently make these decisions with an eye on the political authorities, and their legal base for deciding is often confusing, outdated, and not well understood. In view of the many complaints by both local and foreign investors about administrative abuses, this might be a far more productive area for reforms than the establishment of commercial courts. Donors, however, usually do not understand administrative law, and, in the case of the MDBs, it is often seen as overly political. Models for better practices are scarce and usually very context specific. The whole neoliberal consensus also works against developments in these areas, as they are seen as adding rules when the goal is deregulation.

The criminal justice area poses fewer theoretical and practical problems. If reformers have ignored its economic implications, it is only because they have been fixated on commercial and civil justice, or on other aspects of criminal justice reform. Economists have been quicker to capture the relationship—noting the direct and indirect costs of criminal activities as well as the tendency for businesses to exit from a city or region with extremely high crime rates. This is another area where the right and the left hand seem to function in mutual ignorance. And yet it is arguably, along with administrative justice, the most propitious target for making court actions more business friendly.

In summary, although placed in the section on efficiency, a strategy aimed at market development might better work in other areas. Increased efficiency in handling commercial cases is important to those businesses that take them to court, but a positive impact would require a more sophisticated focus on the causes of

91. Chapter 5 reviews all these issues in greater detail.

92. As discussed in Chapter 5, there are some important exceptions. In both Costa Rica and Colombia, *amparos* or *tutelas* may be presented without an attorney.

delay transcending what can be produced through automation and courtroom reorganization. Targeted procedural reform, more proactive judging, expedited enforcement mechanisms, and curbs on appeals, especially those by the state, would be more helpful. Improvements in the handling of administrative and criminal cases might be more positive in eliminating problems of most concern to investors. In both instances, the goal is to curb abuses by augmenting the courts' efficacy (as well as efficiency) in dealing with them. Furthermore, the benefits would also affect ordinary citizens who have their own concerns with bureaucratic abuses and criminality. For judges who dislike the new paradigm and the emphasis on restricting demand, this may also be a more acceptable, if more challenging, route. It emphasizes the court's role not just in resolving disputes, but also in changing out-of-court behavior. This message underlies the support for the new paradigm. Courts may not be the most effective or efficient means of resolving the bulk of social conflicts, but, assuming they can target their activities appropriately, they can have a major impact on the way citizens and government behave and interact.

THREE DEVELOPING A PROFESSIONAL, INSTITUTIONALLY INDEPENDENT JUDICIARY

Judicial strengthening—commonly understood as the development of a technically proficient, professionally oriented, organizationally autonomous court system—might logically have been the first step in the reform process. Instead, it was displaced by the initial concerns about the quality of criminal justice and the donors' emphasis on efficiency. As explained, participants in these other two areas either assumed they could advance their cause without immediate reforms to the institutional structure or preferred to ignore the issue out of an inability to deal with it simultaneously, or at all. Nonetheless, judicial strengthening has been a continuing theme throughout the twenty- year period, if only activated periodically.

I have separated this definition of reform from the objective of enhancing the courts' checks-and-balance functions. The two are related through their use of the term "independence," but, both historically and in the minds of many reformers, they represent different ways of conceptualizing reform's fundamental purpose. Judicial strengthening privileges institutional and individual independence as the courts' ability to control their own resources and actions, and the individual judge's freedom from irregular pressures in making his or her decisions.[1] Programs pursuing these objectives involve efforts to create more effective forms of judicial governance, introduce "budgetary autonomy" and larger budgets, improve appointment and career systems, and otherwise ensure that the judiciary functions as a technically proficient institution, with a minimum of external intervention in its operations and an adequate capacity to monitor and control its own performance. When Latin American judges talk about enhanced independence, this is generally what they mean.

---

1. Latin Americans frequently stress the need to consider both types of independence, though recent reforms have focused largely on the institutional dimension, assuming, possibly erroneously, that one follows from the other. Traditionally, Europeans have been less preoccupied with insufficiencies in the first type, for example, usually leaving administrative and budgetary control with a ministry of justice. They also appear more sensitive to the conflicts between the two dimensions. See Langbroek (2003), for a discussion of the importance of giving individual judges room to develop a "personal style," in the context of Dutch debates over the role of higher courts in establishing interpretational guidelines. In Brazil, despite or perhaps because of the judiciary's high level of political independence, both types of autonomy receive considerable attention. There is an ongoing debate as to whether the lower-level judges are excessively or insufficiently influenced by the upper levels of the judicial hierarchy. See Ballard (1999).

A second sort of independence, relating to the judiciary's performance of its checks-and-balance functions, has been slower to embrace the goals of the judges' themselves. It was first promoted by local and foreign jurists. Donors often endorse this goal but have not contributed to it directly, because of its markedly political implications. Whereas many Latin American constitutions historically afforded the courts some judicial review powers, they have been observed in the breach.[2] It is only in recent years that some courts have begun to exercise this role more energetically. The developments here and programs to advance them will be discussed in a later chapter.

Because of the somewhat disjointed attention to judicial strengthening, its three main components are treated separately. Taken together they may comprise a strategy, but one with its own internal parallel tracks. A possible fourth component, the issue of general legal education, is also briefly discussed. Although potentially relevant to all five strategies, it has received minimal attention since the late 1970s. Its placement in this chapter is thus somewhat arbitrary and highly hypothetical. The final sections of the chapter review the overall advances, the interactions of the four lines of action, and their level of integration with the other major reform areas.

JUDICIAL APPOINTMENTS AND CAREERS: THE CRUX OF THE MATTER

Of the three factors most often mentioned as undermining the judiciaries' status as an independent, professionally oriented institution, appointments and career systems have been the most central. Both are seen as intimately related to the quality of judges and other personnel, their consequent ability to perform adequately, and their vulnerability to improper influences—bribes, political pressures, requests for special consideration from family, friends, and political allies, inherent prejudices, and the like. Although the traditional expectation was usually early entry (often as a courtroom staff member) and service until retirement within the judicial ranks, few countries had legally recognized career systems. In many cases, this did not prevent the expectation from being realized, but a desire for legal recognition and more recent departures from the traditional practice have made creation of a formal career a widespread goal. Here, as in the appointment systems, the major emphasis has been on "quality at entry." Except for training programs, far less attention has been paid to the opportunity to shape and improve the performance of those within the system.

2. In formally recognizing these powers, the Latin Americans followed the U.S model, deviating considerably from the European tradition. More recently, many have also added constitutional courts, following the postwar developments in Europe. See Chapter 5.

Early History

Most of the region's judicial historians see the problem as a recent development, a result of actions taken under the de facto governments of the mid-twentieth century and the later democratic opening. They usually argue that, before that time, and despite the absence of well-defined appointment and career systems, less formal practices produced levels of institutional cohesion and professionalism congruent with the needs of the era.[3] Judges were chosen from among members of the traditional upper and upper middle class, often on the basis of contacts and recommendations, but judicial vocation was duly recognized and internal socialization took care of further job training.[4] Young lawyers or law students often entered the judiciary as clerks or secretaries and gradually worked their way up the ranks.[5] Although salaries were modest, the profession retained a positive image, reflecting the social status of those recruited to its ranks. Judges coming from families of notables could be depended on to endorse establishment views, and, in any case, most of the conflicts they oversaw were of minimal political significance.[6] Those assigned to more remote provincial courts were another matter, but if they sided or connived with the local landowner and other elites, this was easily overlooked. More socially concerned or ethically sensitized judges in the capital city might worry about irregularities in the periphery, but they usually lacked means of tracking them and possessed a certain institutional interest in not stirring up trouble needlessly.[7] Just as judicial leaders reached an understanding with national elites, judges in the countryside usually had their own local political allies.

Emerging Problems and Their Origins

This comfortable coexistence ended toward the middle of the past century. As new political forces began to contest the hegemony of the traditional establishment, the judiciary was pulled into the conflicts, and governments increasingly exercised irregular controls over the selection and behavior of judges. Throughout the region, judiciaries became more circumspect about dealing with politically sensitive issues. Most often this meant cases affecting the personal interests of political

3. For a typical argument, applied to El Salvador, see Oliva et al. (1991, 32).

4. See Delazay and Garth (2002), chap. 13; and Hammergren (1998e, 136–42, 212).

5. Sometimes they started still lower. A former president of the Costa Rican Supreme Court began as a messenger. Most did not start quite that humbly, but an informal apprentice system was the usual way judges were socialized into their jobs. Even following the adoption of career systems, law students and recent graduates commonly take administrative positions in many countries as a way of getting a leg up on the selection process. This gives them first hand knowledge of judicial practices and often, internal sponsors, who can still influence judicial appointments.

6. Dezalay and Garth (2002, 226).

7. Hammergren (1998e, 138).

elites, their families, friends, and allies, though protests of rights violations and other constitutional questions began to make a more frequent appearance.[8] The courts' cautious posture was frequently not sufficient to protect them from further intervention. In politically convulsed countries like Bolivia, supreme courts were routinely removed and with them much of the rest of the bench. In others, political strong men took a more personal interest in placing their own judges. It was reported that, in Peru, the dictator Manuel Odría (1948–55), commonly held champagne toasts with his new supreme court justices, the night before they were officially appointed.[9] Odría, like many heads of state, had the advantage of an appointment system allowing him to nominate justices for approval by an assembly he also controlled. As was less common, he also directly appointed lower-level judges, via the Ministry of Justice. In the majority of countries, where high courts chose lower-level judges, the trick was simply to ensure the supreme court adequately understood its responsibility for avoiding judicial rebellions and crushing them when they occurred.

During the 1970s, as traditional dictators like Odría ceded to more activist military governments, these kinds of interventions became more common, as did the pressure from political leaders on judges ruling on a wide variety of cases. Regimes, on both the political right and left, seeking to alter rather than maintain the socio-economic status quo encountered resistance from judges who still believed their mandate was to uphold constitutional and legal guarantees or simply to honor the values of the former establishment. This brought more irregular dismissals and appointments to protect the new policies. In Argentina, the transition occurred earlier, in 1947, when after eighty-four years of relative tranquility, the new Peronist government promoted the impeachment of four supreme court justices. Since then governments have routinely used impeachment or its threat to rebuild Argentina's supreme court to their liking.[10]

Authoritarian leaders also used the courts to control political dissidents and thus expected judges to turn a blind eye to due process and rights violations when not asked to enter into the abuses more directly. When as in Pinochet's Chile, a rightist government was matched with a conservative court, the latter often found this ideological turn compatible with its own values.[11] In countries like Peru, with a self-proclaimed revolutionary military government, the judges' conservative stance was more problematic, and political leaders extended their goals to include the

---

8. See Pásara (1982, 88–103), for the Peruvian situation in general, and García Belaunde (1979), for a discussion of the Peruvian courts' treatment of habeas corpus appeals. See also Matus (1999), on the Chilean courts under Pinochet, and Fruhling (1993), for a discussion of the Chilean judiciary's "bounded independence," which he dates to the 1920s. For Argentina, see Carrió (1996).

9. See García Rada (1978, 215).

10. See Abaid and Thieberger (2005); Helmke (2005): Santiago (2002); and Verbitsky (1993).

11. See Hilbink (2003) and Matus (1999). Matus's book was so critical of the courts' performance that it was banned in Chile and the author had to leave the country.

creation of a new judicial mentality.[12] It is doubtful that many judges fully embraced the ideology, but their willingness to pay it lip service would have a damaging impact on internal values and external image. Although there were judges who resisted governmental attempts to manipulate the institution and their own actions, the usual tendency was judicial submission.

The period as a whole was not a positive one for the courts. Most of them emerged from the 1970s and 1980s with a diminished public image and weakened institutional cohesion. Direct political intervention in appointments at all levels meant that judges increasingly looked to external patrons and not to the internal judicial hierarchy to secure, maintain, and improve their assignments. Because of their primary responsibility for ensuring compliance with government preferences, supreme court justices came to be seen as little more than political hacks, discredited in the eyes of the public and of their own institution.[13] Judges as a whole were less frequently drawn from high-status groups and instead took their positions as a means to individual upward mobility.[14] Willingness to tailor decisions to the needs of political leaders soon encouraged other kinds of opportunism. Complaints about selling of judgments and other forms of corruption became more frequent. In the meantime, the nearly universal emphasis on economic growth and development, whether through market mechanisms (Chile) or national planning and a dirigiste state (Peru), had diverted attention from the traditional governance bodies.[15] The judiciary, along with the legislature, political parties, and much of the executive administrative structure (except for ministries of economy, planning, and various autonomous agencies) began to show signs of neglect. Courts may have been most affected, as they depended on other agencies for their budgets and, thus in addition to being functionally circumvented, also entered a period of chronic underfunding.

The situation did not improve much with the democratic opening of the 1980s. The new constitutional governments were forced to pay more attention to democratic institutions, but as regards the judiciary, their early actions were if anything more intrusive than those of their authoritarian predecessors. Here they were

12. See Hammergren (1998e, 142–47).

13. In a few countries, supreme courts served as a convenient resting place for politicians awaiting their turn in government. Thus, in Mexico, where the justices had permanent tenure until 1994, few stayed on the bench very long. See Fix-Fierro (1999, 189). In the mid-1990s, a Honduran supreme court president was forced to resign when the media discovered he was using court funds to prepare his campaign for the national presidency. He reputedly had been placed on the court with the understanding that he would be his party's candidate for the next national presidential elections.

14. In one particularly damning study, Peruvian researchers characterized the judges of the military period (1968–80) as coming from lower-middle-class backgrounds and joining the judiciary as a means of improving their personal situations. Ciudad and Zarzar (1984). See also Pásara (1982, especially chap. 6). Dezalay and Garth (2002, 226–27) make similar arguments about the evolution of the bench in Argentina, Brazil, Chile, and Mexico, adding, however, that the newcomers often embraced the values of the old establishment even more fervently than did its own members.

15. See Correa's (1999, 257–59) argument as to the courts having been sidelined from governmental policy for most of the past century.

motivated by two considerations. First, because elected leaders often relied on clientelism to gain supporters, the judiciary provided a tempting site for patronage appointments. This affected both the judges and their support staff, as well as prosecutors, public defenders, and even police.[16] Second, because these governments, unlike the military, were bound by constitutional rules, they depended more on the judiciary to resolve conflicts over their own decisions and between branches and levels of government. Thus, the judiciary began to exercise an unprecedented political power and one that politicians had even more reason to control.

The result, in the early years of the democratic transition, was a tendency for increased political intervention in judicial appointments and more frequent conflicts with courts that did not support official policies. The courts were most often on the losing side of this battle. The quality of judges declined still further, and the instances of irregular replacements or other manipulations increased. Peru's post-1980 elected governments conducted massive purges of the bench to remove military sympathizers and relied on political loyalties as the primary criterion in replacing them.[17] Honduras, never noted for a well-institutionalized court, vied with Bolivia in the number of supreme court purges, at one time having two courts competing for official recognition. Ecuador's constitutional crisis of 2004–2005 produced both competing courts and then a period of more than a year when the country had no supreme court at all. El Salvador used its justices of the peace, the first and often sole judicial contact for many citizens, as its first-line representatives for the dominant political parties. As their major responsibility was getting out the vote, their dedication to their judicial role was minimal and their fame for malfeasance in its performance widespread.[18] In Argentina, Carlos Menem's creation of four new supreme court judgeships was a blatant, and successful, maneuver to ensure the survival of his economic programs (and probably to guarantee a sympathetic hearing should he or his allies face legal action under a subsequent regime).[19] Menem also took the opportunity offered by the new federal criminal procedures code to stack the federal criminal courts with his political adherents. To this day, the federal criminal courts of the national capital are renowned for the questionable actions and decisions of their judges.[20] The Colombian supreme

16. The practice further eroded any notion of judicial tenure. In Bolivia and Honduras, for example, judges at best could hope to serve out a presidential term, only to be replaced by friends of the new government. See Gamarra (1991, 84–89) for a discussion of the politics of judicial appointments in Bolivia. For Honduras, see Florida International University (1987, 124).

17. See Hammergren (1998e, 147–50).

18. See Hammergren (1998e, 212).

19. See Verbitsky (1993), for an extended discussion of Menem's manipulation of membership of the entire federal judiciary. Abaid and Thierberger (2005) track practices by later governments including the current Kirchner administration.

20. See Abaid and Theirberger (2005), for a lengthy, journalist account that local experts swear is completely accurate. One of the more surprising details for an outsider is that all twelve judges have

court's constant obstruction of proposed legal and constitutional changes resulted in a decision, in the 1991 constitutional convention, to strip it of most of its judicial review powers and transfer them to a new constitutional court.[21]

New Selection Systems

Some of these changes were short-term efforts to stack the bench. Others emerged as part of a more permanent transformation in appointment and career systems. By the early to mid-1990s, the conflict between the discredited bench and the criminal justice and other programs introduced to improve judicial performance were simply too great to ignore. Thus, countries began to adopt measures to decrease political intervention in appointments, encourage merit selection, and create a judicial career with guaranteed tenure. They also built up judicial training programs to orient new recruits, assist in selection and promotion decisions, keep judges up to date on new legislation and encourage specialized career tracks. Both the selection and training programs began to address issues of judicial ethics, if by most accounts, inadequately. A few countries began to collect statistics and introduce courtroom visits as a means of evaluating performance and strengthen their judicial inspection units.[22] Not surprisingly, the transition to the new regimes was frequently accompanied by a total change of the supreme court, as it continued to have a role in supervising selection and career management and also would be the court with which the politicians expected to live for some time to come. In some countries (Peru and the Dominican Republic), the change was extended to the entire bench.[23] Judges had to compete with outsiders for the positions they currently held and, as likely as not, did not succeed in keeping them. In others (El Salvador, Costa Rica, Mexico), the change coincided with the creation of more positions or was superimposed on the traditional ratifications of judges with fixed terms, so it occurred more gradually and less dramatically.

In other countries (for example, Bolivia, Honduras, Nicaragua, Paraguay), the move to instate a judicial career was cut short, but the appointment system was

---

cases pending against them that are being heard by their colleagues. Argentines refer to these as "*casos cruzados*" (crossed cases).

21. See Hammergren (1998e, 239–141) Gómez (1996).

22. Costa Rica has been a leader here and has been active in planting the idea elsewhere—for example, Bolivia and Ecuador.

23. Although Peru has used "irregular" ratifications to purge the politically unwanted, the post-Fujimori council was unique in using examinations to weed out the less competent. This was possible because a majority of judges and prosecutors held temporary appointments (a holdover from the Fujimori period) and thus were not officially within the career. The results of the attempt to select more than 1,800 prosecutors and judges was not an entire success. The initial examinations (held in 2001) produced too few qualified candidates, and, as of early 2006, between 10 and 20 percent of the positions remained unfilled or were held provisionally (interviews with council members, January 2006).

changed in terms of both who selected judges and, to some extent, how they were chosen. Often this coincided with the transfer of part of the selection process to a newly created judicial council formed for just this purpose. Councils are discussed in greater detail below. The important point for present purposes is that where they received a role in judicial selections, the councils were intended to be less political in composition. Except for the Peruvian and Mexican variations, councils do not do the final selection of judges. They screen the candidates and provide the body making the final decisions, either the supreme and superior courts or the executive and assembly (for the supreme court itself) with lists from which they are to make their choices.[24]

An enormous amount of debate has centered on the composition of the councils (whether they should include judicial representatives, what other bodies should be represented, and how the members should be chosen). Far less thought has gone into how they will carry out their role in screening candidates for initial appointments or promotions. Most have opted for some sort of written and oral examination, as well as the traditional review of curricula. Most observers conclude that the process at the most is objective, but a less than perfect means of identifying those who will make good judges.[25] The written tests tend to be exceedingly academic in content and frequently eliminate experienced lawyers and judges, who have long since forgotten how to take university exams.[26] Several observers suggest that the exams favor those who have memorized the law but leave no place for evaluating a candidate's ability to apply it to real cases.[27] Additional indignities include oral examinations that attempt to evaluate the candidate's character by asking about hobbies and musical preferences, psychometric tests that purport to identify judicial vocation, and interviews with family members and children to try to root out inappropriate behavior.[28] The general problem is that those charged with applying the examinations, usually council members, have little idea of what they are looking for and thus are at the mercy of whoever supplies them with the test format.

24. In most countries, the supreme court continues to be selected by the former system. Only in the Dominican Republic, Peru, Colombia, and El Salvador does the council vet candidates to (and in the former two select members of) that body. See Hammergren (2002a), for a discussion of the councils' powers.

25. It is surprising that this has not given rise to another round of studies like those done earlier (see Pásara 1984; and Ciudad and Zarzar 1984) on "who the judges are." There are some exceptions, but they tend to be either fairly innocuous reports sponsored by the judiciaries themselves (León 1996) or attitudinal surveys (Castelar 2003; Sadek 1995b), which, as their authors suggest, are becoming harder to do because of the judges' fear of their participation being noticed by their superiors.

26. This has been a particular complaint in Peru, especially regarding appellate and supreme court appointees (interviews, Peru, December 2002).

27. Luis Pásara interviews, Guatemala, 1996.

28. This last complaint surprisingly was directed against the Costa Rican Supreme Court, usually regarded as a model. The first two are new practices in Peru and are said to have discouraged some candidates, especially for higher-level positions.

In-Service Evaluation

The surprising aspect, in light of the goal of choosing career judges, is that far less attention has gone to in-service evaluation and monitoring. This is often seen as conflicting with the value of (individual) judicial independence. Even when this objection is not raised, the selection committees are usually too busy trying to evaluate the initial candidates to have time to oversee their performance on the job. This is unfortunate because it seems extraordinarily doubtful that any single or series of examinations can accurately predict whether a twenty-four-year-old recent law graduate will make a good judge. Moreover the chances of his or her doing so are probably reduced absent subsequent efforts to monitor on-the-job performance and provide means for resolving weaknesses identified. It is also unfortunate that donors have not become more involved in this process. Many of their own judiciaries have developed better, if not perfect, mechanisms for screening candidates and helping them improve their performance on the job.[29] The oversight can probably be attributed to the fact that most donor project managers have no idea how the systems work in their own countries and thus never think of relying on back-home expertise to help out the courts with which they are working. In addition, project managers coming from countries whose selection systems work no better than those in Latin America may have no better model on which to draw.

The new Latin American systems are generally more transparent than whatever preceded them, but their ability to pick better judges is otherwise in doubt. Although donors support the new mechanisms, their intellectual contribution to developing them has been very limited.[30] Proactive performance evaluation, to identify and resolve problems, remains in its infancy. Where it exists, criteria are often limited to numerical quotas and over time encourage a variety of dodges to move paper as quickly as possible. Inspection units and complaints bureaus are a still more delicate theme, raising the specter of losing parties taking revenge on the judge who ruled against them. Efforts to elicit client input on selections and promotions have provoked similar reactions.[31] Finally, there is the question of the presumed neutrality of the new selection bodies. Many of them have become the target of political factions attempting to reassert their control over judicial selection. Others

29. Despite its different legal tradition, U.S practices in screening federal judges might be useful. See Goldman (1991) and Woodson (1998). For entry-level positions, some of the European countries might serve as useful models.

30. USAID in particular has occasionally made adoption of a career law a condition for continuing support. Although the MDBs have yet to impose this kind of conditionality, they have begun to consider such issues in reviewing proposed loans.

31. In interviews with judges throughout the region, this is invariably raised as an objection. Peru's new judicial council is one of the few bodies to introduce a system whereby the public is invited to comment on candidates to the bench and judges subject to ratification. In Argentina and Paraguay, the national presidents invited civil society participation in the most recent (2004) selection of new supreme court justices. In both cases, the executive was subsequently criticized for overriding the opinions offered.

have been associated with the creation of a corporativist judicial establishment, to the detriment of the independence of the individual judges and the interests of less traditional clients.[32] In short, the aim of creating merit selection systems and professional career tracks has proved less simple than initially imagined. Attempting to operationalize these apparently clear-cut concepts has raised a variety of practical and ideological issues and with them a host of new conflicts. The final section of this chapter expands the discussion of these points.

Training

Although less expensive than some other activities, training usually accounts for a significant portion of the funds invested in reforms. Much of this money has been spent on delivering courses. Programs have also financed infrastructure, equipment, and materials. Training is an activity common to all judicial reform approaches.[33] Criminal justice reforms use training to orient judicial operators (as all staff is called) in the new procedures. Efficiency programs use it to familiarize them with automation equipment and new courtroom procedures, and access and political strengthening reforms add courses to imbue new attitudes and skills. Still, training has been most central to overall institutional strengthening because of its direct linkage to improving human resource quality, internal career development, and general institutional image.[34] The latter factor should not be discounted; many judiciaries seem to want judicial schools because that is what modern judiciaries have. When pressed to address what impact the schools will have, the answers are often much less specific.

Schools are rarely seen as a means of remedying specific performance problems but, rather, as a way of keeping judges abreast of new trends, helping them master the knowledge needed for their next promotion, or improving their scholarly credentials. Most schools seem to aspire to a masters program with a very academic content. Courses are often designed on the basis of what judges want, not what they need to know. Information law, international trade, and new commercial instruments are popular topics regardless of whether most judges will ever handle cases involving them. Critics note that common flaws like an inability to write

32. This is a frequent complaint about the European bodies as well. See Turcey (1997, 147); Devedjian (1996, 193–94); and Provine (1996, 203–4). In Latin America, Brazil is the one country where this is a common criticism, probably because it is one of the few with a well-institutionalized career, controlled by the higher courts. It is not clear how Brazil's recent adoption of an external council will affect the situation.

33. There is a lengthy Latin American literature produced by those involved in these programs, though the theme seems to have been neglected in recent years. See, for example, Correa (1990 and 1994); Buscuñal et al. (1993); Correa (1990, 1994); Guatemala Supreme Court (1994); Haeussler (1993); Instituto Latinoamericano de las Naciones Unidas Para la Prevencion de Delito ye al Tratamiento del Delincuente (ILANUD; 1991); Stanga (1996); and Valenzuela (1991). For an overview, focusing on USAID programs, see Hammergren (1998c).

34. See Hammergren (1998b, 1998c).

concise opinions or to manage their courtrooms efficiently get short shrift.[35] Impact evaluations (measuring the effect of training on courtroom performance) are virtually nonexistent.[36] Nonetheless, training remains very popular with judges, not just because mere attendance in a course provides points toward a promotion, but also because they anticipate that the promotional exams will be based on the course offerings.

Some schools have been more successful in linking training to actual performance. For years, Costa Rica's school used a case study methodology to help develop common criteria for resolving certain types of cases. Where training is employed to introduce new procedures, it appears to have facilitated adoption across the board. Although often justified as a means of improving performance, the most important impacts of the investments in training may lie in other areas. Training has been a means of increasing identification with the institution, strengthening and reshaping the internal culture, and providing judges with benefits, rewards, and recognition. In this sense, it has replaced the old, informal socialization system, and advanced efforts to create a career ladder incorporating even administrative staff. (Of course, this only works if administrators are also included, and they are frequently the last priority of schools with tight budgets.)[37] As with all in-house training, the inherent dilemma is that a program that focuses on internally defined needs and demands can create greater isolation from those of the clients and the broader social environment. Training's role in helping judiciaries regain internal cohesion and improve institutional morale should not be discounted. The new question is how it can be used to increase the satisfaction of service users as well as that of the judges.

A final reason for training programs is the poor quality of judicial candidates and appointed judges in many countries. The problem may originate in the lower attractiveness of the career. It has also been blamed on the shortcomings of legal education programs and an overall decline in their quality in recent decades. This is discussed in greater detail below. It bears mentioning that several judicial schools have had to devote considerable time to remedial training for their judges. Observers also contend that even better law schools provide an education inadequate to the demands placed on judges and practicing attorneys and thus that training is necessary to fill those gaps.

35. Such topics might also combat another common complaint about excessive formalism and an inability to discriminate between cases requiring careful study and those just requiring a speedy, nearly automatic decision. On the latter point, see Beneti (2000).

36. Commonly, evaluations either test judges on what they have learned or ask them to assess the course.

37. Costa Rica, alone in the region, first introduced training for administrative staff and only later added judges. In a few countries (on Peru during the 1990s, see Hammergren 2000a), special courses were set up for courtroom staff and administrators as a means of creating a new profession. Unfortunately, the promises made to the participants, as regards salaries and chances for advancement, were not kept, and many of the trainees have since left the courts. Interviews, Peru, 2002.

Salaries

Budgets will be covered in the next section, but the issue of judicial compensation merits some brief attention here. Like secure tenure, judicial pay has been identified by judges as one of the major contributors to poor performance.[38] Low salaries are said to discourage strong candidates from considering a judicial career, contribute to the subsequent departure of those who can find opportunities elsewhere, and make those who remain more vulnerable to corruption. Salary levels are usually not determined by the judiciary itself. They are often set by national law, or even by the constitution, which may link them to those of other public-sector officials. Although most judiciaries would like to set their own salaries, they have had to settle for lobbying the executive or assembly to increase the legal limits. In 2002, the Peruvian Supreme Court succeeded in having the salaries of all judges (but not administrative staff) doubled, though the judicial budget itself was cut. What this portends for performance remains to be seen. Brazilian federal judges also received a salary increase in mid-2002 as a result of a negotiation with political leaders. In late 2004, they began negotiating another raise for all judges (pegged to salaries of Brazil's Federal Supreme Tribunal [STF] justices), this time trying to tie it to raises for other political officials. Although the ploy failed, one unanticipated consequence of the STF's negotiations was the standardization of judicial salaries across the country, bringing those of lower-paying states up to the nationally defined level. The small minority of state judges whose salaries or pensions exceeded that level (and thus would be reduced) are still protesting the damages to their acquired rights.

In the case of administrative salaries, the situation is more variable. They are sometimes pegged to general public-sector wages, strengthening the government's arguments for not allowing increases. Other judiciaries (Mexico's federal courts for example) appear to have much greater freedom in paying their administrative staff and have taken pains to make increases there as well. Unfortunately, as reported by Mexico's state courts, this has a negative effect on their own human resource situation. Because they cannot match the federal salaries, they lose their best administrators (and judges) to the federal courts.[39]

The arguments about salaries are common to every profession and, as elsewhere, rarely if ever based on a real study of the market or of the alternative opportunities for those with the preferred judicial profile. Although judges often compare their salaries to those of elite private attorneys, it is highly questionable whether this is the appropriate reference group. Arguments as to higher salaries discouraging corruption are similarly dubious. Some of Latin America's better paid judiciaries do

---

38. See, however, Kahn (2002, 173–74), for a review of literature suggesting that, except at the extremes, public sector compensation has no relationship to corruption.

39. Interviews, Mexico, July 2002.

not have a reputation for high levels of integrity, and most are probably earning enough to preclude corruption as a necessity for survival.[40] Nonetheless, whatever the soundness of the arguments, most of the region's judges have succeeded in getting their salaries raised appreciably over the past two decades. Most are also still campaigning for more.

Judicial Ethics

This topic is relevant to several of those already discussed, but sufficiently important to be treated separately. The accusations about corruption and other abusive practices leveled against judges and other sector members in virtually all countries have brought it to the fore.[41] The issue is complicated because it encompasses both actions known to be illegal by those indulging in them and a variety of practices that are more widely accepted, but arguably undesirable.

On the first set of actions, most are already included in existing criminal codes. Although some "typifications" could be updated to reflect modern circumstances and eliminate loopholes, the larger problem is that of identifying and disciplining the offenders. Here the widely adopted remedy of drafting ethics codes and training judges in their contents seems redundant, if not an actual step backward. Corruption is often difficult to prove, but judiciaries could clearly do a better job of policing their own members. The same is true of bar associations, most of which have a truly abysmal record in responding to client complaints. In some cases, the simple explanation for this failure is that judicial and other organizational leaders are themselves part of the problem and may use their powers to expand their own corruption networks. Several of the new judicial councils provide examples. In other cases, professional courtesy and a desire not to air dirty laundry in public play a larger role. When forced to take action, disciplinary bodies are more likely to encourage a voluntary resignation, often with complete benefits, than to proceed with a full investigation and sanctions. Finally, earlier experience with the use of disciplinary bodies to punish or remove politically undesirable judges and a fear that many complaints originate in a client's simple displeasure with a ruling create a certain skittishness about the entire issue. Media coverage and citizen

40. This can be contrasted with the situation in some countries in other regions where absurdly low salaries ($15 to $25 a month in Cambodia or the Democratic Republic of the Congo) appear to be a conscious government policy to keep judges dependent on their whims and also encourage systematic corruption as a means of discrediting the institution as a whole.

41. For one particularly damning criticism of the Mexican federal courts, see United Nations (2002). The report, claiming 70 percent of all federal judges were corrupt, was poorly received by the Mexican judges, who argued, with some reason, that the basis for the claims was rather flimsy—a three-week visit to Mexico by a common-law judge who did not speak Spanish, did not understand the Mexican legal system, and relied for the most part on interviews with local NGOs for his findings. Nonetheless, many Mexican citizens might agree with the assessment. Whether accurate or not, their perceptions constitute a problem for the courts.

protests are forcing some judiciaries and councils to become more proactive, but so far the usual public impression is that the judges (and lawyers) protect their own, even when their own are notoriously corrupt. Although the underlying impediment is political will, as in the case of selection and evaluation, technical assistance in better methods would help. Here the donor community has shown as much wariness as the judges, rarely getting involved in the dirty laundry business.

The second set of accepted, but undesirable, practices poses a different type of problems. Prime targets here are ex-parte conversations and other irregular contacts with interested parties, including members of the government, irregular use of judicial funds, and nepotism. Even when prohibited by law, as is often the case of nepotism, many judiciaries indulge in them, arguing extenuating circumstances or finding ways around the prohibition—for example, making arrangements to hire each other's relatives. Blatant disregard for the law is not, however, unknown. Although nepotism is illegal in Brazil, the new National Judicial Council's order that courts dismiss relatives of judges hired in positions "of confidence" had only a 25 percent compliance rate in the state judiciaries when the ninety-day deadline expired.[42] In both Peru and Paraguay, recently appointed supreme court presidents immediately hired their relatives to assist them, and, in the latter country, one of the justifications for removal of the entire supreme court was its appropriation and use of an airplane confiscated by authorities in a drug trafficking case.[43] Irregular use of sequestered automobiles was also an issue in the threatened impeachment of Argentina's supreme court in 2002. Popular protests and the use of these events as a pretext for removing justices or entire courts may be ending these practices, but it is clear that many judges and justices still believe they enjoy special dispensation from the laws they apply to others.

Ex-parte conversations and other irregular contacts are a more delicate issue, because they have rarely been regarded as damaging, are virtually never prohibited, and in fact are sometimes defended by lawyers and judges as a necessary means of understanding the background to a specific case.[44] The traditional practice of telephone justice (a call to or from the interested government party for direction on how to rule) is now supported by the argument that judges need information on the broader consequences of their decisions as they are drawn into more socially

42. See Weber (2006). A day later (Carneiro 2006), however, the Supremo Tribunal Federal ruled against the temporary injunctions received by 1,682 employees, declaring that the council's decision did not violate its constitutional mandate and that courts not complying with it were in violation of the law.

43. As in the case of several recent supreme court purges (Argentina, Ecuador, Paraguay, and Venezuela) it is doubtful the executive was shocked by these practices, but rather used them to remove court members or an entire court it found undesirable for other reasons.

44. Still another defense, provided to the author by a well-respected and scrupulously honest Peruvian attorney, was that judges ignorant of the law would react negatively to being corrected in court. Thus, he felt ex-parte conversations were the necessary and more diplomatic means of getting his point across.

and economically important issues. Because their training does not allow them to make those determinations, who better to ask than a government representative? It is also argued that the kind of firewall created between the judges and potential litigants in more developed countries is a virtual impossibility in Latin American societies. The story reported to the author by a French judge who asked to be transferred from a community where he knew too many people would be considered amazing to most Latin Americans. Where would he go except to some godforsaken backwater?

Still the problem is not social fraternizing, but rather an explicit avoidance of private contacts with stakeholders in an ongoing case. Because this is a widely shared cultural convention, not limited only to the judges, it most probably will have to be attacked on that basis. Unless judges, lawyers, and prospective litigants can agree on its undesirability, change is unlikely. Here again, judicial ethics codes and training are a weak remedy as they affect only the judges. They may be a place to start, but only as a step prior to taking the issue to society writ large, as it is society that has to change. As for the arguments about the necessity of government consultations to understand the broader consequences, there are other, more objective sources of such information—the use of court experts or the introduction of amicus curiae briefs are two such means. No one wants judges making decisions they do not understand, but the government in power is hardly the most objective witness. Donors have to tread carefully here in the face of a renewed attack on legal imperialism and the imposition of practices "not compatible with local culture." Moreover, it would be an exaggeration to say the objected actions never occur in their own countries, as Latin American jurists are increasingly aware.

In summary, of all the areas related to judicial professionalization, judicial ethics is among those where fewest advances have been made. This is surprising in light of the widespread charges of corruption, and the courts are clearly paying the price in terms of their continuingly poor ratings on levels of public trust. Unfortunately, gains in such areas as secure tenure, higher salaries, and training may both divert attention from the question and make solutions seem less necessary. Why bother with the difficult, when everything else is going so well?

JUDICIAL BUDGETS: BUDGETARY AUTONOMY AND RELATED CONCEPTS

Judicial budgets have been a latecomer to the discussions of institutional strengthening, but they are compensating for the delays by taking a more central role in current debates. For much of the past century, judiciaries' budgets received little attention. Gradual increases in absolute amounts allowed them to keep up with a slowly growing demand by adding courts and judgeships in the capital cities and some provincial centers. Growth was organic and did not appear to follow any long-term plan.[45] Outside the capital, political considerations were often the most important factor in deciding whether a population center got a court or a judge. Overall trends remained unanalyzed by the courts or outsiders. Because courts generally kept few if any statistics on caseloads it is hard to say how well the new additions responded to real or potential needs. Population dispersion patterns and changes in their distribution also complicated matters. As populations became increasingly urban, providing services to those remaining in rural areas became more difficult. Whereas constitutions might mandate one judge for each city of a certain size, judges in many areas were underemployed while those in urban centers began to complain of work overloads. Some countries (Peru) compensated by the use of lay justices of the peace or municipal tribunals (Panama, some states in Mexico, Venezuela, and Colombia, the last two as recent innovations) entirely or partially outside the ordinary court system. With the exception of Peru, little is know about their operations, and for the most part, the ordinary judiciary tolerated, but did not endorse, the practice.

Except in the higher courts, judicial salaries rarely kept up with the rest of the public sector. When judges came from the upper-middle social strata, like university professors, they did not expect to improve their economic positions through their jobs. They often had their personal wealth to maintain their standards of living. As recruitment patterns changed, and both staff and professionals were increasingly drawn from the middle and lower-middle classes, low salaries became a problem, feeding the temptation to seek irregular means of increasing them. In addition, pressures to deliver services outside the urban areas also called for larger institutional budgets to finance new installations. Finally, the recognition of the judiciary's technological backwardness and the desirability of moving it into the modern era, at least on a par with other branches of government, also increased the demand for more funding.

In most of Latin America, courts controlled their own financial administration. Countries like Argentina and Colombia, where a ministry of justice filled this role, were the exception. There were, however, two problems with the seemingly positive normal arrangement. First, courts were notoriously poor financial managers and gave short shrift to hiring qualified administrative staff. The traditional expectation that any and all judicial employees might eventually become judges also meant they preferably recruited lawyers—whose administrative skills were notoriously limited. Second, although courts usually prepared their own budget requests, these had to be approved by the legislature, and at times by the executive as well. They also depended on the ministry of economy or finance for the disbursements of the approved amounts, which frequently came late and incomplete.[46] The judges'

45. See López-Ayllón and Fix-Fierro (1999), for a discussion of trends in Mexico.

46. This is the case in Chile, as reported by J. E. Vargas (1999), one of the few empirical studies on court finances in the region.

poor history of handling their own resources and their frequent inability to present a well-structured and justified request became a further pretext for cutting their allocations, creating a seemingly inescapable vicious circle. The judiciary's solution, logical from its own standpoint, was that it needed budgetary autonomy. This often translated into a guaranteed budgetary earmark (pioneered by the Costa Rican court in 1957) with no external interference in its distribution or use.

In the early years of the region's reform movement, courts did receive higher allocations and in some cases achieved their budgetary earmark.[47] Costa Rica's example was followed by El Salvador in its 1989 constitution, and by Guatemala (3 percent), Nicaragua (3 percent), Peru (2 percent, eliminated in 1993), Paraguay (3 percent), Honduras (2 percent), and Ecuador (2 percent). The constitutionally guaranteed amount was frequently not delivered in full, but many judiciaries at least over the short run found themselves in an unprecedented situation of having funds to increase or supplement salaries, provide additional benefits to their employees, and finance equipment and new buildings. The latter items also benefited from donor programs and from other special arrangements—for example, the auxiliary funds made available to Mexico's state courts in the 1990s, based on interest accruing on judicial deposits, and special funds managed by Brazilian state courts derived from similar sources. Except where this additional funding was part of a formal reform plan, its use was rarely thought out or controlled. Absent a plan, it was almost never programmed from the standpoint of improving services but, rather, as a way of giving the judiciary the dignified image it deserved. Funds disproportionately went into improving or building new palaces of justice and providing better facilities for higher level judges. There was much misuse, if not by judges then by their administrative staff.

Thus, despite the budgetary austerity programs introduced during the 1990s, judiciaries remained a major exception to the overall belt-tightening. Their percentage of the total public budget remained closer to 1–3 percent than Costa Rica's 6 percent,[48] but, in light of their relatively small staffs and limited operating expenses, this moved most of them out of their former abject poverty. Moreover,

47. See Martinez (1997, 27) for a list of court budgets as a percentage of the total national budget. As he notes even those with earmarks often do not receive it all. His figure for Argentina appears to include only the federal courts. Most recent studies in that country and statistics from its justice ministry suggest the percentage for federal and provincial courts is closer to 3.5 percent. While compared to Western and Eastern Europe, Latin America's judge-to-population ratio is somewhat low, judicial budgets as a percentage of the national budget or of GDP currently stand up quite well.

48. According to some sources, Colombia also reached the 6 percent figure in the mid-1990s. Colombia's courts have never had a budgetary earmark and the amount was shared by the several entities comprising "la Rama" (the judicial sector). Nearly half was absorbed by the Public Prosecutor's Office (Fiscalía General). The current percentage has fallen, but Colombia still has one of the most expensive justice sectors in the region and still faces enormous complaints about its performance. Martínez (1997, 27) gives a lower figure (4.62) for 1994, but statistics from the Colombia government showed it as higher for 1995. See Colombia, Comisión (1996).

the amount was often supplemented by off-budget revenues: judicial fees in a few countries, special funds like those of Mexico and Brazil, donor programs, and income from other special sources (running of public registries by Bolivia and Paraguay's courts). Salaries, as well as budgets, were often higher than appeared. Argentine federal judges do not pay income taxes, as a result of their own interpretation of the constitutional prohibition on lowering judicial salaries. Supplementary bonuses paid to judges in Peru and Mexico are not subject to taxes either. In the case of these two countries, this has a longer-term negative impact because judicial pensions are based on the far lower amount subject to taxation. Still, for present effects, when judges argue about being underpaid, they usually do not mention the tax-free portion of their incomes, or when they receive them, other nonmonetized benefits, or special allowances.

By the late 1990s, the situation again changed. Governments facing increased public debt and external pressures to reduce it could no longer afford to exempt their courts from the overall austerity drive. In most cases, this simply meant that the increases stopped, not that reductions would be effected. The courts having accustomed themselves to the years of generous funding and, in many cases finding their further expansion plans nipped in the bud, resumed their drive for budgetary increases and budgetary autonomy. The efforts to obtain constitutional earmarks have stepped up, though most have resigned themselves to 2 or 3 percent. The figures inevitably have no base in any argument except the examples of other countries and the need for judicial "dignification." Courts that spent what they received (and occasionally more[49]) remain unaccustomed to planning or justifying their requests and at most argue that justice deserves more funding, that quality can only be maintained or increased with higher budgets, and that this is the only means of ensuring their functional autonomy.

They have also not been beyond a little political blackmail of their own. Mexico's federal courts, arguably adequately endowed financially, have laid claim to as much as 6 percent of the federal budget; their current request is for 2.4 percent. If they are successful in obtaining it, the reasons are likely to be the federal executive's hope that they will be less assertive in quashing new economic departures—privatization schemes that appear to be of questionable constitutionality.[50] Prior to the 2002 national elections, in which an opposition party (PAN, Partido Acción Nacional) won the presidency but not a congressional majority, constitutionality had not been an obstacle. The Party of the Institutionalized Revolution (PRI) had

49. In both Mexico and Brazil, there are indications that on at least one occasion during the 1990s, supreme courts went well over their official budgets, only to have the government make up the difference.

50. Mexico's courts have also tried lobbying internationally. In a meeting with U.S federal judges (Austin, Texas, April 2001), sponsored by the American Bar Association, and in that same year in a meeting of the Ibero-American Association of Court Presidents (Madrid), the Mexicans tried to get the participants to endorse their claim. Although they were not successful in either case, they returned to Mexico claiming full support.

controlled all branches of government for seven decades and could circumvent the courts by simply amending the constitution. The supreme court, having been selected by the former PRI administration, may have ideological reservations about PAN's programs but also appears well aware that the current political situation enhances its ability to forward its own institutional agenda. The Mexican Supreme Court's other ploy is to seek backing from the state judiciaries by arguing that its victory will set a precedent for similar state earmarks.

Judicial planning capacity is markedly underdeveloped everywhere in the region, with the possible exceptions of Chile and Costa Rica. Colombia is a potential third addition, except that its planning capability does not seem to extend to improving performance.[51] Between this fact and the inability of virtually all courts to specify how larger budgets would improve performance, it is likely that changes elsewhere will also be political, not technical, decisions. In simplest terms, the courts want more because they believe they deserve more, and remain both unwilling and for the most part unable to provide more concrete justifications.

A word should be said on the frequent argument that governments have used the budget to manipulate the judiciary and thus that judicial budgets should be not only large, but also controlled directly by the courts or judicial councils. There actually is little indication anywhere in the region of budgets being used to punish recalcitrant judges and courts and not much more concerning their use as a reward. Because salaries, the most important stick and carrot, are usually set across the board, even in the worst situation there is little sign that judges have had them cut or delivered late to indicate governmental displeasure. The more effective lever in this regard is the appointment system, via promotions, transfers, or removal. Some supreme courts and their presidents in particular have managed special funds that, as in El Salvador in the early 1990s, they might use to reward the faithful. Apart from this, and efforts to buy influence with budgetary earmarks (presumably an ineffective control because of their permanence), budgetary management by nonjudicial agencies does not appear to be the executive's main means of controlling the courts. A refusal to grant more funding might indeed guarantee a less active set of judges, but here too evidence of this having been a major reason for keeping funding low is scarce. In general, courts do not get more funding because there is little practical or political payoff for those taking budget decisions and because of the courts' own failure to demonstrate why it is important.

In terms of a positive impact on performance, budgetary control by external agencies has been neither better nor worse than direct judicial control. On an international basis, ministry of justice administration is not an uncommon practice

51. Since the mid-1980s, Colombia has had an excellent set of judicial performance statistics, collected not by the courts but by the Ministry of Justice and various NGOs. See Nemoga (1988), for a discussion and examples. See also Colombia, Comisión (1996). Whatever its other failings, Colombia's judicial council has kept up the practice.

and in many cases appears satisfactory. The U.S federal courts shifted to direct control in 1939, but other common-law countries have not followed suit. The central problem in Latin America appears to be that the judicial budget has not been well administered by anyone. Whether current levels are too small, excessive, or about right remains undetermined, and in any event depends on what the courts are expected to do. This leads in turn to a third element of the institution-strengthening menu, the creation of new forms of judicial governance to oversee policymaking and performance, as well as ordinary administration.

JUDICIAL GOVERNANCE: THE JUDICIAL COUNCILS, SOLUTION OR ADDITIONAL COMPLICATIONS.

Judicial governance is also a late bloomer but moved ahead rapidly in the 1990s with the creation of judicial councils throughout the region. These structures, modeled loosely on European councils,[52] were introduced as a means of increasing institutional independence. Contrary to the European trends, Latin Americans did this by removing powers from the courts, not the ministries of justice. European councils usually limit their activities to the appointment system and control of the judicial careers.[53] In Latin America, it has also been suggested that they handle judicial administration and thus governance in a broader sense. To date this addition remains an unfulfilled dream of its promoters. Only Bolivia, Brazil at the national level, Costa Rica, Mexico at the federal level, Colombia, Ecuador, and Argentina's federal judiciary have councils with administrative duties. In Brazil and Costa Rica, the councils are internal to the judiciary, and in Mexico so dominated by judicial members it might as well be. Often (Brazil,[54] Colombia, Ecuador, Argentina), supreme courts are exempted from their administrative oversight. The exception was made to avoid further conflicts with the courts.

Whether in its appointive or administrative role, council governance had been introduced primarily to eliminate political interventions in judicial operations. Because of lingering concerns about their political neutrality, most high courts were

---

52. See Rico (1993) and Hammergren (2002a), for a short discussion on the European models and a list of references with more extensive treatments. See Renoux (1999), for lengthier discussions of the European variations, and Ibáñez (1988) and López Guerra (2001), for more on the Spanish model.

53. As councils have become more widespread in Europe, there are now various exceptions to this generalization, but the best-known models (France, Spain, Italy), those inspiring the Latin American adoption, fit the characterization.

54. In Brazil, councils (for the nationally based federal and labor courts) are really advisory and policymaking bodies. They are not responsible for overseeing day-to-day administration or appointments. The Supremo Tribunal Federal (constitutional court) is completely separate from this system. A 2004 constitutional amendment (no. 45) created a new council with some outside members to oversee all of Brazil's judicial systems. As of early 2006, its specific powers remained uncertain as did its budgetary resources.

not seen as vehicles for instilling greater objectivity and professionalism. It was also argued that taking these duties out of their hands would give the justices more time for their principal jurisdictional work. Courts generally opposed the councils, but rarely with success. It is not surprising that the councils' introduction was delayed by lengthy debates over the identity, terms of service, and means of selection of their members, and, after their legal creation, by further conflicts over the actual appointments.[55] Members are usually lawyers, although not always judges; in a few cases, representatives of other professional associations are also included. They may be selected directly by the groups they represent (commonly the judiciary, bar associations, the executive, legislature, and the public ministry) or from lists submitted to the national assembly. Despite their recent creation, several have already undergone changes in their composition. El Salvador's council went from a majority of judicial members to a smaller body excluding judges or their representatives. The latest amendment, in early 2002, added one judicially designated member. Mexico's council was created with a judicial majority (four of its seven members) selected by lottery (*insaculación*). After a 1999 constitutional reform, it is now virtually controlled by the supreme court and its president (who names the judicial representatives). Council size also varies from the five-member Bolivian body to Argentina's twenty-members council (to be reduced to thirteen in 2007). Although a smaller council would appear more suited to making policy, it bears mentioning that the two extreme cases, Argentina and Bolivia, are both known for their ineffective exercise of their administrative and appointive functions.

Aside from the political battles over their creation and their perpetuation within the councils themselves, the principal problem with the councils is that, by composition, structure, and orientation, they were not designed to facilitate a strong role in policymaking. Some observers suggest this was intentional. It seems more likely to reflect their designers' own ignorance about management criteria. As noted, size can be a problem, but this is hardly the only one. Council members are usually chosen because of their ability to represent external interests or their juridical skills and reputation. No one seems to have given any thought to management capability. Where it exists, it is a happy coincidence. Councils function very much like the supreme courts they usually replaced as selection or governance bodies. They are collegial in operation, nonexecutive in outlook, and generally bereft of administrative experience. As judicial selection bodies, they have made some advances over the prior arrangements, but they still have a long way to go in defining what they are looking for in judicial candidates and how they will

---

55. In Argentina, the council was constitutionally created in 1994 but did not take physical shape until 1998. Peru recreated its council (closed by the Fujimori 1992 auto-golpe) with the 1993 Constitution, but it was not organized until 1995, and by 1997 had been so stripped of powers that most of its members resigned. In Bolivia, the Dominican Republic, El Salvador, Ecuador, and Paraguay, there was a two- to six-year lag between constitutional and real creation. See Hammergren (2002a, 10–12).

measure its existence. As bodies responsible for judicial housekeeping and policy-making, they have for the most part been a disaster, albeit not always worse than the supreme courts themselves.[56]

Two noteworthy exceptions in this regard are Costa Rica's internal council (selected by the supreme court and composed of only five members), and Colombia's thirteen-member external Superior Magistrates' Council, divided into a disciplinary chamber, selected by the Congress on the basis of lists provided by the executive, and an administrative chamber with members chosen by Colombia's three high courts.[57] Although the Colombian council has markedly improved its performance in its twelve years of existence, it remains unpopular within and outside the judiciary, and discussions of its elimination continue.[58] Mexico and Brazil's federal internal councils might also be considered exceptions, but the former's aggressively expansionary policies and the latter's more subdued, deliberative role suggest, if for different reasons, a predominantly corporativist perspective and less receptivity to considering user and societal demands. In Brazil, it should be noted, the Federal Judicial Council (which only deals with the federal courts) does not control appointments. These are also managed by the judiciary itself (except for those of the supreme and superior tribunals, the national appellate, and the state high courts) through another series of internal committees organized by federal and state appeals courts. These bodies have also been criticized for their insular outlooks and perpetuation of a judicial establishment. Nonetheless, Brazil appears to have the best-developed selection and career systems in the region, with a minimum of political interference.[59]

It is worth remarking that three of the four more successful councils are organized internally, and that Colombia's administrative chamber, if not internal, is chosen by the judicial hierarchy. Moreover, all are relatively small and in this sense represent an improvement over supreme court management, especially when, as in Costa Rica and Colombia, their members are expected to devote full-time efforts to their councilor duties.[60] The other key to their success is their emphasis on building a strong administrative structure to carry out day-to-day housekeeping and some planning functions. Councilors oversee their administrative staff; they

---

56. Nonetheless, many donors and academic observers continue to see the councils as a positive factor. See World Bank, Legal Vice Presidency (2002, 6) and Ungar (2002, 169–86).

57. Colombia has the most complex judicial organization in the region, with the Council of State, heading its separate system of administrative courts, a Constitutional Court, and a Supreme Court of Justice for the ordinary judiciary. All three bodies select members of the Superior Magistrates' Council, though they are exempt from its administrative control. The council does propose candidates to the supreme court, from which the latter selects its own members.

58. For a far less positive view of the Colombian council, see Saez (2002).

59. See Rosenn (1998) and Bermudes (1999).

60. Full-time service, however, has been a complaint in Colombia. Critics believe it encourages the council members to micromanage. It also raises costs as the council, rather than relying on the official judicial administrative organization, has created a parallel set of advisory offices to serve its needs.

do not second-guess them or perform their duties. Adequate budgets for administrative salaries also appear to be the norm. Excess administrative employment is still the rule in all four countries, but at least this has not been achieved by underpaying staff.

An effective administrative structure, overseen but not micromanaged by the judicial governance body, is a major step in ensuring that courts make good use of their resources and can prepare acceptable budget proposals and ensure that ordinary judges have the staff, equipment, and materials they need to do their work. Even in these cases, there is some tendency to centralize control excessively, something most apparent in Mexico. Colombia and Costa Rica have been more amenable to decentralizing some administrative decisions, though in a country of latter's size this may be less important. Brazil rests at the other extreme. In the federal judiciary,[61] it is the five Regional Tribunals (*Tribunais Regionais*) that have effective control over administration. The Federal Judicial Council, composed of their presidents plus the president and five other members of the *Superior Tribunal de Justiça* (STJ), establishes common policies on the basis of internal consensus.

Centralization is more pronounced elsewhere in the region. When combined with a weak administrative system and less effective governance bodies, it continues to pose problems. In Peru, one fortuitous consequence of the otherwise damaging Fujimori reforms (1995–2000) was the improvement of court administrative systems. Because the reforms were conducted by administrators, they raised administrative salaries and hired more staff. They also consolidated a level of central control that had previously been only theoretical. The administrators themselves recognize the need for greater flexibility, but the Supreme Court, which has resumed its role of judicial governance, neither understands nor seems willing to address the issue. Argentina's federal courts maintain a similar level of administrative centralization and also suffer governance by a council that has too many other internal problems to consider changing the rules. As in Peru, stories abound of courts lacking basic supplies because the order has not been processed in the national capital or having to purchase equipment from a central contractor at prices far higher than those on the local market.

Centralization can also encourage corruption. Decentralized court districts may make deals with local suppliers, but a big central contract for providing office furniture, computers, or even pencils for an entire court system is a far more enticing temptation. Moreover, those controlling the contracts, who do not suffer the direct consequences, face fewer disincentives for buying shoddy goods.

All of this discussion relates to what can be called housekeeping functions, the day-to-day management of court resources to ensure they arrive where and when

61. Brazil also has a system of military, electoral, and labor courts that form part of the national judicial branch, and a constitutional court, the Federal Supreme Tribunal (STF). Each has its own administrative system, with those of the first three organized more or less along the lines of the ordinary federal courts.

they are needed. Internal councils appear to have potential advantages in performing this role as compared with the two usual alternatives—external councils or supreme courts. The advantage is relative and also hinges on who staffs the councils, members' understanding of their jobs, and their ability and willingness to put funds into creating an adequate administrative structure. There is a second governance function that has become still more important in the modern era. This involves the development of judicial policy to anticipate the emergence of new needs, set goals and benchmarks for meeting them, and rethink the institutional mandate and the way it carries it out. Like it or not, judiciaries no longer exist in a static system and cannot assume that business as usual, no matter how efficiently conducted, will permit them to maintain and improve on their levels of performance and their public's satisfaction with them.

As has been argued in previous chapters, most Latin American courts continue to resist this notion. Their standard solutions for twenty-first century needs have been higher budgets and modern technology. Whatever planning capabilities they have are directed largely to securing both. When changing how they operate requires more than the substitution of a computer for a pen, they have preferred to claim this is legally impossible, ideologically undesirable, and an overall perversion of their role. Because this is largely an attitudinal obstacle, new governance structures have been of little help in overcoming it. Individual leaders, whether in a court or an external or internal council, have often been critical, but their ability to advance also depends on building supporting alliances within and outside the judiciary. Internal councils or strong court presidents may have more luck here, because they are already acknowledged as judicial leaders. Lacking this status, external councils, as in Colombia, find it more difficult to overcome judicial opposition and may quickly find themselves pitted against the supreme court as well as a majority of judges. The other common source of opposition is the private bar. Although Latin American bar associations are notoriously weak as formal institutions, they can rally effectively against change.[62] Moreover elite lawyers often have better political contacts than the judges themselves and thus more effective means of making their wishes known.[63]

If creating better, more efficient judicial administration remains a challenge in most countries, instilling policymaking and strategic planning capabilities will be doubly difficult. The need for their creation is still largely unrecognized when not openly disputed, and the existing governance bodies, in both their new and old forms, seem uniquely unsuited for the tasks. Donors and financially generous governments have arguably impeded their emergence, because their budgetary largesse

---

62. Again, Brazil's *Ordem de Advogados do Brasil*, is an important exception, exercising enormous political power.
63. See Dezalay and Garth (2002, chap. 12).

has often strengthened the judiciary's notion that it deserves more funding as a natural right. This free money has further weakened the link between access to resources and performance. Budgeting is always political, but the donors and co-operating governments have made it more so. They also have, not entirely without reason, increased the suspicion that more funds are made available to buy the judiciary's goodwill. This suspicion was awakened with the first donor programs and continues to this day. Donors, like governments, could overcome this impression by demanding that higher funding levels be linked to more efficient and effective performance. Both have their reasons for not doing so, but one consequence of their inaction may be entirely perverse—the judiciary's conclusion that it is indeed owed resources because of what it is, not what it does or how it does it.

THE MISSING ELEMENT: LEGAL EDUCATION

This is a topic that might be treated in a discussion of any of the five reform areas, because it affects them all. Although placed in the chapter on judicial strengthening, it should be emphasized that it has consequences not only for the judges, but also for the wider legal community and, by extension, the way law is practiced as a whole. It is thus surprising that, aside from special training programs provided to accompany the introduction of new codes and procedures (for example, ADR), it has received so little attention. Periodically someone notices that many systemic weaknesses, ranging from corruption to excessive delays and unethical treatment of clients, originate in what is taught or not taught in the region's law schools, but so far very little has been done about it.

One major disincentive for donors is their experience with the law and development movement of the 1960s and 1970s, which placed enormous emphasis on introducing legal training methods developed in the more prestigious U.S law schools.[64] Its participants saw this as a way of making law more relevant to changing social and economic needs. Their self-declared, if somewhat exaggerated, failure in their goals and the energetic ousting of some of their programs served to create the impression that this was not a wise course for donors to adopt.[65] Two other factors discouraging donor involvement are the perceived lag between program implementation and any measurable impact on justice system performance and the sense that the size of the investments might not be justified by the changes produced.

---

64. See Gardner (1980) and Dezalay and Garth (2002).

65. Even in the usually tranquil Costa Rica, students at the National University reportedly burned the library in protest of legal imperialism. Still, despite its participants' negativism the law and development movement did have a direct impact on legal training in a few universities and also created a small core of local jurists with new insights into the role of law. Many of them have been active in reform proposals throughout the past twenty years.

A fourth impediment lies in the reasons for the reported declines in the quality of what was already an outdated system—the emergence of hundreds of new law schools (sometimes without benefit of a surrounding university) throughout the region as an unintended consequence of efforts to democratize access to higher education in the final decades of the last century. Commonly these schools are not regulated and, as a result, may provide little value for the fees they charge. Nevertheless, tightening up the regulations would face strong opposition from their directors and students as well as charges of elitism. For many students, these schools, however poorly they perform, represent the only chance at a professional degree. Similarly, measures to control entry to public law schools, tighten the requirements for graduation, or raise the bar for accreditation as a lawyer face their own threats of violent protest. This factor has little effect on donors, but it does explain the low incidence and limited results of purely local initiatives. There are schools that have adopted new measures, but they tend to be expensive private entities whose students usually seek and obtain jobs outside the public sector. Moreover, many of their graduates operate in a fashion that never requires them to see a court. They have learned and practice preventive law that their well-paying clients require. Unfortunately, this also means their potential positive impact on their own justice systems is very limited.

Aside from its overproduction of lawyers poorly trained even by traditional standards, opinions vary as to what is wrong with the current system or how it might be fixed.[66] The most widely shared criticisms focus on outdated teaching methods (an excessive when not exclusive reliance on lectures with little opportunity for discussions), the premium placed on memorizing the law, the failure to encourage students to think critically or develop an ability to deal with clients and apply laws to real cases, the near absence of attention to professional ethics and skills like negotiation, and a general failure to convey knowledge about how law is actually practiced. The fact that law is an undergraduate program throughout Latin America, even if its graduates are sometimes called "doctors" and thus that students receive little if any training in other disciplines is also commonly cited as a problem. Certain structural factors like low salaries for professors, a consequent reliance on part-time faculty, lack of textbooks aside from codes, and lower use of clinical courses are often mentioned. Some observers also suggest that the way law is taught tends to reinforce the impression that judges must only apply it automatically and uncritically with no attention to the social, economic, and political consequences.[67]

66. For representative examples, and the source of the following comments, see Binder (2005), Burridge (1999), Boehmer (2005), Dezalay and Garth (2002), Pásara (2005a, 2005b), and Pérez Perdomo (2005).

67. This was stressed by one of my reviewers, Keith Rosenn. It is sometimes mentioned by others, though it may be more difficult to sustain today with the emergence of national organizations of "democratic judges," the growth of interest in public interest law, and arguments by judges in some countries (especially in Brazil and the Southern Cone) that their primary responsibility is protecting the poor, regardless of what the law says. Still, however nobly inspired, pro-poor rulings uninformed by an adequate

However the specific problems are described, there is agreement on their direct negative consequences for judicial quality, because most judges are now recruited from the less prestigious and less innovative programs. There is an even more diffuse negative impact on their performance because of having to face an army of poorly trained, ethically challenged, and generally desperate lawyers whose survival strategy too frequently hinges on stringing out a case as long as possible or until the client cannot pay any more. Judicial training can address if not resolve the first problem by ensuring that those who reach the bench get the additional training and orientation their law schools did not provide. It cannot fix the larger problem of the abusive when not incompetent private practitioner. This suggests a dilemma similar to that discussed in the chapter on criminal justice reforms—the extent to which a targeted set of behaviors can be changed without addressing the broader environmental constraints. In short, what are the realistic prospects for improving judicial performance when the principal interface between the judiciary and the citizens served is motivated by a host of perverse incentives?

One partial solution may lie in the otherwise lamentable emergence of a two-tiered legal community—consisting of a minority of well-trained, proficient practitioners and a mass of undertrained and often underemployed private and public lawyers.[68] There are signs that the minority in some countries has reached a size and level of impatience sufficient to impose greater control over all their members. For example, in the past two examinations for entrance to the bar conducted by the São Paulo branch of Brazil's national bar association, the acceptance level dropped precipitously. Still, one does not know whether the transparent efforts to control the supply of lawyers will also enhance the quality of those who got through the filter. Moreover, this is just one example, and it is a tactic that comes very late in the chain of events. More encouraging is the increasing attention by local experts to the entire problem of overproduction of poorly trained professionals and a new series of demands for changes to the legal education system. Because the benefits for the state are neither more immediate nor evident than those for the donors, and the costs to both are high, it may indeed take movement from within to inspire a serious remedy.

RESULTS AND IMPACTS

The combined judicial strengthening activities—career and appointment systems, budgets, and new forms of governance—have changed the face and capabilities

---

understanding of their broader consequences may have their own perverse effects. Thus, the argument by Rosenn and others on the need for multidisciplinary education still holds.

68. For an elaboration on this argument, see Dezalay and Garth (2002).

of Latin America's judiciaries over the past two decades. They might have done more with attention to some missing elements such as legal education and ethics, but that cannot detract from their accomplishments. While having to overcome enormous obstacles, not only in the form of active opposition, but also a thoroughly discredited institutional image, the move to introduce merit selection and judicial careers has arguably improved the quality of the profession and removed some of the worst abuses and abusers. Judicial corruption and incompetence remain a significant problem in many countries, but these are usually those that started late and have not moved to a career system. They also are countries where the pool of candidates poses problems of its own, because of inadequate legal education, and the generally lower quality of the legal profession. Many countries conducting entrance judicial examinations for the first time find they have to lower the cutoff standards if they are to accept any candidates at all.[69] Even so, the fact of having to pass an examination for entry helps in filtering out the most incompetent or those who simply do not take the challenge seriously.

Higher budgets have generally been accompanied by salary increases, making judgeships more attractive to more qualified candidates and also removing the absolute necessity of ceding to material pressures. Career systems, where they have been introduced, have also reduced the fear of political reprisals for good-faith adjudication. Where increased resources are better managed, because of improved governance and administrative systems, judges also work in more pleasant circumstances and enjoy such additional benefits as training programs, libraries, and study grants. Making such benefits available is often a first priority of new governing bodies, especially those recognizing the importance of building identification with the institution. Whereas supreme courts often spent any excess on their own privileges, and sometimes created an excess where it should not have existed,[70] council governance tends to be more egalitarian in its emphasis, in part because it sees this as a way of improving overall performance and in part because it recognizes the need to appeal to its judicial constituency.

The immediate consequence has been a strengthening of institutional ties. Judges can now take more pride in their work and expect more benefits from their institutional loyalties. This is an important part of institutional strengthening, the advantages of which should not be underestimated. It also may make judges more receptive to increased control over their performance, via improved statistical systems and such novelties as judicial visitations—itinerant inspection teams that

69. This was the experience of El Salvador in the early 1990s, of Peru in 2002, and of the Dominican Republic in the mid-1990s (interviews, all three countries).

70. Throughout the 1980s in particular, there are numerous cases of supreme courts using their financial windfalls to their own ends, and creating them, where they were not automatic. When the U.S. government began planning its post-Noriega judicial reform program in Panama, the supreme court first listed the highest priority needs as a new palace of justice, and computers and Volvos for themselves. Anyone who has witnessed the often squalid conditions in which trial court judges work can appreciate the irony.

evaluate the way judges run their courtrooms. Courts and councils have also campaigned for higher salaries for judges, and sometimes for administrative staff, and have sought additional benefits (including housing loans, tax exemptions, and even, in Peru, funds for funeral expenses). In summary, in combination the three principal avenues for upgrading the judiciary's professional quality, institutional cohesion, and ability to direct its internal operations have paid off. As indicated by popular opinion surveys and, where they are available, other more objective indicators of performance (levels of congestion, backlogs, delay, the percentage of cases decided on the merits and not resolved or rejected on more formalistic criteria) the effects are less dramatic.[71] Conceivably, the first set of impacts is a precondition for attacking the others. Still, there are doubts of whether more satisfied judges are ready or motivated to address concerns about the overall quality of what they produce, and for that to happen more attention will have to be turned to the principal missing element, the quality of overall legal education, and its impact on what is channeled into the courts.

SOME CAVEATS: THE LIMITS OF INSTITUTIONAL STRENGTHENING FOR ITS OWN SAKE

The problem and the danger are that this emphasis on improving the lot of the judges and their staff has rarely been translated into improving services to clients or looking for means to do work better. The more pleasant, less threatening working environment has inspired some judges, individually or in ad hoc groups, to explore these issues, but this has rarely emerged as an institutional policy. Training, for example, is frequently offered as a benefit to judicial employees, but its content is based on what they want to learn, not an analysis of what they need to know. As the training director of one Mexican state judiciary noted, "we do not see our role as solving problems," but rather of improving the overall quality of staff. The question is how these abstract qualitative improvements translate into user services. Presumably a happier, more intellectually satisfied staff will treat court clients better. In that same court system, however, judges seemed completely unconcerned about the poor facilities provided by the court for public defenders (nine of them housed in a room the size of a large closet) or the fact that most clients hired their own attorneys. In light of the level of poverty in Mexico, this suggests either that the poor do not have legal conflicts or that they are not taking them to court. In Mexico, as in most of the region, except for criminal cases, legal representation is required for all plaintiffs—civil defendants who cannot find free counsel or afford to hire a lawyer cannot fully participate in the proceedings.

71. As observers are increasingly noting, public approval of court performance has been declining since at least the mid-1990s, in some cases, dramatically. See Galindo (2003).

The argument rests on anecdotal evidence, but, if not conclusive, it is worrisome. Peruvian judges interviewed in 2001–2002, during the lengthy breaks they enjoyed between hearings, appeared unconcerned about their light workload or its relationship to the impact the hefty judicial fees (used to augment their own salaries) might have on obstructing access to poor clients. In 1998, a visit with a Bolivian departmental court to inspect the terrain it was purchasing for a new judicial vacation club was interrupted by a brief interview with officials of a small town requesting their own judge. The court had no funds to finance the latter. In country after country, new court constructions appear largely underutilized, and new computer equipment often remains untouched. Courts suggest the need for higher budgets to replace staff on training, because it would be unfair to expect them to attend courses on their own time. Nevertheless, Peru's judicial school has a budget that affords its director and director of training only half the new salary of a first instance judge. The court successfully campaigned to raise judicial salaries but overlooked all administrative staff and its school as well.[72]

Those improvements that do not directly enhance the working conditions of judicial employees seem an attempt to satisfy the needs of private attorneys — Internet filing, notification by e-mail, and courtroom terminals designed to show the client (that is, the attorney) the status of a case. The assumption that all attorneys now have e-mail may be erroneous, and it certainly is not true of their clients. Some courts have begun programs to reach out to the broader public, but often as an afterthought. Services to attend the poor majority are usually neglected. Still less attention to small claims courts, whether belonging to the ordinary court system or to municipalities, has already been mentioned. Peru's experience is typical. President Fujimori's reforms provided Lima's court district with state-of-the-art courtrooms and computer equipment for its civil courts. Criminal courts were largely neglected except for those judging suspected terrorists. Lima's Northern Cone, a neighboring court district serving poorer clients, has its main facilities housed partly in an old warehouse. Lima's justice of the peace courts still lack computers and consequently keep very poor track of the cases filed. Peru's lay justices of the peace remain dependent on foreign donors for their training programs and equipment. Although they belong to the ordinary court system, they still do not receive salaries or any expense allowance. Mexico's municipal courts are "where the poor go" and are entirely dependent on municipal funding. Interviews with Mexican judges suggested no knowledge or curiosity about how they functioned.

One important exception to this general rule is found in the small claims courts and ADR services financed by Brazil's state and federal courts.[73] The experiment

---

72. In 2002, the salary problem was temporarily resolved by appointing a judge as director. She continued to receive her judicial salary. Her successors have also been judges.

73. There is a vast and growing literature on these courts. See Arantes (1997), Batista (1999), Bermudes (1999), Rodycz (2001), Sadek, ed. (1995b, 2000, 2001a), Watanabe (1986).

began in two states (Rio Grande do Sul and São Paulo) in the mid-1980s, was recognized in the 1988 constitution, and was further encouraged by a 1995 law. The courts allow pro-se (self) representation and feature oral hearings; like the ADR services, they have been created in marginal neighborhoods to afford access to the poor. It is no longer clear that the poor are the majority users (the middle class also has small claims), and there are now criticisms about an excess of work and overly formalistic procedures, as well as of inadequate training of the community mediators. Nevertheless, the services are used (excess demand may be a consequence) and have improved the judicial image. At the other end of the judicial spectrum, Costa Rica's constitutional chamber of its supreme court, which likewise allows direct access without formal representation, has also been an image enhancer, building the judiciary's reputation as a protector of the rights of all citizens, especially of the disadvantaged.[74] Brazil's lower-level judges have in fact laid claim to a pro-poor stance and, until 2004, used it effectively to lobby against giving higher courts the ability to set binding precedent.[75] According to the trial judges and their supporters, the high courts are more sensitive to the needs of political and business elites.

Judicial populism is also not the answer. These examples, which only tend in that direction, are cited because they are so rare and because they do demonstrate the room for moves on that front. The real question is how to get the courts to look beyond improving their own working conditions and potentially increasing their social isolation, to examine the social reality in which they operate and ask how they can better meet its needs. Courts worldwide have rarely done this on their own. Where they have acted, it is usually because of external complaints, coming from the government, the private bar, or concerned citizens groups. Absent such pressures in much of Latin America, at least in sufficient quantity to provoke a response, the judiciary's reaction to its new resources is only logical. In that sense, the anticipated belt tightening might not be a bad thing. Courts suddenly facing hard budgetary constraints may have to start thinking beyond their own comforts. Donors, who represent the principle source of additional funding, must then be careful that they do not ease the situation. A new, largely unprecedented insistence on tying grants and loans to results is highly recommended. For donors operating in grants this is easier; for the MDBs it is difficult, because they run the risk of not consolidating their loans. This will be called political meddling, but it is no more so than an insistence on cutting government employment, privatizing state companies, or reducing the dropout rate in schools. Unless the donor community takes this charge seriously, it risks undercutting its own announced purpose of improving the administration of justice for all citizens and especially for those who currently do not participate in its benefits.

74. See Barker (2000) and Wilson et al. (2004).

75. See Ballard (1999) and Sadek (2001b). The constitutional reform of late 2004 gave the Supremo Tribunal Federal the ability to declare its constitutional interpretations broadly binding—via a device called the *súmula vinculante.*

RELATIONSHIP TO OTHER PROGRAMS

For the most part, institutional strengthening efforts as explicit reform objectives have run on their own separate track. There are obvious potential overlaps with other areas, but most have not been recognized or realized. Efforts to improve recruitment and postentry training have often been coordinated with criminal justice reforms, but only to the extent that candidates for criminal court judgeships will be tested in these materials and provided on-the-job training after the fact. Courts and councils have included new equipment and infrastructure in their wish lists as part of their own definition of judicial strengthening, often arguing about the impact of such additions on enhanced efficiency. Most recently, as discussed in the next chapter, they have also added ADR programs to the list of things for which they require financing to decongest and expand access to their own dockets. Their own demonstrated inability to program these additions, however, raises questions as to the sincerity of their proposals. Courts have become better about lobbying for budgets, but the improvement may be largely in the area of manipulating public relations. The missing quality is improved judicial governance; the control center from which overall performance improvement should be investigated, defined, and orchestrated. Courts are opposed to the concept, local reform lobbies seem not to have recognized or organized to promote it, and donors and governments funding reform programs seem to avoid touching it, out of concern for being charged with violating institutional independence or engaging in political interventions.

Improved governance will become a more necessary part of overall institutional strengthening as the additional funds available to judiciaries dry up. At that stage, they will have to become more efficient, as regards their ongoing activities and those they still wish to add. The most important potential role for whatever body exercises this function will be coordinating the various partial reforms and deciding how to balance their conflicting demands for more resources. This is not yet a part of the new paradigms for the judicial role, but it is a first step in that it will force court systems to prioritize the services they wish to provide. More computers, more ADR, more training, and more courtrooms, built to accommodate an increasing number of oral trials, cannot be financed indefinitely. The quality of the decisions eventually taken would be aided by more assistance on planning and budgeting techniques and on building and interpreting statistical systems to support them.

CONCLUSIONS

Institutional strengthening remains a task half accomplished for Latin America's court systems. Those that have advanced furthest in the area have recouped a part of their former prestige, enhancing the quality of their human and material resources, and improving their capacity to administer both. They have also rebuilt institutional morale so that judges and support staff can feel good about their jobs and well compensated for doing them. Nevertheless, many courts have a long way to go even in this regard. Their reforms either stopped far short of the intended objectives or were subverted by political agendas. For example, Argentina's federal courts, whose judges are a cut above the intellectual average and enjoy some of the highest salaries in the region, still have a reputation for corruption and inefficiency more befitting of some of their poorer neighbors. A thoroughly ineffectual judicial council and the damages worked by former president Menem's court-stacking maneuver are partly to blame. Inefficient resource management, which has left the courts poorly housed and dramatically overstaffed, is another factor. The situation of countries like Bolivia, Ecuador, Honduras, Guatemala, Nicaragua, Paraguay, and Venezuela is more easily explained. Political machinations have stopped the full reform package short of its goals, subverted innovations (for example, Bolivia, Ecuador, and Paraguay's judicial councils) or reversed them (Chavez's elimination of Venezuela's council and subsequent court-packing measures or Gutierrez's sacking of Ecuador's supreme and constitutional courts and the council), and continued to provide incentives to judges to keep their old vices. Ironically, Guatemala's extremely generous donor funding, a result of its successful peace process, appears to have aggravated the problem, inundating the courts with resources they will be hard pressed to use well.

Even in these less successful examples, there has been some progress in building a more technically proficient, professionally oriented, and independent court system. Almost universally, however, the benefits continue to accrue first to the judges, second to the private bar, and last, if at all, to the ordinary citizens. Because courts are in no danger of elimination, their failure to develop responses to new political, economic, and social needs has lower internal costs. Courts will always receive public funds and, in some cases, continue to receive more because it suits governments and donors to fill their coffers. Complete institutional strengthening also includes a better fit with external stakeholders, and, in the best of worlds, these are more than opportunistic politicians and donor agencies.[76] Because so much change, in this and other areas, has been initiated externally, not from the normal users but from other domestic and foreign actors, the institutionalization process has tended to increase rather than reduce the courts' relative isolation. Because it

---

76. Dissatisfaction with progress made under the early programs is now provoking a second round of recommendations, most of them coming from within the national legal communities, and some from political leaders. Examples of the latter are proposals forwarded by presidents Kirchner in Argentina and Uribe in Colombia to reform the judicial councils. Examples of the former are more numerous—see Eguiguren et al. (2002) on Peru, which includes suggestions on both the judicial career and judicial government.

has also increased their internal satisfaction, the pressures to consider additional transformations have also declined. The current challenge for would-be reformers is thus a far difficult one—how to convince the region's more self-sufficient judiciaries that it is worth their while to question the new, more comfortable status quo. Otherwise further reforms will operate around an empty core, cajoling courts to adopt new practices they neither need nor want, but might accept if someone pays them to do so. This is no one's definition of institutional maturity, and their role in perpetuating it should give the local and international reform community pause.

Access to justice holds an odd place in judicial reform programs. Logically, it could be the all-encompassing goal—that of ensuring that citizens share equally in the benefits of a well-functioning justice system. Theoretically, many of these benefits, like those provided by a public health, education, or security system, can be enjoyed by citizens who never receive direct attention. The guarantee that services will be available if needed is important, but it is a condition for, not the essence of, the public good provided. For justice, that good can be described as juridical security, rule of law, or a widely recognized normative framework that actually shapes the actions and interactions of private and state actors. For those not familiar with this distinction, it bears repeating that the public or private nature of a good is determined not by the identity of its provider but rather by the divisibility of the benefit.[1] Individualized services, for example, preventive health care, are private goods (even if delivered by public agencies), whereas indivisible benefits—for example, a healthful environment—are public goods.

The emphasis on access, another later addition to the reform agenda, tends to feature the private good element, as the increased use of courts and related, usually publicly provided, services by traditionally excluded populations, the poor and other marginalized groups. True, the public good derives from broad and equal access for all citizens to services intended to resolve their disputes and rectify alleged violations of their legally and constitutionally protected rights. Real use, not abstract protection, a more effective legal framework, or a reduced level of conflicts, however, has become the usual indicator of success.

Because judicial services have not been equally available throughout the region's history, remedying the situation is important. Where exclusion is a long-term practice, its termination may require more than simply removing barriers. Abstract protection of rights is not much good if significant portions of the population do not believe they have effective means of protesting violations. Limited

---

1. See Shavell (1997) and J. E. Vargas et al. (1998, 2001). Vargas uses the traditional public and private good distinction whereas Shavell speaks of public and private motives for accessing justice. The latter has the advantage of avoiding the debate over whether any measure of private benefit makes justice essentially a private good (with varying degrees of externalities) or whether a public good can have private externalities.

access, whether real or imagined, undermines the public good effects; where the rule of law functions only for those with funds to pay for a lawyer or who understand they are entitled to free representation, it will serve as a guide to only a narrow segment of public and private actions. Citizens with insufficient resources will either lack protection or will find other, less socially desirable means to resolve their conflicts and demand their rights. Resolution of conflicts need not be limited to the courts, but unless alternative means operate in the shadow of the law they will subvert rather than reinforce the preferred normative framework.

Thus, the emphasis on expanding the private good aspects of judicial services is intimately linked to maximizing the public good or externalities. The linkage merits further exploration. As discussed below, defined as a simple one-to-one correspondence (more private benefits mean an equivalent increase in the public goods element), it poses some real problems. Not the least of these are the budgetary implications of expanding existing services to meet potential demand and subsidizing those additional expenditures required even of users who receive "free" court services.[2] Although proponents of access enhancement focus on equalizing use of essentially individualized services, they usually stick to a notion of the indivisible quality of justice when questions of rationing or setting priorities for use are raised. When the fundamental right of access to justice becomes equated with the absolute right of access to court use, the public good itself may be endangered. The service providers lose all control over what is delivered and with it their ability to direct resources into the most socially productive channels. The functional equivalent in public health would be making the provision of treatment, its content, duration, and state-incurred costs entirely dependent on the preferences of the patients. No public health system would survive long on this basis. Traditional justice systems have often done so, but only because of the existing barriers to broader use. Once those physical, financial, operational, and attitudinal barriers are removed, they will find themselves facing a new set of challenges. Access-enhancement programs have so far not created that situation, but their underlying logic seems to drive them in that direction.

HISTORY OF DEVELOPMENT

The early emphasis on criminal justice discouraged attention to the issue of access, at least as an individualized service. Some theorists have attempted to argue that criminal justice is also a private good. Most see it as more nearly purely public in

---

2. For example, although clients may have court fees waived on the grounds of poverty, they still need legal counsel and may also be responsible for other payments—those required for expert witnesses or DNA testing for paternity cases.

the sense that its major benefits (a presumed reduction of criminal activity, greater citizen security, and a strengthening of the normative framework) cannot be individualized. This is arguably true even of what Latin Americans call "private crimes" (offenses against honor or ones private image) or of the use of criminal proceedings to claim civil damages. Individuals do access private benefits through these mechanisms, but this does not detract from the commonly enjoyed deterrent and normative strengthening effects. In any event, these are lesser uses of the criminal justice system, not the main act.

Criminal justice reformers did worry about individualized access in one sense, the provision of public defense services to indigent defendants, who traditionally have been at the mercy of the system, and of strengthening other guarantees to ensure that due process rights of individuals (including not only the defendant but also the victim) were adequately respected. They rarely used the term "access" in this regard, and thus for the most part criminal justice reforms can be thought of as efforts to advance "access to justice" as enhancement of a public good, with some private externalities. As discussed below, one of the major arguments against nonjudicial (that is, private) settlement of criminal disputes is that they tend to invert this formula, privatizing the issues and leaving it up to the parties to decide on how or whether the normative framework will be enforced.

Although access to justice has always been part of the reform discourse, its emergence as a separate theme with its own repertoire of actions thus came somewhat later, in part as the vision of the court's other benefits and services came to the fore. Here again several factors converged to promote this development:

- Efforts on the part of national governments and judiciaries to update noncriminal legal codes, including commercial, family, labor, and other civil law areas, as well as public (administrative) law. In all of these areas, the identity of users is more important in defining both the public and private good elements.[3]
- Charges, largely expressed by national and international nongovernmental organizations (NGOs), that the benefits of legal and judicial reform were accruing largely to economic, political, and judicial elites.[4]
- Donors' emphasis on poverty reduction and efforts by their judicial reform staff to ensure their own programs complied with it.[5]
- A better understanding of court use and the discovery that the usual clientele

3. For example, to the extent family law is intended to protect the family as an institution, access limitation inhibits this goal. Even legislation intended to enable market development (a public good) would have limited impact absent wider access.

4. See Correa (1999) and other chapters in Méndez et al. (1999), for arguments about the limited benefits to the poor from the criminal justice reforms. See Galanter (1974), however, for an argument about the difficulties of designing reforms that benefit the "have-nots."

5. See chapters in Domingo and Sieder (2001), for a discussion of current donor aims, all of which now emphasize poverty reduction.

was less than representative of the entire population and of the variety of barriers to access incorporated in current legislation, court practices, and location.[6]

- Demands from potential users themselves for access to these services and to the rights they presumably protected.
- The emergence of alternative dispute resolution and its attachment to the judicial reform programs
- Courts' use of the argument about the need to increase access as a means of justifying higher budgets, and the adoption of some programs to demonstrate their dedication to providing fuller services

These many contributions to putting access on the reform agenda have produced an even greater number of methods for furthering its attainment. Access enhancement is conceivably the most diversely focused of the reform approaches and, not surprisingly, the least strategically developed. To the extent access enhancement has been equated with getting more, and more diverse citizens to courts or courtlike services, it affords carte blanche to anyone who can propose a means of broadening use or removing traditional barriers. Where the only target is expanding service use, any and all means are automatically welcome. To the extent proponents have been adverse to prioritizing demand or rationing supply, discussions of costs and benefits or comparative impacts have been extremely unwelcome. There has also been a remarkable inattention to the nature of unmet needs, their implications for individual and collective well-being, or the full range of reasons why people might not take them to court.[7] The access "strategy" has been to let a hundred flowers bloom, and so far no one has thought to do any pruning. In the process, proponents have substantially widened our understanding of the ways access can be blocked and of the potential short-term benefits of eliminating the obstacles. They have also been extremely innovative in developing new mechanisms. They have not been able to measure satisfactorily the presumed longer-run advantages for the immediate beneficiaries or for society as a whole. Before addressing these issues, the major lines of activity merit exploration.

6. Until recently, most evidence was anecdotal and apocryphal, though even the experts tended to believe most civil court users were businesses and banks, except in small claims courts. Empirical studies are knocking some holes in that notion but still suggest court users are hardly representative of the entire population. Analysis of a random sample of cases filed in Lima's justice of the peace courts in 1998 (Gonzales et al. 2002) did find that banks and private pension funds were among the most frequent plaintiffs. The district court's own belief that justices of the peace handled predominantly family and labor matters turned out to be untrue. Pásara (1982, 30) reports that twenty-five years ago, child support cases ranged between 20 and 25 percent of filings in three urban centers outside of Lima but were only 8 percent in Lima itself.

7. A focus on barriers is one thing, but what is needed here is a market survey and some means for ranking the importance of what is not submitted for judicial resolution. Grossman et al. (1982) would be a useful tool for access enhancers with its emphasis on how conflicts escalate into judicial cases. So far, their methodology seems only to have been adopted for elites in other regions (Hendley et al. 1999).

PROGRAM COMPONENTS

Expanding the Number and Improving the Distribution of Normal Services

This is always the judiciary's first answer to improving access, on the basis of its usual assumption that it is too overburdened with work to attend to more clients. As discussed above, this initial assumption is open to question, but we will ignore this issue temporarily. Numerical and territorial expansion was a judicial goal even before reform became a conscious drive. It was motivated less by access considerations than by a desire to expand the penetration of the state and of its courts into areas that, for all intents and purposes, had existed outside the formal rule of law. Access to judicial services was a by-product. Because the expansion was territorially rather than client targeted, its benefits for groups marginalized by their socioeconomic status or ethnic identity were minimal. To the extent they felt the new presence of the legal system, it was more likely to be as its victims, as the defendants, and most often losing parties in both criminal and civil actions. Still, the presence of court and other sector services did constitute a potential resource, and, over time, some nontraditional clients learned to use it, both in their conflicts with each other, and occasionally with higher-status groups.[8] Courts made no special concessions to their lack of familiarity with the rules or other disadvantages, so any progress on this front was entirely up to the users.

In the early years, national integration was more important than workload in motivating the expansion. By the 1930s, both factors came into play, accounting for the addition of judges and courts in urban areas, where population growth and increasing conflicts began to augment demand substantially. The most dramatic changes came in the closing decades of the twentieth century. As Sergio Lopez-Ayllón and Héctor Fix-Fierro document for Mexico's federal judiciary, the 1970s saw an enormous expansion in numbers, the creation of an entire new level of courts, and an internal redistribution of workload.[9] For the most part, this phenomenon went unnoticed outside the judiciary. This slow organic growth, followed by sudden acceleration, appears to be the case for other countries, though evidence is not very systematic. It occurred not only at the lower levels but also for appellate courts. Nonetheless, in light of the costs of the appeals process, it is likely that the benefits of this expanded service did not affect poorer clients, except

---

8. Research on litigation in rural Peru during the late nineteenth and early twentieth century demonstrates, for example, a surprising number of cases initiated by indigenous communities. These were usually land disputes, often directed against other communities, but sometimes involving claims against medium and large individual holders. See Contreras (1991, 203).

9. See López-Ayllón and Fix-Fierro (2000). See also Fix-Fierro (1995 and 1999).

to the extent that if they won at the trial court level, it was likely to be a pyrrhic victory.[10]

From what we have learned about the multiple barriers to court use, the argument that more courts and more judges will open the way to new clients appears of doubtful validity. Broader geographic distribution solved only one problem—reducing the distances traveled to get to a court in the first place. It did not take care of legal and court fees, lack of familiarity with the processes, linguistic barriers, distrust, costs of additional documents, speed money and bribes, or simple judicial prejudice. Moreover appeals courts still tended to be located at best in major urban centers, and anyone wishing to take their case to the supreme court, had to go all the way to the national capital. In some countries, for example, Bolivia and Peru, even major criminal trials were conducted in departmental capitals, so that those interested in or charged with these crimes could often not do their business close to home.[11] A similar problem has emerged with some of the new codes. For example in Paraguay, despite the addition of hundreds of justices of the peace to serve rural populations, the absence of prosecutors (required to do the investigation) in rural areas means that only misdemeanors can be handled there.

More recent efforts to take justice to the people have thus combined improved physical distribution of facilities with other services, attempting to attack the additional barriers to access. More of the same, even if more conveniently placed, is clearly not the way to resolve more fundamental problems of unequal access to judicial protections. Because many of these additional services have also been pursued on their own track, they are discussed in more detail below.

Legal Assistance

Legal assistance programs for both criminal and civil justice are usually the first and preferred answer offered by nonjudicial proponents of access-enhancing reforms. They are particularly important in Latin America because in many countries, one cannot be heard in courts except through an attorney. Criminal defendants, are an obvious exception, but absent formal representation, they are unlikely to be heard either. In fact, lack of legal representation keeps many pretrial detainees incarcerated needlessly, and often for lengthy, possibly illegal, periods. A lawyer's first service may be getting the detainee out of jail or speeding his trial date. Often, securing a defendant's release was tantamount to a not-guilty verdict,

10. Hence, the claim, made by one of the leaders of Peru's agrarian reform of the 1970s, that in the first 150 years of the republic, no Indian had ever won a case in the supreme court. Guillermo Figallao, as quoted in Cleaves and Scurrah (1980, 156). As Contreras (1991) notes, however, they did win cases at lower levels.

11. Bolivia's court system remains extremely centralized. There are relatively few trial courts located outside the departmental capitals and they only investigate, but they do not try cases of any significance. See Gamarra (1991, 92) and Chemonics (1996).

because the usual delays with the pretrial investigation, perhaps extended by a few well-targeted payments, could mean the case would never be adjudicated. These well-known facts, combined with the initial interest in improving criminal justice, thus meant that the first legal assistance programs focused on providing subsidized council for indigent defendants.[12]

Latin America's prior experience with public defense was not positive. The usual practice was the reliance on *defensores de oficio,* lawyers assigned to individual courts to handle criminal defense of those who could not afford a private attorney. Whether salaried state employees or paid by the case, the *defensores de oficio* were inevitably insufficient in number, often poorly motivated, and frequently corrupt. Their services were supplemented by pro bono work of bar associations, legal clinics attached to universities, and nongovernmental organizations (NGOs). This patchwork arrangement still did not meet the real demand, and it also was of very uneven quality.[13] Some of the most effective defense was done through NGO groups, but they frequently limited their clientele to political cases or victims of human rights abuses. This was partly for ideological reasons and partly as the only means they had of rationing their resources.

One conspicuous exception was the Public Defenders Office (PDO) established in Costa Rica in the 1970s.[14] Using a simple but effective nationwide organization, the office provided services of such high quality that even those who could afford private attorneys often preferred to use it. As a consequence, in the mid-1990s, the Costa Rican PDO was forced to amend its principles of equal access to all, even those who had sufficient resources for paid counsel, and introduce a system of payments on a sliding scale. The office has also attempted to provide counsel for civil cases, but resource limitations have kept this on a minor scale.

Not surprisingly, the Costa Rican PDO has become a regional model. Its members have provided technical assistance in Ecuador, Peru, Bolivia, El Salvador, the Dominican Republic, Colombia, and Guatemala to create similar programs. The most successful adopters (El Salvador, Bolivia, and the Dominican Republic) now offer reasonably adequate, state sponsored services to indigent criminal defendants.[15] None has attempted to replicate Costa Rica's initial practice of free service for all comers, and all have so far limited their attention to criminal cases. Even here, resources are usually insufficient, and there has been some effort to

12. For a review of some of USAID's early programs, see Hammergren (1998b, 15–34). The Ford Foundation has long supported NGO legal services in Latin America. See Fruhling (2000) for examples, though, as he notes, much of the emphasis has shifted to public interest law.

13. Chinchilla and Schodt (1993, 53) note that in the 1990s, Ecuador had only twenty-one defenders for the entire country and that other court-appointed counsel tended "to result in the delivery of poor or unfulfilled legal services."

14. See Rico et al. (1993, 112–17), for a brief description. See Hammergren (1998c, 15–34), for details on this and other experiences.

15. As noted below, progress in Bolivia appears to have succumbed to political intervention.

coordinate activities with other service providers—mainly university legal clinics and NGOs.

State-sponsored services face several obstacles. The old group of *de oficio* defenders has sometimes opposed their creation as a threat to its own source of livelihood. Incorporating its members into the new service is often not a realistic option, because of their customary abuses and inattention to their clients.[16] Resources are rarely sufficient to meet demand, and funding cuts are a constant threat. Providing free counsel for "criminals" is only slightly higher on the list of public priorities than improving prison conditions. If the services are independent of other agencies, they may have problems getting resources from congress. When they are dependent on the courts, public ministry or ministry of justice, they are usually not a first priority of the parent institution. Politicization of the services has sometimes occurred. When the Bolivian political parties recognized the potential for filling the 110 positions with patronage appointments, they fired the incumbents on the spot and replaced them with party loyalists.[17] For all these setbacks, the public defense offices once created have managed to survive and over time have on a whole improved their coverage and quality.

Criminal defendants were an obvious first priority for legal services. Expanding court use by the poor also requires additional assistance programs. Even if pro-se representation is allowed, and in many countries it is not, most courts are not set up to handle unrepresented clients. Thus, they are likely to be at a great disadvantage, if they even manage to get to court. In the noncriminal areas there is an enormous need for subsidized legal services for clients who cannot afford a private attorney. Governments rarely provide them. To the extent they exist, they must come from other sources—largely NGOs and legal clinics associated with universities. Quality varies, supply is always limited, and often the services depend on donor funding for their very existence.

Governments and courts that have tried to provide legal aid for poorer clients with civil complaints (some Mexican state courts, Costa Rica, El Salvador, for family cases) usually fall far short of meeting the potential demand. In a few countries (Argentina) the growing use of contingency fees—or, in labor cases, services supplied by unions—may begin to fill the gap. In Brazil, lawyers representing workers in labor courts commonly receive their fees only once, and if, they win the case. Because Brazil's labor courts tend to be worker friendly, the lawyers seem satisfied except for the delays caused by employer appeals. Even in combination,

---

16. This proved a problem in the Dominican Republic when USAID attempted to convince the supreme court to adopt the defenders system USAID had been supporting through an NGO. The existing *defensores de oficio,* known to be inefficient and corrupt, fought the change, unsuccessfully, despite being offered the chance to join the new state-financed organization. See Hammergren (1998b, 24). Guatemala's early efforts to establish a public defense service were first opposed by the universities. Their motive was apparently not financial, but a concern for the survival of their own legal clinics.

17. Interviews in La Paz, March 1999.

these various alternatives remain inadequate. The usual result is that clients with few resources either do not get to court or fall prey to the army of underemployed lawyers who will charge a small fee for filing a complaint, only to abandon them later when their funds run out.

Not all legal assistance means representation in court. A few countries (Peru, El Salvador, and Ecuador) have sponsored successful programs of free legal advice. In the former two, these are state financed. In the latter, the programs are funded largely through donor-subsidized NGOs. The Peruvian program began in the 1980s with donor assistance.[18] Its operational costs are now fully financed by the Ministry of Justice (which also handles public defense), though the ministry is seeking donor support for expansion. The program consists of legal assistance offices in poor neighborhoods, usually in large urban centers. The intent was never to provide representation in court, as the offices were for the most part staffed by law students with a single lawyer overseeing them. It was instead to help orient clients as to their legal rights, refer them to other legal services for actual representation, and give assistance in taking care of problems that did not require court action—for example, getting birth certificates and other documents required for access to other public services. The number of these offices remains small (currently about thirty), but they have been very popular. Their impact on client welfare has not been evaluated. Still, evidence from Peru and other countries indicates a substantial demand for these kinds of services. The poor themselves frequently cite their own ignorance of the law as a major obstacle to accessing its protections.

The Salvadoran example also benefited from donor support. It builds on an organization, the *Procuraduría General* (formerly *de los Pobres*, of the Poor) with a long history of providing legal and social services to citizens with limited resources.[19] The most important aspect of those services involves assistance to women seeking child support. The office gives them information on their rights, offers conciliation services with the husband or companion, and, if an extrajudicial agreement cannot be reached, provides legal assistance for an eventual court case. Demands on the office have increased considerably following the 1994 enactment of a new family code strengthening the legal responsibilities of the fathers of children born in or out of wedlock. Despite donor assistance in upgrading its service provision, the office remains severely underfunded. There has been no serious evaluation of the quality of its services, or how they might be further improved.

The Ecuadorian example encompasses a number of NGOs providing legal and social services to women. It depends largely on donor funding. Several donors and

18. See Hammergren (1998e, 88). USAID renewed its support to the *consultorios* in the post-Fujimori period, but, because the ministry had combined them with its conciliation program (not greatly favored by the donors), it had considered ending it (interviews, Lima, December 2002). A recently approved World Bank loan will finance the combined service modules.

19. See Mudge et al. (1996), for a discussion.

NGOs are involved, so this is less a coordinated program than a case of informal interactions inspiring a common menu of offerings. It is similar to efforts conducted in several Latin American countries and, like them, has benefited from donors' interest in gender-based approaches to broadening access. The Ecuadorian example is mentioned because the World Bank has documented its program there in a publicly available report.[20] Cases commonly handled include domestic violence, child support, and divorces. Donors have funded NGOs providing legal assistance to other groups as well, but the programs aimed at women tend to be most popular and thus receive more support.

Collective Litigation and Public-Interest Law

In light of the nearly insurmountable task of supplying individualized legal representation to the mass of potential clients, those interested in promoting broader access have begun to look to other solutions. Here the approaches begin to diverge depending on how reformers define the benefits they are pursuing. Most still seek to provide individualized services but try to overcome the inherent inefficiencies and resource limitations of getting new clients to court in the usual way. The one exception is the growing emphasis on collective litigation, which instead tries to secure rights for groups of citizens or prevent their systematic violation. Although this approach can still be counted as a strategy for expanding the private good element of court services, it pursues a more direct impact on the legal framework itself rather than looking to help citizens resolve their individual complaints and conflicts.[21] Presumably many of the complaints will be automatically resolved once the underlying legal principles are altered, thus reducing the necessity of seeking judicial remedies. This is especially true of legal actions intended to alter the content and delivery of public services provided by other government agencies (for example, demands that fees be lowered or eliminated, that certain activities be added, or that benefits be increased); of collective actions against public or private entities accused of violating legal rights (for example, complaints about unfair employment practices and environmental and consumer complaints); or of efforts to claim individualized or collective compensation for damages done to a group of individuals.

20. World Bank, Legal Vice Presidency (2003b). The report does try to transcend the usual body-count evaluation, focusing on the further benefits (winning legal cases, collecting on claims, school attendance rate of children) accruing to users of one of the clinics. Despite a framework emphasizing the law enforcement (and thus public good) impacts of the services, the benefits measured are still individualized.

21. It is here where the neat public-private goods division begins to break down. Like "test cases," such litigation has direct private beneficiaries, but its defenders often argue for the bigger impact on the rule of law itself. Here Shavell's (1997) emphasis on public and private motives, not goods, may be more useful.

The latter example most closely approximates the U.S. class action suit. This type of collective litigation, however, remains legally difficult, if not impossible, in many Latin American countries. Restrictions on standing, limitations on who can represent such complaints or additional requirements concerning how complainants can be joined to the action make true class actions suits a minority of collective litigation. In some cases (Brazil), governments have added legislation to prohibit class actions against certain issues of particular interest to them—for example, those having to do with pension and public-sector wage disputes where immediate satisfaction of the demands of the many individuals affected would literally bankrupt the country. For many of these complaints, class actions might be unnecessary if high court decisions on rights violations set binding precedent.[22] Because they usually do not, the result is an enormous number of similar cases, usually producing the same ruling, filling the court dockets. The obvious solutions, expanding the possibilities for class action or extending the impact of binding precedent, are resisted by governments because of the well-recognized fiscal implications.[23]

Other types of litigation with multiple beneficiaries seeking recognition of collective or diffuse rights have had more success.[24] Many countries have developed a variety of legal remedies for entering the claims. Brazil may be the most advanced, not only for the number of options available, but also because the Public Ministry has the representation of such interests as one of its basic functions.[25] The ministry's role allows it to sue for relief in the name of a group which is identified but not individualized. This usually means that the outcome or benefit is not individualized either. Brazil also allows duly organized private and not-for-profit organizations to represent collective and diffuse rights cases. Duly organized means the entity must have existed for at least a year and have furtherance of the specific interests as part of its legal mandate. This discourages the ad hoc creation of a group solely to pursue a new claim.

Collective and diffuse interest cases have been given more leeway than class actions as they do not produce individualized payments for damages. In Brazil,

22. This concept is discussed in greater detail in Chapter 5.

23. As reported in the *Gazeta Mercantil* (Rio de Janeiro), January 7, 2003, the new solicitor general (Advogado da União) asked the courts to delay judgments on suits initiated while his party was in opposition. Of most concern were cases dealing with the monetary correction of mortgage payments set during the Collor government and indemnization for Cardoso's intervention of the sugar and alcohol industry. The disputes' estimated value is 120 billion reais (roughly U.S. $40 billion in 2003). In late 2004, the executive's efforts to remove the *súmula vinculante* (binding constitutional interpretations) from its judicial reform package led to an admission of the financial threat it posed. Nonetheless, the measure passed.

24. Collective interests or rights are those pertaining to a group of citizens; diffuse rights are shared by all members of a society (the right to clean air, a healthful environment, and so forth).

25. See Bastos Arantes (2002) and Sadek and Batista Cavalcanti (2003).

where a fine is assessed this is paid into a common fund to be used to support future litigation. In most cases, the relief offered is either the termination of an injurious action or an order, difficult to enforce, that the quality of a service or product be altered. Where those covered by the judgment wish individual compensation or a repayment, they may still have to file a separate action. Judgments favorable to the complainants can pose an enormous threat to government or private activity, but the considerable opportunities for appealing decisions can also delay the impact.

One other limitation on the impact of collective litigation is that by its very nature it requires a concrete and usually, single defendant. Alleged abuses perpetrated by a multitude of public or private actors are not its natural targets. They might be were the additional obstacle of binding precedent not present. While it persists, findings against a practice indulged in by a large number of potential defendants will at most affect the actions of those singled out in the case. This limitation has not reduced the enthusiasm of proponents of this approach. It does narrow the impact on the day-to-day concerns of potential beneficiaries, many of which involve conflicts or complaints not lending themselves to this treatment. Collective litigation can make a difference in the lives of the poor. It is not the universal solution to all the problems posed by limited access.

Special Courts and Special Procedures

The two approaches discussed above (legal assistance and collective litigation) seek to augment access within the existing institutional framework. The next approaches take a different tack by attempting to alter the ways judicial and related services are provided. The first involves the creation of special courts organized to remove some common obstacles to access. It may in its own fashion be every bit as radical as public-interest law, in that it directly challenges many longstanding assumptions as to how courts will work—the need for legal representation, many notions about necessary due process rights, and even the role of the judge. The argument underlying this strategy is that the normal court processes and protections are simply inappropriate for use by many potential clients because of costs, complexity, delays, and the inherent advantages enjoyed by well-heeled parties with expensive counsel. The poor are particularly affected, but the emphasis is often on the size of the claim rather than the identity of the client. Even for those with adequate resources to pursue a major legal action in the ordinary proceedings, having to do so for a small debt or similar dispute may be a major disincentive to court use.

Nonetheless, the first efforts in this area (beginning in the 1970s or even earlier), targeted groups of clients and were intended to handle cases where marginalized populations were most affected. These include special agrarian courts (for example, Peru, Costa Rica, and, most recently, Mexico), labor courts (for example,

Peru, Argentina, Brazil, Mexico), and family courts.[26] Family courts were already present in many countries. The adoption of new family codes in the 1990s inspired their creation where they did not exist and altered their organization and procedures where they did.[27] Some special courts lie within the ordinary court system; others are tied to executive ministries. Aside from their topical specialization, these courts are distinguished by several other characteristics. They often use simplified, oral proceedings, include conciliation among their means of resolving conflicts, and may allow pro-se representation. As opposed to the usual emphasis on judicial neutrality, judges in these courts are frequently expected to give special treatment to parties presumed to be at a disadvantage (tenant farmers, workers, and women). For this and other reasons, the labor and agrarian courts in particular have come into disfavor and in some cases have been reabsorbed into the ordinary court system (Peru) or lost other elements of their special status (for example, Brazil's labor courts which lost their *classista* judges, nominated by employers' and employees' associations).[28] Mexico's recent creation of executive tribunals to hear land disputes is an exception to this trend. As reported by Guillermo Zepeda, the courts, created in 1992, have been relatively efficient in distributing titles and resolving title disputes, but they have hardly produced the broader benefits initially promised.[29]

Although sometimes very successful in representing the interests of the poor, this principle, explicit in their creation, can be successfully subverted by the usual defendants (employers, land owners, male spouses). Especially where judges were insufficiently aggressive in discouraging lengthy delays, appeals, or tactics to impede execution of judgments, the proposed protection of the favored client could be easily undermined. The reabsorption of these tribunals into the ordinary court systems has other explanations. On the one hand, the ordinary judiciary often campaigned for the transfer on the basis of the principle of jurisdictional unity. In less magnificent terms, this simply means that ordinary judges begrudge sharing their powers with other courts. On the other, the ideologies giving rise to these special systems have fallen in disrepute. Neoliberal economics has no place for conflict resolution that explicitly gives the advantage to the economic underdog. In the present era, the only special courts they usually endorse are those for entrepreneurs,

26. For a discussion of Peru's agrarian courts (created during the 1968–80 military government), see Cleaves and Scurrah (1980) and Hammergren (1998e, 72–75, 144–45).

27. El Salvador is an example, with passage of the code in 1994 and creation of the courts in 1995.

28. Under Brazil's Labor Party government, however, the labor courts are again gaining power. The 2004 constitutional amendment on judicial reform extended their jurisdiction and added judges to the highest appeals court in the labor system, the Tribunal Superior de Trabalho. The government also plans to add 300 labor judges, despite the fact that labor judges have the lowest caseload of all national courts.

29. Zepeda (2000). One of the goals was to broaden access to credit and thus create a class of productive small farmers. Unfortunately, clear title was hardly sufficient to do this. Also as land disputes may involve other issues, litigable in the ordinary courts, the separation of the two systems has some disadvantages.

not their workers.[30] Mexico's exceptional instatement of the agrarian courts is explained by its connection to the official termination of the land reform.

The pro-poor courts do frighten investors, and it is not always clear they advance the interests of poor clients. Jurists designing them sometimes imposed their own views of what the beneficiaries needed or wanted without bothering to consult with those they were attempting to help. For example, an aborted proposal to create an agrarian jurisdiction in El Salvador in the early 1990s drew heavily on legislation from Franco's Spain and Mussolini's Italy. Its paternalistic protection of the farm family had little to do with the Salvadoran reality, where land is scarce and keeping the agricultural workers in the rural areas not a reasonable goal. Many discussions about how spousal abuse should be treated in family (or criminal) courts also seem to work in an empirical vacuum, bereft of both statistical data and ample consultation with victims.[31]

Contemporary efforts to use special courts to broaden access are more likely to take another tack, focusing on creating small claims jurisdictions. They target the poor more specifically only as regards the geographic placement of the new services. Two especially successful and well-known efforts are Peru's justice of the peace courts and Brazil's small claims courts. Although the Peruvian example has a long history and the Brazilian courts are a recent innovation, they share many characteristics: a jurisdiction defined by the size of the claim (or in criminal cases, by the likely penalty), simplified, oral procedures, use of conciliation, limited potential for appeals, and pro-se representation. The Peruvian peace courts are of two types. The professional justices of the peace are lawyers and commonly work in urban areas. The far more numerous lay justices of the peace are located in rural districts where they often are citizens' first and only contact with the formal justice system.

It is the lay justices that have received most international attention. This may have saved them from elimination. Throughout the history of the institution, Peru's lay justices have never been paid and receive no compensation for their expenses. This situation reflects the ordinary courts' less than enthusiastic acceptance of their existence. Nevertheless, replacing more than 5,000 lay justices with trained lawyers, as had been suggested by some high court officials, would probably have guaranteed

30. In both Peru and Mexico, entrepreneurs and bankers are currently campaigning for their own special courts within the ordinary court system. Panamanian entrepreneurs were also making this argument in the mid-1990s, contending that removing their cases from ordinary civil courts would give the latter more time to attend the disputes of the poor. Donors wax hot and cold on the topic; at present a majority of their members appear to favor them. The bankers achieved partial victory in Peru in 2005 when seven commercial courts and on appellate court were created in Lima. It appears the model will be expanded, though the vast majority of cases are simply debt collection.

31. Jurists frequently debate the likely impacts of criminalization, arguing that it may enhance the risks of violence to the woman complainant and will also, if successfully pursued, cut off chances of support (as the abusing partner will be in jail). Of course, this is all argued in the air—no one has any evidence to support any of the views.

their disappearance in many of the remote areas where they operate. There is also reason to believe their services would have been less satisfactory, because the lay justices are encouraged to combine formal law and local custom in making their decisions. In the late 1970s, Germany's Naumann Foundation began a program to train the lay justices in the elements of the law and their own responsibilities in applying it. The program, which continued for ten years, was run for most of that time by a German judge who also published several books and articles on the experience.[32] Although many lower-level judges collaborated with the project, the Supreme Court seemed to merely tolerate its existence. Nonetheless, the German judge's publications drew additional international support served, establishing Peru's lay justices as an important experience in taking justice to the people and spreading their fame beyond the national borders. With the termination of the German program, a local NGO, IDL (the Institute for Legal Defense) has taken over the training efforts, receiving grants from several donors to support its work.

Until recently, Peru's lay justices were selected by the superior courts of each district, usually on the recommendation of local notables. In 1999, their popular election, mandated by the 1993 constitution, occurred for the first time. According to IDL, this has changed the composition of the group.[33] Whereas once they were older, more conservative community leaders, there are now younger justices, including both women and individuals who have migrated back to the community after living in larger cities. This is a less tractable and more activist population that may be less inclined to honor the preferences of the local establishment. Whether they will retain their popularity with local users remains to be seen. A further threat to the traditional system is the suggestion that the elections are run formally and that the justices are paid a "reasonable salary." In light of estimates of S/100 million (roughly U.S. $30 million) for one set of elections, the proposal may be a nonstarter. Although some compensation is doubtless due, making these fully salaried positions is likely to change the composition of the group dramatically, attracting lawyers and other professionals less attuned to community norms and values.

Brazil's more recent experience began in 1984 in two states, São Paulo and Rio Grande do Sul. It was modeled on the example of the U.S. small claims courts, and was intended as a means of extending court services to the poor.[34] The 1988 constitution recognized the services, and a 1995 law mandated the creation of these entities at both the state and federal level. The courts have since multiplied and have been so successful in drawing clients that they are facing their own problems of congestion. They also have attracted middle-class users, raising questions as to the identity of the primary beneficiaries. The courts in some states have been

32. Brandt (1987, 1990).
33. Interviews with IDL staff, April 2002.
34. In fact early supporters visited the U.S. to view small claims courts there. See Watanabe (1986).

studied by local researchers,[35] but there is still insufficient information on their operations to allow a complete evaluation of their impact or to test a number of hypothesized failings, including a tendency to bureaucratization, excessive delays, and continuing unavailability to the principal target groups. In theory, the courts operate on the basis of oral hearings, which should be held almost immediately after the claim is filed. Anecdotal evidence reports delays of months or up to a year in scheduling meetings with the parties.

During the last three years, Brazil's federal judiciary has introduced small claims courts to handle the hundreds of thousands of disputes over the recalculation of pension benefits, which arise from devaluations, the accompanying economic plans, and other legislative changes.[36] Many of these courts are highly automated and use template rulings and digital signatures to turn out thousands of decisions per judge per month. Judges estimate that as much as 75 percent of the cases involve no more than the application of an index, determined in a prior ruling from the Supremo Tribunal Federal (constitutional court).[37] While the judges accept that ruling as binding, the administrative agencies have not been willing to apply it on their own, thus forcing citizens to court, and to additional delays, to realize their claims. The example, although clearly expanding access, raises several questions as regards the substitution of judicial for administrative channels. The remedy, what economists might call a second-best solution, is better than the status quo ante, but far more costly and lengthier than making the administrators do their own work. These pension cases are commonly cited as examples of the Brazilian government's judicialization of conflicts to "control the cash flow." The automated courts, however, have proved unexpectedly efficient, so much so that in April 2004 the federal judiciary requested that the amount set aside to pay these claims be increased by 4.5 billion reais (roughly U.S. $ 1.6 billion).[38]

The small claims courts are supposed to encourage conciliation. Brazil's state judiciaries have introduced an additional element involving conciliation services supplied by lay practitioners, trained by the judiciary and provided court housing. Some courts provide mobile units for the conciliators. Here, too, there have been

35. See Bastos Arantes (1997), Batista (1999), Bermudes (1999), Rodycz (2001), Sadek (1995a, 2000, 2001a), and Brazil, Poder Judiciário (2004).

36. These courts handle other issues, but pension claims constitute the bulk of their work.

37. Interviews with the president of the Juizado Federal Prevedenciária, São Paulo, April 2004.

38. By mid-2004, the São Paulo court was making 20,000 rulings a month and estimated that once the problem of inputting the documents was resolved, it could expand this five-fold. The court uses four judges, seconded on a part-time basis from their own courtrooms (World Bank 2005c). Officials from the executive branch show a certain uneasiness about the trends, protesting that the judiciary is cheating by its mass treatment of individual claims or, in one complaint, that the courts cannot make awards in excess of the amount the government is required to set aside for payment of these cases. This is rather like an individual protesting that his credit card payments exceed the amount he has budgeted for them. Interviews with officials from the ministries of finance and of social security, Brasilia, November 2005. The Brazilian bar association (OAB) is also contesting the use of pro se representation in the federal small claims courts.

complaints—inadequate training and supervision, extension of conciliation to crimes (especially family violence) where it may be less appropriate, and an inability to enforce decisions.[39] Once again, much of the evidence remains anecdotal, and Brazilian researchers are only beginning to investigate the operations more systematically.

The suggestions that the approaches work less than perfectly do not mean failure. They imply the need for adjustments, possible reconsiderations of the kinds of cases that should be handled and, for judges and lay conciliators alike, more training and supervision. As in Peru, there is a tendency for the small claims model to benefit from a high level of romanticism on the part of its proponents, who consequently may resist evaluation and criticism. At least in Brazil, there are researchers attempting objective assessments. The danger in a country this large is that findings in one region will be extrapolated to others where they may be less valid. In Peru, the domination of the experiment, first by the Germans and now by IDL, has left the evaluations in the hands of the primary advocates. Although both groups have been willing the admit that some justices of the peace have been abusive, and that the system is far from perfect, their criticism has been tempered by their involvement in the project.

There is also the argument, which has been raised outside Latin America,[40] that the presence of such local courts may take the pressure off the higher-level judiciary to conduct its own reform. This does not yet appear to be the case in Peru or Brazil. Current obstacles to wider reform have other origins. It could be a concern if special courts for elites are created. Losing the business community as a reform advocate would be a real disadvantage in working improvements for others.

Mexico's frequent use of local courts, connected to municipalities and thus largely outside the formal court system, is another matter.[41] In contrast to Brazil and Peru, these local entities are largely ignored in reform discussions, and the services they provide are completely unstudied. In light of the requirement for legal representation in the parallel small claims or justice of the peace courts belonging to the ordinary judiciary, the poor face an enormous obstacle to access there. The presence of these local alternatives effectively discourages attention to this barrier—as those who cannot afford lawyers and cannot find free services "can always take their complaints to the local jurisdiction." Like Peru's justice of the peace courts, Mexico's local bodies (alternatively called justices of the peace, small claims, civic, or municipal courts[42]) have a longer tradition and have provided an

39. Interviews, Universidade Candido Mendes, Centro de Estudos de Segurança e Cidadania, Rio de Janeiro, November 2001.

40. Galanter (2003).

41. State courts sometimes participate in the selection of local judges, but any supervision of their activities appears to stop there. In the Federal District, they are elected.

42. This becomes confusing in that the state court systems often have judges with similar titles.

outlet for resolving small conflicts and dealing with minor infractions. In discussions with members of several state court districts, we could find no evidence of programs to assess or improve their performance or any indication of an interest in knowing what exactly they did. In this sense, the other local alternative, indigenous dispute-resolution systems based on customary law (*usos y costumbres*) may be better understood than these more modern variations.

The idea of breaking down the barriers to court use by introducing courts that operate under expedited proceedings is a potentially useful technique for enhancing access. Nevertheless, its theoretical advantages should not stand in the way of a closer examination of actual practices. There are indications that even in the most successful systems these could be improved. There are also questions as to the feasibility of filling all potential demand even through highly expedited proceedings. If, as Brazilian observers claim, their small claims courts are facing their own backlog problem, either their number will have to increase substantially or some other solution will be required. One suggestion as to the latter is supplied by the still more popular recourse to alternative dispute resolution (ADR).

ADR

When ADR was first introduced as a part of judicial reform programs in Latin America, its acceptance by judges and lawyers was marginal at best. A decade and a half later, it enjoys the status of a universal panacea.[43] Lawyers now understand that it can enlarge rather than threaten their business, and judges interpret it as a means of reducing their workload. The few judicial holdouts are rapidly disappearing. Although discussed here as a means of enhancing access, it merits mention that, aside from the poor, the other usual target user group is commercial firms. Because many firms, and especially those with international ties, were already accustomed to arbitration, the principle obstacle for wider business use had been the recognition of arbitration decisions in the ordinary courts. Availability of services was a secondary concern and was quickly resolved once legal recognition was achieved. Domestic entrepreneurs may be more wary of the venture. Once the legal obstacles are removed, they generally have been willing to try the experiment.

For other groups, the principal obstacles were the lack of services and of familiarity with the concept. Proponents of ADR often claim to be building on preexisting local traditions, as exercised under customary law or practices like that of the *amigable componador* (friendly facilitator). In fact, these were often less widespread than believed, had lost force as people left their traditional communities, or held their own shortcomings in the form of differential treatment of status groups (men

---

43. For a review of practices on a regional basis, see Álvarez and Highton (2000). As Dezalay and Garth (2002, 242–45) relate, the two Argentine authors have been active in spreading ADR in Argentina and around Latin America.

versus women, elders versus the younger, and so on). More important, under its modern format, ADR takes a variety of forms and locations, requires training and often certification for its practitioners, may add additional services, and consequently requires further financial support, either through user fees or government subsidies.

Just to give some idea of the variations on the single theme, the following are some of the options for those introducing ADR as a means of responding to demands and broadening access to services:

- ADR may be court annexed or stand-alone.
- It may be publicly provided or supplied by for-profit and not-for-profit private entities. In the later cases, there may be licensing requirements or government supervision of the services.
- Its practitioners may be restricted to lawyers or may be allowed to come from other professions. (So far no one has suggested lawyers be excluded, but there are those who believe their training makes them unsuitable for the job.)
- It may be compulsory or optional as a prelude to taking a case to the formal courts.
- It may be subsidized or done on a fee basis.
- It may take one of many forms—most commonly conciliation, mediation, or arbitration—depending on the relationship among the parties.
- It may be limited to certain types of conflicts or introduced nearly across the board, including in criminal cases.
- It may focus only on the legal or factual dispute, or be complemented by other social, psychological, and counseling services.
- Any agreement reached may have to be executed spontaneously or may be subject to judicial execution.

As a preliminary note, the term covers a variety of procedures among which the three most common categories are arbitration, mediation, and conciliation. Although all suppose willing participation of the disputing parties (what this means in the case of compulsory mediation is not clear), and the second two require their agreement on any decision reached, they differ as to the role of the mediator, conciliator, or arbiter. Arbitration is the most directive proceeding as the arbiter imposes the solution. The parties' agreement to use arbitration, which often comes prior to the dispute, incorporates willingness to be bound by the arbiter's decision. The difference from a judicial proceeding is the waiving of some formalities and, unless stipulated that this is "arbitration by law," the ability to use additional criteria in reaching a judgment. One concern about arbitration, now being raised in the United States, is that parties may not realize they are limiting themselves to this form of dispute resolution when they sign a contract. This is especially true of consumer debt, credit card applications, or services provided by public utilities. Even if users realize what they are signing, they may be in no position to reject the arbitration clause.[44]

The distinction between mediation and conciliation, the less directive forms of ADR, is fairly clear, except for inconsistencies as to which term gets which definition. What some countries call "conciliation" may be what others call "mediation," and vice versa. In one form, most usually called "conciliation," the conciliator, having discussed the issue in joint meetings with the parties, suggests a resolution to which both are free to agree or disagree. In the other form, most often called "mediation," the mediator may meet with the parties individually, exploring the reasons for the dispute and helping the two sides develop their own solution. Here, too, the decision, though reached by the parties, must be accepted by both sides. Mediation or conciliation (and arbitration for that matter) may exist outside the legal framework in which case compliance with the decision depends on the willingness of the parties to honor it. One advantage of an overarching law is that it can give legal status to the agreement, which is often subsequently registered in court. Another possible advantage is that the services may be supervised by the state, which can also requiring their licensing. This of course can lead to other abuses.

Often a single country has a variety of different services. Only some of them may produce judicially recognized decisions. Less formal arrangements, often backed by community groups or NGOs, may attempt to resolve minor, probably legally irrelevant conflicts that nonetheless impede maintenance of social peace.[45] In fact, there is a whole school of ADR advocates whose primary interest appears to be introducing a new means of conflict resolution and whose attachment to judicial reform programs is more a matter of convenience. These promoters often stress ADR training in schools, to get at the population early, and a variety of additional services to help the parties overcome the various factors provoking a dispute. For example, in a divorce case, the parties may receive social and psychological counseling, the woman may get help in entering the labor market, family and friends may be involved, and so on.[46]

Obviously, much of this broader plan remains on the drawing board. A country that cannot afford free legal assistance for poor plaintiffs is not going to provide self-esteem classes and job training. Nevertheless, as long as this remains in the planning stage, and no one mentions budgets or where they will come from, the

44. For a discussion in the U.S. context, see Williams (2002).

45. Often called "community justice" in the United States, this is discussed in Merry (1993).

46. This approach is promoted by a group of Mexican ADR experts (Instituto de Mediación de México), associated with the University of Sonora. They have had an enormous impact in convincing the courts of the value of the practice, though the issue of costs continues to be ignored. As noted in a joint statement signed during the "First National Congress on Mediation," "It is the legitimate aspiration of all Mexicans to live together peacefully in an environment where conflicts are resolved through dialogue, tolerance, and collaboration" (Mexico, Primer Congreso 2001).

ADR movement has been able to spin out some fairly ambitious dreams going far beyond reducing court congestion or diverting cases from the judiciary. In their most visionary form, they would make the judiciary nearly irrelevant, because their goal is to reduce social conflict to a minimum. True ADR enthusiasts believe any dispute can and should be mediated; less fervent supporters usually draw the line where issues transcending the parties' interests are involved. We will return to this point later.

On the other end of the continuum are the ADR programs that have actually been put in place. Whereas some courts have attempted to provide such services, they usually do not have the funds to do so on a large scale. The Quito (Ecuador) court district for example, which receives about 22,000 civil filings a year, has three mediators working in the main court building. As of mid-2002, they were not even full time, more because of insufficient real demand than for lack of financing. Should they be successful in drawing more clients, it seems unlikely that the courts will be able to fund many more mediators. Several Mexican state and Argentine provincial courts have added services that also remain underutilized at present. The judges' enthusiasm for the approach, however, seems to include an expectation that more funds, from some other source, will be forthcoming to finance it.[47]

In other countries with formally recognized pretrial mediation or conciliation, its use is often compulsory (Ecuador's and Mexico's are not), and relies on a mix of executive financed and independent services. These programs often coexist with judicially administered conciliation or mediation that may be part of certain ordinary proceedings (for example, labor or family law). Two examples are Argentina and Peru. Both countries recognize conciliation as a judicial tool in labor and some family proceedings. Both have also adopted compulsory pretrial mediation and conciliation, respectively, for other civil cases in a few court districts, in the expectation of expanding it nationwide. In Argentina, publicly financed services, provided through the Ministry of Justice, are free to users. Clients may also pay for private mediation. In Peru, all services are privately provided, raising an enormous initial complaint that they thus pose another barrier to poor users. As of late 2003, the law only applied to Lima and two provincial cities. As the minister of justice who introduced the program admitted,[48] it would be hard to reverse the proposal for further expansion because of the 5,000 lawyers who had invested their own funds in certification programs "in the hopes of so resolving their own employment problem."

Peru's program has not been in effect long enough to evaluate. Argentina's has been evaluated and claims success in resolving a third of its cases.[49] Of the remainder, half "disappear" and the rest go on to the courts. The statistics are impressive

---

47. As USAID has paid for American Bar Association assistance to the Mexican effort, and the World Bank is including it in a proposed project, the expectations are likely to be met over the short run.

48. Interview, April 2002.

49. See Garavano et al. (2000, vol. 2, appendices).

but leave a further question of whether the mediation caseload is additional to what the courts would have received (thus expanding access) or duplicative (thus reducing court congestion). Conceivably, the answer is some of both. That also remains to be determined.

This question is not unique to Argentina and is one of several deserving further exploration. ADR may be an effective way of expanding access, reducing court congestion, or both, but there has been virtually no work in Latin America testing those propositions. It is likely that the answer varies according to what is adopted. Those kinds of fine distinctions seem not to be contemplated by its proponents. Costs are another ignored factor. ADR is not free, and it is not clear that it is more cost-effective than the judicial alternative.[50] Who pays makes a difference concerning access, and overall costs and cost-effectiveness must be considered as part of the decongestion argument. Effectiveness will have to be measured not only in the speed of decisions, but also client satisfaction, compliance rates, and further burdens on judicial enforcement mechanisms. ADR proponents claim their decisions are more responsive to user needs and thus more likely to be executed. This should hardly be taken as another axiomatic principle. "Good" decisions that are not carried out spontaneously will require judicial enforcement. This need not detract from their value. Many judicial decisions require coercive enforcement as well.[51]

Because ADR is not one single phenomenon but rather a vast series of possible arrangements, a negative assessment of one experience does not discredit the lot. It may be more appropriate for certain kinds of clients or certain kinds of issues. It has often been suggested that ADR is most appropriate for disputes between equals, where preservation of relationships is key or technical issues are more important than legal ones. These are hypotheses meriting empirical testing. They are often not accepted by those who believe ADR is the best means of resolving any dispute.[52]

Something more should be said about this last argument, because it also affects how systems will be designed and applied. Whatever else it does, ADR tends to limit the dispute and its resolution to the immediate parties and to those closest to them. It tends to be private, its results are usually not publicized, and it is up to the immediate participants to decide on the amount and allocation of penalties, damages, and other retribution. Whereas more moderate advocates argue about its occurring in the shadow of the law,[53] those who see it as a social healing mechanism

---

50. See Hensler (1994), for a review of these issues in the United States.

51. Enforcement also appears to be an issue in Brazil's small claims courts, though one no observer has yet targeted. Readings of transcripts of proceedings reproduced in Sadek, ed. (2001a) suggest that nonpayment of judgments is a real problem.

52. Having been involved in a public debate (Puebla, Mexico, May 2002) with a Mexican ADR guru who claimed everything, even homicide, can be mediated, I can attest to this fact. In the abstract he is right, but the operational verb is "should" not "can."

53. This term comes from the United States and refers to decisions being taken within the legal framework, though including other considerations.

often do not insist on that element. Their goal is to defuse, resolve, and discourage conflict by helping the parties understand their differences and reach compromise positions. The judicial model is quite different—conflict resolution is in some sense a means to its end, and that end is the enforcement of a normative framework. That framework may discourage future conflict, but only because it sends a clear message as to how deviations from its content, whether civil or criminal, will be treated by the courts.

In the simplest terms, the ADR and the judicial model, taken to their logical extremes, offer two methods of reducing social conflict, the first by helping individual disputants resolve their differences and teaching them to seek compromises, the second, by using decisions on their disputes to enforce social norms. There is probably room in any single society for both mechanisms. Not all conflicts are equally central to the legal framework, and when they are not private resolution may be appropriate. Where transcendental social norms are involved, private resolution may not be adequate.

There are some conflicts too important to society to let the parties decide. Many of these are on the criminal side. For example, mediating or reconciling the "dispute" between the family of a murder victim and the murderer is entirely possible. Many traditional societies do this through what is called "blood money." Accepting this arrangement in a modern or less egalitarian society would mean a very wealthy individual could virtually carry out the murders he wished, whereas a poor one might have problems negotiating minor property damage. Several Latin American countries introduced reconciliation with the victim as one way of resolving criminal disputes under their new codes. They have since had to limit the types of cases and number of times it could be done.[54] Aside from the concerns about undermining criminal laws, this was a reaction to the discovery that friends of the alleged perpetrator would sometimes visit the victim to discuss the merits of mediation and the danger of not accepting it.

The concerns are not limited to criminal law. There are also commercial, family, labor, and other civil norms that societies as a whole have an interest in having enforced. Here, even more than in criminal law, interparty negotiations are quite feasible. They may be less desirable from the standpoint of upholding standards. Modern societies' greater reliance on law, as opposed to custom or social pressures, to shape behavior has thus motivated reexamination of such basic principles as the right of the parties to a civil dispute to define the legal issues covered. The notion that the parties decide whether to initiate a civil action remains, but in both civil and common-law countries their further control over its development is increasingly

54. El Salvador's Juvenile Code (Código de Menores) has been amended since its (1994) enactment to restrict mediation to infractions and minor felonies (not rape, murder or aggravated assault) and to limit the times a single individual may use mediation as a means to settling his debt with justice (and his victims).

questioned.[55] This goes far beyond the topic discussed here. It does introduce a final consideration on ADR, its relationship to access to justice, and the further purpose in advancing the latter.

ADR has been explored in the section on access because it is most often proposed as a means to enhance it. Its additional purpose (mentioned in the chapter on efficiency) of relieving court congestion is also seen as access enhancing—as in the argument that, as courts become relieved of many kinds of cases, they will make room for new clients and new kinds of conflicts. Under either guise, ADR is offered as a complement to court services, most suitable for monetarily less significant disputes or those where the legal issues are less central and a win-lose solution less appropriate because it would put a longer-term relationship at risk. Presumably its advantages lie in reduced complexity (and thus a more rapid response), lower costs (particularly important in conflicts over small amounts), and its ability to encourage compromises revolving around factors the law cannot consider. Questions have been raised about the first two assumptions in particular. Even studies that have not validated them admit "user satisfaction" remains critical in arguing for ADR's use.[56] The enormous variety in the forms ADR may take make it difficult to generalize, which suggests that any adoption should be considered as an experiment and tested against its results on the ground. Access enhancement and court decongestion are two valuable objectives. Still, it is premature to conclude that ADR in any of its forms does or does not advance them or that it is the best way of doing so.

More ambitious backers promote ADR not as an alternative to court services but as a preferable substitute. They are seemingly less interested in judicial reform than in creating new patterns of social interaction. Here they have much in common with proponents of public-interest litigation. Both groups have attached themselves to the judicial reform movement opportunistically. Their goal is not to reform the judiciary, but to use it or the reform movement to reform society. Neither transcendental goal seems to have been recognized by the other access reformers, though, in the end, its compatibility with their own objectives is highly suspect. Faith in ADR's particular silver bullet appears to have declined in the U.S and Western Europe. As is common for many reform exports, it is still on the rise in Latin America.[57]

---

55. For a discussion of civil and common law developments and some waiving of the dispositive principle see Jolowitz (2000, 185–204, and passim).

56. See Hensler (1994).

57. Much the same can be said of the abolitionist movement in criminal justice—the belief that crime is a social construct and could be treated by discussions between victims and their assailants. The Netherlands, once at the forefront of the movement (and one of the few European countries to adopt legislation based on it) seems to have taken a turn toward a law and order philosophy. See chapters in Fennell et al. (1995). Abolitionism never flourished in Latin America, but it is an important contributor to the philosophy behind the new criminal procedures codes.

Customary Law

This might be considered as a subset of ADR. It is treated separately because it usually has different backers and because the justifications and presumed benefits for the two programs are different. Customary law is a way of increasing access to justice, but to one's own justice and cultural identity, not that of "the nation." Although customary conflict resolution often involves consensus building or some sort of conciliation, this is only part of the package.[58] Both the procedural rules and the distinctive values applied represent far more than a means of settling disputes. They are also vital to the community's preservation as a social unit and to the individual member's definition of self. Like language, dress, social practices, and kinship roles, they are part of a movement for cultural equality within culturally plural nations.[59]

Many Latin American countries have large indigenous populations, and many of their members still rely on traditional dispute-resolution mechanisms rather than the formal justice system. This is partly a matter of preference and partly a reaction to their difficulties to getting to the ordinary courts and their poor reception and results once they do arrive. The response on the part of the nonindigenous population has typically gone through three stages: nonrecognition of the situation, a call for incorporation of the affected groups into the formal system, and, most recently, efforts to recognize the traditional mechanisms, "so long as they do not violate constitutional rights and principles."[60] As far as can be determined, and that is not very far, the indigenous populations do not have a single, unambiguous response to this most recent formulation.

The situation is further complicated by several historical developments. In some cases, "traditional" community law has been much eroded, and efforts to redefine and reinstate it threaten additional conflicts within the affected communities.[61] Moreover, much traditional law depends on social pressures for enforcement; where communities have been opened to outside influence, this may no longer be effective. This effect is aggravated by the fact that many community members, because of their contact with the outside world, no longer accept traditional values, especially as they relate to deference to elders, prohibitions on certain modern practices, or compulsory participation in customary rites and rituals.[62] Finally, the notion

58. See Nader (1990) and García S. (2002), for two discussions of the traditional dispute-resolution mechanisms.

59. See Stavenhagen (2002), Sieder (2002), and Yrigoyen (2002).

60. For discussions of the third approach and its incomplete implementation, see Van Cott (2002), Sieder (2002), and Yrigoyen (2002).

61. During the civil wars in Guatemala, the army had a conscious policy of undermining the authority of community notables. Whatever success they had in that endeavor will obviously affect the ability of these same notables to enforce their law.

62. Interviews in Guatemala with Minugua (UN Observation Mission) officials, July 1995. They noted that this was a particular problem with young men who had been conscripted into the army. On returning to their villages, they were no longer willing to accept the wisdom of their elders.

of communal law often confronts individual with group rights. This poses problems for community members and for formal courts which might be called on to resolve their internal conflicts.[63]

During the past two decades, several Latin American constitutions have added articles recognizing the right of indigenous communities to impose their traditional rules and conflict resolution practices on community members.[64] In the abstract, this has been widely applauded. As suggested above, its concrete application has not been easy and, in many cases, has not advanced far.

This is an access-enhancement mechanism in the sense that it extends state-recognized justice to groups normally outside the physical reach of ordinary courts. For community members who reject communal values or who are not affected by normal sanctions (shunning or denial of the right to participate in certain common practices), however, it does not appear satisfactory as either a means of resolving their problems or of meeting the needs of those they affect. Even before the move to formal recognition, it was beginning to be realized that many members of traditional communities live with one foot in each world and that they have often indulged in their own version of forum shopping—attempting to direct conflicts to traditional or formal courts depending on where they believe the outcomes will most favor their positions.[65] This phenomenon raises other questions concerning individuals' rights to choose the legal system under which they will be judged. Recognizing these rights would work further damage to the strength of communal values. Refusing them would conflict with the individual freedoms presumably prized by the larger society.

An intelligent discussion of these issues would be greatly aided by more knowledge about the indigenous values and conflict resolution arrangements as currently practiced in the different countries of the region. It would also help to know more about the beliefs and preferences of members of the different communities. The existing information, most of it collected by legal anthropologists, is minimal. More recent efforts to expand it, many of them donor funded, are of very uneven quality. Although the recognition of indigenous law is part of a broader demand for cultural equality, even the extent of support among the presumed beneficiaries remains unknown. Because this is a political movement, its leaders are usually not very welcoming of objective studies of the validity of their claims. As the experience with elections of Peru's justices of the peace suggests, these are not static cultures, and their traditional leaders may no longer represent majority views. Efforts to increase

---

63. This is a particular problem when customary practice is recognized as an alternative source of law. Presumably those affected by it have a right to appeal, but that right may run counter to custom, especially if it involves the intervention of ordinary courts.

64. These include Guatemala, Colombia, Nicaragua, Mexico, Paraguay, Bolivia, Peru, and Ecuador. See Van Cott (2002) and Stavenhagen (2002).

65. See Sierra (1995).

the community's ability to make it own policies, including those involving its normative framework, can, ironically enough, increase internal conflict and hasten internal change. At that point, speaking in terms of customary law may no longer be accurate. We may instead have to talk of allowing room for local preferences. How that jibes with efforts to enforce stable normative frameworks and equal protection of rights remains to be seen.

Other Services

There are a number of other devices that have been used to enhance individual access. Most work on eliminating specific barriers, aside from those of costs or legal representation. They include the introduction of interpreters or the conduct of court services in native dialects, for countries where the poor often face linguistic barriers; public information and education programs to make nontraditional clients aware of their rights and the means to access them; training of paralegals to do outreach among poor populations; courses to sensitize judges and mediators in the needs of disadvantaged clients; special facilities and access for the handicapped; and provision of information kiosks and officers in court building.

Among the programs receiving most attention are efforts to provide "one-stop" shopping or *casas de justicia* (houses of justice) in poor neighborhoods.[66] Such services are useful for any client, and in fact some have been placed in wealthier neighborhoods. The general argument, nonetheless, is that the poor are especially frustrated by the need to visit a series of offices before finally discovering the one where they should initiate their legal action. Where all the principal legal actors (judge, police, prosecutor, public defender, medical specialists, and social workers) are housed under one roof and where there is a single intake mechanism, this seemingly endless search for the right starting point can be entirely eliminated. Colombia, Peru, and Brazil have taken a lead in this innovation. Brazil's experiments usually involve a wide range of government services, as opposed to the more justice-focused programs in the other two countries. As usual, most of these ventures remain unevaluated. One common complaint is that the facilities continue to work without their full staffing.

When, as in Peru's IDB financed program of "justice modules,"[67] the initial

66. Although their introduction was proposed in Peru in 1986, the country that has gone farthest with them (with considerable USAID assistance) is Colombia. See USAID, Center for Democracy and Governance (2002, 49–50).

67. Inter-American Development Bank (1997) describes the initial project. The idea was to construct eighty all-purpose structures in rural areas so that citizens would find all services in one place and could be directed to the most appropriate one. In addition to a judge, each module was to have a prosecutor, public defender, police officer, and a social or medial worker. Because of problems with government compliance in supplying the necessary staff, and some questions about the contracts for infrastructure, the original scheme was cut back to about half the proposed modules.

agreement is with one agency (in this case the courts), others presumably included may lack funds to provide personnel. In addition, physical infrastructure may not take their needs into account. Peruvian members of the Public Ministry, Public Defense, and police note that the justice modules give them inadequate office space, and have cited that as another reason for a less than full participation. Another problem with these arrangements is that interagency coordination is apparently voluntary. There is no single entity responsible for ensuring all the parts work together or finding solutions when they do not. Because the new structures presume a more user-friendly service from all participants, there are further questions of whether the individual parent agencies are taking steps to ensure the necessary changes in business as usual are made. In short, the one-stop services, like many other innovative mechanisms, are conceptually interesting, but their promise of increasing and improving access depends on far more than their physical creation.

RESULTS AND IMPACTS

The increasing attention to access with its primary goal of expanding court use by nontraditional clients has successfully redirected a part of local and donor resources into creating a wide variety of new services and drawing clients to them. It has also produced efforts to reorient existing services to increase their suitability to the needs of nontraditional users. Virtually every country in the region, every large donor program, and many smaller contributors can point to recent innovations in both areas. ADR activities have probably grown most rapidly. Legal assistance, especially for criminal cases, and public information campaigns are also notable for their frequent appearance. Use levels vary, but, for the most part, the services appear to be working to capacity, and some already face their own congestion problems.

Courts and donors have begun to collect statistics on clients served and in some cases, as in Argentina, to attempt to track outcomes, absolutely and in terms of impact on ordinary court use. Efforts to draw in target groups through the use of advertising campaigns are also notable. User surveys taken in conjunction with individual programs often show positive client reactions and a demand for the expansion of the services offered.[68] Over time, public opinion polls have frequently shown that services targeted to poor groups are among the most trusted or popular of the sector's outputs. This appears to be true of Peru's lay justices, Brazil's small claims courts, Peru's legal service clinics, and various public and private legal assistance programs.

---

68. See World Bank, Legal Vice Presidency (2003b).

The visible results still leave any number of unanswered questions. A first has to do with the simple numerical significance of these programs. By now most participants realize they must provide some quantitative gauge of service levels, but many stop with the number of clients attended, with no further indication of what was done for them or with what eventual outcome. Even with a further breakdown, by consultations, representation in court, cases won, and so forth, it is difficult to get a handle on the real service levels. In the end, the numbers pale before the size of the imputed target population. Although statistics are usually provided without any point of reference, like court caseloads, they often seem low if compared with whatever international standards are available. As of mid-2004, Colombia's public defenders were handling an estimated fifty cases per year; in mid-2002, Ecuador's court annexed conciliation services in Quito were seeing a few dozen clients per month. Comparisons are difficult because statistics are often given at the program level, which makes it impossible to track level of effort per service provider (namely, how many clients were seen by each staff lawyer, or by each mediator, as opposed to those treated by the unit). In general, two conclusions can be hazarded. First, efficiency levels could often be improved, though with part-time or volunteer staff this may be difficult. Second, no matter how efficient the individual unit, expanding current partial coverage to the entire national population would require a major financial investment.

With respect to the first point, although many service providers complain of being overstretched, part of this results from poor management and a related lack of policies to optimize resource use. Where clients are accepted on a first-come-first-served basis, staff does its own selection individually or cases are not divided into tracks by urgency, level of effort, or types of treatment, work quickly expands to fill the time available. Many organizations are not prepared for more sophisticated planning and furthermore, staffed partly with volunteers and imbued with a sense of revolutionary purpose, resist the very idea of rationing or rationalizing their offerings. The courts operate in a similar fashion, accounting for their own sense of being overwhelmed. Nevertheless, they have rarely shared the emphasis on attracting new demand and have benefited from the many artificial barriers preventing its creation.

Improved efficiency and a more hard-nosed approach to selecting and dealing with clients could expand the coverage of the programs already in place. This would doubtless displease many members and lose some who are currently willing to work for free or at reduced salary levels because of the psychological benefits of participating in a nonbureaucratic, ideologically driven agency. Even then, the increased coverage will still be insufficient, thus leading to the second point. Here, one need only look at the World Bank's work with women's NGOs in Ecuador. The program was supported by small grants (forthcoming from a loan to the Ecuadorian government) totaling about $400,000 over the five-year period. It served about

15,000 women.[69] At first glance, extending the program to 300,000 women (a modest number, considering the level of poverty in this country of 10 million inhabitants) does not seem unduly costly—$8 million, or $1.6 million per year, less than 4 percent of Ecuador's judicial budget of $40.25 million. The program, however, worked with NGOs that were already in operation and in the cities where they had offices. Expansion would imply creating additional offices and additional NGOs and thus a substantial up-front investment. It also would require more supervision and training, as new organizations might not function as well. There is the further question of where one would get the staff and how much the additions would cost. Expansion hardly seems impossible. It might well be more costly than the initial venture. (Bank figures also do not take into account the funds these same organizations were already receiving from other donors.)

Such simple extrapolations deserve additional caveats. As has happened with Brazil's small claims courts, the quality of services tends to drop with program growth.[70] In Brazil, this is partly because service provision has not kept up with demand, but the recruitment of judges who are less dedicated to the principles of the experiment also receives blame. As programs grow, they become bureaucratized, so supervising staff and keeping them motivated become more difficult. Moreover, increasing service availability at one point in the system requires increasing the supply elsewhere. More legal services mean more court cases, and eventually more courts and judges, as well as police, prosecutors, and defenders. More trials mean a greater demand for appeals, and so on.

This sounds like an argument for increasing the use of ADR in its court decongestion role; however, an effective pretrial program can also channel more cases to court—the parties, having begun the process but not reached an agreement, may decide to go the additional step. Perhaps the third of the caseload that Argentina's services send on to the courts is additional to normal filings, and, even if not, cases settled out of court still require judicial recognition and may need judicial enforcement. ADR advocates usually promise greater chances of spontaneous execution because the parties agree to the solution. This is another untested hypothesis. It also raises another issue. Most documentation of service levels does not include a follow-up, to see whether judicial or extrajudicial agreements are actually enforced.[71] Given what we know about enforcement problems throughout Latin American, this seems an egregious oversight. Even as an individualized service, access to justice must go beyond access to courts to include satisfactory execution

69. See World Bank, Legal Vice Presidency (2003b). The 15,000 number is also all consultations. The number of women assisted in pursuing child support cases, the crux of the experiment, was not indicated, nor is it clear whether each consultation was for a different client.

70. Interviews, Brazil, with Maria Teresa Sadek and Kazuo Watanabe of CEBEPEJ.

71. The World Bank, Legal Vice Presidency study (2003b), is an exception. It did find a higher rate of enforcement for cases in which women were represented by the NGOs. Still, child support, if not forever, is often for at least a decade, and we do not know how future payments hold up.

of judgments. Numbers of judgments or negotiated settlements are only part of the story. This in turn raises the issue of the downstream impacts in improving the lives of the beneficiaries, one of the major justifications behind the access movement. Before turning to it, another mundane funding issue should be raised.

Most of the innovative programs remain small, and many have relied on donor or other special funding. The obvious concern is sustainability, and it extends to programs relying solely on government funding. Where courts and other governmental agencies have provided monies, the programs often benefited from temporary gaps between increased funding for justice and the judiciary's ability to use it. As budgets have stopped growing, or as funders have found other uses, these special services become less attractive. Donors are a temporary stopgap by definition. Their own priorities and budgets change, and they never adopt a program with the idea of funding it forever. When their assistance eventually ends, NGOs or governmental programs they support have to find other ways to carry on. Donors and the recipients of their largesse are well aware of this, but, so far, the problem of long-term sustainability remains unresolved. The fact that the hundred flowers will not bloom forever could provide an opportunity for culling the most promising ones, but even for them financial sustainability is a major challenge.

Culling ought to mean looking at impacts, costs and benefits, and comparative advantages. In all these areas, there are a host of additional questions. As noted, efforts to document results have usually begun and ended with a body count—number of clients served. Clients are usually not distinguished by socioeconomic status, except insofar as can be inferred from their geographic origins or the nature of their complaints. Moreover, the body counts are almost never compared with the potential clientele to give a picture of how much demand remains unattended. This is true even of such areas as representation of pretrial detainees, where the calculation of potential demand is relatively easy. Additional information that might facilitate assessment of the quality of the service is usually not provided and follow-up (whether judgments or agreements are enforced) to measure impact is never done. This is fairly standard procedure for the introductory phase of such services in developed countries, but there providers are now being required to develop more sophisticated impact indicators, not always, it bears mentioning, with great success.[72] Impact assessment is expensive and requires methodologies beyond the financial and intellectual abilities of many service providers. Nonetheless, without it, it will be extremely difficult to assess individual programs and to compare their results.

Assessment will also be difficult given the further benefits claimed, differing targets, and varying services offered, as well as the different mix of public, private,

---

72. The industrialized common law nations—the U.S, Australia, Great Britain, and Canada—have taken the lead here, but they have had problems getting beyond the traditional body count.

and external financing. It is difficult enough to rate and compare alternatives on the basis of a simple body count—how many clients they attend—compared to overall costs, in light of the diverse ways of accounting for both sides of the equation and the inevitable variations in quality. How does one weigh ten consultations against a full-blown representation in court? Does it make a difference if the former are unwed mothers looking for information on social services and the latter is an accused, but indigent, rapist? How does one compare the costs and benefits of a fully state-financed program with one drawing on volunteers, both at present levels of performance and in terms of potential replicability? If the consultation includes psychiatric counseling or information on job opportunities, should it count more (how much?) than one featuring better legal information? And should not legal information also have a follow-up to ensure it has been useful? Are the lower overheads of offices relying on volunteers an advantage? Are they sufficiently monitoring the volunteers' work? Should state-supervised and -certified services be given extra points? Is the supervision worth the added costs?

To the extent the aim is to reach new clients or divert business from courts, it is necessary to determine who is using the services, for what purposes, and with what final effect. A compulsory pretrial program, which becomes an additional barrier to court use, as many have predicted for Peru's user-financed conciliation, may indeed reduce court workload but reduce access as well. A program that becomes a sort of revolving door to the courts, either because it produces few agreements or agreements that are not honored, imposes public or private costs without changing either access or court use. Such programs, like subsidized legal services, have costs beyond those they incur directly—in increasing court workload and that of other, state-financed institutions.

Many of the additional questions address externalities that individual programs cannot be expected to assess; however, if the programs' existence is justified in terms of reducing levels of societal conflict, improving the lot of groups of citizens (women, indigenous populations, parties to collective litigation), or decreasing courts' work, someone will have to work out the figures. This is where the atheoretical, nonstrategic nature of the access programs causes further headaches. To the extent they are joined only by their emphasis on expanding services, they lack a common view regarding their further benefits.

Except for those programs that justify increased access only as a fundamental right, most do argue for the improvement they will work on their clients' lives. This is true of those expanding access to ordinary court services and those creating alternatives. Because they usually, but not always, attract clients by subsidizing use, this raises questions about other kinds of alternatives, and it is one where ADR may come up short. Where subsidies are offered, use is likely to increase unless the service is virtually ineffectual. (An example is the host of recorded information and complaints services provided by the U.S. government as well as many private companies—they are so nonuser friendly that I suspect they leave the impression that no one needs information or has any complaints). If clients are offered other means of resolving their problems or other uses of the subsidy, they might make different choices. Ecuador's World Bank–financed women's legal aid program may indeed have increased the level of school attendance among the children of beneficiaries. Bus fare or a school lunch program might have done so as well and possibly at a lower cost per child.

With regard to all access-enhancement programs, one should thus ask whether their normal clients prefer that public funds be spent here as opposed to on other services—for instance, education, health, or public security. Because the question is never posed, clients' use of the subsidized legal services may not reflect their real preferences. From an individual and societal standpoint, the problems handled through these subsidized programs might be better resolved in other manners. If we take the case of women seeking child support, a theme common to many of them, there are clearly many alternative to Ecuador's NGO model: criminalizing nonsupport, thus raising the stakes for scofflaws, and taking some of them to court to drive the lesson home; providing subsidized state services for ordinary civil complaints; expanding conciliation or mediation outside of court; or providing more state programs for children in need. Each of these has political and financial costs, as well as differing and so far undermined rates of success in advancing the principal objectives (getting food and other essentials to children of indigent families). There is another goal, fomenting responsibility paternity, which could produce different rankings of the options.

It is obvious that child support is not the only issue, and a similar exercise for other common complaints—debt collection, landlord-tenant disputes, division of property following a divorce or death—might produce different alternatives and rates of success among them.[73] Exploring each issue may not be the most efficient way of deciding on the worth of subsidized legal services, but it bears mentioning that most of those services are organized and financed without a prior "market survey" of the intended clientele, even in terms of their purely legal needs. And yet it is the resolution of their problems and the consequent improvement in their lives that are offered as the ultimate justification. The fact that people use subsidized services begs the question of which are most effective for resolving which problems and whether, indeed, other nonlegal or nonjudicial means will produce the results more efficiently.

If we cannot yet answer that question, the higher-order debates about impacts on democracy, market growth, citizen security, or poverty reduction are not even worth tackling. The briefest summary of the consequences of the access-enhancement

73. For a discussion of common legal issues affecting the poor in Chile, see J. E. Vargas et al. (1998, 92–96).

activities as a whole, and for the most part individually, is thus as follows: they have apparently increased use of courts and related services, and expanded it to groups that once faced insurmountable barriers, but we do not know how much of the potential demand they have covered or whether their coverage includes the most needful cases, either absolutely or within the categories they have emphasized. Specialization of focus is largely ad hoc (women, indigent defendants, rural populations) rather than based on an overall consideration of where limited access is most harmful. Within each category, few organizations have attempted to set further priorities, and service is often on a first-come-first served basis. Moreover, at both an individual and societal level, their real and potential impact on improving people's lives or in reducing basic inequalities and other social problems remains unknown. Until these downstream consequences can be documented for the effort as a whole and for its varying approaches, access enhancement will remain like charity—a nod in the direction of soothing social consciences but otherwise a shot (or several) in the dark. Probably, like charity, there are important impacts, but for investments to be made in a more rational fashion, the access enhancers will have to better define their aims and strategies, and develop means of measuring their success.

RELATIONSHIP TO OTHER PROGRAMS

Access-enhancement activities are characterized by their own lack of coordination. It is thus not surprising that they tend to operate independently of other reform strategies. The few obvious exceptions are criminal defense, commercial arbitration, and the frequent justification of access enhancement as a complement to the efficiency outputs of court modernization programs. In only the first two areas is access enhancement directly integrated into the overall strategy—and even there improvements could be made. Criminal justice reform commonly suffers from its own lack of integrated planning, a result of the failure to coordinate the activities and development plans of the various sector actors (and external funders) involved. Because it is new, less popular with governments and citizens, and often less successful in pressuring for funding, public defense is usually the weakest element in these programs. Efforts to improve judicial impact on commercial and economic development remain largely a collection of activities, with no attempt to develop an overarching strategy to coordinate them. In terms of the relationship to overall efficiency enhancement, most of these reforms focus on within-court operations. Some access-enhancement activities (procedural simplification, small claims courts, ADR) may figure in their own schemes, but efficiency reformers have not promoted them independently and have usually not taken the separate access-enhancement movement into account in working out their own plans and projections. From both sides, these are parallel efforts that may interact positively, but no one appears to be pushing for a convergence.

In more basic institutional strengthening programs, access also receives short shrift. Whereas courts often mention broadened access as a justification for their efforts, it is difficult to identify elements of their usual plans with any direct implications for advancing it. The one exception is demands for higher budgets to allow the addition of courts and judgeships. When funds are obtained, however, their use does not often feature a distribution based on where client needs are greatest. It is not unusual for them to go into building or upgrading appellate and supreme courts, or trial courts in urban centers, rather than creating facilities in poor neighborhoods or rural areas.[74] Brazil's small claims court program is one important contrary example, though it most benefits urban residents. As regards training, judicial selection, and monitoring and evaluation, the premium in institutional strengthening efforts appears to be on academic professionalization (thus, the great popularity of master's programs), specialization in modern legal themes (commercial and international law), and other elements to improve the judiciary's image. It is true that many courts have added public relations offices to "educate the public," but much of this education seems directed toward image enhancement rather than making services more accessible. As a profession that has suffered enormous discreditation in the eyes of other elites, the judiciary often seems most concerned with raising its value for this reference group, not in improving its popular image on the basis of services provided. Many judges throughout the region still resist the notion of being service providers—they serve the law, not the citizenry. The important exceptions are usually at the lower level of the hierarchy where they have little impact on policy decisions.

One interesting convergence of the access and other strategies occurs in the area of the checks and balance functions. As discussed in the next chapter, this theme also divides the judiciary. Supreme and constitutional courts entrusted with judicial review powers have become increasingly important in protecting individual rights, including those of the poor. Some, like Costa Rica's constitutional chamber, can lay claim to being champions of the downtrodden. Mexico's federal courts have proposed an expansion of their *amparo* functions (as well as of federal public defenders who might represent poor clients) to give them a similar role. Nevertheless, the drive here is not for generalized access to all court services, but rather a consolidation of these functions in the upper level courts. This notion of enhanced access tends to coincide more with that of the public-interest lawyers—rather than with the many other strands of the access movement. As discussed in chapter 5, the

74. Often overlooked, for example, are the difficulties poor clients will have in getting to new consolidated judicial centers, as recently occurred in Salta (Argentina) and in several Brazilian states. Locating the centers outside the congested urban areas solves the judges' and lawyers' parking problem but is little help for clients who depend on public transportation.

division does not always go in this direction. In Brazil, it is the lower-level judges who claim to recognize the poor, characterizing the higher courts as elitist.

There is another basic issue concerning the relationship of access enhancement to other reform elements—the question of sequencing. Much like the criminal justice reformers, access advocates have not been willing to wait for a larger reform, despite others' arguments that access to a highly flawed system may be worth very little.[75] An underlying theme in many access programs has instead been that greater access will itself promote system change—removing biases, fighting corruption, and forcing judges and other system players to do their jobs better. We have a few examples where this tactic appears to have worked. In El Salvador and several other countries, better-trained and more aggressive public defenders appear to have forced judges to take due process rights more seriously. In Ecuador, members of women's legal service programs claim to have sensitized judges to women's issues. In several countries, where indigenous groups have begun to appear in courts, judges become more aware of their problems. It is clear that court systems that effectively exclude the poor are likely to underestimate the extent of their legal problems or their own potential role in resolving them. By the same token, these court systems will probably not treat the first poor clients very well, and where their vices extend beyond prejudice to corruption, incompetence, or inertia, these early experiences may discourage further attempts.

Rather than treat this as a chicken-and-egg proposition, the dilemma would appear to argue for a simultaneous (and, one would hope, better coordinated) or iterative approach on both fronts. Strengthening the judiciary first, without attending to access, could reinforce isolation. Pushing access without other improvements may be costly, unnecessarily difficult, and unrewarding. The current tendency to parallel, but less coordinated programs is not quite the answer. Still, like all the partial approaches, it has been the easiest for the participants to adopt.

This leads to some final considerations, as addressed below, on the overall aims of increased access—realization of a basic right, a means of helping individuals resolve their concrete problems, a way of furthering collective interests, or a shortcut to creating a conflict-free society, strengthening the rule of law, or promoting social revolution. As with judicial reform in general, the access movement has benefited from considerable ambiguity as to its real goals. Until these are more explicitly defined, it will be very difficult to determine which of its elements are most valuable, and which merit further promotion as part of an overall reform package.

---

75. In addressing a World Bank group (First Global Law and Justice Reform Conference, Washington D.C., June 2001), Julio Faundez thus noted that we may be doing no favor to poor citizens in giving them access to a corrupt, dysfunctional court system. His comment was intended to be provocative and also was made in the context of countries where traditional dispute resolution still works. Nonetheless, it poses an interesting dilemma. See also Faundez (2005b).

SOME ADDITIONAL THOUGHTS ON THE THEORETICAL AND PRACTICAL DILEMMAS IN DEFINING THE CONCEPT OF ACCESS

Limited access to courts and to the private and public goods they provide is an undeniable historical trait of Latin American societies. It is also obvious that the poor and other marginalized groups were the chief victims of the status quo ante. As Peruvian critics like to say, justice is not for the poor because they cannot afford it and not for the rich because they do not need it.[76] No one denies that this situation requires change, but it is increasingly apparent that an improvement involves far more than just getting the poor to court or to some alternative forum. Unfortunately, most of the access promoters have not developed their ambitions much further than that.

Access as an Absolute Value. Access to justice, conceived as an actor's right to certain individualized services, cannot increase infinitely. Greatly expanded access and thus greatly expanded court use will either increase court congestion, thereby putting its own limits on access (especially for those who cannot tolerate lengthy delays) or require the expansion of services. Initially, this expansion may be done by making judicial and complementary operations more efficient. Over the longer run, budgets will have to be increased. Much like health, education, or police protection, there are limits to what the state can provide and decisions to be made as to priorities (one dollar spent on justice versus one spent on health, or the trade-off between funding ADR and more public-interest cases). It appears to be particularly difficult for many jurists to accept this fact. They are not used to the notion that rights (whether to health, education, or justice) must be measured against resource constraints and thus that some kind of rationing will be necessary.[77] This does not mean that access cannot be increased or distributed differently. It does mean that any remedy will still have to recognize the impossibility of an infinite growth in services and thus that implicit or explicit policies will exclude some uses and users. The preferred solution would appear to be facing those limitations head on and making explicit decisions about how and to whom services will be provided. Otherwise it is likely that spontaneously developed rationing systems will perpetuate or even worsen inequities.[78]

Expanded access has other costs. One disadvantage of making access too easy is that it discourages the development of alternative means for resolving or avoiding

76. This line is usually attributed to Luis Pásara, but he himself says he does not remember having invented it (private communication with the author).

77. And even when they admit that other kinds of rights are subject to budgetary limitations, justice often appears as an exception. "The provision of an adequate system of justice available to all cannot be treated as another budgetary item, to be juggled with all other claims in the disposal of such income as a government gets" (Fox 2000, 88).

78. Because such systems are likely to rely on a tolerance for delay and an ability to keep paying counsel, they inevitably favor the better-off.

conflicts. Where creditors can depend on the courts for debt collection they will be less cautious in making loans, and privately financed credit bureaus and similar services will not develop.[79] Where every minor squabble among neighbors can go to conciliation, there will be less inclination to work through or tolerate their differences. Government agencies, which are often major users of court services, may send disputes with clients to courts rather than resolving the problems at the source. Here lengthy delays work in their favor as they are better positioned to wait them out than are most private citizens. Even where the government stands to lose (both because of the monies invested in keeping the case active and the delayed rewards—for example, in a tax collection case), its agents will not bear the costs and in fact may benefit from the appearance of productive activity. In short, although increased access is a desirable goal, more attention is required to the form it takes and who benefits from the change.

Access as a Means Not an End. This formulation may raise still more juridical hackles, but at the very least we should recognize that access can be both a means and an end of judicial reform. Conceived as a right, access to justice is an end, and the problem of its rationing becomes difficult. Conceived as a means, the question is no less thorny, but its focus shifts to the results being pursued. The answers are as numerous as the definitions of justice: the traditional response that the purpose was ensuring that individual conflicts were resolved in accordance with the prevailing legal norms is now joined by an emphasis on guaranteeing other individual rights, enhancing juridical security and predictability, reducing crime, deterring the escalation of conflicts, protecting citizens against government abuses, enhancing the status of the traditionally marginalized, and even revising the legal framework. It should also be recognized that "access" to the social benefits (public goods) of justice is available to all members of a society (and to many nonmembers) regardless of whether they ever take a case to court. As one of my colleagues likes to remind us, the 80 percent of the population who only see the inside of a court on television can still enjoy the enhanced physical and juridical security a well-functioning justice system is supposed to deliver.

Because the various goals are not necessarily compatible, it is not likely that a single strategy of access expansion will serve all of them equally. In fact, radically expanded access can create a short-term setback in several—for example, the goals of deterring conflicts or increasing juridical security.[80] Assuming an enormous gap between the formal legal framework and actual practice, access programs can call

---

79. Economists and lawyers of the law and economics school have actively explored this and other issues related to the nonjudicial means for contract enforcement. Such means range from the value of reputation to hostage contracts and services providing information on creditors. See, for example, Stone et al. (1996) and Sherwood et al. (1994).

80. The latter is a particularly concern in Colombia because of the very diffuse handling of individual protests of rights violations. See Amaya (2005, 344–47). Uprimny (2001, 32) offers opposing arguments.

attention to the problem by seeking rights for citizens normally not enjoying them. Still, the way divergences are worked out is not guaranteed either. However the courts initially decide, the political powers are likely to have the last word and may well determine it is better to forego overly ambitious legal ideals rather than having to implement them.

In short, although one of the recent motives for expanding access is the notion of a social revolution by judicial fiat, the political cards are stacked against its realization.[81] Despite a current tendency to judicialize politics,[82] the courts are really not organized or empowered to make basic decisions on policy, and if they enter very far into that realm they will most likely provoke an unpleasant reaction.[83] More modest ambitions—giving more individuals a peaceful, legal way to resolve their conflicts and thereby enhancing the reach of the rule of law in private to private and private to public dealings—may be more realistic, but even here resource limitations will require choices being made. The real challenge is how to use the courts to leverage extrajudicial reconciliation, still in line with the legal framework, but reached through other means, or to encourage compliance (the deterrence effect) so that the overall level of conflict and rule violation is reduced. Expanding or more appropriately, altering access is a part of the solution. Doing this effectively will require a much closer look at what courts already do and the potential for changing their activities.

We return to this theme and its implications for strategy building in a later chapter. Although access enhancement is possibly the most atheoretical and least strategic of the many approaches to judicial reform, it is potentially the most fruitful entrée for combining the partial models. In all of the partial approaches, the underlying question is "why?" Those pursuing the access route have provided many possible answers, wherever their subsequent activities eventually have taken them. They may not be great theorists, but, in their efforts to justify their programs, they have given us a great deal with which to work. Before returning to that topic, one further strategic approach requires examination.

81. See Pásara (2004), for an argument as to the need to modify our expectations on the results of judicial reform.

82. See Tate and Vallinder (1995).

83. Current discussions in Colombia about eliminating the Constitutional Court or severely limiting its powers are one example. President Uribe is said to favor these approaches.

One frequent criticism of judicial reforms is that they are overly technical and insufficiently political. Though most often addressed to donor programs, the comment is equally applicable to many purely local efforts. The judiciary is no ordinary provider of public services. In Latin America it has long been considered a political power as well, a status assumed to influence how it operates and broaden the impact of its actions.[1] Many of the justifications for undertaking reforms emphasize their positive consequences for overall political stability, democratic governance, and the protection of citizen rights. Yet, to the extent reform programs attempt to change organizational outputs, they have focused nearly exclusively on improving services and service delivery much as they might in a health or education project.

Because of the prohibitions on their political involvement, the multilateral development banks (MDBs) may receive this comment less as a criticism than a validation of their policies. For other donors and for self-financed reforms, it merits further reflection. Of course, even the most technical reforms have political repercussions. The development banks are indulging in a convenient fiction by pretending that speeding up handling of cases, rewriting commercial codes, or helping judicial leaders track the performance of individual judges does not affect the "authoritative allocation of values." Still, over the short run, the impacts of these efforts are highly incremental and largely limited to individual parties. Even access programs, as we have seen, have so far demonstrated the most modest of effects despite the potential political impact deriving from their activation of new clients. In recognition of these limits, public-interest lawyers have adopted more ambitious tactics, but a revolution by judicial fiat is a long way off.

Because the courts' political function is so intimately tied to their "public service delivery," it is conceivable that the current emphasis on the latter could have more important effects on the former. Where judges are encouraged to apply the law in a timely and equitable fashion and to rule against abuses by public or private actors, their cumulative impact on conflicts over the distribution of private

---

1. The European tradition is more ambiguous here. In France, the judiciary was traditionally a political authority, not a power. The U.S. version appears to be winning acceptance universally. In Latin America, its influence is evident in the courts' formal independence, in many cases, since the earliest constitutions.

and public goods could make a significant difference. That it has not happened is partly a result of the incomplete implementation of efforts to improve the quality and quantity of their services. It also derives from the limited resources usually assigned to elements such as access enhancement, which might accelerate the effect. Concerning political impacts in the narrower or broader sense, there are several additional impediments:

- In many instances, the legal framework is a limiting factor. It is not surprising that on both the procedural and substantive side it often favors the interests of established elites with respect to the values it protects and the remedies it offers. The situation is nicely summarized by Anatole France's observation that the law in its magnanimity falls equally hard on the rich man or poor man who steals a loaf of bread or sleeps under a bridge.
- In those cases where constitutional guarantees or secondary laws appear to offer more potential for challenging the status quo, there may be limitations on how such claims can be pursued (restrictions on standing, who can represent these actions, and how additional parties can be joined to them).
- Legal and other barriers may restrict the courts' ability to override governmental actions, policies, and decisions or limit the broader effects of any such ruling.

This chapter examines most closely the third factor, with some attention to the first. The second was discussed in the chapter on access. Here we review considerations affecting the judiciary's status as a coequal political power, one that not only enjoys independence as regards its internal actions, but also exercises controls (checks and balances) over the other branches of government. The point is not the judiciary's ability to foment social and political revolution, though many who promote enhanced judicial power have just this in mind. It is rather its ability to increase the consistency between officially stated values and norms and the real behavior of public (and private) actors and agencies.

Like internal institutional strengthening, the attention to the judiciary's politico-constitutional role has been slow to develop. It has received little impetus from the donor community. A combination of factors explains this situation. Even bilateral donors are reluctant to get involved in this overtly a political project. In addition, they often are not very attuned to the issues. One important element, administrative law, is not widely understood. To the extent it is addressed, it is commonly incorporated in other program areas, most usually public-sector or administrative reform.[2]

---

2. Here the interest is typically in improving structures and processes, not review mechanisms, either administrative or judicial. Legal change is often a part of administrative reform, but only to the extent that new ways of operating must be formalized. It is not uncommon to find that new administrative codes do not fit well with the rest of a country's legal framework. This obviously poses additional problems for any kind of judicial review.

It is not surprising that, when defined in this fashion, the judicial implications are typically ignored. While often endorsing constitutional review powers, donors have developed no more detailed explanation of what this means or how its effective exercise might be promoted and assessed. Finally, on the MDB side, there is an institutionalized ambiguity about the courts' ability to check governmental actions. Many staff economists are not happy about courts interfering with economic and regulatory policy and thus are quite satisfied with arrangements limiting those powers.[3]

The pressure for change has instead come from other external groups and occasionally from the judges themselves. International and local nongovernmental organizations (NGOs), along with some independent jurists, have been the most active proponents. Their early successes in introducing change frequently benefited from the relative ignorance or inattention of political leaders. As in the case of the donors, judicial review powers struck many politicians as positive in the abstract and furthermore were often already incorporated in their constitutions. Here the challenge is to encourage courts' exercise of these functions. In other cases, constitutional and legal changes are also required. Until recently, there was little active opposition to the proposals. They sounded progressive and no one, including the proponents themselves, fully anticipated the results.[4] These have sometimes been dramatic. As a consequence, reformers who activated their campaigns later are encountering considerably more resistance.

HISTORY

Latin Americans follow a mixed tradition with respect to the judiciary's political status and actions. As members of the civil law family, they to this day embrace the principle that judges do not make law.[5] Judges are supposed to apply laws, not

---

3. A World Bank publication on institutional development thus notes that economic policymaking should be insulated from public pressures, and that more participatory decision making is most appropriate in other service areas (Girishankar 2001, 9). The fact that most first-generation reforms were enacted using irregular decree power with a minimum of transparency was rarely seen as problematic by followers of the Washington Consensus. See Santiso (2001) for a critique.

4. See Merryman (1985, 1996) and Dainow (1967), for a general discussion. It bears mentioning that Latin America's experience in expanding judicial review appears to run counter to trends identified in Eastern Europe. The explanation there (see Goldstein 2004, Solomon 2004, and Trochev 2004) focuses on elite interest in protecting themselves against majoritarian pressures arising in the democratic transition. In Latin America, traditional elites seemed to ignore this potential. As discussed in Chapter 3, their self-protective maneuvers were more likely to take the form of controlling judicial selection, not limiting or expanding judicial review. Mexico may constitute an exception. See B. Magaloni (2003).

5. See Aucoin (1992, especially 446–55), on the French tradition. Still, in Latin America as in Europe, judges have frequently indulged in what only can be called law making. It is commonly noted that all French administrative law is really judge made (albeit by special administrative judges) and that French tort law has been elaborated on the basis of only five articles in the civil code. One major difference is that judicial law making is far less systematic in Latin America, in part because of a frequent failure to publish judgments. See Amaya (2005) and chapters in Friedman and Pérez-Perdomo (2003), for a discussion.

reinterpret them, and their decisions usually affect only the case in question. By training and orientation, Latin American judges were expected to use the law as written, not to second-guess the legislators as to its intent or constitutional soundness.[6] Not all have gone as far as Paraguay, which constitutionally gives the Congress the right to determine the meaning of any law, but the sentiment remains. Latin Americans also absorbed the prohibitions on judicial intervention in executive policy arising in postrevolutionary France.[7] This doctrine continues to influence judicial structure, the legal framework, and judges' sense of their own responsibilities. During the latter half of the twentieth century, increased political intervention in judicial operations served to remind judges who strayed from that principle.

Despite their civil law origins, the region's countries were also influenced by their neighbor to the North, the United States. Many early constitutions went far beyond civil law conventions in recognizing the judiciary as a separate branch of government and according it formal independence. One result is the reduced, often nonexistent, role of the ministries of justice in managing judicial affairs and the frequent vesting of judicial governance powers in the supreme court itself. Some constitutions also gave the high courts (and sometimes lower ones, as in Argentina, Costa Rica prior to 1989, and Mexico for its federal courts), the ability (uncharacteristic of the civil law tradition) to declare a government action illegal or unconstitutional or of deciding not to apply an unconstitutional law. In a few cases (Costa Rica after 1989, Chile after 1925), the high court's decision on a law's unconstitutionality had binding effects on the rest of the judiciary and might thus force its retraction. At the very least, via a writ of habeas corpus (often called *amparo*[8]) courts could enjoin certain government actions (often, but not always, privation of liberty or of freedom of movement) on the basis of their violation of constitutionally guaranteed rights. Under diffuse systems of constitutional control, where any judge can accept an *amparo* or refuse to apply a law he or she finds unconstitutional, such decisions are always subject to appeal to the higher courts.

Historically, courts' use of these powers was subject to considerable self-restraint and outright political manipulation. Under the military governments of the 1970s and 1980s, many judiciaries distinguished themselves by their failure to treat even habeas corpus requests (protesting illegal detentions) seriously, finding all manner

6. In El Salvador, following constitutional amendments in the early 1990s emphasizing due process rights, judges hearing criminal cases often stuck to the letter of the still unreformed criminal procedures code, insisting that it was this law that should guide their actions. Throughout the rest of the decade, donor agencies, and especially USAID and the UNDP, worked to change this response, largely through a series of training programs.

7. See Merryman (1985, 1996) and Aucoin (1992).

8. Formerly, as in Peru, the writ of habeas corpus was used for any violation of constitutional rights, but in practice was restricted to the right to freedom of movement. As more countries adopt generous lists of protected rights, habeas corpus usually has the more restricted legal usage, and *ampao, tutela* or some similar mechanism covers other rights.

of formalistic pretexts for dismissing them out of hand.[9] With the democratic open-ing, there were some significant breaks with this tradition. During the Alan García administration in Peru (1985–90), García's attempts to take over the private banks were hindered by the bankers' successful presentation of writs of *amparo* (protest-ing violations of their constitutional rights) to lower-level judges. Although each *amparo* affected only the case in question, García retracted his more ambitious plan on the assumption that the judiciary would continue to foil his efforts.[10] In Mexico, *amparos* also have a long history of successful use by those able to afford lawyers specialized in the material. Because it can be used to overrule state court decisions, the *amparo* affects more than executive actions.[11] The problem with many of these exceptions is the overwhelming popular suspicion that they were no more justly motivated than the actions they protested. Latin American jurists studying their courts' use of their judicial review powers cite endless examples where the courts pulled back from applying them in a manner contrary to government pref-erences and interests or used them only to favor economic elites.[12]

Constitutional review powers were not the only judicial checks on government actions. Many countries had special judicial or administrative courts to deal with other types of disputes between private and public actors. Those in the judiciary, usually located in a specialized administrative jurisdiction (called "*contencioso administrativo*), handled disputes ranging from public employees' complaints about unfair dismissal or disciplinary practices to private actors' protests of tax assessments, public-sector contracting, or arbitrary application of a regulation or law. Specific responsibilities and organization vary broadly. As a general rule, this is the judicial specialization least understood by the ordinary citizen, and is not well handled by many otherwise competent private lawyers.[13] As cause or consequence, these courts are little used and in recent years have been further eclipsed as new forums for protesting government abuses are introduced.

Often the administrative courts were created outside the ordinary judiciary. In Paraguay and the Dominican Republic, administrative disputes are heard by the tribunal, or *Cámara de Cuentas*, the body responsible for external control (auditing), and technically a part of the judiciary only in the former country.[14] Colombia stands alone in the region in its use of a completely separate system of administrative

9. See García Belaunde (1979), Matus (1999), and Carrió (1996).
10. See Asheshov (1988).
11. See Fix-Zamudio (1979).
12. See Hilbink (2003), for a very critical discussion of the Chilean court. See García Belaunde (1979) and Rubio and Bernales (1988, 209–23), for discussions of the handling of habeas corpus requests by the Peruvian supreme court.
13. Administrative law poses its own problems in more developed countries as well. For a discussion of some issues and current trends, see Bell et al. (1998, 167–201), Brown and Bell (1993), Longley and James (1999), and Provine (1996, 185–90).
14. Paraguay's tribunal lost the control function in 2004.

courts controlled by a *Consejo de Estado*.[15] These courts are not attached to the executive, but rather exist within the judicial branch on an equal footing with the ordinary court system. In other countries, extrajudicial administrative courts are appended to executive agencies, functioning more like the U.S. system of administrative tribunals. The most common are tribunals functioning under the revenue agency or ministry of finance to handle disputes over taxation. Mexico's federal fiscal courts, created in 1939, now also see other administrative disputes. The Federal District and some Mexican states have adopted a similar practice.[16] Some "administrative tribunals" were administrative only in the sense of being tied to executive agencies; most of the complaints they heard were between private parties.

There has been some tendency in recent years to incorporate these tribunals into the ordinary judiciary. The trends are not consistent, even in single countries. Peru fully judicialized its labor and agrarian courts in the 1980s.[17] The administrative tribunals created or strengthened under the Fujimori administration (1990–2000), however, retain their separate status. During this period, bankruptcy cases, competition law, and consumer complaints were transferred from the ordinary courts to an independent regulatory agency, Instituto Nacional de Defensa de la Competencia y de la Proteccion de la Propredad Intelectual (INDECOPI), and its internal tribunals. In the mid-1990s, Ecuador incorporated several administrative jurisdictions into a new judicial area of *contencioso administrativo*. It left the special court handling juvenile issues with the executive. At about the same time, Bolivia likewise moved most of its half dozen administrative courts into the ordinary judiciary. Its mining courts have been moved back and forth for reasons apparently dictated by the public and private interests represented.[18]

The susceptibility of decisions by executive administrative tribunals to judicial appeals or review also varies across countries and over time in each one. Usually their decisions may be appealed, if only on the basis of due process or rights violations. Some appeals lie only with the higher-level ordinary courts. In Peru, the decisions of the administrative tribunals attached to the tax (SUNAT) and competition agencies (INDECOPI) can only enter at the level of the Supreme Court.[19]

15. See Santofimio (1996, 321–42). The practice copies the French model, albeit with a certain time lag. The Colombians are only now introducing a lower level of administrative courts in line with French developments occurring several decades ago. Until these courts are created, administrative cases will continue to enter with what are in effect appellate courts, located in the departmental capitals.

16. See González Oropeza (1996, 64–67), for a discussion of Mexico's administrative courts.

17. These were really only administrative courts in the sense of being tied to executive agencies; they heard complaints arising between private parties. The courts created under the Fujimori government hear both private-private and private-public complaints.

18. See Dermizaky (1997).

19. COFOPRI (land titling in the slums) also imposed its own deadlines for citizen appeals of its decisions (five rather than the standard fifteen days for administrative appeals and fifteen rather than thirty for judicial ones.) Its law also denies judicial appeal of the titles it issues—only the intent to issue a title may be appealed (interviews, Lima, April 2001).

This constitutionally dubious arrangement is based on the agencies' own decision and gives them a special status as opposed to other regulatory and administrative bodies. Administrative tribunals, as in Argentina and Brazil, may rely on the ordinary court system for the forcible collection of amounts they find due from private citizens. Or, as in Mexico and Peru, the tax courts can enforce their own judgments. Based on these four cases, it does not appear that location is the major determinant of successful enforcement. The Peruvian and Brazilian systems appear to function better than their counterparts in Mexico and Argentina.[20]

One consequence of these multiple arrangements is that in a single country citizens often have a variety of means of protesting government actions. The alternatives can be mutually exclusive—as in Bolivia, where plaintiffs at some point must decide on a further appeal via the administrative channel or recourse to the judiciary's *contencioso administrativo* jurisdiction. As regards the judicial route, often there is a further choice between a constitutional action, offering an injunction but no recuperation of damages, and an ordinary civil or administrative action in which damages may be claimed. Criminal actions against administrators require still another route, via the criminal courts. Most citizens cannot be bothered with the latter and make their other choices on the basis of the likely payoffs and delays. Peruvian lawyers note that, where time is important and a preemptive action still makes sense, clients usually prefer *amparos*. Where the damage has been done or a remedy is less urgent, they seek redress through ordinary civil, administrative, or labor proceedings, depending on the nature of the complaint.

In recent years, and even before the changes discussed below, most countries saw an increase in citizens' use of these forums to seek redress from government abuse (as well as by others hoping to prevent actions that, objectively speaking, might be considered legitimate—for example, payment of taxes, assessment of fees, or awarding of government contracts to competitors). This increased use is a consequence of the explosive expansion of legislation regulating private activity, the return to constitutional government, and related changes in the courts' structure and operations making them a more credible avenue for complaints. However slight the change, it demonstrated the inadequacies of existing arrangements.

First, long-term neglect has meant that the legal framework, especially regarding ordinary (nonconstitutional) judicial review, is often underdeveloped, internally contradictory, and vulnerable to its own abuses. This is true of that part regulating the administrative or judicial review process and of the laws defining the legal basis for administrative actions. Many countries still lack a single administrative procedures law; where one exists, it is usually patched together out of preexisting legislation with no particular concern for resolving inconsistencies or filling gaps.[21]

20. See World Bank (2003a).

21. Peru enacted its first administrative procedures law in 1967. It remains in effect, with a series of partial modifications, but changes in the political climate have not augmented its consistency. Under

Second, the instruments for accessing constitutional rights were inadequate for many kinds of abuses, especially those affecting groups of actors or second- and third-generation rights. Protective measures like the traditional *amparo* are generally restricted to ongoing actions. If the damage has been done, or the action is periodic but not continuous (for example, police harassment), courts often deny this recourse.[22] Third, judges and government lawyers participating in the process are often insufficiently trained and motivated and lack the resources required to do their jobs well. Judges frequently cite the abusive motivations of the parties on all sides—private clients who see the proceedings as a way of cheating the government or circumventing normal rules, government officials who refuse to honor judgments (especially if they involve returning money to the plaintiff),[23] and government lawyers who are typically instructed to appeal every decision against the state.

The most frequent response to these problems is an increased attention to constitutional judicial review, both as it exists and as regards further development. This has sometimes brought dramatic increases in use and impact, albeit with other negative consequences. Attention to ordinary (administrative) judicial review has been less consistent and brought fewer immediate effects. Arguably it is the area where most work is needed. Most abusive actions are not inherently about constitutional issues, but if that is the most effective channel, private parties will find ways to use it, citing violation of guarantees to equitable treatment or other first-generation rights.

Before turning to the recent changes, a few words are merited on the judiciary's role in curbing criminal abuses by public actors. The growing attention to the issue of corruption has increased the importance of this function and to the fact that, as traditionally organized, it was extremely ineffectual. A first problem was the political intervention in the judiciary and the consequent disincentive for judges to accept denunciations, investigate them, or reach verdicts against governmental, political, and economic elites. These were not the only problems. As judiciaries become more politically independent, they are encountering additional obstacles, many of them legal.

On the one hand, existing legislation defining corrupt, criminal, or abusive acts for which individual officials might be held accountable is very weak. It is commonly

---

the Fujimori government, several powerful regulatory agencies introduced into their own organizational laws articles modifying the general provisions. These included limitations on where judicial review would occur and the deadlines for making an administrative or judicial appeal. Local experts agree this situation should be remedied. Considering Peru's other problems, it seems doubtful this will happen soon. Bolivia's administrative legal framework contains many internal contradictions and gaps. Apparently Bolivian law drafters often do not check for potential inconsistencies with the existing framework.

22. Interviews, Peru, April 2001.

23. In Peru, the Defensoría del Pueblo has documented the instances of nonpayment by various government agencies, finding the municipalities are the greatest offenders. See Peru, Defensoría del Pueblo (1999, chap. 3). A similar comment was made by judges interviewed in São Paulo, Brazil.

so outdated that it excludes the most likely forms of modern abuses or defines them so generally that its application becomes almost discretionary. On the other, individualization of responsibility for many actions is not well defined. Thus, an agency may be ordered to cease an objected practice (or do what it has avoided doing), but there is no way of establishing responsibility for the actions or inaction giving rise to the complaint. This is less true of criminal acts, where defined. Absent a criminal charge, however, there is no real disincentive with respect to the same officials' making future arbitrary or questionable decisions. At the most they may be asked to desist, but without further consequences. Moreover, judges often lack the ability to force compliance. At best, they may rely on one of the parties or the public prosecutor to enter a complaint about failure to comply, but have no independent contempt powers.[24]

Many countries offer special protections to a variety of government functionaries with regard to their susceptibility to ordinary criminal action. Often justified as a means of protecting officials from politically motivated attacks, the practice has its roots in a far older tradition of special *fueros*, or legal regimes, for certain public and private groups. Its corporativist base conflicts with the modern notion of a rule of law applied equally to all citizens. This is particularly evident in current debates over the jurisdictional powers of military and police courts. It also affects the special procedures required to carry out a criminal action against civilian officials.

Frequently, these officials must first go through an impeachment proceedings (*juicio político*) before a criminal case may be initiated. The purpose of the proceeding is to strip them of their political immunity. The group enjoying this special status may be quite large, including not just ministers, congress members, and judges themselves, but also vice ministers and directors of ministerial departments, governors, mayors, and additional lower ranking officials. Officials faced with criminal charges enjoy other advantages. Once losing their political immunity, the criminal proceedings against them may take a special form and are often so complex that a case simply never ends. As in Bolivia, where an action involves several officials, all may enjoy the special proceeding accorded to the highest-ranking member. Moreover, the statute of limitations for their alleged crimes is commonly relatively short, they may avoid charges originating in one position by getting themselves appointed or elected to another,[25] and where monetary damages are involved, they may avoid legal action entirely by paying back the amount in question. (Tax dodgers in Argentina also enjoy this privilege, as well as periodic tax amnesties.)

24. West (1992, 322) notes that French administrative judges also lack enforcement powers but suggests that "the administration, when liable, usually does comply voluntarily with the judgment, even if on occasion it takes some time to do so."

25. One of the most egregious examples is the automatic appointment of all Central American presidents to the Central American Parliament, on leaving office. This gives them immunity for life. For this observation I am indebted to Judd Kessler and Andres Barreto who are conducting a study on political immunity in the region.

Ironically, resigning ones positions can be an effective tactic in some countries, leaving the individual in a sort of juridical limbo, accused of a crime that only a public official can commit or that must be tried through a proceeding to which he is no longer entitled. Often, the resignation ends anyone's interest in pursuing the matter, and, at times, a forced resignation is the real objective of the accusation.[26] Those who resign, even if later tried in ordinary proceedings, do not lose their rights to hold other political office, a sanction imposable only under the special proceeding.

Between these legal impediments and other less legally blessed manipulations, it is no wonder that so few of the region's public officials are successfully prosecuted for corruption and other criminal acts. Because the judiciary usually enjoys similar immunity, its members may resist challenging that of other public servants. The judiciary's public credibility, however, is increasingly linked to its willingness and ability to accept criminal charges and conduct trials against public and private elites. Its perceived reluctance to do so has negative effects on its public image. Moreover, its ability to bring powerful figures to trial is critical to its role in ensuring that the official rule of law is consistent with the law as applied and practiced.

As the above suggests, the impetus for moves to enhance the judiciary's political role comes from a number of quarters. There is first the concern that it protect citizens against abuses of their constitutional rights and ensure that constitutionally guaranteed services be accessible to all citizens. This is a difficult charge in an era where courts are expected to uphold rights arising in constitutions that "were never meant to be enforced."[27] Over the long run, it may require broader political reflection on what rights a society wants enforced and possible constitutional amendments, but, over the short run, the judiciary's charge is to enforce what the constitution says.

Second is the concern that the judiciary enforce ordinary laws, ensuring that government agencies act according to their legal mandates and that they make their decisions in an impartial manner. The underpinning for this charge lies in constitutional guarantees to equitable, unbiased treatment. It can also be handled as a question of mere legality rather than constitutional abuses. That this continues not to be the most common practice is directly related to the persisting underdevelopment of the relevant legal framework.

Third, is the concern that courts act against public-sector corruption and crime, regardless of whether there is a private plaintiff. In the current era, this may be the

26. Interviews in both Bolivia and Ecuador, whose Contralorías use a system of *glosas* (forced repayment of funds by officials who cannot account for their use), suggested it was often utilized as a way of getting rid of politically unpalatable bureaucrats. Once the individual resigned, the repayment was no longer pursued. See Hidalgo (1996), for an explanation of the *glosa* system in Ecuador.

27. The comment comes from Bruce Wilson. For an elaboration of the argument, see Wilson et al. (2004).

acid test of the courts' political role. Citizens less concerned with rights or legal violations of their own situation are well attuned to the emerging revelations about official corruption. They are mere spectators to the events, but their faith in the courts and other justice-sector officials hinges at present on how they deal with these cases.

PROGRAM COMPONENTS

It is probably misleading to speak of this as a program, taking into account the several motivating factors, the diverse groups involved, and the consequently different actions they have produced. In general, the three principal areas—constitutional review, legal review, and powers to adjudicate cases against government actors—have been pursued independently of each other. Within each area, the level of coordination of actions is often not high. Most progress has been made in the constitutional arena. The other activities have received less attention and so have produced less change.

Constitutional Judicial Review

One of the announced and presumably automatic consequences of increasing the professionalism and institutional independence of the courts (as regards internal operations, budgetary autonomy, control of employees, and so forth) was that it would enhance their political role in a broader sense. Better courts were expected to improve their own image and credibility and have a similar effect on the overall political system. It was assumed that greater institutional independence would allow the courts to contest the actions of other government agencies, following the initiation of the legal complaint by some other public or private actor. The judiciary's political engagement is always assumed to be reactive, though some newly empowered Latin American courts have broken even that rule. This reactive role is extremely important. It serves to counterbalance the judiciary's lesser political accountability.

Institutional independence has visibly reduced the courts' susceptibility to external manipulation of ordinary judgments—those affecting private parties in civil or criminal cases. Judges selected for their intellectual qualifications, further trained in their responsibilities, paid reasonable salaries, and no longer fearful of immediate dismissal for an inconvenient decision have shown themselves more willing to decide according to the law and less vulnerable to monetary rewards for doing otherwise. The impact on cases involving public actors was not as automatic. In countries where political intervention had been extreme and where courts were believed to have tolerated or cooperated openly with it, many citizens remained skeptical about their willingness to take another tack. Critics suggested that political allegiances still counted and that judges had in fact been placed by prior governments with this in mind. The most famous example is Carlos Menem's stacking of Argentina's federal criminal courts,[28] a strategy that appears to have paid off.[29] When individual judges were not directly affected, the political loyalties of those overseeing the judicial careers could still weigh on their decisions. Whether located in supreme courts or judicial councils, they were believed to transmit the executive's message to the trial judges. Finally, the existing legal framework often posed further constraints. Rights traditionally subject to constitutional protection were believed inadequate, and the ability of courts to enforce them was severely constrained.

The wave of constitution drafting or amendments following the return to democracy in the 1980s, thus incorporated measures to strengthen the courts' powers, create additional constitutional courts or chambers, add means for accessing rights, and introduce new organizations to investigate, denounce, and sometimes act as plaintiffs in cases involving alleged violations. Where constitutionally guaranteed rights were deemed insufficient, the new or amended documents included additional ones. The move to strengthen constitutional guarantees and the institutional framework for protecting them was contagious. Countries that had not suffered repressive, de facto governments (Colombia, Costa Rica) during the prior period joined in the new trends. The example of Colombia's 1991 constitution is not atypical. Whereas the prior constitution (enacted in 1886, but substantially amended since) had thirty-six articles defining the rights agenda, the current document has 101.[30] As elsewhere, the expanded charter elaborated on the basic first-generation (political and civil) rights and added a host of second- (socioeconomic) and third-generation (diffuse and group) rights, embodying a national decision to construct a social state of rights (*estado social de derecho*).

Constitutions written or amended during the late 1980s and early 1990s tended to take the same direction. The one exception is Peru, which in its 1993 constitution reduced rather than expanded the rights guaranteed by the state. Although many contemporary governments might wish to follow suit, the political costs of shortening the list of guarantees, especially in the second- and third-generation areas, were usually too great. Rights also proliferated in secondary legislation, for example,

28. See Verbitsky (1993), for a discussion of the court packing, and Carrió (1996), for a review of the impacts on decisions. Helmke (2005) differs slightly in arguing that toward the end of a weakened administration, justices will rule against their former sponsors. She says nothing about lower-level judges, and Argentine experts (Abaid and Thieberger, 2005) suggest that those placed by Menem show a remarkable lack of concern for any criticism (and they imply, for the law).

29. As is widely discussed in Argentina, the same supreme court that upheld Menem's privatizations and freezing of bank accounts in the early 1990s, proved a headache for emergency measures adopted by his successors. See Chapter 8 for more details on the Argentine situation.

30. See Saez (2002, 3).

family and juvenile codes promising respect and special treatment to the family, to third-generation (senior) citizens, and to the child.

Constitutional Courts. In some countries, the ultimate protection of these rights was entrusted to the existing supreme court. Distrust of its inclinations and the influence of European developments often lead to another solution. In the inter- and postwar period, continental Europe broke with the civil law positivist tradition of restricting the courts' ability to review executive and legislative actions. This was usually done through the creation of a new entity, the constitutional court. These bodies, which some observers see as appendages of the legislative rather than the judicial branch, were usually staffed by judges chosen "outside the career" (that is with no need to have served in the ordinary judiciary or to be appointed as the latter were), who often held fixed terms and whose powers were limited to reviewing the constitutionality of laws and regulations. Constitutional challenges frequently could be entered only by certain high-level officials, by requests forwarded by a fixed number of legislators, or through petitions signed by thousands of ordinary citizens.[31]

In Latin America, many supreme courts already had some constitutional review powers, however infrequently they might exercise them. Still, they generally spent more of their time on other types of cases—*casación* (an exceptional appeal questioning the legal basis for judicial rulings), third instance reviews (really de novo trials), trials of political officials, certain other cases reserved for their original jurisdiction, and judicial governance. In adopting the European model, Latin Americans often left the supreme courts with their original powers while creating a new body with enhanced capabilities and some overlapping functions. Latin Americans also had a better developed set of vehicles for protesting violations of individual rights, via habeas corpus, *amparo*, *tutela*, or Brazil's *mandado de segurança*. Whereas constitutional courts might review these writs in the last instance, they were usually left to enter wherever they traditionally had done so—with individual judges, with appeals or specialized courts, or at the supreme court.

Colombia's current system thus allows the presentation of a *tutela* to any judge. Its Constitutional Court can select the protective actions it chooses to review; *tutelas* nonetheless constitute 67.5 percent of its caseload.[32] In Peru, the arrangement is similar, though Peru's Constitutional Court reportedly reviews far fewer *amparos*. In Costa Rica, however, the 1989 law creating a constitutional chamber within the Supreme Court directed all *amparos* to this body, removing them from the oversight of other judges. El Salvador has adopted a similar practice.

Most Latin American countries seemed to favor separate constitutional courts,

---

31. Schwartz (2002, 34–36), however, notes an increasing tendency to give standing to individuals, though usually only as regards the impact of a law, not its application.

32. See Saez (2002).

though only about half succeeded in introducing one. Costa Rica (and later El Salvador) presents an interesting intermediate model—the creation of a special constitutional chamber within the Supreme Court. In Costa Rica, the members are appointed by a larger congressional majority but serve under the same conditions as the other justices.[33] Their decisions regarding the unconstitutionality of a law are binding on all other judges (including those in the other Supreme Court chambers) and thus in effect nullify the law. The effects of their *amparo* rulings, however, are limited to the single case—that is, an act found in violation of some basic right is not more broadly prohibited. Costa Rica's model is also unusual in that citizens can access the chamber directly without legal representation and without fully specifying the right in question. (This is also possible in Colombia.) The chamber does the rest of the investigation. *Amparos* account for at least 40 percent of the chamber's workload (now reaching 10,000 annual filings). Despite their limited application, *amparo* rulings have been effective in reversing broader government policies.[34] Apparently, the authorities realize that the chamber's rapid and consistent resolution of these complaints does not leave much room for stubborn persistence.

In this sense, Costa Rica's centralized constitutional protections offer an interesting contrast with the diffuse system found in most other countries. Along with El Salvador, Nicaragua, Paraguay, and Uruguay, it constitutes the exception to the general rule. (Mexico's system is also diffuse, but restricted to federal, not state courts. Like the five exceptions, it does not have a separate constitutional court.)[35] The advantages and disadvantages become most apparent in a comparison with a few countries (Brazil, Argentina, Colombia, and Peru) where diffuse protections are widely accessed. Through its own variation on the *amparo* (the *mandado de segurança*), Brazil's lower-level courts have also been active in overruling government actions. Brazil, however, is a much larger country (172 million as oppose to Costa Rica's 3.5 million inhabitants) with many more judges, and its government has a policy of appealing every negative ruling. Between the consequent delays in reaching a firm judgment, the fact that higher courts do not always uphold trial court rulings, and the enormous variation in the latter, it should come as no surprise that the impact on policy is weaker than in Costa Rica. Furthermore, as discussed below, Brazil's high courts (along with those of most Latin American countries) are limited as to the wider impact (binding precedent) of their decisions. This is equally true of Costa Rica's *amparo*, but Brazil's diffuse system significantly raises the chances of inconsistent decisions on similar issues.

33. This includes fixed terms that are renewable subject to the approval of the National Assembly. See Barker (2000), for a discussion of the chamber's history.

34. See Wilson et al. (2004).

35. In Argentina, there is no separate constitutional court, and final reviews lie with the supreme court. Discussed in more detail in Chapter 8.

In Peru (except in Lima during the 1990s when specialized public law courts existed), Argentina, and Colombia's diffuse systems, citizens can likewise enter a protective action directly with any judge. In Colombia, legal counsel is not required. Direct access to the constitutional court is not available to individuals in either Peru or Colombia. (Argentina, it should be remembered, does not have a separate constitutional court). In countries of their size (24, 36, and 40 million inhabitants, respectively), diffuse control may be a necessity. Here as in Brazil, the down side of the equation is the greater variation in the responses. As these protective actions nowhere produce *ergo omnes* (broadly binding) effects, the negative impact on juridical security may be as much a function of the sheer number of rulings as of their decentralized handling.[36] Until Costa Rica's chamber developed a computerized system for documenting its jurisprudence, its members complained that they were producing their own contradictory responses.

The constitutional courts' additional review of protective writs is a consequence of Latin America's earlier development of these mechanisms. The principal purpose of these bodies was to develop judicial review in another area—that of deciding the constitutionality of positive law (that produced by the legislature or through its delegation of powers, by the executive). There are further variations in the impact of the decision, the circumstances under which it can be requested and the ways the case may be submitted for consideration. Abstract review (that is, not related to any specific legal case) is a frequent and for Latin America, completely novel practice. Some countries allow or require it before a law goes into effect. Peru places deadlines on the postenactment consultation. Abstract review can usually be requested only by specifically defined parties—again high-ranking officials or large numbers of citizens or members of congress. In Costa Rica, the chamber has no such deadlines and does most of its constitutional review as a consequence of issues raised in real cases after the law has gone into effect. This enhances its power and allows it to make its rulings on the basis of problems emerging over time or as its own sense of how the constitutional issues ripen.

Brazil's Federal Supreme Tribunal (STF) stands at the other extreme, in that only its decisions on the constitutionality (but not unconstitutionality) of a law constitute binding precedent for other judges. This has not prevented lower-level judges from continuing to grant injunctions against laws the STF has upheld.[37] Although the STF must notify the relevant government agency (or the Congress in the case of a law) of its findings of unconstitutionality (including the failure to implement

36. Argentine judges, however, have traditionally treated supreme court decisions as though they were broadly binding. There are signs this may be changing. In Colombia (Aymara 2005; Younes and Mejia 2003), the situation is considered to be more chaotic with 4,000 judges all interpreting the constitution according to their own appreciation. Here the situation is further complicated because of the ability of other high courts (the Supreme Court, the Council of State, the Procuraduría General, and the Judicial Council) to offer constitutional interpretations.

37. See Ballard (1999, 256–60).

a constitutionally guaranteed service), the response to the order to retract, nullify, or introduce the affected measure is often delayed or circumvented.[38] Still, like the Colombian and Costa Rican bodies, its decisions have forced government to reverse or revise policies on many occasions. This offers an interesting contrast with the Chilean supreme and Peruvian constitutional courts, which can declare a law unconstitutional with broadly binding effects. In Chile, the supreme court received this power in the 1925 constitution but has always been chary of using it. A constitutional tribunal created in 1980, and enjoying abstract review powers, does not appear any more active. In Colombia and Costa Rica, the constitutional bodies have been accused of imposing their own ideological agenda. In Chile and Peru, they have been criticized for a lack of activism.[39] Much of the difference appears to stem from the orientations of court members. Thus, following the activist performance of Colombia's first set of constitutional judges, it was predicted, that their replacements would be chosen far more carefully.[40] As Peru's case demonstrates, inactivity can also be a consequence of a legislative base overtly intended to curb the court's powers.[41]

A third area of activity involves the constitutional courts' role in reviewing the constitutionality of ordinary (that is, nonconstitutional) judicial rulings. Latin American constitutionalists are divided on the advisability of this function. Costa Rica's drafters decided against it, and thus this is one area where its constitutional chamber enjoys less power than many similar bodies. Judicial rulings are reviewed in the last instance through chambers of *casación* in the supreme court, or in special appellate courts. Colombia's constitutional court does have this role, as do Mexico's federal courts vis-à-vis state tribunals. In these two cases, there are complaints about the workload this places on the higher courts and the creation of a "fast track" or additional appeal that undercuts the powers of the ordinary courts. Supporters claim

38. In the case of federal laws, Article 52 of the 1988 Constitution gives the Federal Senate the exclusive power to "suspend the enforcement, in full or in part of laws declared unconstitutional by the final decision of the Supreme Federal Tribunal" (Rosenn 1998, 27). According to Rosenn, members of the STF insist that the Senate may not reexamine the decision or refuse to suspend the law. This has not prevented the immediate enactment of a similar piece of legislation. Because of an apparent oversight in constitutional drafting, STF findings of unconstitutionality are not binding ergo omnes on lower-level judges.

39. In Peru this appears to be changing. In 2002, the Constitutional Tribunal struck down a 1998 administrative action dismissing 400 employees from a privatized state enterprise, finding it incompatible with constitutional guarantees. It has also begun to review judgments against terrorists. Peruvian judges speak of an "*amparización*" of justice—a tendency for citizen complaints to be channeled through the *amparo* mechanism—encouraged by fast-track treatment and a more sympathetic final review from the Constitutional Tribunal.

40. This appears to have been accomplished. The court's new president, Manuel Cepeda, has expressed concern about the judiciary's impact on the public budget via its handling of *tutelas*. His recommendation, however, is that the legislature enact laws defining the status of social and economic rights guaranteed in the constitution, a task he does not believe corresponds to the constitutional court (Amaya 2005, 246–47).

41. In addition to the usual restrictions regarding standing, the organic law for Peru's Constitutional Tribunal requires agreement by six of its seven members to declare a law unconstitutional.

the practice increases juridical security by ensuring that one entity reviews and decides on the issues raised.

The Mexican example raises some doubts here, largely because these decisions usually rest with the federal appellate courts that are not known for their uniform viewpoints. The situation becomes more complicated in instances where federal and state judicial divisions do not match, meaning that cases arising in a single state may not all go to the same federal courts. Ultimately, the Supreme Court may be asked to provide a uniform ruling. In the meantime, the consequences are anything but juridically secure.

Supreme Courts with Constitutional Review Powers. Not all countries have opted for separate constitutional courts. Some that did delayed their creation or simultaneously enhanced the constitutional review powers of the ordinary supreme courts. The most extreme example is Colombia, where the ability to rule on constitutional issues is shared by five bodies: the Constitutional Court, the Supreme Court, the Judicial Council, the Council of State (head of the administrative court system), and the Procuraduría General.[42] As several observers have commented, the arrangement takes judge shopping to a whole new level. The parties attempt to couch their question to ensure it goes to the forum where they believe they will get the most favorable hearing. In Peru, Ecuador, Chile, Bolivia, and Guatemala, where a supreme court now shares constitutional review powers with a constitutional court, this phenomenon is less common, partly because access to the constitutional court is highly restricted.[43] Also the new bodies have usually not been sufficiently active to produce inconsistencies. Nevertheless, the potential remains. Experts working in other regions have suggested that the dual system has its advantages.[44] It remains to be seen whether this will be the case in the Latin American countries opting for this solution.

Although a separate constitutional court was for a time the preferred regional solution, many countries could not get the required constitutional amendments enacted or, if enacted, have yet to create the new entity. The fallback and sometimes preferred option has been to enhance the constitutional review powers of the supreme court. In Mexico, this was done through a series of reforms in the late 1980s and early 1990s. The Federal Supreme Court of Justice ceded much of its responsibility for receiving *amparos* to the lower federal circuit and district courts and now concentrates on other constitutional issues. This still gives it an enormous

42. This body, part of the public ministry (which in Colombia really is, as the Latin American saying goes, a function not an organization), is responsible for pursuing administrative actions against public officials and representing the interests of society in civil and criminal cases. It also houses public defense and the human rights ombudsman. The Fiscalía General contains the rest of the public ministry function, criminal prosecution.

43. See Eguiguren (1998), for an early discussion of Peru's tribunal.

44. See Schwartz (2000), for a discussion in the context of Eastern Europe.

workload, but its most important cases are those involving the constitutionality of enacted law and bills.

In Argentina, Paraguay, Venezuela, Nicaragua, Uruguay, and Panama, proposals to create a separate constitutional court did not prosper and the supreme courts exercise the ultimate authority. Because of their many other functions and their inability to select their cases, all have an overwhelming workload and little time to spend in reflecting on constitutional issues. The same problem afflicts many constitutional courts. Part of this is self-inflicted. Colombia's constitutional court sees more than 7,000 cases annually largely because it chooses to review so many *tutelas*. Although Argentina's supreme court now has more discretion in selecting the cases it will review, it still hears several thousand a year.[45] This may be the worst of situations, because, in addition to the large caseload, the court usually offers no explanation as to its criteria for selecting cases and is not very communicative as to when it plans to hear them. More generally, the law as written and as interpreted does not leave either supreme or constitutional courts much leeway for filtering their caseload.[46]

Apart from their large workload, and in fact contributing to it, a major issue for supreme courts is the broader impact of their decisions. This is usually addressed as the question of binding precedent, the extent to which a court's single decision, whether over an individually protested right or the interpretation or constitutionality of a law, will become the general rule to be followed by other judges and by the government itself. The issue is a thorny one for a tradition where judges are not seen as making the law and where the independence of the individual judge is also valued.[47] The need for some ability to set precedent is gradually being recognized, if only to reduce court congestion. Although the practical need is acknowledged, the substantial impact on the judiciary's collective powers and on that of the upper level courts as opposed to trial judges has proved a major obstacle to resolving the dilemma. The frequent stopgap measure—declaring that a certain number (often three to five) of similar decisions by the supreme court constitutes binding precedent—has not been much help. There are always ways to prove that the sixth case is different.

45. The Argentine supreme court's certiorari-like ability to select the cases it will review has not significantly reduced its caseloads. Currently, it receives upwards of 12,000 filings annually and decides on about half.

46. Courts can reject cases, after an initial inspection, for lack of merit or failure to file properly. Observers (Magaloni and Negrete, n.d.) have documented the use of this practice by lower-level courts to control their workload. No one has yet to associate it with the region's supreme or constitutional courts, except under authoritarian governments (for example, Peru and Chile) as a pretext for not accepting protective writs.

47. A further, rather bizarre argument against binding precedent proffered by Brazilian judges is that their promotions hinge on an evaluation of their decisions. If they are tied to binding precedent, they believe they will not have a chance to demonstrate their legal skills. See Ballard (1999, 262).

Except for oddities like Brazil, this is usually not an issue as regards decisions on the unconstitutionality of a law. Where constitutional or supreme courts are expressly given this function, their decisions are usually broadly binding. It does affect the far more frequent individual protests of rights violations. Where these challenge not the law itself, but rather its application, decisions, even by the highest court do not have *ergo omnes* effects.[48] In many countries, the consequence has been to clog the courts with hundreds or thousands of similar cases that will eventually be decided in the same manner. Famous examples include the amounts due on bank accounts frozen under the Collor regime in Brazil, decisions on public-sector pensions and severance pay in Argentina, Brazil, and Colombia or illegal taxes levied by Brazil's municipal authorities.[49] In Mexico, many of the *amparos* against administrative and judicial decisions are also repetitive, and each one must be adjudicated separately. The problem is easily understood. The solution seems obvious, but so far remains beyond the grasp of those who must endorse it.[50]

New Rights and New Mechanisms for Accessing Them. As a reaction to de facto governments, and in some cases under them (Peru's 1968–80 military regime),[51] the 1980s and early 1990s saw a marked expansion in the rights given constitutional status. Constitutions of the era often added second- and third-generation rights to the normal first-generation freedoms and expanded the scope and content of the latter. Brazil and Colombia are among the most extreme examples, but many other countries did not lag far behind. In the constitutional amendments adopted in 1994, Argentina greatly increased its constitutionally recognized rights by incorporating all those included in international conventions to which it is a signatory.

By the mid-1990s, the regionwide embrace of neoliberal economic policies, the accompanying efforts to reduce state expenditures, and the privatization of many services left most countries with a host of promises their public-sector budgets could in no way fulfill and which their administrations frequently had little wish to honor. Only Peru, in its 1993 constitution, took steps to reduce the constitutional guarantees

48. They do have these effects in Costa Rica, as regards other judges, but under a concentrated system, that is unnecessary—no one else hears these cases.

49. As of mid-2004, the Argentine government was considering rescinding a decision made under Menem that allowed the appeal of disputes over pension amounts to the supreme court. It is estimated that 60 percent of the cases reaching that body have to do with this issue—and that nearly all appeals are entered by the government.

50. The civil law tradition, it is true, does not embrace binding precedent, but in Europe lower-level judges tend to follow higher court rulings as a matter of "various aspects of the judicial *esprit de corp*" (David and De Vries 1958, 117). In elaborating on this point, the authors mention a concern for institutional image, a "shared responsibility" for decisions, judges' desire to save their own time and that of litigants, and a concern for preserving juridical security or litigants' ability to count on decision-making patterns.

51. See Rubio C. and Bernales (1988), on Peru's 1979 constitution, the impact of the military ideology, and the difficulties of its application. See also Bernales (1996), for a comparison with the "Fujimori" constitution.

and so establish a balance between official aspirations and real capacity.[52] Some countries have followed Brazil's example in assigning a special category to many of the new rights. They are now considered as programmatic (statements of intent to deliver them, once the government creates the necessary laws, institutions, and budgetary resources). As such, they are not subject to the same absolute guarantees as the more conventional civil and political rights. This novel departure emerged when legal activists began to press for their full recognition and new forms of collective litigation threatened a way around the usual case-by-case decision-making. In most countries, lesser levels of activism, a continuing focus on first-generation rights, the absence of provisions for collective litigation, and the courts' tendency to rule conservatively made it unnecessary.

Despite the rights explosion, first-generation rights frequently remained an issue, as traditionally defined and further elaborated. Efforts to reform criminal justice systems and eliminate customary abuses kept legal activists sufficiently occupied in most countries. Though often explicitly prohibited by new codes and constitutions, it would take more than legal strictures to end such practices as automatic pretrial detention, forced confessions, inhumane prison conditions, and denial of access to counsel. It was principally in countries where the abuses were minimal, like Costa Rica, , or that somehow missed the criminal justice reform movement, like Brazil, that attention focused on new areas. Continuing emphasis on first-generation rights was also encouraged by popular reactions to new government policies and scandals and by the availability of new mechanisms for accessing them.

The advance of neoliberal economics and resulting cutbacks in public employment, pensions, and other benefits or in subsidized services directly affected many second-generation rights and were occasionally attacked on that basis. They also raised issues related to more fundamental political and civil rights, ranging from the recognition of unions and collective contracts, through the permissibility of organized demonstrations and protests, to citizens' ability to participate in and demand information on new policies. Individuals affected by the loss of acquired rights (job tenure and benefits) also took their cases to court, but the premium was on protecting their traditional forms of fighting public and private employers and service providers. Mobilized workers and ordinary citizens also began to demand more access to government information, a right promised in most constitutions, but lacking the complementary legislation to put it into effect. The response has been slow. It is only in the past few years that countries have begun to enact freedom of information laws.[53] Prior to their passage, citizens relied principally on the new *habeas data* writs. They usually guaranteed access only to information kept

52. For a discussion of the changes, see Bernales (1996).

53. In early 2003, both Argentina and Mexico took the lead in introducing new freedom of information regulations. Because of congressional delays in enacting the law, Argentina still relies on an executive decree that does not affect the other branches or levels of government.

on the complainant. At the time of its inclusion, *habeas data* was a reaction to abuses by government security forces. It was not conceived as a means to information on how other types of policies were made and implemented.

As this detail suggests, one of the primary obstacles to citizen complaints continued to be the absence of satisfactory channels for making legal protests. Most of the new mechanisms—adding to the traditional *amparo* and habeas corpus, more specific instruments like *habeas data,* Brazil's *mandado de injunção* or Colombia's *acción de cumplimento*[54] (the latter two protest government's failure to take a constitutionally guaranteed action)—relied on the individual complainant and, apart from a positive response to his request, had no broader effect. Tailored to an era when the principal concern was state repression directed at individuals or organized groups, they were of little use in attacking the denial of positive rights to collectivities. In this regard, Brazil has gone furthest in introducing new forms of collective litigation. Its government has also been quick to place limits on the possibilities for true class action suits, using executive decrees and general legislation to exclude complaints over specific issues.

Activists in other countries have shown an interest in promoting the adoption of collective remedies, so far with limited results. In Brazil and elsewhere, groups have had most luck with collective litigation in noneconomic areas (for example, environmental rights) and those not directly affecting the public budget (consumer rights). Still, this is a moving target. In the early twenty-first century, courts in Argentina, Peru, Brazil, and Colombia were beginning to accept collective protests in areas of more direct interest to the state. In Argentina in 2002 and after, it was the lower-level judges, not the supreme court, who took the most radical stances, aided by private and public actors willing to place these complaints. These decisions involved the government's emergency economic measures—freezing of bank accounts, formulas for converting dollar accounts and debts into pesos, and cuts in salaries for public employees. This put the supreme court in a delicate position. If it overruled the judges, it risked losing whatever leadership it retained and possibly ending the traditional acceptance of its judgments as binding precedent. Upholding their rulings might shift the blame to the judiciary for the macroeconomic consequences.

Even less conservative courts have been wary of accepting claims with predictably major impacts on the public treasury. Costa Rica's constitutional chamber was willing to declare the transit law unconstitutional and to accept an *amparo* over a patient's rights to HIV/AIDS medication but stopped short of overruling the central bank's ability to set the exchange rate. Brazil's STF has not always needed an executive decree to keep it from ruling on certain emergency economic measures.

---

54. See Santofimio (1996, 401–7), for a discussion of the various remedies in Colombia. See also García Villegas et al. (1996), for a discussion of early uses of *tutela* in that country and its impact on caseload.

With respect to the 2004 constitutional amendment expanding its ability to create binding precedent, observers suggest the STF will use it very carefully, especially in light of the executive's warnings about the economic impacts. Governments have not been adverse to applying still greater pressures. When President Nicanor Duarte Frutos of Paraguay instigated the 2004 replacement of most of the supreme court, his displeasure over their predecessors' rulings on measures like the new civil service law (which would have facilitated removing nonperforming public employees) clearly had a role. The new court appears to be on a short leash concerning policies backed by the government, and its members' appointment was informally conditioned on their nullifying the former justices' ruling on their own permanent tenure.[55]

New Actors (Ombudsmen, Public Ministries). The heightened interest in constitutional review powers also encouraged the creation of new bodies or the assignment of additional powers to existing ones concerning the investigation and representation of cases of alleged violations. The late 1980s and 1990s saw the creation of *defensorías del pueblo* (human rights ombudsmen) throughout the region. Most cannot take cases to court, but they can help citizens investigate and bring public attention to their complaints. As discussed in the next section, some of these entities have moved into areas more related to ordinary judicial review (legal, but not constitutional, abuses). Most first focused on traditional first-generation rights, targeting abusive actions by security forces, including both the police and the military. As these abuses become less common, there has been a tendency to address third-generation rights—protection of the environment, women, children, the aged, and ethnic minorities. Because these organizations usually have limited funding, they have had to ration their efforts, often emphasizing high-profile cases, publications, and educational work.

Another interesting variation is Brazil's assignment of representation of rights cases to their public ministries.[56] Throughout the region, these bodies traditionally had a split responsibility for representing social interests and overseeing compliance with due process rights. Their actions had typically been restricted to offering nonbinding dicta in noncriminal cases and prosecution in criminal ones and, somewhat contradictorily, ensuring that the rights of the defendant were respected. In recognition of the inherent conflict of interest, the latter role is increasingly transferred to the ombudsmen or public defenders. In Brazil, the public ministries have an additional role of investigating abuses of collective (group) and diffuse (societywide) interests and representing these cases in court.[57] This has led, on the

---

55. See World Bank (2005a, 41–47).

56. Technically, the Defensoría del Pueblo is part of the public ministry, but in most countries, the title "Public Ministry" is held by the entity responsible for prosecution and the defensoría is a separate organization.

57. See Arantes (2002), for a discussion.

one hand, to increased activism in investigating government corruption and, on the other, to their exercise of public-interest law. Several state public ministries have earned considerable fame for their work in both areas. There are indications, however, that this may be at the cost of attention to normal criminal prosecution.[58] Except for Venezuela, other countries have not followed Brazil's example. Investigation of all but criminalized rights abuses remains with the *defensoría* or various legal NGOs, and it is the latter that represent the case in court, either on their own or on behalf of aggrieved citizens.

Ordinary Judicial Review

The expansion of constitutional review mechanisms and the rights they protect has been the primary emphasis of those looking to increase the court's political powers. To a large extent, this has discouraged reexamination of a second type of judicial review, that concerning the consistency of governmental actions with ordinary law. The judiciary's administrative jurisdiction, whether new or of longer standing, has experienced extremely slow growth or even stagnation. The few exceptions are situations where government economic policies have produced massive dismissals, cutbacks in pensions, or affected the value of bank accounts, debts, and interest rates. Having exhausted the administrative remedies, those affected often end up taking their cases to court, sometimes alternating constitutional and normal administrative actions. For example in Peru, judges reported that cases first went to the labor courts to protest an unfair dismissal. When that failed—or the agency found another way to avoid reinstating them—they might enter a second complaint over severance fees or their pension, taking it to the public law courts. Cases arising in alleged administrative abuses have substantially increased the workloads of the judicial and executive administrative tribunals throughout the region.[59] They have not otherwise altered their operations or the laws shaping them. In effect, the courts have been handed the responsibility for deciding on a one-by-one basis, hundreds or thousands of similar complaints that might be resolved by a single government decision. That decision, however, would either be universally unpopular or financially catastrophic for the public treasury.

The present arrangement holds real advantages for the government. Not all potential plaintiffs go to court. Proplaintiff rulings can usually be delayed, and, once

58. In interviews with police and *promotores* (prosecutors) in Recife (Pernambuco state) in November, 2002, it became apparent that the latter's role in investigating police malfeasance was not contributing to a smooth working relationship between the two bodies. This may help explain a very low clearance level for criminal investigations. Data supplied by the public ministry indicated that, of 2,917 homicides reported in 2000, 1,392 were investigated by the police, 138 were referred to the proecutors for criminal action, and 100 were sent to trial.

59. See Younes and Mejia (2003), for data on Colombia's administrative courts.

they are delivered, enforcement becomes another problem. In Argentina's social security courts, where the issue is now pensions, the government's first response was to pay the complainant with ten-year bonds. It switched to cash payments only when the 2001 devaluation reduced the value of the peso by two-thirds. In Brazil, government agencies had the constitution amended to legalize delay. The change effected in 2000 allowed them to pay claims in incremental installments over ten years. Only small awards involving salaries or pensions (*alimentos*, or sustenance) must be paid "immediately," or within 90 days. As the bill for *alimentos* grows, the government is seeking additional changes allowing it to pay even these amounts incrementally. In Peru, workers winning an unfair dismissal complaint often find that their position has been eliminated, there is no budget to rehire them, or that for some other reason, the agency will not comply.[60] Unlike an ordinary civil action against a private party, there is no possibility of seizing state assets to make good on the payment. Brazilian judges do have this option, but are understandably reluctant to use it. As a general rule, plaintiffs winning claims for payment against government agencies can expect compliance to be slow or possibly nil. Governments often do not do much better collecting payments when the award is in their favor, but the odds are more clearly on their side.

Because so many problems originate in the legal framework, the few jurists specializing in administrative law have begun to suggest changes. These begin with a call for a better definition of administrative procedures and of the internal process for reviewing complaints. At the very least this implies standardizing the rules governing administrative actions and consolidating the massive collection of agency-specific regulations. These regulations have accumulated over decades, reflecting different views of the administrative function, different approaches to the role of the state, and the ability of temporarily privileged agencies to acquire exceptional status as regards their internal procedures and their susceptibility to external review. In light of the many vested interests affected, the universally limited understanding of the issues, and the absence of a consensus on the most appropriate solutions, even countries enacting new laws do not seem to have produced solid improvements.

Administrative law specialists are sufficiently scarce in most countries as to facilitate their reaching an internal consensus on a better model. They are, however, also prone to their own magic bullets and axiomatic principles, especially when they lack practical experience in the public sector. Attracting wider support for their proposals and getting them safely through the executive and legislature can be daunting. The administrative experts often have more luck with narrowly targeted experiments—for example, the introduction of conciliation into disputes between public and private parties (such as Peru and Ecuador's recent experiments with

60. Peru, Defensoría del Pueblo (1999, chap. 3).

contract disputes)[61] or efforts to strengthen the oversight powers of internal and external control agencies. Such innovations do not directly effect judicial operations except by diverting cases to alternative forums or reducing some of the abuses on which courts might be expected to rule. Although strengthening internal administrative systems and controls is important, it has no necessary impact on citizens' ability to seek protections from abuses. In fact one evident danger of this approach is that it may further insulate the administration from external oversight and protests—and possibly eliminate the sense of their necessity. Once political and administrative principals are better able to monitor and control the actions of their nominal agents, reliance on service users as a source of information or on the courts to investigate and remedy abuses may appear both superfluous and unwelcome.

It is not surprising that measures to put the administrative house in order overwhelmingly prioritize top-down control, not horizontal or bottom-up accountability. The trend is reinforced by the donors' tendency to treat these issues as public administration, not judicial reforms. It is also encouraged by the development banks' emphasis on controlling the public-sector deficit, holding down spending, and increasing revenue collection. It is true that there have been nods to transparency through the Internet publication of budgets and tenders, but very little thought has gone into how individual complaints will be channeled or what follow-up mechanisms will be introduced. Civil society is now invited to help control waste and fraud with the assistance of twenty-first-century technology. The ordinary citizen who believes the phone company or tax agency has overcharged her is stuck with methods developed decades, if not centuries, earlier—the suggestion box, an administrative appeal process of dubious utility, and a judicial review system with an outdated legal foundation, certain internal biases, and an inadequate enforcement mechanism.

Absent practical suggestions on how to reduce the legal obstacles, one of the more interesting innovations has been the use of *defensorías de derechos humanos* (or *del pueblo*) to investigate administrative abuses and promote negotiated solutions. The most advanced in this area is Peru's *defensoría*, which has added this to its initial human rights focus. Although its limited territorial reach and budget have restricted its impact, the *defensoría* has done its own investigations on many common complaints (usually about fees for privatized public services) and has successfully negotiated the resolution of some individual cases with the companies in question. Its impact on overall policy has been far more limited, if not nonexistent, but many of its interventions occurred under the prior Fujimori government, an administration hardly receptive to this sort of oversight. It remains to be seen whether

---

61. Peru has a special administrative court attached to CONSUCODE, the organization charged with overseeing public contracting. In Ecuador, the Procuraduría has attempted to introduce conciliation for such conflicts.

the institution will continue this emphasis under new leadership and under a government that may allow it to move into the high visibility, third-generation rights favored by its counterparts in other countries. Its initial preference for more basic administrative monitoring duplicates the role traditionally played, with some success, by the original Scandinavian prototypes.

Peru's ombudsman does attack these issues with an ideological bent, and this colors many of its studies. Still, its efforts to document performance and engage both the public and the government in discussions about overall policy are important and could enhance the courts' own role. The courts can do little against an agency with the right to set its own fees, decide how and when complaints can be registered, and limit the judiciary's ability to review its decisions. By calling attention to the resulting inequities, the *defensoría* can provoke legal change and thus give the courts more leverage when called upon to intervene. Until that happens, the current tendency to constitutionalize every instance of administrative arbitrariness is likely to continue. This raises the stakes for all parties, often produces less than optimal solutions, and encourages governments to indulge in bad-faith litigation. When the issue is rights, negotiation is usually not an option. The advantage of administrative law is that it leaves the way open for compromise and for workable, generalizable solutions. Its final advantage and most important one regarding the courts' political power is that it provides a way for changing administrative practices and not just for remedying their damages.

Table 4 summarizes the situation of constitutional and judicial administrative review in the region's courts. It is current as of late 2005. In view of the frequent changes in the region, it is subject to modification at any moment.

Legal Actions Against The Powerful

The traditional impunity of powerful public and private actors has its roots in legal provisions and their political manipulation. Newly independent, reformed courts escaped some of the political pressures, but they still cannot act unless a case is brought to their door. One exception is Ecuador's supreme court, which in the early 1990s, as a result of personal battles between the national vice president and the supreme court president, took apparently unilateral action against the former. The constitutional basis for this action remains questionable. It did result in Alberto Dahik, the vice president, fleeing the country, but it also brought the removal of the chief justice (albeit, formally for other reasons). More typically, the courts' hands remained tied by the special procedures required before a criminal case can be commenced and by the frequent reluctance of state prosecutors to conduct the investigation and press charges.

Discussions of the need to place limits on official immunity and to simplify the procedures for trying government officials have only commenced. They face

Table 4 Constitutional and administrative review mechanisms

| Country | Constitutional Judicial Review | | | Administrative Review[1] |
	With Constitutional Court	With Supreme Court or Chamber	Wholly Concentrated or Partly Diffuse Control[2]	
Argentina		X	Diffuse	Judicial
Bolivia	X	X	Diffuse	Judicial
Brazil	X		Diffuse	Judicial
Chile	X	X	Diffuse	Judicial
Colombia	X	X	Diffuse	Separate system regarded as within the judicial branch
Costa Rica		X Chamber	Concentrated	Judicial
Dominican Republic		X	Diffuse	*Cámara de Cuentas* (audit agency) is administrative court outside ordinary judiciary; tax cases seen by a separate, executive *Tribunal de Contencioso-Tributario*
Ecuador	X	X	Diffuse	Judicial, with Administrative Tribunal, single instance; decisions may be appealed to supreme court only for cassation
El Salvador		X Chamber	Concentrated	Judicial
Guatemala	X	X	Concentrated, lower level judges must seek supreme court guidance on suspected unconstitutionality of laws or actions	Judicial
Honduras		X	Concentrated; lower level judges must seek supreme court guidance on suspected unconstitutionality of laws or actions	Judicial
Mexico		X	Only federal courts, but deconcentrated within them system	Executive by sector— tax, administrative, land, labor—and municipal small claims

| | Constitutional Judicial Review | | | |
Country	With Constitutional Court	With Supreme Court or Chamber	Wholly Concentrated or Partly Diffuse Control[2]	Administrative Review[1]
Nicaragua		X	Concentrated	Judicial, Supreme Court. Law on *Contencioso-Administrativo*, which would have created lower level courts, declared unconstitutional
Panama		X	Diffuse	Judicial and Administrative (by sector and municipal courts)
Paraguay		X Chamber	Concentrated; ability to interpret laws shared with Congress	*Tribunal de Cuentas* (formerly audit agency[3]), part of ordinary judiciary
Peru	X	X	Diffuse	Judicial and executive, by sector, tax, customs, contracts
Uruguay		X	Concentrated	Judicial, but with separate Administrative Tribunal for requested annulments of administrative decisions
Venezuela		X	Diffuse	Judicial, but with specialized administrative review courts

Notes:

1. Excluded here are quasi-tribunals within executive agencies that may constitute the last instance in an administrative appeal, but whose judgments can be appealed judicially for reasons other than violation of constitutional rights.

2. With the exception of Costa Rica, El Salvador, Nicaragua, Paraguay, and Uruguay, where constitutional issues are directly referred to the supreme court or its constitutional chamber (the first two), all systems are mixed to some degree, with some issues (usually questions of abstract challenges to laws) reserved for the supreme or constitutional court. Here the distinction refers to whether an individual protest can be made to a lower-level judge, and whether that judge may reach a decision on it, subject of course to later appeal.

3. Until October 2003, the *Tribunal de Cuentas* also functioned as one of two supreme audit agencies. A law enacted in that month eliminated the second chamber that had this power. A protest of unconstitutionality, filed by employees of the chamber, was rejected by the Supreme Court in late December of that year. The Tribunal now only sees administrative cases in the first instance.

enormous obstacles to their further progress. No one is willing to sacrifice their special *fuero*, suspecting, often accurately, that the next step would be a case against them. Making the sacrifice nonretroactive may be the practical solution, but this is in effect an amnesty. Many political activists will not accept that decision easily. In the meantime, most public attention has ignored these details and instead focused on suspected complicity or incompetence on the part of judges and prosecutors, including in actions against their own peers. The suspicions in many cases appear well founded, though they still discount the role of legal and resource limitations.

In the best of circumstances, corruption is difficult to prove.[62] In Latin America, it becomes still more so because of investigators' lack of skills and experience combined with legal and structural obstacles (inaccurate property registries, legal limitations on the release of information on bank accounts and other holdings, restrictions as to who can testify against defendants, and inadequate protections for witnesses). These additional constraints are difficult to eliminate because they benefit other groups (economic elites, foreign investors) and embody certain cultural values. Latin Americans' resistance to releasing information on their business operations and wealth is comparable to U.S citizens' resistance to the creation of a nation-wide identity card. It may appear illogical to outsiders, but cultural notions about privacy can be as strong as objections based only on intent to deceive.

The new criminal justice systems have rarely proved more effective in dealing with this type of crime. Underdeveloped and often politically infiltrated public ministries are one problem. The *garantista* (due process) focus of many codes typically benefits the white-collar criminal more than the plebian. With luck, the latter may get a free public defender; the former can pay a lawyer to use the new guarantees to undercut the charges against him. One consequence has been a renewed effort to create special bodies to investigate these high-profile crimes. Sometimes they are ad hoc creations (as in the case of Peru's special prosecutors appointed to investigate Vladimiro Montesinos, the eminence grise behind the Fujimori regime). In other instances, they are more permanent entities like Argentina's Anti-Corruption Office or Ecuador's Commission for the Civic Control of Corruption. Much like the *defensorías*, these offices lack the power to prosecute a case (although Argentina's Anti-Corruption Office can serve as *querellante*, complainant). They can publicize their findings, thus putting more pressure on the prosecution and courts to take action.

The longer-term solution lies in legal change and the institutional strengthening of the official investigative bodies. Procedures need to be simplified and immunities reduced. "Typifications" (definitions incorporated in the criminal code)

---

62. The Greylord case in Chicago is a case in point. Although eventually resulting in the indictment of some seventy officers of the court (including a few judges), it took years and the involvement of the U.S. Department of Justice to collect sufficient evidence. See Special Commission (1998).

of crimes require updating to capture the forms most common in the current era. This means adding crimes of recent origin and eliminating those that no longer make sense. In both Bolivia and Ecuador, some of the most severe sanctions currently apply to purely formalistic errors—essentially the failure to get the necessary signatures authorizing an otherwise legal expenditure. Although the monies were not misspent, the accused may be liable for repaying the entire amount. As this suggests, penalties may also need altering to put them into conformity with current priorities. It bears mentioning that the comptroller's office of both countries traditionally devoted most efforts to catching these formalistic errors, leaving little time to investigate more serious kinds of corruption. One additional reason for revising the penalties is their use in determining the statute of limitations (*prescripción*) for crimes. Where, as is often the case, the penalties are low, crimes are only prosecutable for a short period.

Aside from an inadequate legal framework, the biggest setback to handling suspected corruption is the sad state of those charged with investigating the alleged crimes. The criminal code reforms usually give this responsibility to the public ministries. In most countries these organizations are still a long way from being able to develop credible cases against political actors. Sometimes the impediment is misplaced loyalties, but agents motivated to get convictions often lack the skills to develop a case theory and collect the critical evidence. Judicial training is also important for judges to understand the types of evidence likely to be offered and to sensitize them to the issue involved. An administrative judge interviewed in Bolivia in 1999 noted, that lacking training, she had to ask her teenage son to help her read the financial reports presented as evidence in cases of suspected malfeasance.[63]

RESULTS AND IMPACT

For all the attendant problems, the judiciary in most countries now enjoys more political weight in checking the actions of other branches of government. Newly empowered constitutional and supreme courts and some lower-level judges have made surprisingly contrary decisions, stopping government programs, taking forward criminal actions, and granting rights to private complainants. Their rulings are not always consistent, have engendered enormous controversy, and have encouraged proposals to place constraints on their powers. They have also provoked direct government intervention via the replacement of a majority of supreme court

---

63. Just to make it clear, this judge would not have been asked to rule on any criminal responsibility, but her findings might have been submitted to the prosecutor's office for further actions. Here as in Ecuador, criminal charges are usually dropped, and the amounts to be repaid decreased or eliminated, in return for the defendant's voluntary departure from his or her job. Unfortunately, this practice makes the entire operation a handy dodge for getting rid of inconvenient employees.

justices—as most recently in Argentina, Ecuador, Paraguay, and Venezuela. Still ordinary citizens and political activists are increasingly seeing the courts as a channel for voicing their protests about state abuses. They may not have great faith in judicial efficacy, but they are willing to chance it.

From the standpoint of voice and individual remedies, the results can be considered positive, if falling short of the aspirations of many. Aggrieved citizens now have a variety of options to pursue, and some of them do lead to compensation for damages or the reversal of ongoing abuses. Satisfaction is hardly automatic and there are many pyrrhic victories, a positive ruling that will never be enforced. This equally true of demands that the "notoriously corrupt" be brought to justice. Criminal actions are more frequently initiated today, but very few of the allegedly guilty are actually convicted.[64] Here again, the process has advanced, but not yet to a successful conclusion.

From the standpoint of impact in actually discouraging abuses and improving government performance, the results are more doubtful. This is the public good aspect of the judiciary's oversight role. Individual justice is important, but, much like the resolution of private conflicts, its more vital role is in shaping future actions. More citizens are successfully making claims, but the odds are so long, and the chances of any specific public actor being held accountable so slight, that the disincentive effects seem virtually nil. Lack of enforcement capability or of *ergo omnes* effects (widely binding precedent) further dilute the impact.

Ironically, the judiciary has more impact on halting major government policy initiatives than in stopping municipalities from collecting illegal taxes or ensuring that public offices deliver services on an equitable basis. In the first instance, the judiciary interprets the rules as they apply to a single defendant. Noncompliance is obvious and may threaten a constitutional crisis. In the second, a new interpretation may not even be required, but the responsibility for deviations is divided among hundreds or thousands of individual public actors. As a ruling against a government agency commonly means only that the losing party must reverse a specific action (usually without reimbursing damages and often with an ability to delay any repayment ordered), the wider consequences are slight. The same official or agency is free to apply the objected practice to the next victims who will also have to seek judicial remedy. For criminal actions, rules are less ambiguous, and there is by definition individualization of responsibility. The impediments to success, and thus to any disincentive effect, lie more in the complexities of the process and the variety of actors whose cooperation is essential to making it work.

64. For example, of the more than 600 cases of suspected corruption investigated and referred to the courts by the Argentine Anticorruption Office between 1999 and 2002, none had yet gone to trial by early 2003. Private communication from Director of Planning and Policy for Transparency, Anticorruption Office. With the entrance of a new national administration in mid-2003, the situation is slowly improving, but by late 2005, with more than 1,000 investigations forwarded, none had resulted in a conviction.

The obstacles to changing this situation and enhancing the courts' ability to alter governments' basic operating procedures are several-fold. First, the victims are usually interested only in securing a personal remedy. That is an entirely rational behavior, in light of the impediments to achieving anything more and the lack of additional payoffs for a more altruistic approach.[65] Second, governments themselves have little reason to want the courts to increase their ability to make them behave.[66] Third, donors either do not appreciate the issues or, as in the case of the development banks, fear the repercussions for their most cherished policies. Thus, individual constitutional complaints become the preferred strategy for all the obvious stakeholders—and to some extent for the courts themselves, as constitutional law continues to have far more prestige than mere administrative applications. This is unfortunate, but changing the situation will require a longer-range vision on everyone's part and a willingness to sacrifice individual short-term gains for collective, longer-term benefits.

RELATIONSHIP TO OTHER PROGRAMS

Proponents of increased judicial activism often seem to work in a strategic vacuum. Because much of their success does depend on changing laws, they seem inclined to assume this is all that is needed. Their obvious preference for the constitutional dimensions has complicated their project by overburdening that jurisdiction, turning all issues into questions of rights and thus overlooking the potential for leveraging incremental changes in government performance via the far less sexy, ordinary judicial review. The courts have cooperated with this tack. Constitutional law enjoys the same privileged place in the judicial world that it does in the academic sphere. This contrasts dramatically with administrative law, where few aspire to work, and with rare exceptions, often do so by default. Constitutional cases get press attention; administrative ones receive yawns. Judges (and prosecutors) handling suspected corruption are still another breed. When they are serious about their tasks, they seem more interested in fighting vice than in developing an institutional role. In fact, many of them are dismissed by their colleagues as publicity-seeking vedettes.

General efforts to enhance the courts' political power, if most usually in the

---

65. Altruism is generally less successful in civil law systems because of the lack of binding precedent. In common-law countries, government's increasing tendency to negotiate out-of-court settlements is a recognition that a contrary ruling would set the standard for other cases.

66. See, however, B. Magaloni (2003), on the reasons why an administration might increase the courts' oversight role. Her arguments, though similar to those used in the context of Eastern Europe, refer largely to macro policies and politics in the face of likely changes of the party in power. They explain why constitutional review powers might be enhanced but do not extend to administrative review or corruption cases where the macro concerns have less relevance.

constitutional sphere, do benefit from actions in other areas—the criminal justice reforms' emphasis on due process rights and the access strategists' efforts to get marginalized groups to court, whether individually or collectively. They also benefit from the institutional strengthening programs' successful reduction of the possibility for external intervention in judicial decisions, appointments, and budgets. These apparent synergies, however, are more coincidental than intentional and have had other unanticipated consequences. As a result, and as elaborated in the next section, the combined impact has its negative as well as positive side.

EMERGING PROBLEMS

The speed with which judiciaries have acquired their new roles and powers has produced predictable misuses and abuses. They have been compounded by citizen expectations as to how the more autonomous judges will deal with their concerns and by the efforts of political actors, within and outside the government, to manipulate their operations. To the extent anyone anticipated the downstream consequences of empowering the third branch of government the visions were undoubtedly different and continue to be so.[67] Moreover, despite widespread criticism of the immediate results, there is no visible consensus on what ought to be different. Latin America is now experiencing the judicialization of politics, and, as elsewhere, it has costs.[68] It also continues to experience the politicization of the judiciary, albeit with important changes in the means and content of that process. Whereas before politicization meant that the entire judiciary toed the political line set by governmental elites, today political allegiances often divide a judiciary no longer controlled by any one party, faction, or ideological strain.

The new style of politicization, combined with greater autonomy, can put the judiciary out of sync with the other branches of government or further distance it from citizen expectations. Outgoing political parties often timed their judicial reforms to ensure a new court or bench favorable to their own policies and concerns.[69] The administration that follows is then faced with the choice of either tolerating an unsympathetic court or violating constitutional principles to replace it. In

67. For an interesting and critical discussion of the concept of judicial independence in the context of the United States with some comparative examples, see chapters in Burbank and Friedman (2002).

68. See Tate and Vallinder (1995), for a global view.

69. The 1994 constitutional reforms in Mexico also replaced the entire supreme court. Observers usually credit the ruling party's (PRI) expectation that it would lose control of the two other branches of government and its wish to ensure judicial support for its agenda and protect its members from legal action. The new justices now have fixed terms. Their relationship with the PAN executive elected in 2000 has been difficult. See González Oropeza (1996) and B. Magaloni (2003). Menem's court stacking in the early 1990s (Abaid and Thieberger 2005; Carrió 1996; Helmke 2005, Verbitsky 1993) is another example, accomplished here not by removing judges but by adding positions.

post-Fujimori Peru, post-Pinochet Chile, post-Menem Argentina, and post-Zedillo Mexico, the governments initially opted for the rule of law, despite the threats to their programs. Only Chávez in Venezuela took another tack, sacking all the justices and placing a court more sympathetic to his cause; however, he can hardly be counted as a constitutionalist. Under the Kirchner administration in Argentina and the Duarte administration in Paraguay (both entering in 2003), there has been another sea change. Both presidents publicly announced their intent to replace a good portion of the supreme courts and, within a year of taking power, had fulfilled their promises. The actions have been popular. Both courts suffered from terrible reputations for abuses, corruption, or outright incompetence. Nevertheless, a minority of observers, while agreeing renewal was needed, has expressed doubts about the methods used and the precedents they set for further political intervention. In late 2004, Ecuador's President Gutiérrez outdid the others' record by sacking the supreme court, constitutional court, judicial council, electoral tribunal, and various executive officials. This time, the public was less supportive. Popular protests led to Gutiérrez's ouster and arrest. In late 2005, after several abortive attempts, a new court was seated.

The problems extend far beyond being saddled with a less than ideologically compatible or otherwise unsatisfactory set of judges and justices. Patience and time can shift the bench's composition. The additional difficulties are more transcendental. Increasing judicial independence is a classic example of a reactive reform, based on eliminating a broadly criticized status quo with little or no consideration as to the further characteristics of the new order. It is these issues that now require more reflective attention.

Many problems originate in the courts' sudden assumption of their new powers and their consequent lack of preparation or institutional policies for wielding them. When even the United States, the path breaker in the area of judicial review, is still debating whether its courts have applied it with excessive or insufficient zeal, it is no surprise that countries with far less than 200 years to study the issues are having their own doubts as to the courts' role. Ten years ago one might have pointed to U.S. judicial principles like ripeness and judicial restraint as guides. The concepts are still important, but their application is now perceived as far more ambiguous as is the U.S. model as a whole. It would be convenient if new policies could be developed through a lengthy process of internal reflection, ample study and commentary by academic jurists, and popular discussion. Latin America's courts, however, are too busy making decisions to have time for contemplative action, and many of their members may lack the necessary talents and background. Meanwhile, their actions are often so divisive that outside commentary and broader debate have themselves become politicized. Moreover, many courts do not seem interested in outside input, interpreting their autonomy as placing them above external views.

One frequent observation, which does merit immediate attention, is that many court members have their own political axes to grind. These can be purely personal or institutional or involve a separate political agenda. Courts have been involved in what can only be called personal vendettas against political actors or, alternatively, have shown an excessive loyalty to recognizing the interests of those who placed them in office, even after the latter have left power. Those accusing them of these biases often seem poorly informed,[70] but there have been enough questionable verdicts in favor of former patrons to raise a red flag in several countries.

Courts' rulings on issues directly affecting their own interests are another dimension of the problem. There is no easy solution here. The entire judiciary can hardly excuse itself from deciding on cases affecting its own pensions, as well as those of other public workers, determining the applicability of national law to its own operations, or deciding where certain inconvenient issues will be aired.[71] Reaching a decision is the judges' responsibility, but the public can expect that they do so as objectively as possible, with a clear recognition of their less than disinterested status, and with ample explanations of why they decide as they do. Unfortunately, many courts caught in this bind have been anything but transparent about their reasoning process and thus, rightly or wrongly, are perceived as having decided solely on the basis of self-interest. A conviction that autonomy means not having to explain to anyone when combined with an apparent inability to see the larger impact on their own credibility or the public good can be deadly.

On the first point, many Latin American courts seem to operate on the assumption that ordinary rules about transparency and accountability do not apply to them.[72] This is doubtless a holdover from the period when they were so unimportant that no one cared what they did. In light of their enhanced status, a continued failure to publish statistics, judgments, and detailed budgets or to accept new policies on assets declarations, contracting, and external audits will not go unnoticed. It also puts them out of sync with new citizen demands for greater transparency from the entire public sector. Courts justify their policies by arguing that releasing this information will reduce their independence vis-à-vis the rest of

70. One example is a January 2003 ruling by a Peruvian trial judge (in an anticorruption court) ordering the *excarcelación* (release from preventive detention) of Vladamiro Montesinos in one of the cases against him. The reason was excessive delay in bringing the case to trial. As Montesinos faces many other charges and is already serving a nine-year sentence for one conviction, he remains in prison. Still, President Alejandro Toledo and many citizens demanded the judge be investigated.

71. Three examples are a decision of the Brazilian Supremo Tribunal Federal on a matter affecting state pensions (including their own), the Paraguayan supreme court's constitutional interpretation to give its members permanent tenure, and the Argentine supreme court's ruling that judges should not pay income tax, as it would violate the constitutional prohibition on reducing their salaries.

72. See Motta (2001), for a discussion of the Argentine court's rulings on general questions of citizens' right to information and the effects on their own operations. As Abaid and Thieberger (2005, 18) note, this was one of the motives for the threatened impeachment. See Hammergren (2002b), for a treatment of the general problem of judicial accountability in the region.

government and some private actors. What they fail to take into account, or perhaps consider and reject, is the notion that the accountability is to the citizen-user of their services. This is the crux of their failure to grasp the bigger picture—the idea that, under a rule of law state, they are responsible for ensuring that the law is applied equally to all, including to themselves.

These same issues also extend to charges that the new courts, and especially those tasked with constitutional review functions, are promoting their own political agenda, not only interpreting the law but also setting the direction of public policy. The criticism comes from both the right and the left. Colombia's Constitutional Court and Costa Rica's Constitutional Chamber are often criticized for a social state of law mentality (resting, it is true, on constitutional guarantees inspired by this ideology).[73] The Chilean Supreme Court has been described as applying the 1980 constitution to the letter of its neoliberal, promarket intent.[74] Mexico's PRI-selected justices are viewed as unnecessarily obstructing the Panista efforts to loosen up the former ruling party's statist ideology.

These courts and others accused of excessive dedication to an outdated political project can base their actions firmly in their respective constitution and secondary law. The question is how far they should go in using those documents to direct policymaking, especially but not exclusively, when popular sentiment and government policy are moving in new directions, or when the laws themselves, as is all too common, are drafted with insufficient analysis of their consequences. It would be an exaggeration to suggest all courts are sensitized to this last, very critical issue—the likelihood that the laws or constitutional provisions they are asked to apply are themselves a recipe for disaster. Those that are have occasionally come to this realization long before the laws' executive and legislative sponsors.[75] Wherever the recognition originates, the courts inevitably face the same dilemma—blatantly ruling against a legal or constitutional provision or applying it and being blamed for the consequences.

Courts have other options. They can refuse to consider a case for reasons of form or substance, limit the effects of their decision, or issue a ruling that indicates a preferred direction of action without explicitly defining its contents. These are the principles of "political restraint" and "ripeness" as developed by the U.S Supreme Court—waiting until the social and political climate seems to dictate a more rigid

73. See Fuentes and Amaya (2001); Amaya (2005) on Colombia; and Wilson et al. (2004) on Costa Rica.
74. See Hilbink (2003).
75. This appears to be the case of the Brazilian courts' role in determining which legally mandated index should be used to adjust pensions and other government payments. Surprisingly, several judges interviewed maintained that, until recently, the Ministry of Finance had never intervened in the process, apparently oblivious to the economic consequences. The judges hearing these cases were the first to recognize that millions of small awards could add up to very large amounts, many subject to "immediate" payment. This recognition is facilitated in Brazil because the courts directly manage the payments, receiving funds from the affected agencies designated for that purpose.

or just different interpretation of constitutional guarantees or until the other branches can remedy their own mistakes. Although Latin American constitutions, rich in guaranteed rights and strictures on institutional powers, do add complications, courts can also rely on the concept of programmatic rights (those that express aspirations rather than absolute guarantees) or broaden or narrow the interpretation of mandated or prohibited functions. Their frequent refusal to do so seems most often a consequence of their own political convictions or an inadequate appreciation of the damage they might do.

Courts' frequently greater caution in dealing with economic issues suggests that they can waive their principles and ideologies when fearful of provoking a catastrophe. Examples include the Mexican court's decision on *anatocismo* (upholding the constitutionality of compound interest), the Brazilian Supreme Federal Tribunal's decision to allow Collor's freezing of bank accounts, and the Costa Rican chamber's last-minute resolution not to override the central bank's ability to set exchange rates. One suspects that one reason courts dash in to force policy directions is that they simply have no idea of the possible repercussions. As they begin to appreciate them, they may well exercise greater caution and take advantage of the ploys for avoiding definitive decisions. Still, the ultimate remedy of readjusting legal norms is not the judiciary's responsibility and rather lies with the other branches of government. Where the others neglect to do their part or, still worse, continue to enact ill-advised legislation, there is not much the judges can do.

On a purely institutional level, the judicialization of politics and politicization of the judiciary also have costs for internal cohesion. This is common to all judicial bodies. (One has only to look at the current U.S Supreme Court to appreciate the phenomenon). The difference in Latin America is the greater role of purely partisan loyalties and the underdevelopment of a corporate sense of common purpose. Latin American supreme courts, like Latin American judicial councils, or judiciaries as a whole, include far too many members who interpret their role only in the most individual sense. They rarely seem to have an appreciation for any kind of collective product or for the notion of how their decisions can affect the future of their societies. As a consequence, high courts are often divided by purely idiosyncratic or outdated political identifications. These can be so diverse and so esoteric that they defeat outsiders' attempts to understand them. The "blue" and "white" factions in the Argentine judicial council are one example, but at least they represent only two positions.[76] Trying to understand the divisions among the thirty members of the Ecuadorian Supreme Court or the fifteen Salvadoran justices can be an exercise in frustration.

Constitutional tribunals despite their novelty and the tendency to limit their

---

76. See Ungar (2002, 179), for an attempt to explain these differences.

members' terms can be equally perplexing.[77] It has been said that Colombia's first group of activist constitutional judges was an unwelcome surprise to many politicians and that future appointments would likely be made to counteract such tendencies.[78] Observers also claim, however, that, as the same judges neared the end of their terms, they began to decide differently, possibly with an eye to securing another government position. As noted earlier, the Peruvian Constitutional Tribunal, despite being saddled with a law intended to curb its impact, has become more aggressive in overruling policy and past judgments. Given the need for six of the seven judges to overrule legislation, this does suggest more internal unity. Because of their smaller size and workload as compared with supreme courts, the constitutional bodies may have more success in forging a common perspective even within their short tenures. That may eventually make them more predictable, though not necessarily in directions that coincide with executive preferences. It is one thing to reach agreement on constitutional interpretation and another to develop strategies for an effective checks and balance role. The latter appears to take much longer, is not solely the judiciary's responsibility, and is still evolving in the industrialized nations.

Many of these emerging problems arise from outdated legal frameworks, defining both substantive law and the balance of powers itself, and from the shortcomings of other governmental institutions. Some, however, stem from the fact that judicial independence, of both the political and institutional variety, progressed more rapidly than internal reform, leaving countries not just with politically incompatible courts, but also with judges whose integrity, intellectual talents, and view of their responsibilities are still very much in question. Time, and a better evaluation and disciplinary system, could deal with this, but it also raises the issue of judicial accountability, the absent element in the new equation. This is not an easy topic for any society, and certain international trends indeed seem to place courts, whether national or international, above the other branches of government and thus with little accountability to anyone. It is in this line that one could interpret the efforts by the Inter-American Human Rights Court or its African counterpart to seek funding from international agencies so as to not depend on the states on whose actions they will be ruling.[79] Much human rights doctrine seems to give the courts a primus inter pares status—the check on other branches of government that is never balanced. Whereas most proponents of this line would doubtless like

77. This practice follows the European model, intended to make the courts more compatible with changing political priorities. See Aucoin (1992, 450 and passim). French members of the Conseil Constitutionnel serve nine-year terms (except for former presidents of the republic, who hold lifetime appointments). German members of the Federal Constitutional Court serve twelve-year terms.

78. See Gómez (1996).

79. Members of the Inter-American Court were exploring this possibility in the late 1990s. More recently the African body has tabled similar suggestions. Both courts face problems in collecting quotas from member nations, but they also see the device as a means of ensuring their own independence.

to see Latin American constitutional bodies reformed and restaffed before they receive this status, they clearly do not view accountability as a major issue. For ordinary citizens and for governments, it is important. Especially where judges serve long careers and are socialized into institutional attitudes, the opportunity to have some say in early appointments does not seem sufficient. There are no obvious solutions. Just as the courts' role in checking governmental abuses could be improved, their vulnerability to some sort of outside check also requires further exploration.

CONCLUSIONS

Regardless of whether efforts to increase the courts' political role can be considered a reform program, the activities included in this area have had a visible impact on Latin American societies. To date, the impact has raised many issues, ranging from the need to improve the incumbents' capabilities to questions about how far they should go in overriding and shaping government policies. The absence of a coherent strategy has not impeded dramatic changes. It has placed their desirability in question. For the most part, citizens appear to favor the new judicial activism and demand more where courts have not fully assumed this role. Nonetheless, dissenting voices are being heard, not only in terms of impacts on the government's ability to make policy and otherwise attend to business, but also as to the content of the rule of law being realized. Where judges take sides, even for the most altruistic reasons, their ability to reshape the rules to their own ideological preferences raises serious issues of accountability and legitimacy. A recent study in Brazil provoked strong, if divisive, reactions with its findings that judges (especially lower-level and younger ones) believed their responsibility for protecting the weaker parties to a case superseded the need to uphold other legal values, like the enforcement of contracts.[80]

Although there are many intended and unintended interactions with other strategic goals, the most important are clearly in the area of internal institutional strengthening. Courts freed from the traditional sources of external influence are now able to check government actions and nullify legislation on the basis of their own reading of what is constitutionally permissible. Their reactions to the situation are as varied as the differences in their composition, skills, and powers. The results have been criticized for imposing overly narrow appreciations on new government initiatives and impeding efforts to balance the public budget. Courts that take constitutional guarantees seriously can drastically increase government's fiscal responsibilities. Nevertheless, despite their powers of obstruction, the tribunals have been remarkably ineffectual in decreasing systematic abuses.

80. See Castelar (2003).

The problems involve more than the courts. In some sense, the constitutional framework itself is out of balance. Apart from the courts' own shortcomings, the situation is not conducive to a sustainable rule of law. Latin American countries are famous for having social welfare constitutions financed by Third World budgets. The situation was tenable as long as most citizens did not claim what was promised. As they begin to do so, constitutional rigidities extract a high price. During the return to constitutional democracy, political leaders relied heavily on extra-constitutional measures or exaggerated use of executive decrees to get things done. As courts begin to rule against such mechanisms, governments' room for maneuver narrowed. This is not the courts' fault. Most blame should go to the governments for failing to transcend the practices of expediency and find ways to work within the law. Finally, the constitutions commonly recognize a variety of rights and privileges claimed by certain status groups.[81] These entitlements, though not available to all citizens, comprise commitments that must be honored. In addition, these and other groups have laid claim to "acquired rights," based only on tradition, not on any constitutional recognition, and sometimes without any other legal foundation. In short, Latin America's courts are being asked to apply and work within a set of rules not designed for full and simultaneous enactment in the real world. That they are being asked to do this on the basis of little experience and possibly with inadequate skills and knowledge complicates the task, but their own shortcomings are the least of the problem.

If Latin Americans want a positive system of checks and balances, one that ensures a lawful, equitable, and successful pursuit of their developmental goals, they may well require a reassessment of the framework on which it is based and of how far they want their courts to go in enforcing it. Judges can find clever formulas to avoid requiring the impossible, but those are stopgap measures, not the basis on which the rule of law normally operates.[82] Reaching a new consensus will not be easy, and any short-term agreement will likely require further adjustment. The courts must participate, but they cannot be responsible for the entire process. The necessary decisions far transcend their present or future responsibilities, but they are essential to their expanded roles.

81. These may range from the special legal *fueros* offered to the military, police, and political appointees and the recognition of indigenous communities' right to operate by their own laws to the explicit or implicit recognition of certain acquired rights won by classes of public or private employees.

82. One interesting example is a September 2004 decision by Brazil's STF, determining that the non-payment of taxes on pensions is not an acquired right and thereby could be altered by law. In light of the Brazilian Constitution's protection of acquired rights, the STF's only room for maneuver is in deciding whether a long-standing practice constitutes a right.

PART II PROBLEMS AND REMEDIES

SIX JUDICIAL REFORM AS A PROBLEM OF FOCUS: WHY THE PARTS
DON'T ADD UP TO A COHERENT WHOLE

Judicial reform is a new discipline, but not so new that it escapes questions about
its intellectual and practical value. In the past few years, external observers and
long-term participants have begun a serious reexamination of its accomplishments
on both dimensions. This process is not likely to end soon, especially regarding
the more transcendental questions about reform's ultimate objectives and purpose.
There is an emerging consensus that neither these nor a series of more immediate concerns are likely to be advanced without direct attention to some basic flaws
in the disciplinary development and its application to real problems. Here critics
have pointed to a series of issues, ranging from a tendency to design and execute
projects in a near informational vacuum, through an absence of systematic efforts
to build and test theories and strategies, to a simple failure to draw on lessons
of experience or to consolidate and disseminate them adequately. The problems
may be inevitable given the field's dominance by practitioners and advocates more
inclined to action than to contemplation. However, they are sufficiently serious to
threaten its immediate utility and longer-term survival.

In this and the following chapters, the focus shifts from partial approaches to
three larger issues: how to turn approaches into strategies, how to ensure they are
based on experiential knowledge, and how to combine the separate lines of action
into a single reform. Some of the problems giving rise to this emphasis have already
been referenced in the discussion of the five approaches. The present chapter
explores the phenomena more systematically, focusing on the differences between
strategic and tactical reforms, and between knowledge-based and ad hoc programming, and proposing explanations for why ad hoc tactics have so often been
the "strategy" of choice. In the three final chapters, suggestions are forwarded as
to how reform efforts might become more grounded in the lessons of experience,
how they can shift from a tactical to a strategic focus, and how concerned reformers can improve their chances of effecting these changes.

An earlier version of this chapter was published in Spanish in *Revista de CLAD: Reforma y Democracia*,
2002, no. 23: 41–80.

TACTICAL PROGRAMMING CONTRASTED WITH THE STRATEGIC IDEAL

The preceding discussions of strategic approaches to reform exaggerate the orderliness of many real programs. Whether intentionally partial or self-consciously holistic, they too often are characterized by low levels of internal coordination and weak empirical and theoretical foundations. Within each of the approaches discussed, there are elements of a strategy. This hardly means that everyone working in an area operates from that perspective. Some participants seem to be along for the ride, using the assumed existence of an overarching strategy to justify whatever they propose to add. This presumed connection, virtue by association, reduces their inclination to justify their contribution on the basis of lessons learned elsewhere. Activities are included because of their prima facie logical fit, not because of what experience has taught about their efficacy. Many participants seem completely oblivious to the fact that their proposals are not novel, and that a review of past efforts might suggest ways to improve their impact, or in some cases, recommend against their adoption in any form. Moreover, in larger programs, the partial approaches often coexist as disconnected stovepipes—parallel activities which are never successfully integrated into a common effort that might maximize their complementarities and overcome their inconsistencies.

The reform efforts mounted during the early and mid 1980s could not be described as strategic in any but the most rudimentary sense. They rarely began with an analysis of the overall judicial system and its weaknesses, identified causal relationships, set prioritized objectives, defined sequences of activities to achieve them, coordinated inputs, or identified obstacles and key assumptions affecting their success. Instead they tended to pick off problems as they found them, and propose isolated activities as remedies. This was certainly true of the early law-based approaches to criminal code reform. They identified the problem as an outdated procedure and proposed to remedy it by enacting a code incorporating a series of "axiomatic principles." As it developed, the problem far transcended procedural rules, the principles are hardly axiomatic, and new laws proved an insufficient means to alter behaviors. The tendencies are also seen in USAID's first intervention in El Salvador in the mid-1980s.[1] Having identified impunity of human rights abusers as the problem to be solved, project designers went no further in analyzing its causes and instead created a program based on three activities: formation of a special investigative unit, protection for judges, and financing of a forensics laboratory. Not surprisingly, the results were minimal.

Contemporary reforms can still be divided among those with a strategic focus and those which are tactically organized. The difference is not the breadth of the activities adopted. A strategic reform may eventually feature a few activities in a

---

1. See Mudge et al. (1988).

fairly narrow area, while a tactical one may include dozens of discrete actions, organized into several components. The distinction instead lies in how the program elements are chosen and organized. Strategic planners work in the context of a broader systemic analysis, proceeding from the most general to the most specific categories. Their methodology can be best understood in terms of the schematic diagrams they use to lay out their programs. The most famous is the logical framework, a chart starting with goals and purposes, and working down through results, benchmarks, outputs and inputs. Another less complicated method uses a pyramid (or two pyramids, as a prior version also diagrams the identification and causal analysis of problems) to illustrate the relationship between the ends pursued and the individual activities, programs, and intermediate results.

For example, as illustrated in the strategic pyramid, a reform aiming at improving the court's economic impact (goal) might have the objective of improving court handling of debt collection cases, pursued by decreasing delay in case processing, raising the chances of getting a judgment, and facilitating access for small and medium clients (components). Activities involved might include legal reform, improved case management, readjustments to fee systems, and judicial training and monitoring, each in turn requiring a series of inputs. Most projects are far more complex, with multiple objectives and components for each, and a host of activities and inputs associated with them. A more detailed depiction would also indicate the connections among the various lines of action. For example, an activity like training will be used in several or all of the components, although the content will vary according to the specific impacts pursued. Separate training programs might be established for each objective. It is usually more practical to create one training program incorporating the multiple targets. This second option also allows for a measure of cross-fertilization. A training activity focusing on procedural efficiency can simultaneously sensitize participants to dealing with nontraditional court users.

Equally important, but still more often overlooked is the accompanying, inverted pyramid, illustrating the problem analysis. The selection and further design of interventions is based on the logic outlined here, where a series of externally perceived problems (low investment, lack of credit availability, higher transactions costs for businesses) is linked to a number of "perverse" internal behaviors (slow processing of cases, unenforced judgments), which in turn are traced to institutional factors (incentives, informal rules, organization and distribution of resources), and then to underlying causes (for example, the motives of powerful external actors). Although the underlying causes may be few, they often are not susceptible to direct change. Thus, the strategic pyramid is more likely to work at the intermediate level of institutional factors and the behaviors they produce, attempting to mitigate or short-circuit the causal impacts or overcome causes of a historical nature (the origins of the perverse incentives, although often no longer actively supporting them). By inverting the analytic pyramid, the intent is not to highlight reductionism

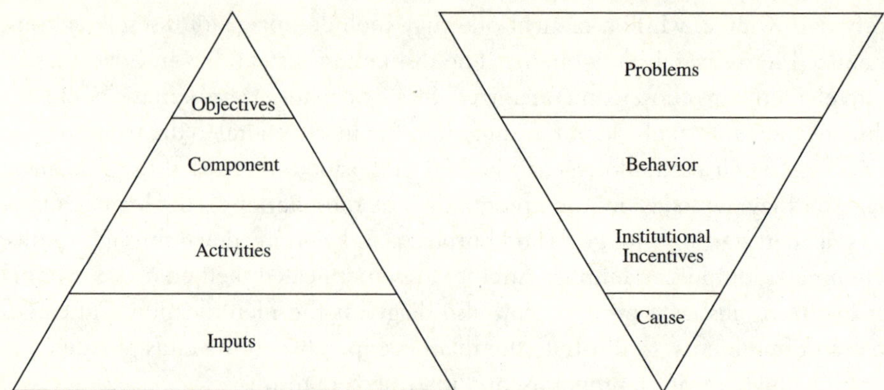

Fig. 2. Strategic and causal pyramids: (a) strategic pyramid; (b) diagnostic pyramid.

and magic bullets, but only to demonstrate the way in which a particular institutional arrangement gives rise to a series of problematic actions.

Its susceptibility to being presented schematically does not guarantee a strategy's effectiveness. It does allow outsiders to understand, evaluate, and monitor the plan. Evaluation of the strategy's likely success focuses on the internal linkages and the assumptions (which also must be stated) as to why they will hold. These assumptions encompass both the reasons (based partly on theory and partly on experience) for believing that activity X will lead to result Y, and the context-specific conditions which might interfere with the connection. To the extent the strategy lays out its goals, specific objectives, components and outputs, activities and inputs, it allows tracking of progress and eventual success. A strategy for institutional reform is not a blueprint. It is predictable that many slips will occur along the way. Still, knowing more or less what is expected to happen permits those charged with implementation and those reviewing it to assess the internal logic and catch errors requiring further corrections.

Tactical approaches short-circuit this process in a variety of ways. They often start at the bottom of the strategic pyramid (with activities or inputs) and eliminate the intermediate steps. They rarely work in terms of complex causality (the behaviors, attitudes, or incentives that may encourage an objected practice), prioritized problems, or strategic assumptions. In El Salvador, impunity was a political more than a technical problem. Police who had orders not to go after high level suspects would not act differently with a forensics lab. Judges selected for their political leanings and susceptible to arbitrary removal had reasons other than physical fear for deciding as they did.

Tactical solutions often work on the logic, expressed by one consultant, that if country X has 1,000 judicial weaknesses, attacking any of them is an improvement. While sometimes described as programming toward targets of opportunity, the opportunity appears to refer to the activity, not its downstream impact. Strategies also use tactical targets of opportunity. The difference is their selection not only for their immediate feasibility, but for their hypothesized utility in leveraging further change. Alternatively, tactical programs frequently identify interventions by arguing that if a well-functioning judiciary publishes judgments or uses computers, than making those additions to one which is not functioning well will improve its performance. In the most rudimentary version, activities are simply selected on the basis of what a donor or technical assistance provider normally does. This man-with-a-hammer methodology often ends up conflating the problem with its solution. The "problem" is that this judiciary lacks a training program; the solution is to provide one. In the larger scheme of things the presence or absence of training is not a problem. It is an observable fact, potentially useful in explaining and modifying behaviors and outputs with more transcendental importance.

Most contemporary reform programs are more tactically than strategically organized. Reform critics often describe them as "Christmas trees"– a hodgepodge of actions joined only by their presumed contribution to a common goal. As the previous discussions indicate, the current situation is still more complex. The various reform areas, strategies, or approaches can be thought of as the trees, each comprising a collection of activities organized around a single theme—modernization, access, or independence. So called "holistic projects," join the trees into a forest; similar activities located in different reform approaches are no more coordinated with each other than they are with the other ornaments on their respective trees.

While planners have an inherent preference for strategies, it must be admitted that the jury is not in on which approach will produce the most positive change over the longer run. Strategies are complex, and thus subject to many points of breakdown. These may stem from flawed analysis, assumptions, and design, or in problems encountered in delivering the various parts in the necessary form and order. As we saw, the efficiency-enhancing programs frequently skipped the recommended procedural rationalizations and went straight to installing computers, thus automating a flawed process. Similar breakdowns occurred in the other approaches, undermining their strategic content. Codes went into effect before organizations were prepared to implement them, and judicial councils and constitutional courts had their initial design subverted by those hoping to weaken their impact.

Strategies select harder objectives and thus face more obstacles. It is one thing to try reducing political intervention in judicial appointments and another to offer to build a school or computerize offices. A tactical approach, letting a hundred flowers bloom, might conceivably alter enough of the institutional context to induce more fundamental changes in behavior. Because tactical approaches often do not define their objectives beyond placing the immediate input, they can avoid evaluation by the more demanding criteria used for strategies. However, the downstream consequences in improving outputs and affecting extra-sector projects (economic growth, equity, political stability) are the ultimate justifications for undertaking judicial reforms, and by that token, should be used to evaluate their results. The question of whether strategic or tactical approaches are more successful in achieving them could be tested empirically; unfortunately, no one has yet thought to do this.

The bias here is toward strategies, and beyond this, a strategy which links the multiple approaches. Chapter 8 looks at some proposals for getting there, although only suggesting what the product might resemble. The ultimate goal, a theory of the judicial role in contemporary society and how it might be improved, is far beyond the scope of the current volume. What is important for the moment is that reform participants recognize its absence and thus the need to consider their present efforts a work in progress. Over the short run, even the partial strategies teased out of the several reform components could use improvements. As discussed in the previous chapters, some are further advanced than others. The criminal justice and the efficiency-enhancement programs can be considered real strategies, despite their oversights and far from perfect implementation. Access, institutional and political strengthening have a long way to go in this regard. They remain highly tactical collections of isolated interventions, lacking a clear vision of their intended end states or how their diverse contributions will combine to achieve them.

KNOWLEDGE-BASED VERSUS AD HOC EFFORTS

A strategic focus is one thing; an effective strategy is another. Efficacy also depends on adequate analysis, sound theory, and a good empirical foundation. Purely tactical actions would benefit from these additions, but they are almost as scare as strategic approaches. One of the real puzzles of current reform programming is how little attention it pays to experience derived from efforts elsewhere or in the same country. As will be further elaborated, part of this stems from the difficulty of accessing information and the premium on doing something now, but action in an informational vacuum as often seems intentional as a product of necessity. Some of the reasons for this behavior are discussed below. To underline their importance, a few examples can be given.

Reform designers, it is true, have become increasingly aware of what can be called the standard elements in any program: training, computers, new appointment systems, legal assistance, and new laws. While they often justify their proposals on the basis of "successes elsewhere," their interest in obtaining more details about the organization of the successful venture, its strengths and weaknesses, or the conditions affecting either is usually extremely limited.[2] The previous

---

2. I will simply note that I have seen donor proposals justified in terms of "lessons learned" in up to a dozen countries, some of which to my knowledge do not have reform programs. Most of those reading the proposals have no basis for making that judgment. Those who do, exercise professional courtesy in ignoring the inaccuracies.

chapters suggested that many reputed successes have hardly been proven as such, and that some might as easily be considered partial failures. The "principles" underlying criminal justice reforms are one such example. Most of them are simply matters of faith. To this day, no one has really demonstrated that an oral, accusatory system is inherently fairer, more transparent, less abusive of human rights, or more efficient in processing cases. They certainly have not demonstrated that it is more effective in combating crime. Granted, most modern criminal justice systems feature some sort of oral hearing and do emphasize what the French call the "contradictory principle" but this is as true of the modern inquisitorial version as more purely accusatorial ones. Moreover, it could be argued that modern criminal justice systems function better because of other elements—more professional staff, higher budgets, better coordination among the parts, more oversight, and an emphasis on certain due process rights that is entirely independent of their respective legal traditions.

The popularity of judicial councils is another example. They were adopted in imitation of European successes when even Europeans were expressing concerns about the problems they created. Moreover the imitations were poor ones and did not take into account the different circumstances in their countries of origin.[3] The benefits of automation in speeding up case processing and reducing court congestion are a third example. As discussed, they may help a judiciary that prioritizes reducing delay keep track of its cases, but absent this very important condition and a series of other changes, have so far not proved effective in their Latin American version. Contrary to an early study that concludes they were the principal input explaining delay reduction in the countries surveyed,[4] it could also be argued that courts which want to reduce delay are more likely to purchase computers. The statistical correlation on which the authors base their conclusion also supports the alternative interpretation—the important variable is the motive, not the automation itself. If it holds, then it is doubtful that giving computers to a court not interested in reducing delay would have much positive effect. Results from many automation programs suggest just such a situation.

A second aspect of this information-free planning is the failure of reform proponents to review the varying organization and outcomes of certain key activities to identify what are often called best practices. With all the investment that has gone into training, the apparent lack of interest in taking a critical look at past programs, including those in the same country, is astounding. Conceivably, people who propose to do training assume they know the best practices, or that they are too obvious to warrant further review. Admittedly, their inclinations are similar, but this can encourage the replication of the same mistakes. They certainly have

3. See Hammergren (2002a).
4. See Buscaglia and Dakolias (1999).

not advanced in resolving some of the evident weaknesses in training's contribution to overall reform: its high costs; unproven impact on performance; and limited ability to alter attitudes and ingrained habits. Too many training programs still follow an academic pattern (remedial lectures on legal theory); assess needs by asking judges what they think they ought to know; evaluate impacts by inquiring whether they liked the course and thought they learned anything; and base their anti-corruption effort on courses in ethics. What appear to be critical choices, like off-site or on-site delivery, course length, use of foreign or local instructors, or linkage to career paths seem entirely driven by resource and other constraints or by ad hoc preferences, not by a review of the alternatives and trade-offs.

There have been recent efforts to hold regional and global seminars to bring trainers together to discuss their activities. Unfortunately, these usually devolve into little more than show-and-tell sessions, in which training directors present their programs in the most favorable light. The exchanges do increase awareness of additional possibilities. Absent a more serious review of the issues, they may result in little more than a broader choice of ornaments for the training Christmas tree. Much the same can be said of programs to foment exchanges among those involved in judicial automation programs or overall reforms. Conceivably, the meetings are a first step in building information network, but their impact on creating a cumulative knowledge base is still very limited.

One immediate effect of information exchange has been the strengthening of another tendency—the increasing fascination with the role of new technology in resolving longstanding problems. Court automation is just one element; others include the use of Internet, distance learning, document scanning, bar codes, DNA and fingerprint data bases, videotaping of court proceedings or videoconferencing hearings, computer mapping for crime control or for programming court distribution, and so on. The technology is appealing because of its promise to short circuit seemingly insurmountable obstacles. Unfortunately, many of these obstacles if left unresolved will limit its impact, and the technology itself is often a second best solution even to the part it can address.

Distance learning is a typical example. Those most versed in its application usually admit that it is at best a complement to more conventional classroom programs, seminars, and face-to-face tutorials. It is not very interactive, fails to hold the attention of many students, and to be effective, requires on-site facilitators who can answer questions and direct discussions.[5] Its biggest shortcoming is that it cannot compensate for inadequate content. Distance learning is a means for transmitting a program. Unless that program is adequately designed, its positive impact

---

5. One common problem, mentioned by several informants, is that students often sleep through the courses, or disappear to do other chores once the lights go off for the video-taped portion. Interactive computerized courses may get around these problems, but they are difficult to design for complex topics not lending themselves to linear presentation.

will be nil. The fundamental challenge of creating a training program which attacks and remedies important performance problems will not be resolved by the use of distance training, anymore than DNA and fingerprint data bases or mapping systems will improve the performance of unreformed police.

In short, while reform participants have not completely ignored experience elsewhere, the overwhelming tendency is to use information selectively to support preconceived preferences or to add to the repertoire of standard activities. Knowledge about what can be included in reform programs has expanded rapidly; knowledge about impacts or the internal and external factors conditioning them is near nonexistent. Participants are also extremely selective as regards knowledge collected on a country where they propose to work. It is extremely common for training programs to be proposed without a review of what other training has been done or is still under way in a given country.[6] The result is that many efforts are duplicative, differing only in their sponsorship or specific target group. Redundancy is not necessarily negative, but any positive impact requires a comparison of objectives, methodological variations, and outcomes. As no one seems motivated to do this or to operate so that it could be done, the potential benefits of duplication are rarely realized. The consequence is that both strategic and tactical approaches continue to operate on testable, but untested hypotheses. Better knowledge management could change this situation, but so far no one seems inclined to promote it.

Before turning to a discussion of some positive actions to remedy the situation, it will be useful to examine its underlying causes. The problems are not accidental. They arise in the historical origins of the reform movement and the incentives and perspectives of those most directly involved in it. In combination they reinforce certain perverse practices and outcomes. While hardly intended to do so, they have effectively impeded the construction of better strategic approaches, based on accumulated knowledge, a concrete specification of the partial goals, and a logical linkage between the selected interventions and some more socially important goal.

STRUCTURAL IMPEDIMENTS TO KNOWLEDGE-BASED ACTION: WHY WE STICK WITH POORLY SUBSTANTIATED TACTICS WHEN WE COULD BUILD EMPIRICALLY TESTED STRATEGIES

Judicial reform, under its current guise in Latin America, is a more than twenty-year-old discipline. Despite its chronological maturity, it has failed to build a consensus among practitioners as to what they are attempting and how they can best

6. Donors are less likely to err here, though they are often not exhaustive in their reviews. Once an externally financed program begins, it is usually inundated by proposals from volunteers, most of whom seem oblivious to the desirability of doing a market survey first.

get there. The failure to learn from the past is still older. Many of the problems experienced today had already been identified by the law and development movement of the 1960s and 1970s.[7] The explanation offered below is hardly novel. It builds on comments made elsewhere by concerned participants, although often informally and rarely in published form. Its intended service is to put them on the table in a consolidated format so that they can be discussed openly. As a reader of an earlier version of this chapter noted, I will not make many friends with this frank a statement. In putting myself so far out on the proverbial limb, my interest is in provoking debate and encouraging the resolution of some very perplexing problems. With this as an introduction, the following are the areas most often identified as impeding the construction of a common knowledge base as a first step to building a consensus on a shared strategy.

Lack of Knowledge of Sector Operations or of Their Real Impact on Extrajudicial Behavior

The positive consequences assumed to flow from a judicial reform are almost daunting in their number. Few development programs rival them in the variety of promises made and presumed beneficiaries. One explanation for the phenomenon is the timing of the movement. It emerged as observers were seeking to explain the disappointing results of other efforts, and thus became a sort of missing link in the development equation. The judiciary was depicted as the forgotten "third pillar" of democratic government, the key to a well-functioning market economy, and the leveler of the playing field for the poor and dispossessed. For an institution which in many countries was a mystery to the mass of the population, this was a radically new image. It appealed to the judges (quite naturally) as well as to those who were looking for a way to exit an apparent developmental gridlock.

A second explanation lies in how little was known about Third World judiciaries, even by those who worked within them. As the "orphan branch of government," (a term used by Latin Americans but applicable far more widely), the court system was largely overlooked by academics, ignored by politicians (except for its role in producing friendly judgments), and usually lacked its own ability for self examination and monitoring. Judges and lawyers frequently had no idea of real caseloads, use patterns, clearance rates, delays, and sometimes not even the number of staff or courtrooms. No one really knew which conflicts went to court, why, and with what immediate results and longer-term consequences.[8] One important role

---

7. Gardner (1980) is still the classic overview of the program.

8. Such knowledge is not that widespread, even in the more developed countries. U.S. researchers took the lead here. See Jacob (1955), for an early example, and Daniels and Martin (1995) and Galantar (1998), for more recent efforts to explore conventional wisdom about the incidence and impact of civil damage suits. Judiciaries in some other countries (see Australian Law Reform Commission 2000; Ontario Law Reform Commission 1998) have begun to commission studies of their own caseloads. A few European

of early reform programs has been to fill in some of the knowledge gaps, both by increased contact with and observation of the sector and through the installation of statistical and monitoring systems to allow the courts to keep track of their business.[9] In the meantime, there was plenty of opportunity for speculation on what the courts did, how they did it, and with what broader effects. This speculation provided the basis for program design. Once the fundamental patterns were set, it became very difficult to contest their underlying assumptions.

Some errors have since been recognized, if not always with much effect on programs. An initial assumption that judges made bad decisions out of ignorance gave rise to a plethora of training programs. Their often minimal impact on the quality of judgments has since drawn attention to other factors (incentive systems, political interference, out and out corruption, the poor performance of other sector actors) that often play a bigger role. The massive efforts to draft new legislation (sometimes simply translations of laws from more developed countries) produced similar disappointments, calling attention to the need for contextual modifications, the limited impact of the legal framework in shaping the behavior of judges, lawyers, or their clients, and to the additional institutional changes required for even a good law to have an effect. The initial successes in getting new clients, and especially the poor, to the courts, were marred by the discovery that judgments might still go against them, or when in their favor, face the enormous obstacle of adequate enforcement. Equipment provided to automate court operations was often underutilized or simply served to speed up poorly designed, inherently inefficient procedures. The assumption that it might reduce operating expenses, and especially those for veritable armies of underprepared staff, ran afoul of the courts' traditional use for patronage employment, sponsored by politicians or by the judges themselves.[10] In short, the quick remedies based on an initial identification of the

researchers are investigating cross-national and historical patterns of court use. See, for example, Blankenburg (1994, 2000a, 2000b) and Wollschlater (1990, 1998). Poor record keeping and statistical systems do not ease the process, hence the importance of recent efforts to standardize statistics within and across European countries. See, for example, Blank et al. (2004), Contini (2000), and CEPEJ (2002, 2004). See Sousa Santos et al. (1996) and Pastor (1993), for statistically based analyses of court use and performance in Portugal and Spain, respectively.

9. Now that statistics exist and are more publicly accessible in a few Latin American countries, local and foreign academics have begun to use them to analyze court performance and challenge some conventional understandings of the judiciary's role and impact. See Buscaglia and Ulen (1996), for an early regional overview. Sousa Santos and García (2001), on Colombia, and Hernández Breña (2003), on Peru, feature more detail and more sophisticated methodologies. Piaggi (2000) builds on earlier work to review the size and composition of caseload in Argentina's civil and commercial courts. Rubio et al. (1994) makes a first stab in Mexico but is hampered by limited access to court statistics.

10. Courts, like any public employers, are usually reluctant to introduce innovations as labor-saving devices, especially when those savings come through dismissing staff. Thus, automation plans commonly focus on giving a computer to every staff member, a sort of guarantee that they will have a place. In one discussion with court authorities, when it was pointed out that judges might no longer need thirty or so staffers assigned to support their work, the chief administrator explained he was finding other courtroom duties for them to perform.

most obvious shortcomings or on purely theoretical arguments soon confronted the realities of a far more complex situation in which simple solutions might create as many problems as they resolved.

Even as reformers achieved a better understanding of internal procedures and thus some success in altering them, the larger issue of the downstream impacts has remained unresolved. On the one hand, the immediate broader benefits of a reformed system were doubtless oversold. If, as several macro economic studies have attempted to demonstrate,[11] well-functioning court systems are associated with political stability, strong market economies, and greater social equity, there is the question of the direction of causality and of the myriad contributing factors. On the other, assuming judicial reform is a necessary if not sufficient condition for advancing these goals, there remains the issue of identifying the critical linkages so as to accelerate the change process. If judicial performance does affect investment decisions, what aspects are most important—is it delays, corruption, or poorly designed legislation in the commercial and civil courts; the courts' failure to curb administrative abuses; or the sector's (and not just the courts') inability to discourage ordinary crime? Can we generalize about the answers or must they be treated as context specific? As regards impact on the poor, is the problem best addressed by enhancing access and fair decisions for individuals, or should more attention go to collective interests or perhaps to cases not directly involving the poor, but nonetheless affecting their well-being (for example, administrative, competition, environmental, or land use law as they shape the actions of governmental and private elites)? And finally, what role can and should the courts play in broader governance reform? Can they do this without considerable prior internal reform to their own operations? What are the dangers posed by an independent, but unreformed, and possibly unaccountable judiciary? To what extent should courts, and especially newly empowered ones, second-guess policymakers? In countries where constitutions are full of rights never intended to be enforced, what happens when the courts start enforcing them? Is the creation of a fully equal third branch of government always a stabilizing factor, or can it promote new, potentially destabilizing conflicts?

The overriding assumption that judicial reform, however defined, was always positive encouraged little attention to these questions of detail. Experience over the past two decades suggests this is an important oversight and can no longer be tolerated. The kind of general information collected on court performance has not been shaped to provide answers. It has largely aimed at a composite, often descriptive picture which does not distinguish among the varying consequences for different clients or from different types of action. Just as all judges are not corrupt, all

---

11. See Kaufman et al. (1999 and 2002) and La Porta et al. (1998). Pistor (1995) and Berkowitz et al. (2001) offer critiques of the latter's arguments on the negative impacts of the civil law tradition.

delay is not bad, and all output does not merit being made more effective. The current need is for other kinds of investigation, targeted specifically at these issues and at otherwise disaggregating the judicial product.

Participants' Lack of Preparation for Institutional Reform Programming

The initial ignorance about court operations and impacts was matched by the novelty of judicial reform programming for all participants. This was as true of judges and governments as it was of assistance agencies and other external allies. Although many judiciaries and jurists had discussed for years the need for reform, when the moment came to undertake the programs, they were frequently at a loss as to what to do. Commonly, preexisting proposals featured new laws, higher budgets and salaries, and increased independence from other branches of government. Originating within the sector, they were usually short on attention to improved performance or output. To the extent anyone considered these issues, they were assumed to follow from the initial changes.

Confronted by offers of increased funding from their own governments or foreign donors, the judges often had few ideas as to its potential uses—especially as many of their traditional remedies either did not require much funding (the case of new laws) or could not be financed through the new resources (salaries, for example, which donors could not fund, and which were often set by national legislation). As elaborated below (see section on disciplinary biases), the judiciaries were not attuned to the notion of development projects, but rather requested their quick fixes—legal change and more funds for their normal operations. Over time, and benefiting from others' suggestions or what they saw occurring elsewhere, they became more ambitious in their efforts, but usually only to the extent of expanding their shopping lists (adding buildings, equipment, and training programs). Even today, most judicial leaders find it difficult to think of using reforms to change how things are done, alter the content and mix of service outputs, or redefine and rework the benefits they provide for society. They envision reform as a means of enhancing their performance of their traditional role, not as a chance to reexamine and possibly modify it.

Courts, while often well aware of their failings and poor public image, have been reluctant to attack these head on. Sometimes this is because their own leadership is very much involved in the undesirable practices; more often it is a reluctance to air their dirty laundry in public. Additionally they may see the problems as insoluble, lack ideas as to how to attack them, or interpret this as someone else's responsibility. Especially where internal procedures and organization are set by law, they may find innovation psychologically as well as legally impossible. Even in countries which average a constitutional amendment every few months or a new constitution every few years, judges commonly protest that something cannot be done because the constitution prohibits it. Contemplating changes theoretically feasible under existing law may be equally difficult. Judges by nature, training, or self-selection are rarely risk takers, and thus commonly resist altering practices at most supported by tradition and how things have always been done.

The lack of preparation was not limited to the judiciary or other national stakeholders; it also affected their external allies. While judicial reforms should, it is said, be a product of national demand, there is no denying that assistance agencies have had a major role in their initiation and development. "Donor" interest has helped put reform on the development agenda[12]; it provides financing for activities, and it helps determine which local stakeholders will have a part in the process. Donors have added to the objectives officially and unofficially pursued. They are often under considerable pressures to undertake these reforms because of foreign policy agendas (the most famous being the U.S. government's war on drugs), domestic lobbies (businesses with interests in the affected country, aggrieved citizens who have fallen afoul of local authorities, or human rights or other civic interest groups), or in the case of multilateral developmental banks (MDBs) and agencies, a perceived relationship to their other policies (economic growth, helping the poor), a search for new areas in which to introduce programs, or the interests of internal factions (often a legal department looking to expand its activities).

Whatever the reasons for their involvement, all assistance agencies faced a major initial problem—this is a new area in which they had little in-house expertise. Bilateral donors enjoy the mixed blessing of being able to call on their own national legal agencies. Although this provides them with staff with some credible experience, it has several disadvantages. First, national experts are experienced in working in functioning systems; their ability to create functionality, as well as their skills in cross-cultural work, is far more questionable. Second, borrowing staff increases the chances of adding their own agendas, which may be at cross purposes with what the donor agency wished to promote. Third, the agency providing staff may eventually decide the donor agency is superfluous and so usurp the program. USAID's use of experts from the U.S. Department of Justice, as well as other governmental and nongovernmental agencies, provides ample evidence of all these problems, though it is likely its experience is not unique.[13]

Bilateral and multilateral agencies alike still faced the challenges of developing in-house project managers and designers and repertoires for the new programs. In doing so, they usually relied on their traditional resources and protocols. In-house lawyers or project managers seconded from other sectors became rule of law advisors, and modalities and activities commonly used for other programs were simply

---

12. In the interests of economy, the term "donor" will be used to cover grant- and loan-giving agencies.
13. See Salas (1999).

adapted to the new area. That the MDBs used loans and long-distance management to do this work is not because it was most appropriate format, but rather because it was how they always operated. If all donors relied on the same general-purpose contractors and consultants, that was because this was what they had at hand. If judicial programs tended to duplicate contents, not only across countries, but also across regions, this was because time was short and alternative ideas scarce. Differences in programs (a greater or lesser reliance on technical assistance, accompaniment, provision of equipment, or training and conferences) are most easily attributable not to objective need, but to how donors operated in other areas. Small donors did small projects, and larger ones provided massive funding with no necessary relationship to what was actually required.[14]

Lack of preparation did little to harm the popularity of these programs, which especially within the assistance community grew to assume an importance quite disproportionate with the amounts invested.[15] The development banks first dragged their heels because of restrictions on political involvement. By the early 1990s, they found their way around these obstacles and were advancing rapidly. Timing, the multiple benefits claimed, the apparent lack of negative consequences, and the ease with which outsiders accepted their importance all helped, as did the surprising willingness of partner governments to accept grants or negotiate loans for their creation. Because no one knew what a judicial reform program should do (though they often understood, or thought they did, the evils it was to eliminate) virtually anything counted, and advances and partial victories could be declared without much fear of contradiction. In the longer run, this optimistic triumphalism presented its own problems. Once agency or political leaders had announced their dedication to the cause, it would be difficult to tell them their underlings had set off on the wrong foot. Clever politicians often found means of surreptitious backsliding, manipulating the contents of an "improved" law or making minor adjustments to inconvenient institutional innovations. Rule-bound assistance agencies lack this kind of flexibility and, faced with the prospect of first having to tell the board, the congress, or some other authority that they had made a mistake, generally preferred to defend their programs up to the point of absolute collapse (or when a change of administration makes it possible, to blame errors on their predecessors).[16]

14. Commonly funding levels are set before projects are designed so that planners are asked to create an $X million project, not to resolve a given problem.

15. For the external observer, the millions or tens of millions of dollars invested in a typical program might seem enormous, but compared to amounts spent in other sectors (or to a large donor's total country "portfolio") these are modest expenditures.

16. The classic example is the U.S. government's efforts (with the cooperation of several other donors) to "stand up the Haitian justice system." Despite clear evidence that things were not working, this was so linked to the Clinton administration's foreign policy goals that it took a change of government to allow an admission of failure. See United States General Accounting Office (2000).

Changing Political Role and Importance of Courts

The creation of a strong, independent judiciary has not been a universal priority of the reforms, but all of them increased the courts' political weight, if only in terms of the number and types of clients and cases they would handle. There have been additional, independent reasons for this shift—most notably an increasing worldwide emphasis on rule-based dispute resolution and at least nominally constitutional governments, an increase in social conflicts occasioned by the breakdown of traditional forms of control, the importance of international standards and conventions, which at the national level have been left to the courts to interpret and apply, and an increasing tendency for political actors to transfer politically sensitive decisions to the courts, which they might attempt to control or simply leave with the final responsibility. This last tendency, the judicialization of politics, is most apparent in the developed world.[17] It is also making inroads in Third World countries. The requirements of mass-based electoral politics have left traditional politicians increasingly unable (because of legislative gridlock) or unwilling to make certain decisions that only seem destined to lose support in some quarter.[18] The judiciary has often leapt into the breach, not realizing it faces the same lose-lose proposition. No matter how it decides it will alienate some important social group. In view of its less direct accountability, however, the negative consequences, at least over the short run, are not obvious. With few exceptions, judges cannot expect to be voted out of office and so in this area can depart from their usually conservative stance.

Over the longer run, the implications for judicial reform or the role of the judiciary are less certain. Activist judiciaries and especially constitutional courts or chambers have made decisions that put them into direct conflict with other branches of government and place certain high-priority programs in jeopardy. Whether this will lead to increased political interest in controlling their actions or a popular or elite backlash is unclear, but some sort of reaction seems inevitable. Furthermore, many courts have not accompanied their heightened powers and independence with any effort to increase transparency or accountability. This was never a part of the initial reform programs, and participants have been slow to acknowledge its importance. It is a very controversial, when not entirely unpopular measure with judges, and even its backers are hard pressed to describe how it

17. See Tate and Vallinder (1995), for various treatments of the phenomenon.

18. A trivial, but dramatic, example was the ruling by a Brazilian judge, in the last days of 2003, ordering Brazilian authorities to finger print and photograph Americans entering the country in line with practices instated against Brazilians (and other foreigners) entering the United States. He based his decision on the "principle of reciprocity," as recognized in international law. Whether the principle constituted a mandatory rule, and whether a federal judge had the ability to force its recognition remain moot points. The Brazilian public loved the ruling, and the government was spared having to take its own decision.

should be enacted. Practices followed in the industrialized nations are not uniform, nor is their acceptance among judges and citizens. Along with the issues of the judicialization of politics, the courts' role in ruling on or shaping government policies, and the expanding powers of international law and tribunals, it is an area where more rather than less debate can be expected over the coming years and where the apparently simple concept of judicial reform runs into a far more complex modern reality.

For the most part, reform proponents have avoided or ignored these issues out of a fear of complicating their work, alienating their judicial allies, or because they just do not recognize them. A certain amount of backsliding, as well as manipulation of reform programs by political leaders, suggests this may not be the wisest strategy.[19] Ideological and tactical considerations pose enormous disincentives. Opening this Pandora's box risks creating divisions among the apparently unified supporters of reform, would offer the first suggestion that reform might have a down side and would doubtless raise questions about its other presumed benefits. Thus, the emerging changes in courts' political role have further dampened enthusiasm for this and other types of inquiry.

Disciplinary Biases

One of the greatest influences on the development of reform programs has been their dominance by judges, lawyers, and other members of the legal profession. This is true as regards national actors and external experts. In contrast to other kinds of institutional reform where mere participation in a comparable entity hardly constitutes expertise (no one claims that any bureaucrat is automatically an expert in public administration reform), this is usually seen as a primary and often sufficient prerequisite for participation in judicial programs. Unfortunately, as is true of most professional training, preparation for performing well in a stable system has no necessary relationship to being able to create or improve one. As Richard Posner, a U.S. federal judge, has recently written, "The focus of a traditional legal education is practical; it is on how to be an effective lawyer. . . . Such an education, followed by practical experience as a lawyer with a good firm or in a good government agency, can form a highly skilled professional, which is to say someone who can 'work' the system. But it cannot supply the tools essential for

---

19. Here we might count discussions of the elimination of judicial councils (actually accomplished in Venezuela), continued postponements of the enactment of career laws, and recent modifications to criminal procedures codes seen as too soft on criminals. It is clear several countries with activist constitutional courts or chambers would like to reduce their powers. Recent actions by several national presidents (for example, Fujimori in Peru, Gutiérrez in Ecuador, Kirchner in Argentina, and Duarte in Paraguay) suggest they are finding ways. The judiciary has made its own reversals. The Mexican supreme court promoted a constitutional amendment giving it the majority vote in the new federal judicial council.

understanding and improving the system, because it cannot cultivate the requisite external perspective."[20]

Legal training in fact may constitute a particularly bad background for this second task, because of its emphasis on advocacy, and on rules and their application to individual cases. Narrowly focused advocates are often excellent in implementing new ideas and practices but, by the same token, not whom one would consult as to the wisdom of their introduction in the first place. A program designed by true believers is likely to favor disproportionately elements they want to work, not what experience or cold empiricism indicates to have the greatest chances of success or the highest payoff. Nonetheless, lawyers and judges have held their ground as the determinants of the content and direction of judicial reform and, to a large extent, have convinced outsiders that this should be the case. This has had an impact on shaping programs and on the analysis of their goals and achievements.

Domination by legal experts has contributed to what are increasingly called "guild reforms," designed to the needs, demands, and perspectives of the legal community or just of the judges. Even when lawyer advocates attempt to design programs to the interests of outside groups, they frequently err in second-guessing the presumed beneficiaries.[21] It might be easier to ask, but there has been a notable reluctance to do much canvassing of outside opinions. Disciplinary biases have also meant, inter alia, a tendency for programs to emphasize purely legal (that is, law) reforms, a reluctance to give equal weight to the views of other stakeholders (the clients for the legal and judicial services[22]), and, somewhat ironically, an insufficient appreciation of the varying qualities of inputs from other disciplines.

The legal community has come around to accepting the necessary inclusion of outside experts—in administration, information systems, training, and public relations. Nonetheless, this new, "multidisciplinary" approach has two important caveats. First, it usually means that the nonlegal experts are expected to contribute only in their limited areas. Overall planning and agenda setting continue to be lawyer dominated. Second, their disciplinary biases often make lawyers superbly bad consumers of these alien inputs. One additional reason for the disappointing results of past reforms has been an insufficient vetting of the nonlegal elements. As a consequence, infrastructure is often unsuited for judicial needs (because the architects are not specialized in that area), automated systems are overpriced for the benefits they deliver (because the informatics experts are allowed to create what strikes them as most appropriate, which all too often is not what the users

20. See Posner (2001, 1).

21. For example, insistence by legal drafters that the new agrarian laws for El Salvador and Costa Rica set a minimum length for tenant contracts ran into the fact that the intended beneficiaries (small renters) often preferred greater flexibility (interviews with Costa Rican informants).

22. In Latin America, judges have often been reluctant to include lawyers in reform planning, except for a few well-recognized local jurists or those accompanying international missions.

need), and training programs do not serve their intended ends. Lawyers, like all professionals, tend to discount the complexity of other disciplines, on the assumption that their products and experts are fairly interchangeable.

The guild outlook also has negative impacts on review and evaluation. Law is hardly an experimental science, and the legal penchant for using evidence to prove a point, rather than test a hypothesis, carries over into notions about evaluation, when they are actually entertained.[23] Judges in particular resist being contradicted and usually do not welcome subjecting their pet schemes to some outsider's assessment. Furthermore, as another observer (also a lawyer) has noted, law tends to be a backward-looking discipline, emphasizing conformity with principles rather than the results produced.[24] These may please critics who want to see judges stay out of policymaking and is a refreshing reminder that results (commonly expressed in monetary terms) are not the only values to be considered. It is, however, hardly a good strategy for a development project.

There are noteworthy exceptions to all these generalizations. A legal expert who understands scientific evidence, appreciates results, and recognizes the limitations of his or her expertise can be the most effective of reformers. Still, these are not qualities normally associated with professional formation, and, when they occur, it is usually a happy coincidence, not an intended effect. The more radical idea, that judicial reform is not about lawyering but about institutional development and thus requires an entirely different set of skills and talents (as well as considerable familiarity with sector operations), has been strongly resisted. Until it is accepted, or until lawyer-reformers acquire these other outlooks, efforts to introduce strategic and empirical elements into judicial reform planning will be extraordinarily difficult.

Ease of Entry and the Expanding Range of Participants

The legal profession's dominance of the judicial reform movement has guaranteed one thing—a seemingly limitless supply of reform experts, in effect anyone with a law degree, possibly complemented by some international exposure. This phenomenon is both a product of and a contributor to the difficulty of establishing additional criteria for evaluating expertise or quality. It also explains the continuing reemergence of the same ideas, as newcomers reinvent wheels already tested and sometimes discarded by their predecessors.

Virtually everyone starts by proposing some kind of judicial training. This is the easiest kind of program to set up and the one where a legal education appears

23. For a very critical view of lawyers' approach to experimental research, see Epstein and King (2001).

24. See Saez (1998).

most relevant.[25] There are hundreds if not thousands of law schools, judicial colleges, bar associations, and independent practitioners prepared to undertake it. A variation on this is skills transfer, training intended to enhance local professionals' capabilities in performing certain parts of their work— for example, oral trial techniques, or developing and handling of certain kinds of evidence (ranging from finger prints and DNA analysis to forensic accounting). There is ample room for these kinds of improvements, but a collection of skills does not make a professional, and a haphazard selection of which ones are transferred can distort on-the-job behavior.[26]

Conferences, tours, and exchanges are another easy favorite. While they are usually valuable only in the context of a larger program (as complements to the main act), they continue to be proposed as stand-alone activities. Another frequent idea is to take a program that has proved successful in one country, usually the one from which the proponents come, and export it more broadly. Linguistic, cultural, and other institutional barriers (not the least of which may be a radically different legal system) are often ignored. Aside from a tendency to repeat the same suggestions, new participants often show a disturbing lack of interest in what has already been attempted or is occurring simultaneously in the countries where they propose to act. That is not entirely their fault; as discussed below, this information can be difficult to obtain.

All of these proposals require funding. Two factors work to the newcomers' favor. First, there are numerous private foundations and small assistance agencies that are also interested in establishing a foothold and that may be attracted by a modest proposal and the chance of discovering new talent. Second, many of the new entrants have their own political strings to pull—and may be quite successful in convincing a minister of development (from a nation providing assistance) or a counterpart in the country where the reform will be undertaken to insist that they receive financial backing. Nationalism, whether of the assisting or assisted nation, has its part here. Larger bilateral donors have begun to untie their technical assistance (in part because their experts already have a sufficient foothold), but smaller ones and targeted countries may be less inclined to this sort of neutrality. National loyalties have more than symbolic value. Helping to shape a country's laws and legal system can have downstream payoffs in terms of future economic relations.

An influx of new participants could be a source of innovative ideas. The unfortunate reality is that it has created more redundancy and repetition. For the situation to be otherwise, two conditions would have to be met: first, newcomers would need

25. This begs the questions of whether a knowledge of the law qualifies one to teach it, whether legal knowledge is what is needed, whether lawyers automatically know how to train judges, or how the would-be trainers will determine the needs in any given country.

26. For example, an emphasis on oral trial techniques might encourage too many cases to go to trial rather than reaching out-of-court settlements. It is also common for skill-transferrers to overlook the ways the local laws or legal culture may affect their application.

easy access to information on others' experience (as well as an incentive to utilize it); second, those controlling the points of entrance (in essence the national or international funders) would need this same information and their own incentives to exercise quality control. Both conditions imply some entity or group's claiming intellectual ownership of the programs. In other areas, this is done by professional schools or associations. To date, no such entity or threatens to emerge in the area of judicial reform.

Academic-Practitioner Divergences of Interest and the Weak Role of Research

The existence of a peak professional association or program would also be helpful in fomenting policy-relevant research. Because no such entity exists,[27] what work is done tends to have a less practical focus, largely because its authors come out of academic disciplines and, quite naturally, respond to the academy's notion of what constitutes important research. The main practitioners are lawyers, political scientists, and most recently economists, but they are practitioners in the academic not the policy sense. Most of them have little, if any, involvement in actual reform programs. Thus, even if they wished to be useful to reform designers and implementers, they would have considerable difficulty in determining what that meant in concrete terms. This is particularly unfortunate because of the persisting knowledge gap, not only in terms of the current operations of judicial systems, but also in terms of their presumed impact on extrajudicial goals and the simple question of how reform programs have done. It is not clear whether the academy would recognize the value of research directed toward these questions, but it would be of considerable help in orienting real programs.

In general, researchers from the three main disciplines, as well as those from a smattering of other backgrounds (psychology, sociology, anthropology, criminology, comparative law), have tended to focus on the macro questions—in law, the differences among legal systems and their evolution over time; in political science, the role of courts in upholding or contesting power structures; in economics, the costs of judicial dysfunctionality. They have rarely done this in terms that would guide a reform planner in deciding where to make an intervention. The grand

27. Some reviewers dispute this statement, citing academic entities like the Law and Society Association, the International Comparative Law Association, the Committee on Comparative Studies of the International Political Association, and comparable sections of other academic organizations. One could add the international divisions of professional organizations like the American Bar Association, or the Federal Judicial Conference. Their very number, their status as subsections of organizations dedicated to other ends, and the relative lack of communication among them or any sense of who is leading the charge are, however, indicative of the problem. That those interested in these issues are beginning to organize is an important first step, but one that falls far short of the creation of a disciplinary home with a principal emphasis on reform.

variables holding the researchers' attention are usually not those reform programs can manipulate. For example, if social inequality explains 90 percent of the level of violence in any given society, that gives the would-be reformer little practical foothold; he or she probably will have to work with the variables explaining the other 10 percent. It may be intellectually interesting to know that civil code systems generally provide less protection to investors than do common-law ones, but for the reformer the question is which details (specific legal provisions or institutional arrangements) account for the difference. They may not be able to change the entire system, but they may be able to produce alterations in the critical parts.

For the reformer, the grand between-category differences are usually less important than the within-category ones. The common-law/civil-law difference is one example. On average, one tradition may produce better results in some areas than the other. The reformer is less interested in averages than in how to improve the functioning of the system within which he or she is working. Possibly, as many Latin Americans had argued, an accusatorial criminal justice system is, on average, more effective in combating crime and less abusive of human rights than an inquisitorial one, but there is also enormous room for improvement in how each operates. That is where most of the reformers' work is directed and where the researchers have tended not to focus. Much the same can be said of training, which, on average, probably does not work (because so much of what passes for training is extremely poorly designed). Still, those averages hide considerable within-system variations that, once again, are what reform is about. These differences, more visible in case studies than in statistical analysis, are important to the reformer. They are not the stuff on which academic careers are based. If judicial reform, like education or medicine, had an applied sister discipline, it might promote this kind of research. For the meantime, acquiring this information means either that reform agencies must do it on their own, or somehow convince academics it is worth their effort to indulge in these deviations from their disciplines' preferences.

Relative Absence of Broadly Based Review and Evaluation of Results

Many of the basic contributing elements have already been anticipated in the above discussion. No one likes being evaluated, so the situation of the judicial reform movement may not be all that unusual, and thus the resistance to evaluation and review not that insurmountable. Evaluations of judicial programs are unusually scarce, however, and relatively inaccessible to those interested in reviewing them. Few national groups promoting reform have undertaken them on their own, even in developed nations. The Rand Civil Justice Institute's recent review of the U.S. civil justice reforms suggests some further problems.[28] The significance and implications

28. See Hensler (1994), Rand (1996), and McArthur (2000).

of the findings are still under debate. Although they appear to demonstrate that the reforms were less successful than promised, or even claimed after the fact, the reforms' defenders have questioned the evaluation design and the inferences drawn from its results. There is the issue, for example, of whether the evaluation tested the impact of a specific reform strategy as applied to a concrete and possibly nonrepresentative group of courts or of the more generic approaches the reformers sought to introduce. Proponents of differential case management or of ADR (alternative dispute resolution) might be willing to accept that, in the form both were introduced in the courts surveyed, they had a disappointing impact but not that the results demonstrated their ineffectiveness in general. The finding that the courts where these measures had greatest impact were those that used them before the reform might indeed support that argument. One could conclude that the measures were effective and that the problem was a failure to encourage their wider adoption. In any case, the experience demonstrates both the need for empirical testing of results and the difficulty of carrying it out. Most judicial reforms are inherently complex and cannot be designed to meet rigorous experimental standards. In the face of political sensitivities, the various interests affected, and the risk that negative findings might undermine an entire effort, evaluation becomes a thankless task for which the intended beneficiaries may see little positive justification.

Assistance agencies, foundations, and other external actors have been less able to avoid evaluation. It is usually part of their standard operating procedures or required by those who approve or supply their funding. Nevertheless, much of what they have done is far from satisfactory either as a means of improving their own programs or of building a broader knowledge base. To a large extent, evaluation continues to be treated as an inherently unpleasant, bureaucratic exercise. Despite considerable differences in how they handle it, the experiences of USAID and the World Bank are two cases in point.

USAID is undoubtedly the agency with the most frequently evaluated programs. Until it shifted to a management by results mode, midterm and final evaluations were required of every project. They are now optional and, not surprisingly, far less common. The agency's programs have also been evaluated by a wide variety of external organizations— NGOs, the U.S. Congress and its Government Accountability Office (GAO), and USAID's independent inspector general.[29]

USAID's own evaluations were commonly done by contracted external experts. Evaluators usually worked in teams, with individual members chosen for their expertise in specific areas. The final reports, often running to more than a hundred pages, provided remarkably critical, detailed examinations of individual projects based on lengthy and sometimes repeated field visits. They offer a wealth of information on the target systems, the project operations and accomplishments, the

---

29. See, for example, United States General Accounting Office (1992, 1993, 1997, and 2000).

problems encountered, and suggested improvements in design and implementation. Their impact on improving program and project design was far less significant, impeded by several factors:

- Although USAID has both an evaluation office and a central rule of law unit, design and supervision of evaluations is highly decentralized. The lack of a standardized format or prior agreement on the substantive issues to be covered makes it extremely difficult to compare the results and thus to reach general conclusions about lessons learned and areas for overall improvement.
- The reports were simply too lengthy and as a result not widely read. Although publicly available, they are difficult to access and often remained in draft form in the individual field missions.
- Because many of the evaluators were also consultants to other projects (that being the logical source of expertise), they were often perceived, sometimes correctly, as having an ax to grind or a less than objective viewpoint.
- The evaluators seemed to interpret their role as identifying mistakes rather than encouraging improvements. They usually failed to prioritize the problems they did encounter or focus on elements that were amenable to modification.
- Because evaluations were contracted for individual projects, they tended to be reviewed at that level. USAID never introduced a means for a systematic, comparative review.
- Although midterm evaluations did produce some internal corrections, they were often conducted and reviewed too late to have much impact. In light of the limited review of final evaluations, it is unclear what effect they might have had.

For all their problems, the USAID evaluations offered an enormous potential for improving program design. That this did not occur cannot be blamed on the evaluation process itself. The evaluations would clearly have benefited from more guidance as regards length, format, key questions, and intended products and applications. Though demonstrating the value of field observation, they also suggested the need for more systematic review, and not only at the project level.

The external reviews of USAID projects have been no more systematic, shaped more by the agendas of the evaluating group than by any inherent interest in (and sometimes knowledge of) judicial reform itself. Their impact on the targeted project or overall program ultimately hinged on the political clout of the evaluating body. The GAO gets action; an NGO usually does not. Over time, USAID has developed a better relationship with many of its external reviewers, some of which can now be said to take a more constructive approach to their tasks. Still, others continue to see their primary mandate as finding problems, often in very narrow areas.

The World Bank's experience has been quite different. Although the bank has an evaluation office that oversees the process and imposes a standardized format, the most common evaluation document, the implementation completion or close-out review (ICR), is usually prepared by or under the direction of the responsible project manager. Like the periodic grading of project progress (also initiated by the same manager), the ICR is assessed by other staff, but the procedure does raise questions as to inherent objectivity. The ICR, like the bank's quality review programs, is essentially a desk exercise—based on available documents and interviews with staff and other informants, but with little or no direct field observation. It may eventually be published, after a lengthy and highly bureaucratic internal process. As the bank has completed few projects, it is impossible to estimate how many of these documents will finally be available to the public. Formal midterm reviews are almost nonexistent. Project managers instead hire consultants as necessary to assess individual project elements. The results are available to in-house staff— though one suspects rarely consulted—but not to the public.

The World Bank has done a few field evaluations of projects, usually as background documents to its CARs (country assistance reviews). Conducted by one staff member or external consultant, they may be based on one to several weeks of field observation. Although they uncover details not visible in a desk review, the findings will be limited to the single evaluator's expertise, which is unlikely to cover all project elements adequately.[30] The simple, standard outline for the exercise does structure the results, forcing the evaluator to list achievements, lessons learned, and recommendations, but the focus is open-ended, leaving the author to decide which details are worth covering. The background papers are available to bank staff, but only if they choose to look for them. Although they are referenced in the final country assistance report, the latter is usually devoted to economic themes.

The limited public access to bank documents and to bank operations in general has probably discouraged external evaluations.[31] Private researchers and NGOs have thus focused their attention elsewhere. The one prominent exception, a Lawyers Committee review of the World Bank's first judicial reform project (in Venezuela), was done in cooperation with the bank.[32] Its critical findings had a significant impact on that and other projects. This positive example has not been duplicated. Whether the choice lies with the NGO community or with the bank is unclear. The bank's status as an international organization has for the most part spared it the attention of governmental auditors and investigative bodies.

30. In light of the large investments in automation equipment in particular, it is disturbing that none of the evaluation exercises have called on experts in this area.

31. Since 2002, however, the World Bank has begun to make more of its internal documents available on its web site.

32. See Lawyers Committee and Venezuelan Program (1996).

Although other bilateral and multilateral agencies have conducted evaluations of their judicial reform work, little of it is publicly available. It also appears not to be widely disseminated within the agencies themselves. Most are attempting to strengthen their evaluations procedures, and perhaps most interestingly, to do this at the program as opposed to the project level. The IDB has had one such endeavor under completion for the past three years; the UNDP appears to be attempting a similar exercise; and USAID has initiated a series of thematic reviews of project work (focusing first on case management and then on judicial independence).[33] There have also been discussions of sharing evaluations among agencies, though a first step might be better internal dissemination.[34] A more controversial, but nonetheless interesting, suggestion involves the proposed development of judicial and judicial reform performance indicators as a means of reducing the inherent subjectivity of the evaluation process. Many participants regard this as a dubious, if not outright dangerous, undertaking, largely because of the risks of skewing reform design toward what can be quantified and the inherent difficulties of working across different legal systems at different levels of development.[35]

The limited development and utility of judicial reform evaluations can partly be blamed on the difficulties posed by the topic itself. As suggested by the review of agency experience, there are also some broader problems that may be shared by all institutional development programs, or perhaps development programs in general. The bureaucratization of the exercise, the tendency to focus first on its role in grading individual performance, and the difficulties of finding substantive experts who also understand evaluation (or of evaluators who understand substance) all warrant mention. There is some indication that agencies are attempting to professionalize their evaluation departments (rather than just seconding staff from other sectors); however, professional evaluators, like professional auditors, may still see their role as identifying problems as opposed to fomenting better understanding. The ideal solution, though an extremely costly one, would be to develop evaluation teams of substantive experts. Alternatively, one might rotate substantive experts through the evaluation department, giving them training in evaluation methodologies. The real point is that from the perspective of producing better programs and projects, evaluation should be seen as an intrinsic part of the entire process. Unfortunately, bureaucratic organization and incentive systems rarely lend themselves to that view.

33. For two examples, see USAID (2001, 2002b). Whether the IDB will ever release its study is a good question. Many outsiders believe the report (conducted by external reviewers) may have been too critical; insiders suggest some departments did not find it critical enough.

34. At least among the larger donors it is frequently commented that relevant material is difficult for even insiders to locate.

35. USAID actually tried this in the mid-1990s but gave up when it determined that the suggested indicators were too context specific. USAID (1998).

CONCLUSIONS

For a variety of reasons, the reform movement as organized contains its own perverse incentives and other obstacles to knowledge-based action. Altering this unfortunate conjunction of forces will require an unprecedented amount of cooperation among the various parties and an equally unprecedented willingness to recognize and discuss their own problems. Strategies can be developed without knowledge, but at this stage in the game that hardly seems necessary. We know how to do many things; we often seem not to know why we are doing them. Institutional development should only be done in an informational vacuum when no information exists. To continue in this vein when there are concrete lessons to guide further action is itself perverse.

What should and can be done is another question. The immediate suggestions, elaborated in the next two chapters, focus on two related lines of action: a better system for managing the knowledge we are accumulating and efforts to build overarching strategies or at least strategic options. Improved knowledge management can be thought of as the minimal approach and the logical prerequisite to strategy building. As the preceding discussion indicates, however, it will threaten many vested interests, ranging from countries and donors wanting to declare the success of their investments to academics with their own disciplinary or ideological axes to grind. There is also the question, addressed in the final chapter, of who will take the responsibility for pushing it forward. There is no logical candidate, in terms of either a special interest in and talent for the undertaking or the necessary credibility to have its efforts recognized by others. Aside from the negative impact of the myriad institutional jealousies, within and among organizations and disciplines, any effort to impose this sort of orderly review will run up against a prevailing culture of open-ended entrepreneurialism. Judicial reform has engendered its own "dot.com" phenomenon, in which any one with a proposal has usually found some means to have it financed. Requiring a knowledge-based peer review prior to its enactment into fact will likely be interpreted as a violation of the right to innovate (even if many of those innovations exist as such only in the minds of their specific backers).

Strategy building faces similar obstacles. It could commence simultaneously but, without a knowledge base to inform it, will remain at an abstract level. Some progress could be made by simply convincing those promoting reform programs to articulate and justify the strategies they believe they are applying. Unlike knowledge management, this first step lends itself to decentralized adoption. Donors are the obvious candidates for its implementation, and if they do not like the results, they can keep them confidential. Conceivably, some of the ongoing program evaluations may serve this purpose, though until they are released more widely the rest of us will not know the answer. Also, while articulating strategies is a first, important step, unless they are systematically reviewed for feasibility, internal consistency, and empirical grounding, this will simply encourage another part of the entrepreneurial culture—the development of fragile strategic frameworks, often little more than elaborate silver bullets. Such frameworks often posit complex causal chains, but they usually rely on highly tenuous assumptions as to the strength of those connections. Abstractly, a single law or a new palace of justice may be able to turn the judicial universe on its head, just as the butterfly flapping its wings in Madagascar causes irreversible climatic disaster on the other side of the world. There is, however, an enormous leap between abstract potential and concrete probabilities, and most of these fragile frameworks do not stand up to that test. This is where strategy and knowledge must come together, to ensure that we are planning on the basis of what we know, not what we hope will happen.

Despite a growing recognition of the importance of this undertaking, progress is best described as incipient, disjointed, and overly redundant.[1] This chapter offers some practical recommendations for accelerating the process, focusing on how reform participants can improve the information used and generated by their individual activities and convert it into a common knowledge base accessible to and utilized by all players. Four key elements in that effort are assessments, monitoring, evaluation, and research. Though discussed separately, they are interrelated and ideally should build on each other. The emphasis on field interventions might seem illogical given practitioners' bias toward action as opposed to reflection. This, however, is where most information originates and where its inadequate utilization poses the greatest costs. In the absence of a strong academic constituency with a vested interest in the discipline's development, the practitioners, for better or worse, still have the major responsibility.

This is in the nature of a lessons-learned analysis. The negative lessons have already been addressed and are not repeated here. They do suggest that the task will not be easy. At the risk of placing excessive faith in the powers of rationality, my assumption is that an analysis of what we know about how we generate, collect, and use information can encourage improvements even in the face of organizational and political incentives for doing otherwise. There is a corollary assumption—the belief that knowledge-based action produces better results than stabs in the dark or uninformed good intentions. This still begs the question of how much you should know before you act and how much time and other resources should be invested in sheer knowledge building as opposed to working actual improvements. An emphasis on immediate action is embedded in most reformers' incentive systems, as demonstrated by their frequent argument that we have enough studies and that what we have has not been useful (or used). Although more resources should be devoted to constructing a knowledge base, I agree that we have made poor use of what we have. More with more would be better. For the present, more with the existing investment is a desirable and feasible goal.

1. The redundancy is evident in the same lessons learned constantly appearing as new discoveries— for example, the need to coordinate activities or the fact that institutional reform is slow and that new technologies or new laws require complementary actions to ensure their impact.

The further development of these arguments is very simple. It reviews how the four activities have been conducted, identifying the strengths and weaknesses of the usual approaches and deriving some lessons as to how they could be improved. Not discussed, but of equal importance, are the subsequent steps required to disseminate the improved knowledge base and encourage its use by the reform community. It can be hoped that the availability of a better product will provide additional incentives and that those involved in its creation will promote its use. Realistically, more direct action will also be needed and more thought devoted to the form it should take.

ASSESSMENTS: THEIR PLACE IN REFORM PROGRAMS

If only as a matter of faith, it is generally agreed that any reform program requires a good prior understanding of the problem to be resolved. This is usually achieved through a diagnostic, assessment, or appraisal.[2] Whatever the term used, the intended product is a presumably objective study identifying the problems of the target system, attempting to prioritize and relate them, analyzing immediate and underlying causes, and suggesting likely solutions. In schematic terms, this means gathering the information needed to fill out the two pyramids introduced in the previous chapter. It is also generally agreed that the assessment should be as broadly focused and open-ended as possible even though its recommendations will likely target only a part of the system. This is a way of avoiding the risk of premature diagnosis—the study focuses on what the authors have already decided is the problem and thus overlooks what may be more important issues. Diagnosis is an iterative undertaking and will inevitably incorporate some preexisting notion of what is wrong. A good diagnostic takes this notion as a hypothesis and is prepared to test and replace it as necessary. Finally, an assessment often requires original fieldwork and data gathering, but it can also be done as a desk study, especially in systems where considerable information and research are already available.

Despite the simplicity of these basic principles, a majority of reform programs do not follow them. Among the situations found are the following:

- No diagnosis is done: in recent presentations, several World Bank officials noted that by 2001 the bank had eighteen projects under execution and twelve sector assessments completed. The situation may be improved by the inclusion

2. As used by the MDBs an appraisal is not an assessment, but rather evaluates (appraises) the feasibility of a proposal that has already been consolidated. Unfortunately, it may be the closest thing to an assessment that the project gets.

of diagnostics as a first phase of a project,[3] but it is a matter of record that the bank and other donors do i.nitiate reform work without a sector assessment to guide it.

- Although a diagnosis is performed, it prematurely focuses on a single issue without examining the broader context. If the topic is judicial reform, one would at least expect a review of the institutional setting and of the way nonjudicial elements impinge on judicial operations. We cannot assess judicial impact on credit operations, citizen security, or poverty without reviewing other contributing factors.

- The diagnosis is more broadly focused but skips over important problem areas. This is most likely when assessors are too concerned with pleasing the client (whether the judiciary, a government, or a major funder) and thus avoid sensitive areas (judicial corruption, incompetence) or themes perceived as less relevant—for example, criminal law or legal education for a funder that cannot or will not work in that area.

- The diagnosis is conducted from one point of view. There are many stakeholders affected by judicial performance. Assessors too frequently consult only with those most easily reached or most vocal in their criticisms. This is also a problem of self-assessments where judges or governmental actors may consider only their own view of the problem.

- The diagnosis is guided entirely by what people think about the system with little effort to test this empirically. Like many of the above problems, this often originates in the scarce time and financial resources provided to the assessors, who are thus forced to rely on what is already "known" about problems and their causes. It is also encouraged by the recent emphasis on participatory assessments—participants' viewpoints are important but do not necessarily constitute the truth of the matter.[4]

- Assessors unfamiliar with what a reform program can do focus on insoluble problems or impossible solutions. This is a particular risk for academics and activists less familiar with or less accepting of the usual political and resource constraints.

- The assessment becomes an inventory of structural and procedural characteristics presumed to constitute problems in and of themselves or to be causes of problems, which are otherwise not identified. This approach would be valid if we had an empirically based model of what a well-functioning system looks

3. Some of these assessments (and certain of the initial twelve), however, were done so late in the course of the project as to have little chance of impacting its design or implementation. See, for example World Bank, Legal Vice Presidency (2003a).

4. This point has been well understood by U.S. researchers for years (see Kritzer, 1983). Recent World Bank–sponsored research, conducted in several Latin American countries, has demonstrated that "conventional wisdom" about court performance is also inaccurate in that region. See World Bank (2002b, 2003a, and 2003b).

like. In its absence, there is little basis for holding that salary levels, the lack of a training program or the contents of specific laws are problematic in their own right.

- An assessment, of reasonable or unreasonable quality, is made, but it is further evaluated in a vacuum — there is no yardstick for determining whether what is found represents serious problems or the universal "norm" (for example, citizens everywhere complain about court delays, even in systems that seem to move fairly rapidly.)
- Finally, there is the frequent phenomenon of multiple assessments, of varying degrees of completeness, conducted by several different agencies, or sometimes by the same one. This problem will not be addressed further here, but it warrants mention because it wastes resources and, absent any effort to coordinate designs or share findings, can also produce contradictions in the resulting programs.

These observations are all taken from real cases. For each of them, examples of the counterproductive results could be provided. Rather than wallow in the negative, the reader is asked to assume that (1) having an assessment before beginning a reform or conducting one as part of the first stage is preferable to not having one at all and (2) the positive principles to be followed are the converse of the situations described above. The guidance thus derived is still fairly abstract, and much more remains to be said as to what a good assessment should look like and how it should be conducted.

Longer and more complex is not always better. When USAID began its administration of justice programs in Central America in the early 1980s, it sponsored a series of very complete assessments, which took as long as a year to conduct and ran to hundreds of pages each. This is now an unaffordable luxury, in terms of time and money.[5] Moreover, in the specific case of the USAID assessments, it is frequently remarked that most of the material collected was never used. Proportionality is thus also critical. Many activities that are less reforms than very targeted efforts to address an obvious problem may require relatively little in the way of an assessment. Whether this is the case at hand is a judgment call. The donation of a couple of computers, software, and training to create a prison registry (and so keep track of prisoners' whereabouts and status) might not warrant an evaluation of the entire prison system. Used repeatedly, this approach could also give rise to a flurry of disconnected activities, each focusing on a discrete problem, with no consideration of their integration, prioritization, or coordination. Before the practice is too far extended, it is in everyone's interest that a general diagnostic be available. Thus, given the large quantity of proposals to conduct training programs, it would be well

---

5. Although, if donor agencies devoted less time to polishing project proposals to fit their internal bureaucratic requirements, they might find funds and staff to carry out more thorough assessments.

to link them to an assessment of training needs, and preferably to a broader study to determine whether training is really where funds should be invested.

The remainder of this section focuses not on partial assessments, but rather on what else we know about the characteristics of a good initial overview. In suggesting how better assessments can be constructed, it elaborates on the four following arguments. First, even when the intended focus is narrow, it is preferable to begin with a broad survey. A proposal to work on court reform requires situating the courts in a broader institutional context and, if with less detail, identifying and collecting information on other agencies and contextual factors that impinge on court operations. Second, whatever the target institutions, the assessment should collect three kinds of information as the basis for its analysis and overall conclusions: purely descriptive, qualitative, and quantitative details on the country, sector, and institutions to be covered; a more qualitative and, if possible, quantitative analysis of institutional operations; and a discussion of the major problems claimed and identified as caused by current operations.

Third, although each assessment is made for and possibly by a specific country, it is becoming increasingly evident that a standardized format would be helpful. This is obvious in the case of international agencies conducting multiple programs. It helps them to interpret the information they collect. Less obviously, it is also useful for a country or country-specific program. In general, a problem is best identified, understood, and resolved in a comparative perspective. It is not uncommon to find reformers proposing solutions that have repeatedly failed elsewhere, describing as highly problematic a situation that is not that bad by international standards, or ignoring other conditions that, by those same standards, might be regarded as requiring attention.

Finally, and especially for a program initiated and implemented by a country itself, some of the following may seem superfluous. Why would they want to pay someone to document what they already know? If the sponsors truly believe that the assessment will never be read, consulted, or otherwise used by those less familiar with the system, they may downplay the general descriptions. Even for internal purposes, however, some of the descriptive material serves a purpose. Population, GDP, and income figures will help in making subsequent calculations or in tracking progress, and even insiders may not have thought about some of the obvious details. Many U.S. lawyers, for example, do not understand that country's administrative court system or what it implies for the burdens on the ordinary courts.[6] In World Bank–sponsored research in Mexico, the Mexican lawyers doing the field work required their own briefing on the specific proceedings under examination.

---

6. A recent international lecture (Mexico City, May 2001) by a former chief judge of the Federal Court of Claims found U.S. lawyers in the audience asking each other what the court did (interviews with participants).

As further discussed below, once we enter the area of judicial statistics and details like caseloads and time to disposition, it is now widely acknowledged that the estimates of insiders are frequently way off the mark.

ELEMENTS OF AN OVERVIEW ASSESSMENT

1. Descriptive section: Description is often seen as a mere prelude to the real assessment and consequently either given short shrift or done with no particular sense of what is relevant and what is not. It is not uncommon to find entire assessments composed of little more than a repetition of legal facts, a restatement of the laws with scant attention to how they really operate. Thus, to facilitate comparisons between countries and ensure the information gathered will be the most useful for country planning, the following guidelines are recommended:

General Discussion of National Context: There are some basic elements of the national setting that are critical to evaluating judicial performance. These include population size, distribution (rural and urban, as well as regional dispersion), per capita income and income distribution, economic base, literacy rates, ethnic and other divisions, and so on. Certain historical information will also be needed—colonial tradition, form of government and any recent changes (for example, re-democratization), recent ethnic conflicts and civil wars, and salient political issues. This is the section where the principal national developmental problems or objectives will be first touched, as a prelude to investigating the role of the justice sector in creating or resolving them. The treatment should be brief, and is largely for outsiders, but it may be helpful to local planners in interpreting what follows.

General Description of Legal Tradition and Basic Organization: Although this general description is primarily for "outsiders" who will either review or make inputs to the reform plan, it may be a useful reminder to insider judges and others of what the entire system comprises. Emphasis here is less on how the system operates than on establishing its basic organizational and procedural parameters. A few basic statistics will be included (how many members on the supreme court, number of court districts, and so forth), but most of these are reserved for the next section.

The following are the usual questions covered: what is the legal tradition (common, civil law, or some subcategory or other mix)? Is there an indigenous or traditional source of law, and what is its legal and organizational relationship to the state system? What are the basic laws shaping the court or justice system, when were they written, and how often have they been revised? How much of the sector's organization, powers, or internal procedures are governed by the constitution, statutory law, or regulations issued by the organizations themselves? What are the major institutions in the ordinary justice system? What auxiliary organizations (administrative and other special courts, administrative and investigative police, bar associations, independent regulatory agencies with judicial powers, and so forth) exist? How is legal representation handled? Are there traditional or communal adjudicatory bodies outside the ordinary court system? If so, how are they organized and where are they located?

Because this is the most free-form part of the exercise, it would be helpful to establish a general outline to be used by those without a strong preference for their own descriptive scheme. This would make the results more useful for comparative purposes and also avoid the omission of important categories. Even experienced reviewers frequently overlook administrative or parallel court systems or ignore items such as the presence, organization, and compulsory nature of bar associations and memberships. The later analysis of operational workings may remind them of their omissions, but a basic checklist for the descriptive section would also be helpful. It might be a joint product of agencies doing many of these assessments. It then could be made available to all interested in conducting one.[7]

Basic Statistics (as Far as Available) on Sector Operations: It is extremely helpful, though often very difficult, to include statistics ranging from the number of judges, court staff, prosecutors, public defenders, and private lawyers to the number of cases filed (by category, district, individual court), the caseload per judge, annual filings and dispositions, backlog, clearance rates, and average times to disposition. Figures on budgets, the funding sources (how much from the national budget, how much from judicial fees or taxes?), salaries, and expenditure categories are also useful as are crime rates (at the various points of reporting, including, if available, victim surveys). The reason for collecting these statistics is to flesh out the narrative descriptions of judicial and sector operations and potential problems and allow comparison with figures drawn from data bases on other systems.

As further elaborated below, single statistics tell us little, and even a complete statistical profile of a country must be interpreted with care. Nonetheless, for a reader with some knowledge of comparative trends, a few key numbers (judges and cases per 100,000 inhabitants, ratio of judges to court staff, prosecutors, defenders and private lawyers, budgets and salaries) provide a much better handle on performance and performance problems than the longest narrative description. This also suggests the utility of a standardized format for data capture and presentation. Experience suggests that some statistics are more meaningful than others and that the manner of their presentation facilitates their use. The lump sum spent on salaries is far less useful than the salary range for different kinds of employees (and this, in turn, is meaningful only when compared with per capita income and salary scales for similar public- and private-sector employees). An understanding of the real workload usually requires several statistics: cases pending, filed, and disposed

---

7. Some such lists do exist although they are not widely used even in the organizations creating them. See Hammergren (1999), for illustrative examples.

on an annual basis and disaggregated by level of court and, if possible, by major types of proceedings.

The availability and quality of statistics are highly variable. In some countries, it may be impossible to get a good count of the judges and lawyers. Individual court districts may have no idea of the size of their caseload or what is being resolved and at what speed. Furthermore, available statistics are often of dubious quality. Used largely for end-of-year speeches by chief justices or other agency heads, they may never be checked and, as a result, be supplied quite casually. Finally, whatever their accuracy they may not be provided in very useful forms. Socioeconomic information on court users is frequently unavailable even in the most sophisticated systems, as are useful breakdowns by type of case or comparable categories across jurisdictions. Despite years of statistical studies of judicial operations in the United States, researchers still find it difficult to make comparisons across state systems. A recent effort to collect comparable statistical data bases on a number of European courts has footnotes as long as the statistical tables—allowing the authors to stress the difficulty, if not impossibility, of making precise comparisons.[8] In such more developed systems, something as simple as an appeals rate is often impossible to calculate.

Nonetheless, statistics are important, and efforts should be made to collect them. They are helpful in determining the relative importance of phenomena identified more impressionistically and can put a different slant on problems reported by local observers. It is rare to find a judiciary that is not described as swamped with work, but figures for annual filings or dispositions often present another picture. In the worst of cases, assessors may have to supply their own statistics, conducting inventories or studies based on smaller samples. Most assessments will not have funding to do this, and thus the absence of a good, reliable statistical system may be among their most important findings. In that situation, they will have to collect what they can, note what is absent, and interpret their findings with extreme caution.

It is important to recognize that the numbers do not speak for themselves and that, where they do speak, it is usually cumulatively, contextually, and comparatively. There has been an ongoing effort in recent years to collect and use court statistics as basic indicators of judicial performance. This, it should be emphasized, is not why their collection is recommended and brings its own problems. Efforts to elevate certain statistics (average caseload, number of judges per 100,000 population, ratio of judges to court staff or to private lawyers, conviction rates, and the like) to the level of indicators (representative of some aspect of the quality of judicial performance) have yet to be abandoned, though most who have attempted

---

8. See Contini (2000). Blank et al. (2004), CEPEJ (2002, 2004), and Douat (2001) are suggestive of advances made in refining concepts and unifying measures, but, as they admit, this is still a work in progress.

this soon discover the practical and logical shortcomings.[9] Are twenty-two judges per 100,000 inhabitants better or worse than eight or thirty? How much (as a proportion of GDP or the public budget) should be spent on the courts? What is a reasonable caseload for individual judges? A good disposition rate? A good appeals rate? To answer these questions we need far more information on the universe of variations, and, even then, any conclusion is far more likely to be a range than a single figure and still subject to contextual interpretation.

In short, statistics, when available, should be considered primarily as a way of enriching the description of the target system, not as a direct means of evaluating its performance. That there is not, and probably never will be, one statistic that can be used to measure the quality of justice is not only a consequence of the multiple values pursued, but also differences in contextual situations. Once a problem has been defined, these descriptive statistics provide a means, collectively and comparatively, of deriving some hypothetical explanations. The number of judges absolutely or per 100,000 inhabitants means nothing on its own. Combined with litigation rates, number of lawyers, and some understanding of the procedural rules and requirements for representation, it can begin to give us an idea of whether a complaint about delay or lack of access is valid or not.

The same need for caution applies to more complex statistics and statistical trends. Although they look more like good indicators, they are usually subject to a variety of interpretations and explanations. Ironically, the same statistical profile might characterize a very good and a very bad system, and, as the situation develops over time, rates and trends may take unexpected directions. More or less is not always better. A high conviction rate for criminal cases brought to trial might mean a well-trained prosecution with a good nose for what should go to court or an easily pressured judiciary. In the latter case, an effort to impose due process rules and curb other abuses may well lower the conviction rate temporarily. A drop in the percentage of untried prisoners (a usual goal for human rights groups) might mean a very selective use of pretrial detention or that other, less desirable means have been found for reducing the prison population. As is frequently observed, crime rates depend on many things besides an effective criminal justice system. A system may be so ineffective that citizens stop reporting crimes. As improvements are made, and citizens' confidence increases, reported crime rates are likely to rise. A 50–50 rate for overturns on appeals might be viewed as positive, indicating that only very difficult cases go to appeal. It could also be produced by a system that operates like a lottery and even worse, a corrupt one.

For those used to dealing with general purpose indicators like infant mortality

9. USAID developed a list of seventy-five indicators in the mid-1990s. The list was relegated to the status of "suggested" indicators after field testing revealed that most were relevant only for a few systems and that the desirable direction of change is contextually determined and may well vary over time in a single country. See USAID, Center for Democracy and Governance (1998).

rates or GDP, the ambiguous significance of candidate indicators for judicial performance will be perplexing. It is a logical consequence of the judicial role, the variations in how it is defined and enacted in different countries, and the complex nature of its output. The judiciary is a reactive rather than proactive institution, and the raw material with which it works (conflicts and rule violation) is shaped by a variety of other forces. Its own statistical systems track the tip of the iceberg (the cases getting to the courts), not the broader social phenomena. Limiting performance measures to how well it deals with the business it receives is tantamount to judging a public health system only by the number of sick people treated. Both measures are important, but both, if used exclusively, would also create perverse incentives. Courts, like public health systems, have a preventive, as well as a curative, role, and if performance evaluation hinges only on the latter they will be encouraged to waste their resources by attracting more business than is necessary and focusing on processing the easy, not the important cases.[10]

2. Analysis of Internal Operations: Because this is the area where most reforms will be directed, it is an especially critical part of the assessment. The objective transcends documenting the output problems (for example, delays, bias, barriers to access), seeking instead to identify how the organization or organizations function and with what results. The immediate challenge is to select those characteristics that are most influential in shaping sector output and defining its quality. Early assessments often did this by measuring organizational and operational details against an implicit model—usually drawn from the assessors' own country. The recognition that function can and should be separated from structure and that there are consequently various paths (or path dependencies) to improving performance has made this less acceptable. It has also removed the implicit yardstick. Fortunately, there are a number of suggested substitutes. In fact, during the past two decades, those called upon to conduct assessments have often seen part of their task as leaving a template that might be used by others.[11] There is still no agreement on which is best and a decided tendency to reinvent rather than adopt some existing proposal.

Presumably this sort of checklist should be short, and its elements should have a direct relationship to predicting output. As many normal inclusions are already covered in the above sections (Basic Statistics, General Description of Legal Tradition and Basic Organization) most of the suggested templates could be substantially

10. In a study of the Mexican federal courts, two researchers found that an evaluation system based on cases resolved tended to encourage the admission of cases that would ultimately be dismissed for lack of merit. Because they counted as dispositions, judges had little reason to reject them out of hand. (Magaloni and Negrete, n.d.) Interviews in February, 2006 with advisors to Colombia's Superior Magistrates' Council revealed that judges kept two sets of statistics to submit to the council—one including their entire backlog for the office deciding on where more courts were needed, and a second, omitting backlog, for the office evaluating judges' performance.

11. A sample of the efforts is found in Hammergren (1999).

condensed. The suggestion here is to treat the judiciary (and other sector institutions covered) as an organization with all the typical requirements for effective functioning. These include a way of selecting appropriate staff, provisions for supervising and directing their performance (without, in the case of judges, interfering with the necessary degree of independent decision making), adequate resources and a system for administering them, and procedural rules congruent with quantitative and qualitative standards for output. Table 5 is one example. It is divided into three dimensions, one covering simple organizational functionality (here called institutional governance) and the others relating to independence and accountability. It is particularly tailored for the judiciary and would have to be slightly modified for other sector institutions, especially regarding the independence and accountability dimensions.

Aside from a reluctance to adopt existing schemes, the biggest obstacle to constructing this sort of assessment format is the tendency for legal professionals to define the problem in terms of the adequacy of the legal framework. Given the often imperfect coincidence between legal requirements and what really transpires, this has not been a very productive approach. It is not improved by an accompanying faith in certain doctrinal principles believed intrinsic to better performance.[12] In explaining internal operations, the principles of neo- and classical organizational (or institutional) analysis are arguably better guides. Judiciaries have special characteristics, but they still must provide adequate incentives to their professional and administrative staff, monitor performance, and manage their resources efficiently. Their failure to do so accounts for many common problems, and thus much reform programming will inevitably focus on these functions.[13]

3. Discussion of the Major Problems Attributed to Sector Performance: Although it may be a hard message for their strongest proponents to swallow, judicial reforms are usually not supported for their own sake but as instrumental means of achieving some larger goal. At the very least such goals involve improving the provision of services already delivered (greater efficiency and efficacy in deciding conflicts and otherwise dealing with existing demand). Often they refer to downstream events, the judiciary's impact on crime, economic investment and growth, the incorporation of marginalized groups, or citizen security. The links between the two levels of goals are not well defined. Efforts to articulate them in any given country often rest on scant and frequently inaccurate understandings of what courts actually

---

12. Many of these are now entrenched in international conventions that often seem to incorporate arbitrary and occasionally ethnocentric assumptions about best practices. Although much of this is so vague as to constitute only a nod toward good intentions, efforts like those in Latin America to stipulate a guaranteed percentage of the national budget for the judiciary are potentially counterproductive.

13. Nevertheless, care must be taken in attempting to improve incentives. The neoinstitutional school has tended to take a reductionist cut on the issue, counting on its ability to second guess what motivates organizational actors and overlooking their deviations from the dictates of the rational choice model. See Sunstein (2002), for a discussion, much of it addressed to the impact of laws, of the limits of this approach.

Table 5 A proposed instrument for assessing judicial operations

(The list includes three dimensions and presumes that an assessment will focus on all of them; a reform program that focuses on only one or two, without taking the others into consideration, may well create new impediments to satisfactory performance.)

	Selection of Judges	Management of the Judicial "Career"[1]	Internal Administration	Resources	Judicial Processes	Legal Profession
Internal Governance	• Judges are selected through preestablished criteria based on job-relevant[2] merit • Candidates are selected from those recommended by an independent professional body • Selection process and criteria are periodically reviewed to ensure they are obtaining the best candidates • In addition to screening for substantive knowledge and skills, criteria also include background checks and other means of identifying (and eliminating) candidates with questionable personal and professional histories	• Training in compliance with code of conduct and process for monitoring compliance, disciplining violators, and appealing disciplinary decisions • Code of conduct includes conflict-of-interest provisions requiring recusal, and public disclosure of assets • Standards for performance (number of cases decided, average time limits, reversals on appeal, service to users, etc.) exist and are monitored to help judges improve their work and, where relevant, to affect decisions on tenure, promotions, transfers, and discipline	• Administrative processes (at the systemic and courtroom level) follow set rules and procedures • Budgets, procurement and management of resources are planned, monitored, and audited • There is a management information system (manual or automated) to facilitate planning and budgetary oversight • Administrative staff is chosen, promoted and retained through objective, merit-based procedures	• Changes in the overall judicial budget are commensurate with the growth of the national budget and reflect increases (or decreases) in demands for judicial services • Staffing, equipment, and offices provided to judges and administrators are adequate to allow performance of their duties • Staffing, equipment, and offices provided to judges and administrators are no worse (no better?) than that for the rest of the public sector	• Procedures for handling cases are standardized and mechanisms exist for ensuring they are followed. • Rules of evidence and standards for evaluating arguments exist and are applied in a predictable fashion. • Assignment of cases follows standardized procedures, does not allow judge shopping, and results in a reasonably equitable distribution of work. • Procedures are reasonably efficient and designed and reformulated in the interests of eliminating unnecessary steps and bottle-necks.	• There is a transparent process for entrance into the profession, based on educational back-ground and other relevant criteria. • Law school curriculum includes professional ethics. • Pre-appointment training and continuing education. • Professional codes of ethics governing the profession are widely known and enforced. • Denial of entry or disbarment is subject to objective, published rules, and is carried out by an independent professional body.

- Promotions, transfers, dismissals, and/or renewal of appointments are based on preestablished, publicized criteria

- There is a transparent appeals process to an independent judicial body for judges in the case of denial of promotion, transfer, or renewal

- Training programs are available and participation is encouraged and facilitated; some sort of entry-level training or orientation is compulsory

- Judges can be prosecuted for nonjudicial misconduct

- Administrative staff has rules of conduct, performance standards, and own career and disciplinary systems

- Adequate training is provided for administrative staff

- Internal resource distribution is based on need and workload

- Judges have the power to move cases along and to punish or deny efforts to create excessive delays.

- Where judicial decisions are not complied with, courts have additional means to enforce them.

- Judicial decisions are reversed only through a regularized appeals process.

- The pre-trial settlement of disputes is encouraged but not forced.

- There exist duly recognized alternative dispute resolution mechanisms, both court annexed and free standing, which provide a viable alternative to judicial processes.

- Where there is a shortage of qualified professionals, there is a provision for lay representation or performance of some legal duties, but these individuals are also subject to rules of conduct.

Table 5 (*continued*)

	Selection of Judges	Management of the Judicial "Career"[1]	Internal Administration	Resources	Judicial Processes	Legal Profession
Transparence/ Accountability	• Public input is solicited as a part of the judicial selection process • Appointments are adequately publicized • Selection process is open and transparent • There are limits on future government employment after term expires	• Standards for judicial performance and ethical behavior are publicized • There is a process for registering complaints about judicial misconduct and a means of follow-up. Information on complaints is publicly available • Public input is solicited as part of the judicial evaluation process	• There is a process for registering complaints about administrative misconduct • Adequate information is publicly provided on the roles and responsibilities of administrative officials attending the public	• Judicial budgets, salaries, and results of audits are publicly available • Judicial requests for additional resources are presented publicly • Proposals for major investments in infrastructure or equipment are presented publicly with opportunity for discussion	• The rules for how cases will be processed are well publicized. • Court users have access to information on the status of their case. • Hearings are publicly announced and open to the public. • Judicial decisions and statistics on case flow are publicized. • Ex parte meetings or conversations with litigants are expressly prohibited. • Press and other non-judicial groups may comment on decisions without fear of reprisals. • Court services are readily accessible to the entire population, and there are no unreasonable geographic, monetary, or legal barriers	• Information as to accredited bar members and any paralegal profession is easily available to public. • Disciplinary actions and disbarments are publicized. • There is an easily accessible process for providing complaints about attorneys' actions.

Independence						
	• Any external input (by other branches of government or private individuals and organizations) to the appointment process is subject to transparent rules and occurs only in accordance with established procedures • Evaluation of candidates is done by a body or office separate from that making the final selections • Judicial appointments are made as vacancies occur, not to coincide with changes in national administration	• Judges have permanent tenure or fixed, renewable appointments • Judicial salaries meet living wage and some reasonable proportion of good wage in private sector • Additional benefits (housing, vehicles, trips, training) are allocated through a transparent process with no nonjudicial input • Where external actors have complaints about judicial performance these can only be entered through the normal disciplinary process	• The selection and further management of administrative staff is handled through objective rules and regulations and is not subject to intervention by officials not legally authorized to provide specific inputs • Whether handled by an external body (e.g., Ministry of Justice) or by the judiciary itself, oversight of internal administration responds to judicial needs, not to the administrators' agenda	• Salaries and budgets cannot be reduced or their distribution altered by other branches of government • When judicial workload reaches unmanageable limits, the judiciary is able to obtain more resources	• Other branches of government do not override or ignore judicial decisions, and when they do, they are subject to legal action. • Decisions and powers accorded to the judiciary are not usurped by other governmental actors. • Judiciary is able to set its own rules for internal operations; where those rules are limited by enacted law, they have substantial input into shaping the latter.	• Access to professional status is managed only according to official rules. • Whether the judiciary or the bar association is responsible for admittance and discipline, it does this without irregular outside intervention. • Ability of lawyers to form professional associations is reasonably open. • Internal operations of bar associations are determined by the members themselves.

Source: Hammergren (1999).

Notes:

1. For countries without true career systems (e.g., where judges are elected or appointed "for life" to a single position), some of these categories will not apply and should not be scored.

2. The kind of explanation offered here is doubtless needed for some other criteria. The term "job-relevant" is used because many merit-based lists, while properly objective, focus on traits of questionable importance to what a judge does—publications, ability to recite laws or entire codes by memory, performance on psychometric tests supposed to reveal judicial vocation. Here, credit would be given for having objective criteria, but graded down for relevance.

3. Independence refers both to that of individual judges and of the judiciary as a whole. The dual definition does pose problems, but it is important in that it distinguishes the judicial model from that of ordinary bureaucracies.

do. The ultimate solution, a good, empirically based theory of judicial roles and impacts, however, is a long-term project. For specific assessments, the immediate task is to inventory and test current complaints and identify other problems that may be less obvious to those standing too close to the system.

Any reform project logically starts with a problem or a desired change in the status quo. Hence, early on and throughout the assessment, information will have to be gathered on what people believe to be wrong, because this constitutes the motivating force for the reform. Initial responses are likely to be vague and not very specific—the judiciary is not modern, the laws are out of date, there is too much delay, judges are overworked, biased, corrupt, or incompetent. Assessors will have to elicit more precision or at the very least some concrete examples of the alleged ills. Ideally, this will provide them with a list of more targeted areas for improvement with easily identified proximate causes (measurable delays or paralysis of cases caused by procedural bottlenecks, inefficient administrative practices, or too few judges or support staff; limited access caused by the physical distribution of courts, high court fees, or requirements for representation; widespread use of speed money or petty corruption caused by low salaries, insufficient supervision, or court practices that facilitate bribes). They are, however, just as likely to find that problems are exaggerated, misdiagnosed, or entirely ignored or that widely touted remedies are unlikely to produce much of any effect. Corruption or delay may be less common or more localized than usually believed. What looks like an excessive workload may be vastly inflated by a large number of inactive cases remaining in the courts. Judges may make good decisions, but enforcement may be avoided. Or local reformers may believe that all it will take is an up-to-date law to increase the efficacy of the criminal justice system or bring foreign investment flooding into the country.

Returning to the medical analogy, assessors are very much like a doctor facing a patient with a variety of complaints and symptoms who has already decided what is wrong and what needs to be done. The patient's complaints and symptoms cannot be ignored, but the self-diagnosis is frequently completely in error. What the patient would like to see fixed with a pill, a shot, or perhaps an operation may require a more complex treatment, including lifestyle changes and other less pleasant kinds of therapy. Because judicial health is a much more subjective state, reported ills and suggested remedies will necessarily be given more weight. Drawing on international experience, advisors can note the costs and other difficulties associated with making certain changes or the likelihood that proposed solutions will not bring the desired results, but in the end what constitutes a better system is in the eye of its users, not in any sort of universal standards.

4. Analytic Summary: Taken as a whole, the three preceding parts of the assessment provide an overview of the situation of the sector or organizations reviewed, list and prioritize the principal problems attributed by the local stakeholders or

found by the assessors, and identify traits and practices accounting for current patterns of operations and output. The analysts' further task is to use this information to derive an overall diagnosis of sector or organizational performance and suggest how it might be improved. Their reworking of the basic information should separate spurious or second-order problems from more basic ones and note where solutions might be more practically pursued outside the sector or organization.[14] Areas where further investigation is required should also be noted; in this sense, the initial assessment can be regarded as a first cut at diagnosis. Whereas the quality of the analysis hinges on the skills and knowledge of the assessment team, the emphasis on more standardized formats is intended to assist their efforts. It helps call their attention to details they might otherwise overlook, simplifies the collection of information, and provides a basis for evaluating the significance of their findings.

Because assessments (and evaluations) collectively constitute our best source of information on sector operations and reform programs, it is particularly important that they be made available to the entire reform community. There are evident obstacles to adopting this in practice. Unless they can be overcome, the discipline as a whole, as well as individual reform efforts, will find their progress limited.

MONITORING

Until the recent emphasis on results management, monitoring of judicial reforms was conspicuous by its near absence. When it was done, the emphasis was on tracking inputs or outputs delivered, not the impact on overall goals and objectives. Although the announced shift to tracking results is important, it poses problems for this kind of project because of how institutional change is accomplished.[15] The underlying logic of any institutional change project is inherently complex, involving a three-stage process in which certain desired improvements in organizational outputs and impacts are defined; they are linked to modifications in internal behaviors; and these behavioral changes are promoted by shifting the mix, composition, and quality of organizational structures, resources, and incentive systems. Until internal behaviors have responded to these shifts, outcomes and impacts are not likely to vary, and, if they do, there may be a temporary decline in quality or quantity while the new patterns are learned and perfected. This suggests a sort of progress by plateaus in which the second-order outcome changes will not occur incrementally,

14. Research in Mexico (World Bank 2002b, 2003b) on debt collection proceedings found many problems originating outside the courts—for example, poor practices in making loans, absence of credit bureaus, corrupt property registries, and lack of debtor education. Studies in Argentina, Brazil, Ecuador and Peru had similar findings. See World Bank (2003a, 2003b), Simon et al. (2002), and Gonzales et al. (2002).

15. "Announced" may be the best description. That anyone is actually tracking progress, even when indicators are included in project design, is not apparent. For the most part, bilaterals stick to inputs and the MDBs remain focused on disbursements.

or not begin to do so, until the first-order changes are relatively complete. In reality, there is still a fourth stage, in which improved outcomes (court performance variables) produce changes in extrajudicial behaviors and thus in overall societal well-being. We would not expect to detect outcome changes (and the subsequent impacts on societal goals) until the internal change process is well advanced. The resulting dilemma can be phrased as two related questions. How do we know anything is happening in the meantime? How can we be sure the long-term goals will ever be achieved?

Only the first is really a monitoring problem, but its solution is closely related to the second. If one cannot monitor progress through incremental improvements to the final objective (whether reduction of delay, improved decision making, greater trust in courts, or downstream impacts like higher growth rates, poverty or crime reduction), one will have to monitor it by tracking progress in making intermediate process modifications. In essence, this means monitoring by benchmarks—the completion of the stages in a change strategy that in the end will produce fundamental alterations in how things are done and thus in the value of outcomes. For example, a delay-reduction effort might start with the establishment of baseline data, proceed through an analysis of process bottlenecks, develop means for changing those not regulated by law and encouraging any needed law revision, introduce improved manual or automated systems, and so on. The benchmarks generally coincide with the project implementation plan, following the chronological order it establishes.

It is also possible, going to a much lower level of detail, to track the impact of these partial internal changes on lower-order behaviors. For example in a project attempting to improve the coordination of police and prosecutorial operations in Panama and thus their success in detecting, investigating and prosecuting crimes,[16] intermediate progress was measured by tracking changes in specific procedures—types of evidence collected, rate of consultations between police and prosecutors, or even something as simple as improvements in the format of the police charge sheet. These are extraordinarily context specific indicators, in terms of not only the specific country, but also the problems identified for resolution. In Panama, it was thought important to encourage police to number the pages of the charge sheet. This thus became an indicator of progress. In a conventional delay-reduction project, behavioral changes might include participants' adoption of new procedures, evidence that once the means to do so are installed, those responsible are keeping track of the progress of individual cases and trying to meet deadlines, or indications that records of individual judges or courtrooms are being monitored. In both examples, internal changes should be visible long before the outcome goal (more

---

16. This was a USAID project, undertaken in the early 1990s. I am indebted to Tim Cornish, a consultant with the project, for providing documents and explanations of the benchmarking process.

investigations completed within a shorter time, higher clearance rate of criminal cases, or reduced average time to disposition and backlog reduction for all cases) shows any signs of impact.

In the end, the significance of achieving the benchmarks or effecting the intermediate behavioral changes hinges on the validity of the overall strategy. If training judges will not produce better decisions, monitoring stages in implementing a training program or judges' absorption of new skills and knowledge will not have much point. This type of monitoring only makes sense in the context of a viable change strategy. The solution to this quandary is not to return to monitoring outcomes and impacts. However much those responsible might want to do so, they will not have visible systemwide results for years. Instead, the emphasis will have to go to improving the quality of strategies and finding ways to test the hypotheses on which they rest. There is, most would agree, considerable room for improvement here. Much of it rests on the other elements of better knowledge management, including improved analyses of country specific problems (assessments), a better use of the lessons of experience (starting with more systematic evaluations to bring them forth), and a concerted effort to explore hypothesized linkages for which empirical evidence is scant (research). This reinforces the relationship already noted among the topics explored in this chapter as well as the importance of increased attention to knowledge consolidation, dissemination and debate.

Among the elements critical to improving the strategic content of reforms, two warrant special emphasis: an effort to ensure that reform programs do have explicit strategies, thus lending themselves to monitoring, ex ante quality control, and ex post evaluation and the use of pilot programs to do a quick check on the anticipated outcomes. As regards the first measure, critics frequently note that large and small programs alike are too often mere collections of activities with only the most tenuous links to their presumed downstream goals. They embody strategies only in the loosest meaning of the term. Forcing their designers to articulate the means-ends changes they presumably incorporate might better align outcomes with inputs (How much impact will a code or a course on ethical behavior have on curbing rampant corruption?), weed out the less likely proposals (Will $19 million of new buildings and $1 million of computer equipment really increase access to justice in a country where judges are believed to be corrupt, incompetent, vulnerable to political pressures, and guided by outdated rules and procedures?), and establish a better base for monitoring and evaluation. This does not eliminate space for innovation. It does mean that an innovative approach will be recognized as such, more closely monitored for results, and modified or discarded if it does not produce them.

Novel approaches can also be tested in pilot projects. Rather than build all the new computer-equipped courtrooms or train the entire judiciary, the proposed measures can be applied in one district to assess their impact and determine how it might be enhanced. Pilots can be used to determine the costs of successful imple-mentation, evaluate competing variations, and make adjustments so that replica-tion, if desired, can be done more economically. Pilots, of course, are special cases and should be evaluated with this understanding. What works for a group of judges who see themselves as having been selected for being in the vanguard will proba-bly have less impact for the entire universe. Pilot projects are no novelty in judicial reform programs. Unfortunately, they have too often become ends in themselves—neither created with an eye to their replicability nor used as inputs to a broader knowledge base. This accounts for a growing skepticism about their value, for which their backers must take a large part of the responsibility. The other part lies in an inadequate evaluation of their results and potential impact, and thus leads to a third element of the knowledge-management agenda.

EVALUATION

Although it is commonly acknowledged that evaluation is essential to program development, this lesson has had little apparent impact on judicial reforms. For the quantity of work that has been done, evaluations are remarkably few, and all too often neither widely consulted nor even available. Everyone reads the evalua-tion of their own project; almost no one reads those of anyone else's work. This suggests an amazing lack of interest in acquiring information and an incentive sys-tem which allows and possibly encourages it. It is also evident that by intent or mere oversight, evaluations are not easily accessible, even to members of agencies which conducted them. The perennial suggestion that major donors share their evaluations is a good sign. It will be difficult to implement, if only because they may not know where they have stored them.[17]

Participants in judicial reform programs seem remarkably resistant to evaluation. Courts and governments rarely evaluate their programs. NGOs seem to regard eval-uations as an infringement of their independence, and major donor agencies have been very lax in reviewing their own work. It has been suggested that this is a con-sequence of a disciplinary bias. Lawyers dominate the programs, and law is not an experimental science. Lawyers are more inclined to argue than to test their posi-tions. Moreover, because of the values involved (justice, rights, fundamental prin-ciples) and the politically charged nature of the topic, measuring or quantifying

---

17. A series of informal interviews with individuals charged with evaluating programs for the UNDP, IDB, USAID, and the World Bank made it clear that none of them had access to all the in-house docu-mentation that should have been available. I suspect, because the work was commissioned by the respec-tive agencies, that this reflects an information storage and retrieval problem, not a conscious effort to keep their evaluators in the dark. It also demonstrates an inadequate internal usage of the documents. Were they being read and used, they would have been easier to locate.

achievements is often regarded as denigrating the importance of the theme. Despite a recent effort by several donor agencies to conduct evaluations of their entire programs, observers are still wondering whether the results will be released and if so, in what form. Preliminary reports from the evaluation teams suggest that their findings may not please agency leaders who have highlighted their dedication to promoting judicial reform.

Aside from evaluation phobia, another major disincentive is that evaluations add to costs. Like assessments, they are seen as absorbing funds that might be put directly into reform, and, because they come at the end, when funds are most likely to be scarce, they are still more obvious targets for elimination. However, in-house policy, including the funds initially allocated for evaluation and monitoring, and decisions, like that of USAID, to make evaluation optional indicate that more than last-minute cost cutting is at work.[18] Nonetheless, the increasing impression that programs are repeating old errors, that strategic programming has if anything weakened over the last years, and that the number of objective pursued has grown with no particular relationship to program content demonstrates a serious failure to learn from and build on experience.[19] Whatever the reason for the inattention to evaluation, it may be the largest single contributor to this situation and an obvious place to work immediate changes.

A first lesson and recommendation is thus that systematic evaluations must be performed because without them there is little way of determining whether programs are producing results and how they might be improved. Results indicators, like those USAID has attempted to adopt and other agencies are also pursuing, are no substitute. They will only serve this role once we have a better understanding of how judiciaries and reforms operate. The further advantage of evaluation is that it not only looks at progress, but also analyzes the path for arriving there. That second kind of knowledge is essential for anyone attempting to replicate a presumed success. It does little good to know that country X has reduced the average time to disposition of cases by 25 percent if one does not know how it did this. Evaluation can also focus on additional consequences and contributing factors. Delay reduction could be achieved by simplifying proceedings, improving in-court management, automation, discouraging filings, doubling the number of judges, or dismissing more cases for lack of merit. Each of these mechanisms would shorten times to disposition, but each has different implications for financial or other costs (for example, reduced access). Perhaps the reduction coincided with a substantial upturn in the economy, which is usually associated with lesser recourse to court services.

18. This is not only for judicial reform but for all programs, and was motivated by the agency's shift to a management by results mode.

19. Donors have not helped here with their mandatory checklists intended to ensure every institutional interest—from gender and environment to fiscal discipline—is covered. The World Bank's "Quality at Entry" questionnaire featured twenty items. Apparently it has been revised to five, multipart questions.

This might mean that the program itself had no impact, as the reduced demand was sufficient to allow speedier processing of the remaining caseload.

Evaluating individual projects is important, but its value is substantially increased when evaluations are compared. Comparison makes it easier to identify the causal relationships and the intervening variables that affect them. Especially in an area as complex as judicial reform, where many programmatic interventions are introduced simultaneously and where exogenous variables can have a still stronger influence, it is all too easy to pick out spurious relationships. Was it the training, the higher salaries, or the internal monitoring that caused judges to speed up their handling of cases, change the patterns of their decisions, or become more resistant to bribes? Could one have achieved the same results with only one of the interventions or achieved more by doubling one of the inputs? Or was the result a consequence of some external change with no relationship to the actual reform? These questions are not easily answered, but there is additional opportunity to weed out the irrelevant or to define the conditions for relevancy when several examples are under investigation.

Thus, a second lesson and recommendation is an emphasis on comparisons of evaluations or cross-project evaluations of single activities—training programs, automation, delay reduction, or changes in basic laws. As this latter effort approaches research we can leave it for a moment, and look further at the process of comparing evaluations themselves. For this to happen the first obvious steps are that evaluations be done, that they be widely available, and that a program or incentives be introduced to encourage comparative study. A second need is for evaluations to be structured to allow comparison. This has generally not been the case. Evaluations, whether done by in-house experts (either in evaluation or on judicial reform, generally not on both), contracted outsiders, or external agencies (a governmental body or an NGO), tend to be shaped by the project at hand and by the specific interests of the evaluators. As a result, they are usually directly comparable only when the same evaluator does them, and that person's interests may still not coincide with those of the parties using the evaluations to improve future programming.

When general protocols are established, they usually are so open-ended that they allow the evaluators to pick and choose what they will review. The World Bank's standard evaluation format (prior situation, strategy adopted, what was done, results and lessons learned) is as good as any but leaves enormous leeway to the evaluator. More specific terms of reference tend to be determined by the project under review and thus often avoid some key questions. (Was this project worth undertaking? Was training or law revision the best way of achieving the desired ends?) They instead commonly focus on whether the inputs were provided as stipulated, the immediate outputs achieved, and how the quality of the individual activities could have been improved. In training programs, for example, attention often goes to the training methodologies, the content of individual courses, and the means for selecting students. A training expert, the usual candidate for this part of the evaluation, is hardly likely to question training's contribution to the overall reform. Where the evaluation is entrusted to one expert, he or she may ask some of those harder questions about less favored elements, but, there again, the standards remain dependent on the evaluator's inherent preferences.

What this suggests is the need for a dual focus in evaluations: one part examining the project at hand (to determine how well it has carried out the proposed actions) and the other focusing on more general questions, both the adequacy of the strategy and the way it addressed certain common problems. For an individual agency doing many evaluations it should be easy to adopt this format. Its implementation will be harder, in light of the inherent limitations of evaluators themselves—their own biases and preferences, a tendency to not want to be overly critical (an evaluator who finds himself declaring even a few strategies not worth following may not be an evaluator for long), and the difficulty of finding people with both specific knowledge and the ability to take an overview. Using generic evaluation experts is usually no solution because of the specialized, substantive knowledge required. USAID's first overview of its rule-of-law programs came under heavy criticism from project managers for just this reason.[20] It was claimed that the authors, coming from other disciplines, never understood the purposes of the projects, conflated their objectives with cause lawyering (the use of existing systems to reach immediate benefits for the poor), and misread the multiple and interactive aims of many of the common elements.[21] Participants have been equally critical of macroeconomic analyses of judicial performance and reform impacts and especially of their efforts to derive composite or unidimensional scores for both.[22] Designing better evaluations is really a collaborative task in which evaluation and substantive experts both have a role.

The third need and recommendation is thus to make evaluation a little less free form, by establishing general standards (the work of the evaluation experts) and common themes and questions (the responsibility of those designing and overseeing programs). The project-specific criteria will be set by the sponsoring agency (assuming there is one) and the project itself. This is the within-system evaluation, the one that focuses on whether the project followed its intended strategy, complied with any rules the sponsoring agency requires, and achieved its proposed results.

20. Blair and Hansen (1994).

21. For example, training which is often used to build support for reform, collect more information on common problems, and provoke judges to take a different view of their role or develop sensitivities to the needs of a wider variety of clients, was relegated to simple capacity building.

22. Many of these analyses rely on surveys or expert opinions to assess quality. A common criticism has been that those surveyed often have a narrow view and that, in any case, even knowledgeable informants tend to misjudge real operations. In one recent study, lawyers from prestigious law firms were asked about the duration of debt collection cases. As several discussants noted, these lawyers probably rarely if ever do such work. See Djankov et al. (2002) and La Porta et al. (1998).

These are important questions for evaluating any specific project, but they are less important in furthering programmatic knowledge. For the latter, the evaluation will be expected to address the adequacy of solutions in advancing certain common objectives—delay reduction, combating corruption, ensuring the selection of the most capable judges, encouraging judges to make speedy, fair decisions, increasing access for marginalized groups, and so on. Once again, selecting these categories will be easier for assistance agencies administering multiple programs, but they are also the ones best situated to compare results.

RESEARCH

Judicial reforms have become very routinized (a mixture of training, administrative restructuring, legal change, automation, ADR, and subsidized services for the poor, with the odd building thrown in to improve the judicial image or reduce the purported perils of renting facilities). This creates a risk that the actions recommended above will only lead to improving a second-best approach. Most reform programs attempt to make an existing process work better but rarely question whether that process represents the best use of resources in advancing high-priority needs. They also tend to take their impact on extrasystem objectives (economic growth, equity, political stability, and citizen security) on faith because of the obvious difficulties of tracking these changes. Better assessments, monitoring, and evaluation are unlikely to tackle these broader issues. However radical its promises, reform like every other human activity tends to follow established patterns for all the usual reasons. Regardless of whether training has ever accomplished any improvement, it is far easier to design a reform program highlighting training than one excluding it. Certain elements are added largely because they are popular— judges want new laws, equipment, training, and buildings. External assistance agencies feature activities conventionally included in all their programs. And, finally, there are the measures arising in preconceived notions about problems and their solutions that are again easier to incorporate than to contest. Consequently, knowledge building based only on actual reform programs is inherently limited. The full range of possibilities is unlikely to be explored because they have never become part of the standard reform repertoire.

Research is thus a vital fourth element in the knowledge-management program. It can examine conventional understandings, test dominant hypotheses, and explore novel solutions that would not be possible in an ordinary reform. Research on judiciaries and judicial reforms is far from nonexistent. As currently conducted, whether by donors, academics, or NGOs, it suffers from some potentially serious problems. First, it is not very coordinated in the sense of pursuing a set of common themes and questions, building on prior work, or confronting differing findings.

Second, many researchers and most practitioners appear to lack a good overview of the relevant body of existing studies. Third, even when sponsored by donor agencies, research is rarely policy relevant in the sense of exploring themes that might improve reform programming.

The explanations for the first two phenomena largely lie in the absence of a well-established academic discipline focusing on the judiciary and its reform. Researchers come from a variety of disciplines. This in itself is desirable, but some of the negative side effects are that content, methodologies, and eventual dissemination are usually driven by the parent discipline's priorities and that published articles are scattered through a vast number of journals, only a few of which focus specifically on legal and judicial reform. The fact that academic careers, access to funding, and publication depend on a disciplinary community less interested in judicial reform for its own sake creates two interlocking vicious circles, which also explain a good part of the third observation. Researchers select topics, questions, and methodologies defined as important by their disciplines and thus tend to keep cross-disciplinary, thematically determined issues off the agenda, thereby guaranteeing they will continue to be seen as less significant. Practitioners' inherently lesser interest in reviewing research is thus reinforced because much research is not relevant to their activities.

These tendencies affect even research sponsored by assistance agencies, which often seems more influenced by academic than practitioner concerns. For example, much of the recent work sponsored by the World Bank has involved the statistical analysis of relationships between aggregate indicators of judicial and economic performance. Its apparent purpose is to demonstrate the need for judicial reform, but beyond that its impact on reform content is dubious. Even discounting questions about concept validity,[23] the further problem is in unpacking the indicators to understand the nature (and direction) of the relationships. Efforts to breech that gap by linking major variations in judicial structure or legal tradition to performance face similar criticisms. The construction of both the dependent and independent variables often involve some fairly arbitrary distinctions,[24] but, even if we accept their findings, the implicit recommendations (change to a common-law

23. These are legion. Most use judicial performance indicators based on surveys or expert opinions. Even in a single country, there are question as to what is really being measured (public perceptions, the perceptions of a small group of citizens, experiences respondents are willing to report, or something else). Cross-national comparisons are still more problematic because of the different perceptions of what is normal.

24. A series of studies (La Porta et al. 1998) focusing on differences between civil and common law systems have been criticized (Pistor 1995; Berkowitz et al. 2001) for overlooking the enormous variation within and cross fertilization between the two traditions. Another study (Buscaglia and Dakolias 1999) relating delay to such traits as computerization of courts, investments in infrastructure, and proactive judges raises many questions as to how the last three variables were constructed, as well as to the posited causal links. Courts that invest in computers may simply be courts interested in reducing delay. It may be that interest, not the computers, which explains their success in shortening time to disposition.

system, or a parliamentary as opposed to presidential one) will not be easy to enact. As discussed in chapter 6, although the grand distinctions (civil versus common law, inquisitorial versus accusatory criminal proceedings) may matter, the emphasis on tracking their impact fails to recognize that they are the least amenable to change. It also overlooks the potentially greater variations within the grand categories (for example, between the inquisitorial justice system as practiced in Haiti and in France). Such within-category variations are intrinsically less interesting to academic researchers because they hinge on a multitude of differences of detail, most of which will not be statistically significant. The obvious conclusion is that, if practitioners are going to benefit from research, they must help define the agenda and finance those studies most likely to have an impact on their own work. Inevitably these will involve more intensive comparisons of a limited number of cases. Because they will be more costly to conduct, it is also important that the themes be selected with care.[25]

As a start toward a new research agenda, the following general topics are suggested, ordered from least to most ambitious:

- A review (possibly as cross-project single-theme evaluations) of the activities (training, automation, law reform) common to most projects to identify variations in approaches, difficulties encountered, costs, and results. This is the most basic form of knowledge generation needed. Although it might not substantially alter the cafeteria approach to programming, it could reduce redundancy and increase efficiency of actions. Despite a recent aversion to the notion of best practices, at the level of individual activities the concept still warrants consideration.[26]
- A review (via cross-project, single-theme evaluations) of progress in advancing the common subgoals (delay reduction, increased access, anticorruption meaures) found in most programs. While more complicated than the above (because it usually includes multiple components and activities), the value of this approach lies in its emphasis on affecting outcomes.
- Research on the factors commonly blamed for poor judicial performance and giving rise to many standard reform policies. Among the high-priority candidates are salaries (for their purported impact on corruption, quality of judges,

25. Aside from the disciplinary biases of the researchers doing macro studies (most of whom are economists) another explanation for their methodological focus is that they can use data bases that already exist. This allows them to do a study covering eighty countries for less than it costs to do original research in one.

26. For some reason certain donors (most notably the World Bank) have become extremely critical of the term. Taken as blueprint solutions, the criticism may be well placed. As more flexible rules of thumb or basic principles for conducting activities, however, "best practices" are demonstrably effective. See Scott (1998), for a discussion of "rules of thumb" in the context of all development projects. For example, we know that training is best done with a needs assessment; that the focus should be not on simple knowledge transfer, but rather on improving concrete practices and behaviors and that repetition and complementary organizational changes substantially enhance training's effect.

efficiency, and efficacy); size and control of budgets (as related to quality of service); variations in appointment systems, selection criteria, tenure, and the use of lateral entry; differences in forms of judicial governance; and equipment and infrastructure.[27]

- Research on some of the overlooked candidate causes of poor judicial performance—for example, the role of the private bar and variations in its organization, power, or the sheer number of private professionals; the influence of educational institutions and patterns in legal training; the effects of judicial fees, prohibitions on pro se representation, legal (il)literacy, and the types of services provided in limiting access to courts; the adequacy of and disincentives for using alternative and community dispute-resolution mechanisms; and the importance of registries, credit bureaus, and other nonjudicial institutions. Judicial reforms are increasingly criticized as too "court-centered," which is to say they do not recognize the role other institutions play in conditioning court performance. Ironically, the best way to improve court operations may not always lie within the courts.

- A simple examination of how courts and other sector institutions really operate and how incentive patterns and other constraints shape their output. Most reforms are based on uncontested conventional wisdom (there are delays, large amounts are commonly at stake, large users avoid the judiciary because they do not trust it, and so on). Many of these assumptions do not hold up in fact, and, to the extent they can be replaced with a more accurate picture of what is occurring, overall reform planning will benefit. On extremely interesting area is the issue of congestion—and why all judges, whether receiving 100 or 2,000 annual filings, feel they have too much work. The simple answer is that work expands to fill the time available, but a closer examination might reveal ways of time filling that do not contribute to a better product.

- Finally, because of the use of extrajudicial impacts as the principal justification for reform programs, more attention needs to go to exploring them. This is the most ambitious part of the research agenda, and the one least directly related to the immediate interests of reformers. Nevertheless, it is critical to ensuring the value of their work. Here the current emphasis on aggregate, multicountry analysis can be abandoned in favor of more intensive exploration of the themes within one or several countries. The macrostudies are suggestive of where one might look; what is now required is an exploration of the specific linkages. If delay is critical because of its impacts on growth or poverty reduction, what kinds of delay are critical for whom and for what? What kinds of compensatory

27. Equipment and infrastructure often constitute the major part of investments in reform programs. Ad hoc arguments and some empirical work (Buscaglia and Dakolias 1999) suggest an impact on performance. However, despite (or because) of their popularity, critics have expressed doubts that are worth pursuing.

mechanisms are adopted and with what results? Do the answers vary across and within different types of legal systems and societies?

There is still a further area of research, or just speculation, focusing on the questions of what justice or judicial reform can realistically accomplish and why it is worth doing. This probably is of limited interest to those sponsoring reforms as part of their public policy agenda, in light of their usual emphasis on resolving specific problems, ranging from insufficient economic investment to excessive criminal and civil violence. Classic research methodologies, whether macro or micro, qualitative or quantitative, will be of less help here, especially because this particular set of questions requires transcending or at least contesting more of our assumptions about what a justice system does, the place of law in contemporary societies, and the role of the organizations that enforce it. Some of the less radical insights may be of use to reform practitioners, but this is an open-ended project that could lead in very different and not very practical directions. A few longtime observers have begun to call for this type of investigation, in part because of their doubts that any of us are working with the "right" paradigm.[28] In a less ambitious form, the exercise is also relevant to the emerging questions, raised in chapter 5, about the constitutional structure of the balance of powers. Ongoing judicial reforms will remain less transcendental in their thrusts—striving to make the existing system work better or to effect less monumental changes in its logic. Still, it is useful to be reminded that there are alternative ways to accomplish whatever judicial systems do and that the dominant model of the judicial function simplifies, but never adequately captures reality. There is, for example, the clear disjuncture between the neoinstitutionalist paradigm of the courts' role in shaping behavior through rule enforcement, and judges' and lawyers' more usual description of their functions as resolving or winning individual and individualized disputes. The two depictions are not incompatible, but, as anyone who has explained the economists' model to a group of skeptical litigators must admit, the gap between the two levels of understanding merits further exploration.

With the exception of this last area, which is best left to political philosophers and theorists, donors will have to sponsor this research. To the extent they can help build a body of relevant work, they may also help legitimate it within the academic community. An obvious first priority is that they reorient their in-house research programs to coincide more closely with programming needs. A second is a larger research budget both for in-house and sponsored work. And a third is that research be reviewed and used. That it has not been so far may be a disguised blessing, but it is time to replace the two vicious circles with a virtuous one. If reform planners are forced to incorporate research findings in their own designs, they will pay more

28. See Faundez (2005a) for some speculation on this point.

attention to what is proposed and what is delivered. When the results are, as is currently the case, contradictory,[29] someone will have to resolve the differences.

CONCLUSIONS

There is a special irony in judicial reform's problems with knowledge management. The sector itself prioritizes intellectual effort and is dedicated to processing information. There are also disciplinary and agency biases at work. Lawyers are not scientists and reformers tend to be activists, not dispassionate analysts. Multidisciplinary contributions are a plus, but the absence of an applied disciplinary base has made their input less practical. It has also discouraged cross-disciplinary dialogue. The various disciplines are present, but they do not necessarily build on each others' work. Both reformers and academics with an interest in the theme, and not simply in advancing in their respective primary homes, will need to overcome these obstacles if the field itself is to survive.

The topic does have more status, as an academic and applied discipline, in the industrialized nations. It would thus be helpful if those involved in Third World reforms paid more attention to the developments in the "North."[30] Some clearly have, but their readings tend to be highly selective, and one suspects they are not following the emerging arguments in full. Otherwise they might put a little less faith in the remedies they adopt, many of which are now being questioned in the countries where they were first introduced.[31] One characteristic of a mature discipline is its development and recognition of major unresolved issues and internal conflicts. Members argue with each other because they agree on where they disagree, and it is this process of confronting contradictions that eventually leads to a better shared understanding. As practiced in the Third World, judicial reform and judicial studies still lack that trait. It is as though the participants had agreed not to enter into conflict and thus to endorse a common dogma. There are exceptions, but they tend to be unwelcome because they are violating the firemen's syndrome by treading on the hose.

Improved knowledge management inevitably threatens that cozy status quo. It requires more work and endangers conventional routines. As always, the basic challenge is to get participants to focus on the long-term losses as opposed to the short run gains. As long as those who control the funding continue to believe that

29. For example, two recent World Bank publications found that salaries were (1) unimportant to and (2) highly predictive of levels of judicial corruption. The different sources of data easily explain the discrepancies, but to my knowledge no one has even noticed them.

30. This is the symbolic North—some very interesting work is also being done in Australia. See Australian Commission (2000).

31. The benefits of ADR and various types of proactive case management are two examples.

judicial reform is important and feasible, there are immediate advantages to working in the dark. In the short term, the funders will not notice the difference, and they might actually be disheartened by reports that things are not as easy or as certain as portrayed. Still, if the interest is in working real changes, as opposed to the merely cosmetic and in enhancing our ability to continue making them, our knowledge base requires continual attention. Better assessments, monitoring, evaluation, and research are a start. If we have collectively failed to ascend the learning curve, that is primarily because we have failed to construct one.

THE CASE OF ARGENTINA

This chapter was first drafted in Argentina in late-2003, a setting providing a number of cautionary lessons for would-be judicial reformers. The lessons derive from the fact that in the prior decade Argentina made notable strides in implementing many of the usual reform recommendations. This was done in a less concentrated and publicized fashion than has been customary in most countries. As a consequence, it is probably misleading to speak of a single Argentine reform. Aside from the constitutional amendments introduced in 1994, many of the changes occurred gradually and with minimal central direction or planning. Nonetheless, the nation's political and judicial leaders have responded to concerns about the sector's poor performance with a series of actions intended as remedies. Taken as a whole, they cover the full range of partial strategies and the activities commonly associated with them.

Most of the changes discussed here occurred at the federal level. Many have been imitated and in some cases anticipated by provincial court systems. It is well to keep in mind that Argentina's judiciary, like that of Mexico and Brazil, is federally organized.[1] The "national courts" of the federal capital (Buenos Aires) belong to the federal system and are divided into *fueros* (specialized jurisdictions) that hear either local or federal cases (as determined by applicable law) in narrower substantive areas.[2] Elsewhere in the country, twenty-three independent provincial court systems exist alongside those belonging to one of fifteen federal judicial districts. There is one set of substantive codes for the entire country, but each province has its own procedural codes.

The Problems

Complaints about judicial performance, at both the provincial and federal levels, have a long history in Argentina. In general, they are not much different from

1. It also bears noting that the three vary considerably as to organizational details, the rules for assigning cases to federal or local courts, and the impact of federal law on state or provincial court operations.

2. See Bielsa and Graña (1999), for a description of the national judiciary. There is also a small set of municipal courts in Buenos Aires. They currently hear only misdemeanor and local administrative cases, but represent a move to give the capital an independent court system.

elsewhere in the region. They originate both within the sector and among its clients, political elites, and the broader public. Complaints from judges and other members of the legal community tend to focus on insufficient institutional autonomy, excessive workloads, and inadequate budgets. Contrary to common regional practices, management of Argentine court budgets and other administrative matters traditionally fell to ministries or secretaries of justice, not to the respective supreme or superior court. Formal executive control of appointments and other career decisions was the normal rule. Typically, this meant the president or governor selected the judges, with some or all appointments ratified by the legislature. The real level of political interference may have been no greater than in countries where the supreme court nominally managed budgets and appointments, but the legal foundations of the Argentine arrangements made them the target of criticisms from reform-minded judges.[3]

With respect to the judges' additional complaints, Argentina's litigation rate is moderately high (roughly 9,500 cases per 100,000 population), but its complement of judges (4,029, or 10.9 per 100,000 inhabitants) and judicial workload (875 annual filings per judge) appear reasonable in that light.[4] There are problems of geographic and functional distribution. Some judicial districts or specialized courts (*fueros*) have far more work than others. Argentina's courts receive less financial support than they would like, but in regional (and global) terms they are among the better off. The judicial share of the public budget has risen over recent years, currently reaching 3.5 percent. Until the economic crisis of 2001, court budgets were sufficient to allow significant investments in buildings and equipment.[5] Budgets also provided for a very large auxiliary staff, working within the courtrooms and in central administrative offices. At the federal level, the staff per judge ratio is about twenty to one; in the provincial courts the ratio is usually lower. As compared to the rest of the public sector, judicial salaries are relatively high. Moreover, judges are alone among public employees in not paying income taxes, thanks to the Supreme Court's interpretation of the constitutional prohibition on lowering their salaries.

3. This qualification is important, as some judges obviously owe their positions to executive backing and thus benefit from the traditional system.

4. Argentina, Ministerio de Justicia (2002).

5. During the 1990s, Argentina was the regional star of IMF-backed macroeconomic policies, basing part of its success on pegging the peso to the dollar. A five-year recession, escalating public and private sector debt, and an overvalued currency produced the crisis of late 2001. The country defaulted on its debt payments, devalued its currency, and only prevented a complete collapse of its financial system by freezing bank accounts and converting dollar accounts and debt into pesos at indexed rates. In the eight following months, real per capita income fell to half its former level, the percentage of the population living below the poverty line rose from 30 to slightly more than 50 percent, and unemployment soared. The crisis provoked the resignation of President Fernando de la Rúa and the creation of an interim government, which decided to advance the next national elections to March 2003. Economic conditions have since improved, but the courts' budget (converted from "peso-dollars" to devalued pesos at a one-to-one ratio), like that of the entire public sector, buys considerably less than it once did.

Contrary to the judicial view, the public has begun to question the costs of maintaining their court system. High salaries, large staffs, and short workdays, as compared to the rest of the public sector, reinforce the impression that at current budgetary levels, the outputs are less than might reasonably be expected. Delays, corruption, and erratic decisions are other mainstays of public criticism. Political interference in personnel and other operational matters has been criticized by jurists and ordinary citizens as a problem in its own right and a source of many others. Judicial competence has been less of an issue than the belief that loyalty to external benefactors biases individual decisions, facilitates freelance corruption, and reduces judges' interest in providing a high-quality public service. Over the past years, the press has called attention to irregular rulings and to judges whose lifestyles seem to far exceed even their generous salaries. Especially during the early years of the Menem government (1989–99), federal judges showed an exaggerated support for his programs and a strong disinclination to pursue investigations of government officials. Many judges, including members of the Supreme Court, had dozens of outstanding complaints against them, but disciplinary actions were infrequent and criminal sanctions or permanent removal far rarer.

At a more pedestrian level, individual judges commonly had thousands of theoretically active files, closure rates for criminal cases, and especially for major crimes, were low, and, though delays in handling civil cases appeared less than widely believed, they still might take several years to come to judgment.[6] Moreover, the procedural rules gave ample opportunity for bad-faith litigation. Party-initiated delay was more important than slow judging, but the point is that the system was not designed to combat it. While procedural codes often established deadlines for each stage in a judicial proceeding, few courts actively enforced them.

Many of these problems had extrajudicial origins—in the legal framework, the actions of other sector agencies, and the role of the public and private bar. The judges, however, did not help their image with an attitude that either downplayed the complaints or dismissed their responsibility for identifying and addressing the underlying causes. Courts were also notorious for a reluctance to provide information on their performance or adopt new standards for operational transparency. Judgments were usually available for public review, but the Supreme Court in both its official rulings and less official statements tended to stress the judiciary's special status as regards measures like assets declarations, ethics codes, or the release of ordinary statistics. In its view, judicial independence exempted the courts from practices introduced by other branches of government and required that the judiciary design its own policies in these areas.

6. See World Bank (2003a) and Garavano et al. (2000).

The Reforms

Although many of these complaints persist to this day, during the past decade a number of actions have been taken to address them. Since the constitutional reforms of 1994, Argentina's federal court system has been under a new form of judicial governance, vested in a twenty-person judicial council. With this change, the Ministry of Justice lost its role in managing the federal judicial budget and its part in selecting members of the federal bench. The council's size represents an effort to prevent control of the judiciary by any other branch of government or political faction. Membership includes representatives from the judiciary, the private bar, the executive, and the legislature. The council's responsibilities for judicial appointments and administration do not include the Supreme Court. The court manages its own budget; the executive names its members subject to Senate ratification. For other federal judges, the council holds competitive examinations for vacant positions and prepares a list of three candidates for each slot, from which the executive (president) makes its selection, which must be ratified by the Senate. The executive is not bound by the order of the lists and may nominate any candidate on them for the position in question. After the council's physical creation (delayed until 1998), however, presidents and many governors, in those provinces adopting a council mechanism, informally agreed to follow the councils' recommendations.[7] Provincial councils are smaller than the federal body and usually limited to vetting candidates. Regardless of whether a council exists, administrative management lies with the provincial superior or supreme court.

Although Argentina's courts only recently escaped from an unusual degree of executive oversight, they enjoyed an equally atypical measure of formal political powers for decades.[8] Argentina's diffuse system of constitutional judicial review dates back to the mid-nineteenth century. Any judge, at the provincial or state level, may refuse to apply a law he or she considers unconstitutional or rule against a government action on the same basis. Judges can offer immediate injunctive relief to parties claiming violation of their rights. These decisions may be appealed and eventually reach the supreme court. Although most supreme court rulings are not legally binding beyond the case in question, lower-level judges normally accord them the weight of binding (not merely persuasive) precedent. Once the court releases its opinion, it is thus assumed to be the final word on the larger issue. In recent years, the country has begun to adopt mechanisms for collective litigation

7. It is not clear how a change introduced in 2004 by President Nestor Kirchner affects this understanding. Kirchner opened the selection process to public discussion, starting with his own nominees to the supreme court.

8. Provincial courts are still subject to executive interference. Since 2000, several governors (including now President Nestor Kirchner) had superior courts enlarged or their members replaced to shape their rulings.

and has further expanded the rights guaranteed under its constitution by incorporating all those included in international conventions to which it is a signatory. A freedom of information law, still under discussion by congress in late 2005, is intended to clarify and regulate the constitutionally guaranteed rights in this area.

Access-enhancement measures have not been neglected. Parties appearing in court usually require legal counsel, but those unable to pay have a variety of options. There is an active group of NGOs promoting public-interest litigation and providing legal services to needy citizens. They supplement the subsidized counsel provided by the state and some pro bono work by private attorneys. Certain governmental entities, a human rights ombudsman and an anticorruption office, are also active in receiving, investigating, and representing complaints about public-sector abuse. Although civil plaintiffs usually must pay filing fees, initial charges may be waived for indigent parties; labor cases do not require prepayment of fees.[9] Finally, Argentina is a regional leader in introducing alternative dispute-resolution mechanisms.[10] Since 1996, pretrial mediation is required for most civil cases entered in the national courts of Buenos Aires, and many provincial courts have begun to provide mediation services on a voluntary basis. Court- and NGO-sponsored mediation is often available free of charge.

In 1991, Argentina adopted a new federal criminal procedures code, implanting a "modern-mixed system." Investigations are still done under the supervision of an instructional judge, but the public ministry now decides whether an indictment will be requested and presents the oral arguments against the defendant if a trial is held. The 1994 constitutional amendments gave the ministry greater political independence; its prosecutors (*fiscales*) have career status and its head, the attorney general (*Procurador General de la Nación*), serves in that position for ten years. Several provinces have adopted similar changes. A few, like Córdoba and Mendoza, introduced codes featuring more accusatorial proceedings, eliminating the investigative judges among other changes.

Immediate Results

One disadvantage of incrementally planned and executed programs is the potential for individual elements working against each other. For example, when the criminal procedures reforms went into effect, the number of federal judges was increased to allow full implementation. Because this occurred before the changes to the appointment system, President Carlos Menem was able to stack the federal bench (including a supreme court expanded from five to nine members) with

---

9. In both civil and labor cases, *costas* (a combination of court and attorney fees) are part of the final award. Judges may assign them to one party, divide them between the two, or have parties pay their own expenses.

10. See Garth and Dezalay (2002, 242–45).

judges loyal to him and his party. Because federal (and provincial) judges enjoy permanent tenure, most of those individuals remain in place. Menem's appointees to the criminal courts, and especially those in the national courts of Buenos Aires, were repeatedly associated with irregularities in both their professional and personal lives and are widely believed to have blocked investigations of official corruption.[11] Members of his "automatic majority" on the supreme court also accumulated numerous complaints about their professional conduct, with the chief justice alone having forty outstanding charges.[12] The extremely negative impact on public perceptions would eventually enable President Nestor Kirchner to force out the *menemista* justices. In the meantime, the situation, as elaborated below, substantially complicated executive-judicial relations in responding to the 2001–2002 economic emergency.

In the post-Menem period, the federal adoption of council governance has reduced complaints about politicized appointments and judicial subservience to the executive branch. Its introduction of competitive, merit selection is also improving the quality of the bench. The council has been less successful in tackling other impediments to performance. Its twenty members are so embroiled in internal battles as to preclude attention to increasing judicial productivity, redistributing court workloads, lobbying for legal change, or identifying and disciplining judicial malfeasance. Instead, reforms in these areas have been introduced in a decentralized fashion by individual federal *cámaras* (appellate courts) or more advanced provincial judiciaries. Changes include installation of automated case tracking and statistical systems; more transparent mechanisms for assigning cases to individual judges; training programs and other measures to professionalize staff; efforts to push judges to comply with legal time limits; modified procedural systems; and promotion of alternative dispute resolution. Most of the innovations and their impacts remain very localized, but there are signs of interprovincial cooperation to encourage their replication. The new supreme court has shown an unprecedented interest in improving federal performance. Under the current rules, however, that responsibility lies with the council in which the court has a minority participation.

Access-enhancement measures have an equally mixed record. Alternative dispute resolution has only been widely embraced in Buenos Aires where it is in fact obligatory. Early studies suggest that it has reduced the number of cases eventually sent to the courts, either because disputes are successfully mediated or because parties decide not to pursue them.[13] In the provinces, progress is limited. Judges, lawyers, and their clients appear to harbor reservations about the intrinsic fairness of the proceedings. Lawyers also resist mediation, or interfere in its operations, because of the anticipated impact on their earnings. Whereas state-financed counsel

11. Abaid and Thieberger (2005) summarize the stories reaching the press.
12. See Abaid and Thieberger (2005, 20).
13. See Garavano et al. (2000).

is in short supply, free services from NGOs and public-interest law groups have increased the access of marginalized populations. Use of the waiver of filing fees remains surprisingly limited. Still, the biggest disincentives to court use are the lack of trust in outcomes, the belief that delays will be lengthy, and the perceived difficulty of enforcing judgments.[14]

It was, however, the courts' judicial review powers that attracted most controversy and criticism especially during and following the political and economic crisis of 2001 and 2002. The judiciary and the supreme court in particular were thrust to stage center in debates over the government's emergency economic measures—salary cuts for public employees, reductions in public pensions, the freezing of bank accounts, the conversion of dollar-denominated accounts and debt into pesos at reduced, but different, exchange rates ("asymmetric pesification"),[15] and the suspension of automatic tariff increases negotiated with the privatized public utilities. The situation pitted Menem's hand-picked "automatic majority" against the opposition De la Rúa administration and, following the latter's resignation, a government headed by Menem's rival for *justicialista* party leadership, Eduardo Duhalde. The *menimista* supreme court had upheld comparable emergency measures in the early 1990s, an action unpopular at the time but eclipsed by the ensuing economic boom.[16] Its members now faced a hostile public and executive and open discussions of individual or collective impeachment for complaints entered over the intervening decade. It was clear that how it handled the new disputes would be instrumental in fending off the threats.

As it pondered its strategy, events moved ahead. All of the emergency measures became the subject of tens of thousands of *amparos* brought by the affected individuals before lower courts. Whatever the initial rulings, they were inevitably appealed and made their way to the court's docket. The government's greatest concern was the bank accounts captured in the *"corralito"* (little corral, referring to the blocking of funds) and the two issues they presented: the De la Rúa administration's freezing of the accounts themselves, in late 2001, and the conversion of dollar amounts to pesos at 1.4 pesos to the dollar, ordered by the Duhalde government in early 2002. Upholding these measures was seen as critical to the government's emergency strategy and the preservation of the financial system. Lower-level judges handling the *amparos* usually ruled against the government, granting injunctions to individual plaintiffs. Bankers refusing to release funds were jailed for contempt of court. On December 28, 2001, the justices upheld the *corralito* by ordering

14. A World Bank sponsored study (Garavano et al. 2000, reported in World Bank 2003a) did not find enforcement to be a major problem. Subsequent research by a U.S. NGO (Henderson et al. 2004) produced contradictory results, most likely because it was done during the economic crisis.

15. Debts were converted at 1.2 pesos to the dollar and accounts at 1.4—hence the term "asymmetric."

16. In 1990, the supreme court (in *Peralta v. Estado Nacional*) upheld Menem's freezing of bank accounts. It also supported measures related to the privatization of public enterprises, an issue not raised in 2001–2002.

Claudio Kniper, a federal appellate judge, to return the $200,000 he had withdrawn from the Banco Ciudad under an *amparo* granted by another judge. Two months later, however, they reversed their position in *Smith v. Estado Nacional.* The decision provoked panic within the government and its informal request that the supreme court suspend all *amparos* for sixty days. The justices' response was a threat to declare the pesification decree unconstitutional, a move with potentially far more damaging consequences than simply unblocking the accounts. The court never made good on its threat, but in March 2003 it again supported the injunctions by ordering the unblocking of an account held by the province of San Luis, leaving, however, the manner of repayment up to the parties.

The justice's decision on another issue, the public-sector salary cuts, was more easily received by the Duhalde administration. Rather than waiting for the hundreds of thousands of affected individuals to take their own legal action, the executive accepted the outcome, returning salaries to their former levels and making retroactive payments. The real costs were reduced by the devaluation that had already lowered the worth of the peso-denominated wages. Still, this complicated any agreement with the International Monetary Fund to prevent further default on the country's international debt.[17]

The *menimista* justices' actions were interpreted as largely defensive. They were known to be negotiating with the Duhalde government,[18] and their decisions in *Smith* and on the public-sector salaries were seen as shots across the bow, to dramatize the risks of not dropping the impeachment proceedings. Their continuing failure to take up *amparos* related to asymmetric pesification and the public utilities was equally strategic, but increased public outrage and strengthened the hand of the incoming Kirchner administration in forcing out a majority of the members. The reconstituted court delayed consideration of the pesification of private accounts for more than a year, until October 26, 2004. Although it upheld the measure, one Kirchner appointee wrote an addendum to the majority decision, urging that for amounts under U.S. $70,000, a one-to-one conversion be used. Many trial judges indicated they would follow his lead. An apparently contradictory decision in late 2005, revisiting the San Luis case to set the terms of repayment, was viewed as not reversing the 2004 ruling or affecting the 45,000 outstanding *amparos* for accounts held by individuals and enterprises.[19] This was just as well for the government (and banks), because the justices ordered that the San Luis account be converted to pesos at the exchange rate in effect on the day of the ruling—less than that of 2002, but still higher than under the pesification decree.

As of early 2006, the new Supreme Court still had not ruled on measures

17. This problem was resolved in late 2005, when Argentina announced it would use its foreign reserves to pay all outstanding debts to the fund and eliminate any need for a further agreement.

18. As documented in Abaid and Thieberger (2005, 11–26 and 43–62).

19. See A. Vargas (2005).

involving public utilities and the conversion of dollar-dominated debt. The continuing delays had one benefit. They gave the government the advantage of time and an improving economic situation. Many individual and corporate account holders simply accepted the reduced exchange rate to get access to their funds or entered into other government-backed agreements with their banks. Some privatized firms dropped their complaints about contract violations; others have gone to international arbitration. President Kirchner's decision not to create his own automatic majority and, in fact, to invite public comments on his candidates also helped. The new justices' diverse ideological leanings and impeccable intellectual credentials created an unprecedented confidence in the court's neutrality. Nonetheless, the Kirchner administration has advanced proposals to redesign the federal council (accomplished in February 2006 via a law scheduled to take effect at the end of that year) and criminal courts, moves long overdue, but again raising the specter of politically motivated intervention.

Some Preliminary Conclusions

Argentina's recent experience provides a cautionary lesson because this is a judicial system (or more accurately twenty-five judicial systems), which has made advances in all the strategic areas. The country adopted a new criminal procedures code (and still has high levels of impunity, especially in white-collar and serious crimes); it invested in computer equipment and legal change to increase court efficiency (with no noticeable improvements); it added mediation services and expanded court units to enhance access (with some positive, but largely unrecognized, impacts); it increased budgets, added new forms of governance, changed means of judicial selection and terms of service (and is still accused of overly politicized judges); and its judges have assumed an active involvement in constitutional controls (complicating relations with the executive and with very mixed reviews from the public and political leaders). Overall, Argentina's judiciary may have received more criticism in the past decade than at any other point in its history. Any improvements are largely unacknowledged.

This lengthy example suggests several tentative conclusions about the judicial reform process and, especially, the interactions among its several components. First, it again demonstrates that high salaries, enhanced independence, new governance systems, and monies for computers and other innovations do not have an automatic impact on the quality of judicial output. This seems especially likely when their provision is not directly linked to this goal but rather occurs because funds are available, there is a wish to look modern, or governments want to show they care about the judicial branch.

Second, judiciaries with enhanced constitutional powers, whether those they are suddenly granted or simply decide to use more proactively, will run into problems determining to what extent to second-guess government policies. If it has taken the U.S. Supreme Court 200 years to get the matter only partially right, there is no reason to suppose others can do so from one day to the next. Moreover, their task is complicated in Latin America because of courts' limited ability to filter the cases they accept for review. Here, the lack of binding precedent is a double-edged sword. While restricting the effects of any single decision, it also considerably expands judicial workloads.

Third, it is very difficult for courts to work on upgrading their provision of ordinary services, adjust to new forms of governance, and master a new constitutional role all at once. Although the specific tasks often center in different judicial bodies, their simultaneous emergence will still detract from their individual realization.

Fourth, although judiciaries need to be attentive to demands from the public, their entrance into judicial populism (playing to the masses) is a distortion of this concept and one they do not manage very well. The Argentine judges' protection of citizens against "government abuses" related to the emergency measures was welcomed by the immediate beneficiaries. The supreme court's actions were nonetheless widely interpreted as a political maneuver. Popular demands to "throw them all out" (*que se vayan todos*) included the justices as well as the politicians.

Finally, where increased independence and other changing political circumstances have augmented the political importance of the courts, efforts to intervene in their operations will continue. Only the forms change, though governments faced with tough political choices can also buy time and save face by sending them to the courts. The Argentine executive engaged in this practice during the decade preceding the most recent crisis. If it now finds itself with unanticipated judicial obstacles, it is partly because it encouraged the courts to handle decisions it was reluctant to take.

Present-day Argentina may be one of the most convincing arguments for a more comprehensive approach to reform. The whole can be more than the sum of the parts, but if the parts are not summed adequately it may be less than their individual contributions. Obviously, Argentina's implementation of the partial approaches was far from ideal. Its recent problems, however, may be less a result of imperfect partial strategies than of a failure to consider how they collectively contribute to a final more perfect whole. Experience elsewhere is comparable, if less dramatic. Colombia adopted similar reforms in the early 1990s, and its courts are likewise criticized for expanding costs, static productivity, ineffective governance, and exaggerated interference in public policy. Following the victory of the opposition PAN in the 2001 presidential elections, Mexico's supreme court (selected by the traditionally dominant PRI) became involved in political conflicts with the executive. It is widely believed to be using its constitutional review powers to leverage its demands for a constitutional earmark that would at least double the federal judiciary's current budget. Peru, having spent nearly $100 million (mostly of its own funds) on its executive controlled reforms of the 1990s, has apparently not reduced congestion, delays, or corruption and may have reduced access because of the introduction of hefty court fees and compulsory pretrial mediation.[20] Throughout the region, increasing backlogs continue to be the rule despite legal changes, the addition of new courts and judges, and extensive investments in buildings and automation. Even countries, like Costa Rica, where judicial leaders have made strides in increasing the quality and quantity of services provided, political leaders and the general public are questioning the investments required to produce these results. A former inclination to raise budgets and meet the courts' other demands is rapidly disappearing as those outside the sector review the benefits delivered.

The demand for reform and further improvements has not disappeared. The assumed efficacy of the standard remedies is increasingly in doubt. Judicial independence, as conventionally envisioned, has begun to look problematic. Courts are exercising their new powers in unpredictable ways and sometimes to favor interests not in line with broader definitions of the public good. Observers now view investments in computers and buildings as "guild" reforms, largely intended to benefit judges and some litigators, but with few spillover effects for the general public. Both within and outside the judiciaries there are signs of emerging disagreements about the benefits of what has already been done in these and other areas and the future steps to be taken. Some of the measures recommended in the preceding chapters will be useful in charting a course, but, as suggested here, much more is needed.

MOVING FROM IMPROVED KNOWLEDGE MANAGEMENT
TO KNOWLEDGE-BASED STRATEGIES

Better knowledge management is obviously critical. It could make an enormous difference in the quality of ongoing work, reducing redundancy and reinvented wheels, focusing interventions on real, higher-priority problems, weeding out less successful practices, and strengthening the linkages between inputs and projected outcomes. Lessons of experience, however, are best suited for improving individual interventions, ensuring that knowledge derived from years of involvement in training, automation, and code drafting is tapped by and built on in new ventures and thus that our repertoire of standard reform components is constantly upgraded. Experiential knowledge is less likely to resolve the larger questions about the ultimate objectives, broader impacts, and overall value of the past, present, and future

20. The fees are an obvious barrier. They can be waived, but as in Argentina, this is rarely requested. Moreover, other charges (for expert witnesses or forensics tests) are not included in the waiver. Compulsory mediation is too new to evaluate, but many critics claim its major benefit is for otherwise unemployed attorneys who have set up their own, fee-based clinics.

efforts or to clarify the relationships among the differing approaches to and definitions of reform. It may improve the quality and reduce the ad hoc nature of reform tactics. It will not necessarily place them within a strategic context. For this, a second and more difficult undertaking is needed. It is one thing to help trainers or informatics experts select the best methods for carrying out their activities. It is another to raise questions about their contribution to partial goals like reducing delay or increasing due process rights and still another to ask how those partial goals fit into an improved judicial process.

This second type of undertaking focuses on the entire strategy-building process and the links among the approaches. Accumulated knowledge is an important input, but the questions addressed are at a much higher level, and some cannot be answered on the basis of what we have already learned. They require further research and a realization that ongoing work is itself an experiment. Strategic reform is as much an attitude as a product. It implies explicit recognition of the underlying uncertainties in any reform program and an equally explicit willingness to test its validity as part of implementation. Obviously, for reformers and reform agencies expected to produce results as quickly as possible, this will not be an easy transformation. The prevailing incentive system works to very different ends.

In the context of current reform programming, strategy building can be envisioned at two levels—as a means of improving the partial approaches or as an attempt to consolidate them into a single, if multidimensional, whole. There is no question of the room for increasing the strategic content of the partial approaches. Even the most developed—for example, criminal justice reform—would benefit from self-examination and self-criticism. For criminal justice the problem is less the absence of a strategy than the failure to evaluate its formal logic against results and so identify corrective actions. The criminal justice reformers have done some of this in moving from an exclusive reliance on legal change to an emphasis on strengthening the organizational implementers. As discussed in chapter 1, however, their approach still overlooks many obstacles, including those arising in the codes themselves, and has never adequately resolved the contradictions inherent to its bifurcated goals. The still more explicit efficiency strategy also requires reexamination and adjustment. Its assumption that delay is the main problem and that new technologies, courtroom reorganization, and some legal change will be sufficient to reduce it remains largely untested. Moreover, the common tactical shortcuts—installing the machines and hoping that they will encourage better practices—eliminate such critical strategic steps as prior simplification of procedures and so increase the risk of retaining traditional bottlenecks and vices.

For the other approaches, a strategy exists only in the loosest terms, as the assumption that enactment of a number of related activities will advance the desired results. Causal links are not well specified except at face value—more services will increase access; judicial independence will be enhanced by removing the traditional channels for political intervention; and institutional capacity for effective self-governance will result from higher resource endowments and more judicial control over their use. Conflicts and contradictions go unrecognized, as do the possibilities for traditional vices to creep back in under a different form.

It would be tempting to insist on first improving the strategic content of the partial approaches to ensure they are better able to produce their anticipated results. This would leave us with five perfected partial strategies and still with the dilemma of how to handle their mutual contradictions and differently prioritized objectives: How to reconcile increased access with delay reduction. How to ensure that a more independent, self-managing judiciary responds to new kinds of societal demands. Or how to deal with contradictions first arising within the partial approaches, but hardly ending there—due process guarantees versus citizen security or enhanced juridical security versus a more socially conscious judiciary.

A continuing emphasis on partial approaches also leaves the question of financial and opportunity costs unanswered. Collectively, the five approaches taken to their logical extremes promise a sector budget far beyond the means of any country. Virtually none of them aims at cutting costs; most work on the logic of more and better services as a result of higher investment and operating budgets. The issue of costs could be addressed approach by approach. It seems more productive to take their combined effects into consideration—how each element contributes to advancing overall societal goals and how the implicit and explicit trade-offs will be handled. Ultimately, this involves trade-offs among the judicial approaches and between judicial reform and other public programs. Is credit availability best enhanced by improving judicial debt collection or by promoting credit bureaus or microcredit programs? Should each poor person deprived of access to educational or health facilities have to take his case to court, or should the respective sector programs simply be expanded to reach more citizens? If the latter is the answer, should the size of the increases be decided by the courts or by politicians and technocrats? Is crime best fought by improving criminal justice, involving communities in prevention programs, or providing jobs for at-risk groups? The questions do not lend themselves to yes or no answers. Nevertheless, it is important to recognize that, although courts can address some social and economic problems, they are often not the best means. Judicial reformers will naturally look for the judicial contribution. They must be prepared to admit that it may be the least-efficient alternative.

These and other questions suggest a need to return to the fundamentals, reexamine the ends pursued through judicial reform, and develop a strategy more in line with real possibilities, priorities, and circumstances. Here, the macroeconomic correlations between levels of judicial development and political stability, poverty reduction, or economic growth will not suffice. The relationships they demonstrate provide little clue as to how the macrovariables are linked. For that, we need a better understanding of what courts do, how they do it, and how variations in each alter their contributions to societal well-being. It is this understanding, rather than the correlations, that would allow us to create a theory and model of the judicial role as a guide to strategy design. Lacking both the theoretical model and the higher level of understanding required to construct it and recognizing that reforms will not wait for their emergence, over the short run we are left with second-best alternatives.

One option is to continue with the partial approaches and the equally partial implicit theories behind them. Let the "market" determine which is attempted and which, by virtue of its results, is maintained. A second, pursued here, is to create mechanisms for integrating the approaches or facilitating the decisions among them by starting with what we do know or agree on and placing the remaining choices, among objectives or among means, in a context where their merits, chances of success, and intrinsic inconsistencies or synergies can be discussed systematically. The resulting "framework for constructing reform strategies" incorporates certain widely shared assumptions as to the judiciary's generic functions (for example, conflict resolution, rule enforcement) and the organizational characteristics needed to perform them. The framework does not further specify the content of those functions (for example, what kinds of conflicts; which rules) or which of them any given reform will emphasize. It is thus a planning tool, not a universal model, and its strategic or theoretical content focuses on how to change judicial behavior, not what ought to be changed. Still, much of what we have learned over the past two decades lies in the first half of that equation, comprising a better understanding of the principal factors shaping judicial performance. After one further brief digression, the remainder of this chapter lays out this framework as an interim solution to the task of making reforms more strategic and enhancing their reliance on experiential knowledge. The suggestions offered are neither novel nor definitive. They provide one way to conceptualize the problems, drawing on the Latin American experience and the current state of its reforms.

A PRELUDE TO THE STRATEGIC FRAMEWORK: USING ACCESS TO RESTATE THE ISSUES

As suggested earlier, the concept of access to justice offers an interesting entry point for examining judicial reform. Once we get beyond the simplistic (and, as I hope to have demonstrated, unrealistic and probably counterproductive) notion that the goal is to give every potential user his or her day in court and begin to ask what we really are pursuing, we face some very basic questions about the role of the legal/judicial system, the nature of its product (justice), the benefits to individuals and societies of court use, the nature and impact of current use patterns, and the potential and reasons for changing them. I am not foolhardy enough to attempt to answer these questions but will note that they are being raised by a growing number of observers, including those in countries with justice systems that are presumed to work fairly well. Among some of their early and very tentative findings, the following are most relevant for present purposes.

First, we really do not know enough about who uses courts or other sector institutions and with what effect. Thus, many of the assumptions guiding reform design tend to be based on fragmentary, often anecdotal, evidence, shaded by ideological predispositions or mere wishful thinking.[21] Second, although it is evident that the individual and societal impacts and benefits of court use diverge significantly,[22] the application of this knowledge to rationalize services is relatively unexplored. Justice may be the only public service where individual use rights are seen as too essential to be weighed against collective benefits.

Third, there is an increasing and near-universal public dissatisfaction with court performance, even in countries where citizens perceive their judges as hard-working, honest, and competent. This suggests a growing expectation gap between what citizens believe courts should do and what they actually deliver.[23] Fourth, to the extent we understand individual decisions to access the courts, they seem increasingly based less on the "legitimacy" of the claim than on a rational calculation of the costs and benefits of taking legal action.[24] Legal counsel may affect this calculation, sometimes in ways that advance only its own interests. The parties themselves, however, are more sophisticated in terms of how the strengths and weaknesses of a specific legal system work to their advantage or disadvantage, regardless of whether a judgment is eventually delivered. Here the legal system is less a neutral means of resolving conflicts than another resource to alter relative bargaining positions or the nature of the issues at stake.

Fifth, although the judicial process is inevitably an expensive way to resolve conflicts, a part of the high costs arise from its monopolistic structure and the control over such factors as supply, demand, fees, and content exercised by legal practitioners.[25] There certainly are judges and lawyers interested in producing improved services at reduced costs, but guild interests are a strong deterrent to many kinds of change. Finally, increased access to courts in the conventional sense has augmented the ability of individuals and groups to claim rights guaranteed in their

21. Although studies on court use began in the United States several decades ago, funding cuts and shifting research priorities curtailed much of this work. In Latin America, it is only beginning. It is also very recent in Europe; see Genn (1999), for a first cut at the situation in Great Britain.

22. A whole school of Chilean research seems to be developing around this issue. See, for example, J. E. Vargas et al. (1988 and 2001). For a related discussion, see Shavell (1997).

23. Although approval levels are higher for developed countries, they still fall in the 50 to 70 percent range. See Martínez (1997), for some examples. Toharia (2003) also notes some interesting differences between citizens' approval of their legal system and of court performance itself. The former figures tend to be much higher than the latter, another indication of the expectation gap.

24. Although not couched in cost-benefit terms, Grossman et al. (1982) is highly relevant to these issues.

25. See Marks (2000), Hadfield (2000), and Tobin (1999).

respective constitutions. The rights discourse features private, rather than public, benefits and costs. The problem transcends the courts, but it does transfer to them a more traditional political logic—supplicants take their petitions to a higher authority to make claims on public resources. This piecemeal approach to public policymaking does not offer the opportunity to consider trade-offs, alternative means for resolving problems, or rationalizing scarce resource use. It not only gives the courts a role for which they are ill-suited, but also relieves political authorities of a fundamental responsibility.

One conclusion to be derived from these partial findings is that the dominant model shaping our understanding of how courts' operate and thus current reform efforts may be less appropriate for contemporary societies because of the dramatic qualitative and quantitative changes in the demands for judicial services. In its most basic form, this traditional model suggests that the justice system, by resolving disputes through the application of legal norms, will strengthen the rule of law, increase juridical security and predictability, reduce conflicts, and bring social transactions more into line with the overall legal framework.[26] It is fairly silent on the norms enforced, but it does assume they will be applied equitably and universally and that all parties will have an equal chance to take their complaints and grievances to the courts.

Part of the growing expectation gap doubtless involves a realization that this is not quite how the judicial system really works. Before we declare the model in crisis, it is worth speculating whether things ever operated that way. The frequent complaint that the courts, rather than expediting conflict resolution, merely give the disputants a different forum and a different set of resources for pursuing their agendas may not be anything new. Parties have always accessed courts as a way of postponing anticipated negative outcomes or used delay and litigation expenses to weaken their opponent's resolve. They have also used the threat of judicial action, or a judicial ruling itself, to force a negotiated settlement. On both the civil and criminal side, negotiated agreements have long been the key to how courts deal with excessive demand, and, although neither the process nor the outcome may coincide with popular understandings of justice, cases do eventually come to closure.[27] On a more positive note, judicial rulings can have an impact beyond that of the cases they actually decide. Extrajudicial settlement is aided by an ability to predict judicial outcomes (namely, what would happen were the case taken to court); in this sense, parties seeking delay do not hold all the advantages. Moreover,

---

26. "Dispute" is used here to cover both civil and criminal issues of fact and law. In the interests of economy, I am temporarily ignoring uncontested matters, which in any event also involve a decision of how to apply the law if not an outright conflict between parties.

27. Some civil code lawyers and judges suggest this is less common to their systems. France (see Doriat-Duban, 2001) is a prime example. Outside France, however, the importance of settlement seems more widely accepted, though not well documented. See Marchal (2003).

where courts are assumed to take their part in the process seriously and professionally, the threat of judicial action does deter noncompliance and so encourages conformity with the legal norms. Although a minority of the individually aggrieved may actually get their day in court, and still fewer may be satisfied with the results, their real numbers are reduced because potential violators do fear the law.

Nonetheless, high costs to individual users and to the public treasury, burgeoning demand, growing delays, the potential for opportunistic abuse, a consequent weakening of juridical security, and increasing public cynicism do imply that the model has its limits and that it may be time to either lower our expectations or change the system itself. Because such changes have direct implications for conventional notions of access rights, their further development bears a short discussion.

One suggested direction of change is to weaken further the connection between conflict resolution and rule enforcement, partially abandoning the notion that courts enhance juridical security and rule compliance through the resolution of an endless number of individual disputes. Recognizing that courts are only one part of a societywide set of mechanisms for resolving conflicts and that not all conflicts are equally important to the rule-enforcement function, we can begin to distinguish among potentially justiciable cases on this basis. Routine disputes could be channeled elsewhere, leaving to courts those of more transcendental significance. The ADR movement and the creation of administrative tribunals or special offices for dealing with routine matters such as consumer complaints address the first part of the equation. These alternative forums also allow the entrance of extra-legal considerations that may be critical to party satisfaction. One wants courts to uphold the general principle that a contract should be enforced as written, but parties to a specific dispute may be willing to negotiate the terms after the fact, recognizing a mutual interest in preserving a relationship or doing what is feasible. The increasing use of small claims courts featuring pro se representation, less formal procedures, limited appeal rights, and more involved judges provides a means to the same end, albeit within the formal court system and with more emphasis on legal issues.[28]

The other side of the equation, defining and helping courts focus on high-priority issues,, is more controversial, but some suggestions have emerged here as well. The increased emphasis on public-interest law among those representing marginalized groups is one example. Having decided that representing individual clients is a very inefficient way of defending the rights of a whole category of claimants, advocates have begun to focus on cases with potentially broader consequences—those that challenge patterns of government or private behavior

---

28. See Baldwin (2000), for the advantages and disadvantages of their use in England. Brazil's small claims courts are discussed in Batista (1999), Bermudes (1999), Rodycz (2001), Sadek (2001a), and Watanabe (1986).

violating the interests of entire groups of citizens. A different approach derives from the argument that most judicial actions have a higher component of individual as opposed to social benefits. It thus proposes charging users a greater share of the real costs of handling their cases or even overcharging them so as to discourage some kinds of use.[29] Here demand is rationalized by involving the parties in the choices on court use. When they have to pay more for court services, they may seek other means of resolving their problems or find ways to avoid their emergence in the first place.[30] These measures obviously conflict with the demand for greater access, but costs could be scaled or subsidies provided to put all potential users on an equal footing. Still, some uses merit discouraging no matter what the social status of the parties. That the rich abuse their access is not because they have different motives, but only the means to exercise them. Allowing unrepresented litigation or increasing the supply of subsidized counsel would increase poorer citizens' opportunity to engage in the same abuses, which in the interests of fairness should also be discouraged.

Demand (and public and private costs) can also be rationalized through the more conventional remedies of procedural simplification and other legal changes and by providing judges with more means to discourage dilatory practices, unreasonable appeals, and frivolous claims.[31] Such methods reduce the workload less by excluding conflicts than by streamlining their treatment. A related tack involves efforts to make negotiation more acceptable and more transparent. Once citizens understand that negotiated settlements are both common and often the only way to reach a solution, they may adopt more realistic expectations as regards their own chances and the process in general.[32]

There is a final dimension to the issue of prioritization. It is the courts' role in public policymaking, a question of both workload and the balance of powers. The rights revolution and the expanded importance of constitutional judicial review, at both the national and supranational levels, have made this a universal rather than a Third World concern. Suggestions of how it should be handled are few.

---

29. This is a principal conclusion of J. E. Vargas et al. (2001) and Correa et al. (1999), though their views may be influenced by Chile's limited experience with fees. Argentina's experience indicates that introducing or raising fees may have little impact on reducing abusive use. See World Bank (2003a).

30. It is often argued, for example, that easy access to justice may discourage potential creditors from the necessary due diligence in making their loans. If they know judicial recuperation will be expensive, they may do more credit checks and otherwise exercise greater caution.

31. It is now a near commonplace observation that one of the greatest impediments to juridical security is the proliferation of legislation and regulations. When even legal professionals are incapable of keeping up with legislative change, the notion of the legal framework shaping societal interactions becomes absurd.

32. In the United States, a part of the bar has in fact begun to worry what will happen when citizens discover the high rate of postjudgment negotiation—settlements of civil cases that are actually made after a trial is held. Although lawyers regard this as natural and a way of avoiding still more lengthy and costly appeals, to the public it often looks like an enormous waste of tax dollars.

Those engaged in the discussion seem to be split between advocates of technocratic policymaking (who thus view the courts' entrance as a negative development requiring explicit limits)[33] and the rights advocates (who call for an expansion of legal guarantees and an expanded judicial role in enforcing them). One could caricature this as a conflict between two disciplines, economics and law, battling for the final word on how public policy should be made and the courts' place in the process. If politics is the art of compromise as well as the authoritative allocation of values, the most logical response to this confrontation is to reexamine and renegotiate the role of law (the courts) and technocracy (the experts) in making policy decisions and to leave some political space for citizens to choose among the alternative recommendations from each set of experts. In any event, the conventional model of the courts' role as that of making the fine distinctions on the application of a definitive legal and policy framework is no longer up to present circumstances. Where the framework is vague, inadequately analyzed, and "never intended for full enactment," the courts easily graduate from applying the law to making policy, a role for which they have little preparation and no real legal mandate. Much the same can be said of sheer technocratic policymaking, but the experts' role in second-guessing popular preferences is the material for another study. The other shortcomings of the traditional model increase costs and add confusion. In this final area, as suggested by the Argentine example, the negative consequences are more serious, for their immediate impact on both policy and the public's faith in all their political institutions. Thus, while a long-term project, a rethinking and renegotiation of the conventional checks and balance system is clearly in order.

The common thread in all these proposals is their tendency to take a systemic view of judicial services and thus of the concept of access. Here the right of access, in its amplest sense, does not refer to specific cases and users, but rather to participation in the individual and collective benefits accruing from society's provision of the best and most equitably delivered justice service it can render. That service includes more than the courts. On the one hand, it extends to alternative mechanisms for conflict resolution and rule enforcement. Such mechanisms will likely exist outside the courts' direct oversight, but their operations should be guided by patterns of judicial decision making, occurring "in the shadow of the law." On the other, it incorporates a legal framework that adequately reflects the rights political society intends for immediate enactment, distinguishes them from statements of programmatic goals, and defines the courts' role in reinforcing both. Where the line is drawn, what a society considers as immediately enforceable rights as

---

33. Here the International Monetary Fund's initial reaction to the Argentine judiciary's rulings against the frozen bank accounts is illustrative. The fund's call was to control the judges who were interfering with rational economic policies. The revised interpretation was that the judges were protecting property rights.

opposed to programmatic guidelines, are questions of values, resources, and political compromise, but, unless answers are attempted, situations like those of present-day Argentina are the likely result.

Within this more complex system, individuals have a right to petition for attention to their specific complaints, but, as in the case of other services (public security, health and education), this does not mean that everyone gets what they want when they want it. Who gets what, when, and how is a question of policy and so transcends the choices of both individuals and service providers. This is particularly important as current patterns of supply and thus use of judicial (and other public) services have a historical origin that may run counter to contemporary definitions of the common good.[34] Any decision to alter these patterns should obviously involve more than the judges, lawyers, and their usual clients. These are political determinations requiring the attention of political society as a whole.

In a rationalized distribution, some judicial or related services may not be provided by the state at all, and others may be provided only if paid fully or partially by the individual beneficiary. Where the provision of services (that is, court attention to certain issues) is considered a high priority, subsidies will be required for those who cannot pay. For other public services, these kinds of policy choices, while difficult, are more easily conceptualized. For justice, this is a novel approach, if increasingly necessary given the growing demand and the costs of augmenting the supply. Where every case cannot have its day in court, it is important to understand the demand, the implications of meeting it, and the potential for choosing what is most critical. This may not mean that all citizens get to take their case to court. It does mean that everyone should participate equally in the benefits of the system and that the decision as of which cases are viewed by courts, which are handled by other state-sponsored means, and which are left unattended is based on contemporary priorities, not the cumulative weight of individual claims.[35]

This revised vision of judicial services may not lie well with those defining access to judicial services as an absolute right. Still, it is less conservative in its operations than current reality, which, for all the rights discourse, in the end depends on market mechanisms (the law of supply and demand) or some less explicit criteria to

34. Argentine judges and jurists frequently appeal to the concept of "acquired rights," *derechos adqueridos*, thus giving a permanent constitutional status to agreements reached through the ordinary tug and pull of interest politics. The position seems unfortunate, as extrapolated to its extreme, it would leave little room for the emergence of new or realigned interests, condemning political society to historical privilege over contemporary demands. Brazil's constitution explicitly prohibits (Article 5) the violation of acquired rights. A September 2004 decision by the Supremo Tribunal Federal suggests an opening to reconsideration; however, the court left the concept intact, ruling instead that the privilege in question (nonpayment of income tax on pensions) could not be considered a right, acquired or otherwise.

35. I would stress that this is not a call for a technocratic solution. Societal priorities should be politically determined, not defined by experts. The latter's role is to explain the trade-offs and implications of specific choices.

determine who actually gets to court.[36] Furthermore, the values it maximizes can be quite revolutionary. They depend less on the rationing system than on the rules being enforced. If the idea is that these rules reverse existing social inequities and create a new social order, the question of whom or rather what issues will be privileged will be quite different from a situation where the goal is to maintain the existing social equilibrium. The revolution does not start with the courts. If a society wishes to produce it, it can use them and other parts of the justice system to this end.

With all their other problems, the notion of rationalizing judicial services according to anticipated impacts on the collective good may be far beyond the grasp of most Latin American countries. In the medium term, they will be more concerned with ensuring that judges are reasonably competent and honest, that the laws they enforce make sense, that geographic and other barriers do not egregiously skew access, and that citizens are adequately informed on how to use the system. It is not too early to think about the model, however, and some of its elements are incorporated in the strategic framework that follows. The framework does not discard the five partial approaches, accepting that their individual goal statements are still the terms in which reforms will be envisioned. Its own approach, however, is more operational and instrumental, emphasizing the organizational and institutional commonalities inherent to any effort to improve performance.

THE OUTLINES OF A COMPREHENSIVE FRAMEWORK
FOR DESIGNING REFORM STRATEGIES

The framework proposed here adopts some additional assumptions following from the arguments offered above and in the preceding chapters. It locates the judiciary within a larger societal system of conflict resolution and rule enforcement and thus does not see these functions as exclusive to the courts. It assumes judicial services are not infinitely expandable and thus that an explicit or implicit rationing system will determine both what is offered and who uses it directly. It assumes that among the basic functions commonly performed by courts, some may be considered less important or even rejected within a given national context.[37] It also assumes that choices as to where the line is drawn in all these cases are essentially political,

---

36. As several judges had noted, the flood of *amparos* in Argentina had diverted attention from more ordinary cases, putting them at the end of the line and drastically increasing the likely time to their resolution. Women seeking child support or individuals and firms seeking to collect debts simply had to wait. *Diario Judicial*, September 17, 2002 (http://www.diariojudicial.com).

37. For some societies this may be the checks and balance role, but in Latin America there may be greater resistance to the notion of courts reducing conflicts by making their decisions more predictable. This appears to conflict with many judges' belief that all judgments should be individualized.

albeit shaped by culture and historical tradition. In combination with the further elaboration of the framework, the results may constitute a model of the judicial role, but it is a very open-ended model, more descriptive than prescriptive and more focused on function (instrumentality) than impact (substance).[38]

The distinction between function and substance is repeated in the model's separation of strategic and tactical choices. In any particular country, the tactical entry points will vary, depending on where concerns and complaints about impact are targeted. Tactical or contextual considerations do not alter the strategic logic; they shape its application to a specific context. If criminal justice is the source of complaints, one would start a reform there, but always keeping in mind that this is a tactic of convenience, not a definition of the general goal. In its most abstract form, that goal can be summarized as creating a productive space for the judiciary within the set of principal governance institutions and ensuring it has the capacity to occupy it well.

The framework is organized around a set of functional objectives, transcending the tactical focus but giving a more concrete cast to the abstractly defined "purpose." These objectives draw from the list of outputs usually attributed to the courts. Thus, reforms attempt to enhance the courts' capacity to do all or some of the following: provide the satisfactory and timely resolution of private disputes and criminal complaints, either directly or through their influence on other forums operating in the shadow of the law; discourage the emergence of conflicts through enhanced juridical security or the predictability of judicial resolutions, based on a consistent, egalitarian application of the legal framework; provide a check on any government tendency to violate the constitutional and legal framework and serve as the arbiter for conflicts of jurisdiction among other governmental bodies; and strengthen the normative framework through its application, interpretation, and, where necessary, detection of inconsistencies and inadequacies requiring attention by lawmakers.

Although the courts remain central to its formulation (and to the following discussion), the framework places them within a broader system of rule enforcement and normatively based conflict resolution. This becomes clearer in the next level, the components of reform, where the partial approaches reemerge, if in slightly altered form. Themes such as efficiency become constants across the components, and specific areas such as criminal justice move to the tactical side (sharing this status with other substantive areas so far receiving less attention). The list of components is the most experientially based part of the framework, referring not to the usual substantive subgoals, but rather to what we now know to be the critical areas for changing system behavior. They thus include:

---

38. I owe this distinction to Alvaro Santos who is using similar categories (differentiating between the courts' instrumental and intrinsic impacts) to analyze donor approaches to reform.

- Basic organizational strengthening—enhancement of the judiciary's capacity (and that of other sector institutions) to control its own internal operations and to respond to and plan for new needs
- Improved definition of ties with and powers vis-à-vis other branches of government and citizen-users—the independence, accountability, and political dimensions
- Improved legal framework—updating of procedural and substantive rules to reflect changing circumstances and to support the effort to rationalize court use
- Development of mechanisms and services to equalize access to judicial services
- Development or integration of auxiliary services within and outside the sector to provide complementary or alternative attention to clients

The components constitute the main areas within which the strategy will be further designed. Each component in turn includes a number of activities or lines of action with their respective inputs. These are the familiar reform building blocks—training, studies, law drafting, reorganizations, outreach, and so on. Because many generic activities are common to most or all components, an applied strategy would seek to coordinate their impacts. Thus, a training program, introduced as part of the organizational strengthening component, would also include elements intended to reinforce any innovations in the other four. In a comprehensive strategy, linkages are not strictly unilinear. At each level of the framework, single items will have multiple ties to the higher and lower strata.

This same logic affects the framework's higher levels. Although certain components are more closely related to one or more objectives, a comprehensive, integrated reform will check for and coordinate their impact on all of them. The components can be worked on simultaneously or sequentially, but the approach to all is gradual and iterative. Where one starts depends on the weaknesses detected, but sequencing should not be taken to mean that each problem is addressed and fully resolved before the next is attacked.[39] The goal is to maintain a balance among the components to avoid over endowing one and creating additional problems (as when the legal framework becomes too sophisticated for the system to apply, or external independence increases without internal reform). Nonetheless, the framework does draw from lessons of experience in suggesting a logical sequence for addressing system weaknesses. This fleshes out its underlying theory or model of judicial change. The following discussion elaborates on this point and on the contents of each component.

In most real cases, the first strategic priority will be component one, some measure of institutional development, strengthening, and reengineering to improve

---

39. USAID's strategic framework as developed in the mid-1990s (Blair and Hansen 1994) did seem to require this absolute sequencing, an approach roundly criticized by actual project managers.

the organization's ability to control and monitor its own operations, manage its resources, detect and respond to new demands, and plan for future changes. This implies attention to several areas: recruitment of personnel, further career management, internal administration, resources, procedural rules, and relations with the public and private bar.[40] As opposed to the ordinary "additive" strategy (any advance in any area is a plus), these represent a composite set of requirements, all of which are important in guaranteeing that the organization functions well. Reforms that focus on only one internal governance area (like reforms that focus on only one component) will not achieve this goal, except in those rare cases where existing weaknesses are limited to that dimension.

Further details as to preferred solutions (for example, council versus court governance or the more specific composition of the governance body) are not included. This is partly because of continuing debates over best practices, but it also keeps the emphasis on functions as opposed to structural arrangements. Obviously, there will be a need for a central governance body to which the various implementing offices, agencies, and committees report and thus supervises and coordinates their actions and sets overall policy. Because its members are likely to lack vast administrative experience, the creation of an executive director (director of administration) responsible for day-to-day administrative oversight and coordination also seems essential. Judiciaries that have numerous administrative agencies reporting directly to the policymakers seem to be too swamped in detail and the internecine battles and turf wars among their subordinates to perform their oversight function well.

With this division of labor, no matter how more specifically organized, the judicial policymakers, backed by adequate information and analysis from their technical and administrative staff, should be able to focus on ensuring the governance activities are adequately performed. The fundamental challenge in most reforms is to get judicial and other sector leadership to understand this restatement of their roles—as a two-part process of developing capacity to monitor and direct organizational performance, and designing and implementing strategies aimed at improving output in response to changing societal demand and needs. For many leaders and ordinary members of the judiciary, the formulation verges on the heretical. They continue to define their responsibilities as simply "applying the law" and thus view reform as at most adding elements to raise the quality of the individual judgment (training, computers, some law revision). The idea that more proactive management can advance rather than undermine performance quality (and especially judicial neutrality) is still not widely accepted. Judges are not prepared to

---

40. The bar is placed here because of its usually critical role as gate-keeper to judicial services, as well as its additional influence in shaping demand for services. However, further development of this subcomponent could also be addressed as a ministrategy in its own right.

engage in it, do not like the change of orientation, and frequently interpret it as incompatible with their jurisdictional mandate.

Of course, judiciaries as organizations are never entirely passive. They do lobby, often quite actively, for certain changes, including higher budgets and salaries, greater independence from outside control, and the like. The deviations, however, are selective, and the corporate culture provides a larger justification for not doing more. If justice were limited to conflict resolution and the number of cases resolved within a reasonable time, the simple answer to this dilemma would be to take reform outside the hands of the judiciary and entrust it to an executive body. This arrangement has been attempted in some countries, most notably Peru in the 1990s.[41] As this and other experiments suggest, the solution is not satisfactory because the courts are not just another public service. They also hold a political role and the functions of checking abuses by other branches of government and deciding on how laws will be interpreted. Moreover, even in basic conflict resolution, their perceived neutrality, and thus distance from domination by the executive and/or legislature are critical. The public good aspects of the judicial role, the enforcement of the legal framework and the authoritative resolution of differences on its interpretation, visibly suffer when judges are seen as standing in for executive branch preferences.

Disappointments with the results of judicially led reform have produced suggestions that attention to the courts' political role (component two), and to the two primary requisites for its performance—independence and accountability—be left for a second stage, and that early reform efforts focus on internal strengthening as it affects ordinary disputes. In the interim, accountability can be taken care of by the perpetuation of outside (executive) supervision and independence replaced by professionalism and technical competence. Professionalized judges, absent full institutional independence, will be counted on to work to the rules (the law) and so to provide reasonably neutral decisions. This can be thought of as the Singapore model, a judiciary with a high degree of professional competence, efficiency, and standardized decision making, but with a limited capacity to check governmental abuses.[42] To the extent judges do the latter, they operate like an internal control system, enforcing the rules the executive wants enforced. Aside from the disappearance of the checks and balance function, the problem with this model is that few governments can avoid the temptation to interfere more frequently.[43] The Peruvian reforms of the1990s may have started as a Singapore model. By the

41. See Hammergren (1998e, 2000a), De Belaunde (1998), Lawyers Committee (2000), and Ledesma (1999).

42. For a discussion of Singapore's experience, which seems to endorse this model, see Malik (2002).

43. One other element of the Singapore model, also decreasing its applicability elsewhere, is the use of extremely high judicial salaries, up to a million dollars annually for justices. This clearly decreases vulnerability to both corruption and antigovernment actions, especially if being caught means losing the position, the salary, and any future as a lawyer in the country.

time they ended, the executive had undermined its institutional strengthening effort with its top-to-bottom infiltration of the courts, including pressures on individual judges and connivance in mismanagement of resources. This not only diminished the political credibility of the judiciary, but also reversed initial advances in increasing the efficiency, quality, and predictability of ordinary judgments because judges knew they were not ultimately being evaluated on that basis.

In light of the high risks of such deviations, it seems best to work on the second component, political independence and accountability, simultaneously instead of waiting until internal systems have been adequately strengthened. One intermediate solution may be to focus on the elimination of external controls (independence from . . .) but delay radical changes in the courts' judicial review functions (independence to . . .). For courts like those of Argentina, which already had extensive checks and balance powers, even if they used them infrequently, the solution is less practical. The other Argentine lesson is that the government itself can encourage greater judicial activism by transferring policy issues to the courts. This is not the only contributing factor, but to the extent it does have a role, governments should be careful about their actions in this direction.

Accountability has been the neglected element in the traditional definition of the political component. Efforts to strengthen the courts' political role have focused instead on increasing the rest of government's accountability to the judiciary. This is not surprising in view of Latin America's history of judicial domination by other political powers and actors and the fact that the drive for its reversal has been headed by jurists and judges who naturally tend to discount the need for what they see as new limits on judicial powers. As a general rule, the only way to ensure that new powers will be used responsibly and advance the common, as opposed to particular, interests is to enhance accountability commensurately. This has posed an enormous and as yet unresolved conundrum in the case of the courts. There are parts of the puzzle that lend themselves to easier resolution. These refer specifically to certain aspects of administrative and aggregate performance.

Courts, like other public entities, use public resources and should be held accountable for their management. It is no great threat to institutional independence to subject them to the same accounting, contracting, and procurement rules as any other public entity. Judges may bristle at having to comply with rules set by the other branches of government, but it is difficult to find a justification for their not doing so. This means compliance with the rules and being subject to periodic audits and other external checks on use of funds, including those they generate independently. The latter includes judicial fees, income from registries where they are run by the courts, and any other independent source of income.[44] It extends

---

44. A further problem of increased independence has been judiciaries' tendency to view the monies they collect as their own funds (*fondos propios*). This is rather like the revenue agency deciding that it

to collections and eventual expenditures where courts are allowed to retain their earnings. Where assets declarations are required of other public employees, judges would also be expected to file them, and, if this is the general rule, to make them available to the public.

In conformity with new standards of transparent governance, courts will also have to comply with requirements for publishing information on their internal operations. This includes salaries, additional benefits, appointments, movement of cases down to the level of individual judges, average resolution times, and disciplinary actions. Judgments (*sentencias*) should also be public, even if the names of the parties are removed to protect their privacy. It is difficult to see how the judiciary can perform its role in strengthening the normative framework if no one knows what it decides. Whatever else functional accountability might involve, at the very least it requires public knowledge of judicial decisions, and not only at the supreme court level.

Beyond these basic points, the further accountability of the judiciary to political and civil society remains a highly controversial issue. As judges are usually not elected and, according to informed observers, should hold permanent or fixed, long-term appointments, there is little check on their potential for distancing the content of their decisions from prevailing public notions of justice or getting more deeply involved in setting public policy than most citizens believe to be justified. There are ways to enhance public input into decisions on hiring and promotions, and even in disciplinary processes, but these are easier to enforce against a few oddballs than against the institution as a whole. Although a solution has yet to be found, some means of midcourse corrections and public input regarding overall institutional performance might also avoid many of the obstructionist battles over hiring and promotion decisions. Where political elites and citizens believe they only have one bite at the apple, they are likely to take unnecessarily exaggerated positions to ensure "their" judges will not at some later point espouse positions contrary to their own interests.

The three additional strategic components—legal change, access enhancement, and the creation or integration of auxiliary services—are an intrinsic part of system improvement, but their efficacy rests on getting the basics right. A judiciary that cannot oversee and control its own performance, lacks sufficient independence to resist external pressures, or maintains ambiguous lines of horizontal and vertical accountability with other political powers and societal groups will have a limited ability to apply more sophisticated laws, meet the demands of new clients,

---

has first grabs on what it collects. The judiciary of the state of Rio de Janeiro in Brazil now accumulates so much income from court fees and interest on judicial deposits that it is loaning money to the executive. In Brazil and elsewhere, the notion that these are public resources and not the judiciary's to manage does not seem to have occurred to either the judges or the rest of the government.

or manage its relationship with a broader system of conflict resolution. A perfect judicial machine that operates under a flawed legal framework, serves a small traditional clientele, and enjoys a functional monopoly, however, is not destined to maximize its role as a service provider and political power. Thus, these three components are vital to improving performance. The trick is to regulate their addition to optimize their impact and guarantee an adequate response.

As elements of the partial approaches discussed earlier, these three components have sometimes been promoted as a way of leveraging radical change. New laws, new clients, and alternative competitive services are seen as creating an accelerated external push on recalcitrant courts. There is some truth in this argument. It has also been taken to extremes. As both Latin America's criminal justice reformers ("we'll enact the law and then work out the details") and those attempting to create full blown, market-oriented legal frameworks in other regions have found, when the law is too far out of sync with system capabilities, it will either be ignored or encourage new forms of misuse. Obviously, some legal change is required to advance internal and external institutional strengthening or clarify court powers and accountability. Moreover, where the existing legal framework creates visible perversities and obstacles to timely, relevant court decisions it would be foolish to insist that it not be touched at all until the courts have reached some higher level of development. The key here is a good measure of common sense and sensitivity to contextual needs and constraints. All reform is iterative and incremental. Legal change is no exception.

The situation of direct access enhancement and the integration of alternative services, the two major lines in the conventional access approach, is comparable. It may be true that one is doing no favor to marginalized populations in giving them access to a completely dysfunctional, corrupt, and biased court system. It also seems doubtful that judicial reform can be "bootstrapped" onto an access-enhancement strategy—a sudden, dramatic increase in the number of poor clients taking their cases to the courts will force the judges to resolve their longstanding performance problems.[45] Alternative services pose similar problems. They may lead to the creation of a second-class justice or simply reduce the pressures for reform of the primary one.[46] Nonetheless, those emphasizing the role of new clients do caution us to the dangers of judicial isolation and highlight the desirability of widening external ties and exchanges as soon as possible. Courts, like every other public service, derive their vision of social needs and values from the clients with whom they come into contact most frequently. If these are usually banks or members of the middle class, the judiciary's notion of what constitutes good service will be posited on their interests.

45. This argument has some currency in the World Bank (among its civil society teams), but, to my knowledge, it remains untested in practice.

46. See Galanter (2003). A common suggestion that special courts be created for commercial disputes reverses the location of the second-class system (now the ordinary courts) but runs much the same risks.

The questions of when the basics are sufficiently covered and thus when external pressures should commence are contextual judgment calls. The answers depend on the weaknesses inherent to the status quo ante and the complaints about its real and potential impacts on external goals There might conceivably be situations where access, legal change, or competitive services represent the ideal entry point because they, rather than internal disorganization or poorly defined political relationships, address the biggest obstacles to altering the courts' perceptions of their own role. Many self-benefiting reforms, the kind where computers, buildings, and budgetary increases seem to serve judicial needs more than any others, might have been avoided had the user base or certain legal elements been modified early on. Even where the kick start comes from these elements, however, this is not a call for an entirely reversed sequencing. A certain measure of client expansion or new operating rules will in turn require attention to system strengthening to facilitate a satisfactory response.

As opposed to the ways most reforms have been introduced, the change strategy encompassed in the framework thus begins with fixing the institutional parameters—as involves internal capabilities, external independence, and accountability—in the context of an overall vision of the judiciary's larger public service and political role. It starts with the premise that order to perform its essential functions, the judiciary's organizational integrity and its relationships with the rest of political and civil society must be defined and incorporated in its structure, powers, and external connections. These orderings are a work in progress and will be subject to continued revisions, but they are a fundamental prerequisite for the enactment of any further reforms. Tactically, they may have to accompany one or more of the other components, but, contrary to past practice, attempting to improve certain aspects of performance without addressing fundamental structural weaknesses is an invitation to sheer cosmetic change.

TAILORING THE STRATEGIC FRAMEWORK TO THE NATIONAL CONTEXT

So what happens to the judiciary's impact on crime, rights violations, or economic transactions? Or to delay, biased decisions, corruption, and excessive costs? These are the contextual problems that motivate reform and create a constituency for its implementation, taking it beyond the abstract pursuit of a better-functioning justice system into the resolution of obstacles to extra-sector societal goals. They define the more specific content and short-term goals of the change strategy as applied to specific cases. They are also the elements that will be used to measure success. They are, in managerial jargon, the results contract for the judicial reform.

Judicial reform is not done for its own sake. It is a means to attain other ends. The strategic framework provides a generic statement of these ends (for example, timely and satisfactory resolution of private disputes and criminal cases) and lays out the equally generic means through which they are best achieved (for example, basic organizational strengthening); however, judicial reforms, like other types of institutional change, achieve their impetus from societal discontent with specific problems—corrupt officials or participants in organized crime avoid legal action, debts are not collected, or those legally entitled to government services do not receive them. These problems are usually symptomatic of broader (generic) weaknesses. They could, nonetheless, be tackled on their own through a variety of ad hoc measures. In a strategic as opposed to purely tactical approach, their resolution is instead linked to the underlying cause, becoming the short-term indicator of success in attacking it. An enhanced judicial capacity to strengthen the normative framework will not be limited to that affecting corruption or creditor-debtor relations, but, if these are the most pressing complaints, this is where actions may first focus. Delay reduction, in general or in regard to certain types of cases, is only one result of a heightened organizational capacity to monitor and improve performance. If this is where criticism is centered, it will be a first test of success. Concrete, contextual problems, in short, provide the impetus for broader reform and set the short-term output goals. However, the strategy looks beyond their attainment to the creation of the capacity to address a multitude of similar problems— those which will doubtless emerge once the most visible ones are dealt with.

Tailoring the strategy to a specific national context thus still incorporates the generic objectives and components. It also respects the importance of sequencing—whether one starts with institutional strengthening and independence/ accountability, or first revises laws and increases access. Even here, the choices depend on not only the state of the system, but also the more detailed extra-system problems requiring resolution. This means that the strategic design should be preceded by a thorough sector assessment, reviewing generic characteristics, system impact on other societal goals, and the most common complaints about both. If the major complaint is the obstruction of business transactions, the high rate of crime or impunity, or a failure to deliver guaranteed rights and services to the poor, these will become the immediate raison d'être of the reform, justifying and shaping activities over the short to medium run. If these problems are addressed as isolated phenomena, the risk is that their resolution will not strengthen, and may even weaken, the system as a whole. Judicial reform requires an underlying strategy, but it also needs context-appropriate tactics, an appreciation of where its impact will be most visible and thus most likely to convince stakeholders of its longer-term value.

The short answer to where the other issues and approaches fit is thus "in two places." They become the indicators of progress in achieving the generic objectives and they influence the identification of specific activities. If reform were simply a question of achieving a more perfect justice system, this would not be necessary, but reform exists in a political space and responds to political pressures. Although the discussion here focuses on a comprehensive strategy, it bears mentioning that the same is true of the original partial approaches. Within their own narrower spheres, none of them has yet to focus on delivering concrete results and benefits; more access or a more accusatorial system are extremely abstract aims. If their promoters wish to build support for their efforts, they will also have to demonstrate the more immediate benefits for an expanding constituency of stakeholders.

Table 6 suggests how the generic strategy can be tailored to individual country needs. The difference lies in the specific activities and indicators, which derive from contextual problems—in this case, for illustrative purposes, delays in debt collection cases, and especially those for small users, and impunity of allegedly corrupt officials.

The table is only an example. Debt collection, corruption, and limited access for the poor have been used as illustrative problems. Where ordinary crime and violence are greater concerns, the desired type and direction of change would be different. The general categories of objectives, components, and activities, however, are standard; it is the content of each that is altered to reflect contextual circumstances.

For both the strategic (columns 1 and 2) and the tactical (columns 3 and 4) elements, the country's starting point and the causal underpinnings of problems identified dictate what will be included, how elements will be operationally defined, where emphasis will be placed, and how activities will be selected. If the judiciary is fairly well organized, already offers a variety of services, and has an adequate legal framework, a program will be very thematically specific and may largely ignore some objectives and components. If it is weak in all areas, the list of results and indicators will be far more extensive and will probably emphasize the organizational elements of component one.

Both results and indicators would vary according to the national situation. This is true not only of the themes selected, but also of the direction of change. Even in the same, thematic area, what constitutes a sign of progress in one country might well represent a setback in another, as, for example, rates of filings and types of dispositions for debt, corruption, or ordinary criminal cases. In a country where courts are generally underutilized, progress might mean increases in all types of filings. Where they are over- or abusively utilized, it would instead dictate reductions in the appearance of certain types of conflicts. Indicators for a strategy seeking to enhance the judiciary's role in combating corruption are also highly sensitive to national context. Depending on the circumstances, progress might be measured by more or fewer filings or convictions. Moreover, for any given country, the nature and direction of indicators can be expected to vary over time. An initial rise in corruption cases, if effective in combating the phenomenon, should eventually produce a longer-term decline. This is similar to the frequent observation that reported crimes are likely to rise and then fall as progress is made in handling criminal cases more effectively.

Table 6 Illustrative strategy aimed at improving debt collection, especially for small users, and improving judicial handling of corruption cases

Level	Definition	Targeted Result	Indicator
Purpose	Enhance judiciary's role within a political system capable of advancing the public good	Greater regime legitimacy	Decreased complaints about official corruption
		More economic growth	More credit available
Objective	Resolve conflicts in a timely, satisfactory fashion	Times to resolution of cases decreased	Debt collection occurs more rapidly
	Discourage conflicts through enhanced juridical security	Composition of case-load changes	Debt collection cases reduced as percentage of total cases heard[1]
	Check on government abuse	Courts review more government actions	More corruption cases adjudicated
	Strengthen normative framework	Inconsistencies in laws and their application reduced	Common legal loop-holes for avoiding prosecution for corruption eliminated
Components	Organizational strengthening	Management information system installed	Times for resolution of debt cases enforced
	Improved definition of external ties and powers	Courts' ability to enforce judgments against government defined	Government payment of debts to citizens occurs; other questionable actions decrease
	Improved legal framework	Substantive and procedural laws updated	Debt collection proceedings simplified; definition, penalties for corruption cases updated to current circumstances
	Mechanisms to enhance access	Small claims courts, subsidized counsel introduced	Greater percentage of users come from less wealthy classes
	Auxiliary services created/integrated	Mediation services introduced	More small debt cases submitted to mediation and successfully resolved

Table 6 (*continued*)

Level	Definition	Targeted Result	Indicator
Activities	Organizational strengthening:		
	Selection of judges	Merit competition introduced	Background checks to eliminate questionable candidates
	Career management	Rules for promotion linked to performance	Judges ranked on ability to decide cases on time
	Administration	Courtroom administration rationalized	Times and outcomes for processing of debt, corruption cases tracked
	Resources	Court budgets linked to performance needs	Courts/judges added or redistributed to rationalize workloads
	Processes	Procedures vetted to eliminate unnecessary steps	Default judgments added for debt cases; appeals limited
	Legal profession	Bar membership made compulsory and based on credentials and ethical performance	Disciplinary committees established and ethics codes enacted
	Ties with other actors:		
	Constitutional powers	Courts' ability to review government policies clarified	Courts' enforcement powers vis-à-vis judgments against government defined
	Rules on accountability	Courts held to same standards as other public offices	Assets declarations introduced for judges; publicly available
	Transparency measures	Courts required to provide information on performance	Statistics on filings and resolution by individual judges published
	Legal framework:	Courts identify and promote changes to procedures requiring simplification	Experiments with single, oral hearings for small debt cases

Table 6 (*continued*)

Level	Definition	Targeted Result	Indicator
Activities (*continued*)	Access:		
	Provision of legal services	Coordination of public and NGO services introduced	Public services redistributed to reach areas without NGO offerings
	Removal of cost barriers	Barriers identified and changes made to reduce them	Filing-fee system altered to benefit small user
	Geographic barriers	Plan implemented to place courts closer to users	Decentralization of court offices to outlying areas in urban centers
	Auxiliary Services:		
	ADR	Program of court-annexed mediation introduced	Courts increase proportion of mediated agreements
	Administrative offices	Routine complaints more susceptible to administrative resolution identified and provisions made for administrative handling	Greater proportion of complaints handled administratively; lower percentage sent to judiciary

Note:

1. This is a context-specific indicator—in the abstract, a higher or lower percentage of debt-collection cases has no particular significance. In the context of a reform aimed at increasing its efficiency and efficacy, a medium-term decrease in the weight of such cases should indicate improved performance (but one will always want to test for other, less positive interpretations).

CONCLUSIONS

The strategic framework laid out above and its illustrative application to a hypothesized case are intended to demonstrate how the various partial approaches might be incorporated into a single reform program. The advantage of starting with a comprehensive outline of this type is that it forces us to consider all the potentially relevant parts of the system. Although any given reform will inevitably focus on a lesser number of interventions, the use of this type of framework reduces the changes of overlooking critical elements. It also encourages consideration of how the lowest level of interventions, the individual activities, may affect more than one component or objective, and it at the very least, forces those promoting activities to place them in the context of the higher levels of the strategy. It may not eliminate the reform Christmas tree entirely. It can reduce the number of ornaments placed on it simply because "this is what one does in a reform," and it can ensure that those that remain have an explicit linkage to higher-order goals.

Better knowledge management can inform the strategy at all levels, but especially at the lower ones. This is where we have learned the most about what works to produce certain short-term results—changes in the internal processes and behaviors of system actors. In turn, the framework can help direct future knowledge management—research—into areas at its higher levels where we are less certain of how to proceed. This is where we still need to ask which lower-level changes are most likely to affect extrasystem economic behavior or how crime rates are impacted by the justice system. In fact, it is the linkages between levels that require the most exploration—knowing how and which kinds of "access" services are really likely to bring targeted groups to courts or, more to the point, advance their interests and produce more timely and satisfactory resolution of their conflicts. Over the short run, such linkages will constitute working hypotheses. They should be specified as such for testing, along with the indicators to be used to detect the expected higher-order changes.

For the immediate future, strategy building is largely a question of discipline. It requires forcing would-be participants to specify how whatever they propose to do is linked to some larger goal and of similarly requiring those backing the reform to articulate their goals, link them to the components and activities, and provide some justification for accepting those linkages. Those who cheat on the linkages will eventually be caught when the indicators they will also have to propose do not demonstrate any change. Over the medium term, this may produce some slightly less ambitious claims as to what judicial reform will achieve and, over the longer run, a better understanding of what we can hope to accomplish by training judges, changing laws, or altering judicial budgets.

Strategic planning will not resolve the final question of the optimal role of the judiciary in a contemporary political system. It should reduce the gap between the promised impacts and the real achievements. That will leave to the experts and the reformers themselves the definitions of future lines of argument and research, but such definitions are also the hallmark of a more mature applied and academic discipline. Once we finally reach the stage of agreeing on what we know and where we disagree, judicial reform will have evolved beyond its current status as a hodge-podge of good intentions to a more systematic approach to considering how judiciaries affect the quality of governance and what can be done to enhance their impact.

The arguments developed in the preceding chapters emphasize the need for a more empirically based, strategic approach to judicial reform, one that coordinates the multitude of activities currently included in reform programs by defining and validating their linkages to longer-term objectives and aims. An improved strategic framework is more than an exercise in abstract theory building. Its practical utility also depends on its being firmly grounded in knowledge accumulated through experience and research. The need for this undertaking arises in the growing sense that two decades of Latin American judicial reform programs have delivered less than promised and are beginning to generate some unanticipated and not always positive consequences.

The reforms have indeed produced changes in the structure, operations, and resource endowment of the sector. This is a demonstrable fact for every country in the region, and only the most willfully narrow-minded critic could hold otherwise. Change is one thing; improvement is another. Despite the quantities of national and donor funds invested, the dramatic growth in the size and national presence of judicial organizations, and the proliferation of new buildings, equipment, organizational entities, procedures, and training and information programs, basic complaints such as delay, corruption, impunity, irrelevance, and limited access do not seem to have dissipated. Public opinion polls indicate no improvement in the courts' public image, and the statistics that are available show little change in the usual performance indicators.[1] In most, but not all, instances, courts are handling more cases, but doing so neither more rapidly nor more efficiently than before.[2] As for contributions to downstream goals such as reductions in crime or

---

1. One hopeful note is provided by CEJA (2005) in its review of the state of justice in the region. In a majority of countries, the latest public opinion surveys do show a slight upturn although still not reaching earlier levels. Moreover, CEJA's first attempt to include clearance rates shows most countries at close to 100 percent. In view of other available information, this part invites healthy skepticism. As mentioned earlier, one predictable consequence of using performance statistics is that those being evaluated will begin to game the system. Taking into account statistics provided by the courts two years ago and the problems the country has faced since, it seems highly improbable that Ecuador's judges, for example, are now processing, or even receiving, an annual average of over 2,000 cases each.

2. The absence of baseline data makes comparisons difficult. It also indicates courts' lack of interest in tracking performance. In Mexico's Federal District and Quito (Ecuador), filings actually decreased in recent years with no visible impact on delay. See, however, the preceding note. The World Bank (Legal Vice Presidency 2003a) documented some improvements in clearance rates in its pilot courts in Ecuador.

poverty or increases in economic growth rates, the most that might be hypothesized is that things would have been much worse without the reforms. There is, however, no empirical basis for supporting even that minimalist assessment.

It is certainly true that judicial reform is a more complex and lengthy process than initially believed. Part of the disappointment is thus a result of overly ambitious estimates as to how fast improvements could be made. Nonetheless, many observers are identifying more fundamental problems that will not be resolved no matter how much more time is devoted to implementing conventional programs. They now talk in terms of guild reforms, which suggests that the investments have largely benefited the judges, not the public or society as a whole. Although new policies have reduced the judiciaries' traditional subservience to other branches of government and political elites, they have not enhanced their accountability to civil and political society or increased their interest in providing a high quality public service in a timely fashion. Indeed, they sometimes appear to have augmented judicial isolation from the expectations and values held by the broader public. With guaranteed salaries, tenure, and other benefits, the tendency to sink into bureaucratic complacency is evident among many members of the region's judiciaries. More independent and better-financed courts have begun to exercise their political weight in ways that often meet with public criticism.[3] This includes instances of judges having opposed policies on the basis of how their own interests were affected,[4] entered actively into policymaking, or overturned government programs with insufficient consideration for the likely results. No one doubts the desirability of judicial checks on government abuses. Such checks, however, should

---

Still, there is no indication of whether this reflects more efficient handling of current filings or the closure of masses of inactive cases via backlog reduction programs. The more common situation appears to be a gradual increase in backlog as a result of increased demand and static productivity. For Mexico, see World Bank (2002b); for Ecuador, see Simon et al. (2002). Peru's results are more positive (Gonzales et al. 2002), but there are signs that initial decreases in delay have been reversed and possibly never occurred outside a few pilot courts.

3. For example, in just one month (March 2005), three actions, originating in different levels of Brazil's judiciaries, brought public outrage. One was the continuing push from the President of the Supremo Tribunal Federal to again raise judicial salaries, starting with those of the Supremo Tribunal Federal justices. A second was the Rio de Janeiro state superior court's (Tribunal de Justiça) nullification of some 6 million traffic fines on the grounds that they violated the right to a prior defense (*"Prêmio à impunidade,"* O Globo, Rio de Janeiro, March 24, 2005: 12). The third was the same court's granting of a temporary injunction to a judge demanding that the officials and residents of his condominium address him as "sir" or "doctor." Satisfaction of the judge's additional claim of 10,000 *reais* (US $4,800) in moral damages is pending the final ruling. (*"Juiz será doutor ou senhor até decisão final,"* O Globo, March 24, 2005: 13).

4. The Argentine supreme court's findings as to the judiciary's exemption from the income tax and from transparency measures like publication of assets declarations and management statistics is one example. Both the Colombian Constitutional Court and the Brazilian Federal Supreme Tribunal have ruled on pension policies that also affect their members. In mid-2003, the Brazilian federal and state judges united to negotiate their exclusion from the executive's proposed pension reforms. The judges invited more ill will by insisting the constitution declared them more valuable than teachers or doctors and that it was not their fault that cane cutters had inadequate salaries and pensions.

not be exercised lightly or simply substitute judicial preferences for those of political authorities.

FACTORS WORKING AGAINST CHANGE

This general impression of insufficient or questionable progress is shared by many working within the programs. It is also evident among external stakeholders, including the very groups supposed to benefit from the reforms and those who are asked to finance them, directly or indirectly. Nonetheless, there are strong disincentives working against an explicit recognition of these doubts or a resolve to act on them.

On the one hand, judicial reform has become a business and as such has engendered numerous vested interests in the standard repertoire of interventions. Ideally, reform designers should be able to deviate from the usual formulas and adjust their activities accordingly. Still, any attempt to question the value of training, automation, or law drafting puts in jeopardy the livelihood of those specializing in their provision. No one wants to be told that what they have been delivering for the past ten years is of dubious value and may have to be eliminated from the menu or radically revised.

On the other, the disagreement over the ends of judicial reform and how they are best pursued often arises in honest differences of opinion. Most reform participants are not callous entrepreneurs, attempting to sell their snake oil of choice. A majority genuinely believe that what they are offering is what societies where they operate urgently need. Purveyors of training may be more easily convinced that they can modify the content of their programs than a fervent believer in the accusatory criminal justice system might be persuaded to forget about perfecting oral trials and get on with improving police-prosecutorial relations. Both the trainers and the criminal justice experts, however, work from the best of intentions. The problems arise in their narrow perspectives on country needs, past experience, and emerging questions as to the efficacy of standard recipes. As discussed in chapters 6 and 7, these limitations are largely the consequences of poor knowledge management and a failure to encourage broader discussions of new issues and gaps in our understanding. Responsibility thus lies as much with the entire reform community as with any individual participant.

Those more emotionally removed from the reforms, but caught up in their progress for extraneous reasons can also pose impediments to change. These are the organizational and political leaders who finance the reforms as one of their star programs or have incorporated them into their administration's platform. Most of these adoptive backers would prefer to declare victory and move on to the next challenge rather than enduring a postmortem on their last effort and the conclusion that it did not turn out that well.

Finally, there are participants who have seen reform as a means of advancing agendas that in some sense undercut the assumed purpose of the efforts. Among them we can count the politicians who have found ways to reassert their control of judicial appointments through the addition and manipulation of a judicial council, the economic elites laying claim to special laws and courts as a means of creating their own captive justice, or the private lawyers who manipulate mediation programs as a new way of increasing their clientele. We might also include here the judges who have welcomed the reforms solely for their provision of more resources, increased salaries, or a greater independence from any sort of external control. Judges have not always been the reforms' principal beneficiaries, and there are many who appear most interested in their potential for resolving user complaints. When their primary concern is the personal rewards, though, they may be the major obstacle to any change in content.

Thus, the new challenge is how, with all these contrary incentives, participants who have begun to question the standard reform recipes can join forces to encourage improvements and so form a constituency to replace the existing alliances. In this essentially organizational and political dilemma the obstacles can be summarized as two interrelated phenomena. The first has been called the "firemen's syndrome"—do not admit there are problems as this will cut off the supply of funds for everyone. Those violating this rule, whether from within or as outside critics, are likely to find themselves excluded from further participation. The second can be described as a reverse principal-agent effect. The agents in this case see the problems, but their principals would just as soon ignore them. Anyone attempting to overcome these barriers confronts a third dilemma, here called the "Archimedes principle" or the question of where one places the lever that moves the world.

The Firemen's Syndrome

With respect to the firemen's syndrome, the disincentives are obvious.[5] Reformers who publicly express doubts about their individual or institutional contribution, which is where one usually starts, may find themselves excluded from the game and replaced by a more optimistic participant. This phenomenon also operates within organizations where several internal factions or departments contribute to reform programming or manage separate projects. Although their relationship is

---

5. I was originally tempted to call this the prisoners' dilemma, but, unlike that game theory model, the incentives here are to cooperate in perpetuating a shared fiction. Whereas the prisoners end up confessing, and so sharing common sanctions, the firemen respect the adage "don't step on the hose," thus protecting their endeavor but sacrificing the potential for improving it. The difference is that the firemen know what their colleagues are doing and can take preemptive measures against defectors. The prisoners cannot communicate with each other.

often competitive, overt intra- and interdepartmental criticism is commonly discouraged, the former for obvious reasons, the latter because it can lessen confidence in the entire effort.[6] For those offering critiques from outside, or insiders attempting to encourage internal, less public debate, there are slightly different variations. External critics, those who have not walked the walk, are rarely positioned to have any special influence. Frequently located in academic institutions or NGOs, they are commonly viewed as chronic complainers with an ideological ax to grind. And because they often have limited knowledge of the situations they are critiquing, their few errors of fact will be used to discredit their entire argument.

There are a few, rare cases where external critics have had an impact on reshaping reforms under implementation or at the proposal stage. The Lawyers Committee's public critique of the World Bank's first Latin American judicial reform loan is one example.[7] The project was redesigned as a consequence, the total funding cut, and the initial ambitious construction program passed over to Venezuelan counterpart support. The overall impact on subsequent World Bank projects in the region, however, has been slight. Many of the weaknesses targeted by the committee's report (failure to focus on corruption as a major problem, dedication of loan funds to buildings and equipment) continue to be staples of project design. Criticism from a broader range of NGOs has also provoked the inclusion of "civil society" elements in the MDB and other donor programs, but in a way that usually verges on the largely symbolic. Commonly, a few NGOs are consulted on project design and an NGO component (grants to local organizations for justice related work) is tacked on to take care of the rest. Organizations persisting in their criticisms may find themselves excluded from the largesse.

Insiders who dare to criticize their organization's strategies or specific projects, even within private forums, are usually treated as disloyal participants unless they can limit their comments to a few positive suggestions. Although one might hope that behind closed doors donors or national reformers could hash out some of the transcendental issues, the firemen's syndrome prevails even here. A serious, fundamental critique is too often seen as impeding progress, threatening timely delivery of a product, and raising issues that "can be treated later" but should not be allowed to interfere with getting the program started. Here teamwork becomes confused with an implicit agreement to perpetuate certain deceptions in the interest of advancing a common goal. Unfortunately, the goal soon begins to resemble

---

6. Within U.S. government programs, there has been a long-standing competition among such agencies as USAID, the Department of Justice, the Department of State, and increasingly, entities attached to the federal courts. In a private conversation, a member of the justice department once commented to the author that he did not understand why USAID openly discussed its problems with projects because this clearly worked against it in the inter-departmental struggle for control of budgets. This may have been a friendly piece of advice, but it also reflects concerns that any one department's admission of doubts could have negative impacts on the others.

7. See Lawyers Committee and Venezuelan Program (1996).

doing or financing projects more than effecting reform. This type of goal substitution can be explained in terms of another concern, that such internal criticisms will
have a negative impact on the views of those outside the immediate planning group.
In their respective organizations, judicial reformers are usually a small minority
assumed to have the necessary expertise for delivering what they promise. When
members begin to cast doubts on that assumption, the expert status of the group
as a whole is threatened. It is far easier to cashier the doubter than to entertain his
or her objections. Would-be critics, well aware of that fact, thus face their own disincentives—if they want to play, they have to support the other players.

The Reverse Principal-Agent Effect

This phenomenon is less frequently mentioned. It is closely related to the firemen's
syndrome and in fact is a source of the latter's strength. It draws on the principal-
agent dilemma as depicted in neoinstitutional economic theory but inverts the
problem.[8] Here, it is not the principal's efforts to control the agent, but rather the
agent's inability to influence the principal's understanding of the basic issues that
counts. I suspect that much of what are usually described as principal-agent problems incorporates this aspect as well. The principal's apparent inability to control
the agent stems at least in part from the failure to understand how the agent per-
ceives the situation on the ground and what he or she can actually do about it.[9]

Most reform programs depend for their financial and other support on political leaders (whether of countries or of assistance agencies) who know relatively
little about the subject matter, but have adopted it as a cause worth backing. These
leaders want successes; they need them to promote their broader and usually un-
related agendas. If they understood more about the real problems being addressed
and the impediments to their resolution, they might be less satisfied with programs
delivering only cosmetic change. As they do not, a well-publicized victory is far
more pleasing to them than a well-argued criticism of what they have already supported or what they are on the verge of promoting. Judicial, like every other type
of reform policy, thus has both a political and technical side. The technical side,
it should be clarified, includes not only technological elements, but also institutional analysis more broadly defined to incorporate incentive systems, informal
rules, human and other resource constraints, and interactions with extrainstitional
actors. Technical input determines a program's chances of producing the promised

8. See North (1990).

9. Both sides of the principal-agent dilemma were in fact anticipated, long before the term reached
its present formulation and currency, in a book written by two political scientists (Wildavsky and Pressman 1960) explaining, to paraphrase the subtitle, why programs designed in Washington were enacted
so differently once they reached the local level. The authors do emphasize the implementers' tendency
to follow their own agendas, but also note that the Washington designers often did not understand how
the implementation context would force alterations to their best-laid plans.

results, but political backing is the source of its ability to be put into effect. Ideally the two elements should work to the same end. Most often they do not, and unless reform proponents are willing and able to work out sustainable compromises, they will either lose their backing or produce technically ineffectual programs.

The challenge here is for the agents—the reform designers and implementers—to find ways to convince their principals—the funders and supporters of reforms—to recognize and give importance to technical problems and shortcomings (including local political and other vested interests impeding their adoption) and back strategic corrections, rather than simply canceling the programs. This is particularly difficult inasmuch as the principals commonly have no particular interest in or understanding of the technical and contextual issues—they may in fact, it sometimes appears, be relatively skeptical about the prospects for substantive change and more attracted by the immediate benefits of association with a popular cause. Reform experts have contributed to this phenomenon, either by not explaining themselves well or by consciously obfuscating the issues. A presumably esoteric expertise not easily accessible to the layperson is itself a source of power, especially when those holding it can ensure their superiors that they have all the unintelligible angles covered. In the battle among experts for the funders' attention, the expert who can deliver the most positive news in the most concise format holds an indisputable advantage. One who insists on qualifying his or her message with caveats and complicated details is less likely to get it across.

If a program appears to be going well, offers an opportunity for positive publicity, and has apparent support from interested stakeholders, that is usually all political leadership requires. A political leader able to announce that he will deliver computers to every courtroom, training to every judge, or put a national legal framework into line with international standards is not going to respond positively to suggestions that none of these measures will produce reductions in delay and corruption, facilitate economic transactions, or enhance access for the poor. As long as the major stakeholders, many of whom may be quite pleased with the new offerings, endorse the changes, technical quibbles will be highly unwelcome. Politicians prefer and need simple stories. They will countenance fine, technical distinctions only if they do not get in the way of less complex explanations and programs. Technical experts thus have to be able to provide them with both—a good story line and a technically sound strategy that coincides with it, even if treating the details in ways that will never figure in the public version. Unfortunately, if forced to choose, the politician will usually opt for the attractive story line and not the better strategy.

The phenomenon is equally applicable to the situation of the head of an assistance agency, a national president, or a chief justice. Only the latter has a predominant stake in judicial reform but that stake may serve very narrow interests and derive from an equally narrow notion of what requires change. For the others, judicial reform is usually a minor item in a long list of programs in their agenda and thus not an area where they want to focus a good deal of attention. Moreover, as technical weaknesses usually involve longer range implications, and political leaders have a far shorter planning horizon, the implied risks will generally appear tolerable. Over the short run, progress in installing novel services, opening courts in new regions, or computerizing case management will suffice to prove success. Doubts over whether such actions will produce any improvement in performance can be easily ignored. In the short term, there will always be ways to document progress, and, in the more distant future, the principals will not have to answer for the consequences. In brief, those closest to the problems and best qualified to evaluate the likelihood of solutions are least-well-positioned to register doubts about their chances of success. The technical expert who fails to recognize this situation, like the internal critic who threatens the prevailing consensus, may find his or her participation in the reform facing a hasty termination.

SOME IDEAS ON HOW TO LEVERAGE CHANGE

A Role for Theory and Its Academic Proponents?

This comes as a digression, but a necessary one in light of questions raised by readers of early drafts. Why was I, with at least one foot in academia, not proposing a theory of the judicial role as a means of guiding future reform programs? The answer comes in three simple parts: my ambitions are more modest, the effort would undermine a principal message as to the conflicting, if often implicit, views of the reformers themselves, and most important, I have my own doubts as to the feasibility of developing a theory that would actually serve this purpose. Theories as to the role of courts and the factors conditioning it already abound. Although usually acknowledging the same set of basic functions, they differ considerably as to their assignment of relative importance or their assumptions of universality.[10] All of the partial approaches have an implicit theory behind them that accounts for where they put their emphasis and sometimes is more explicitly stated to justify their selectivity. The implicit theories of course differ, as do the more explicit theoretical models proposed by the minority of academics directing their attention to judicial reform. For the academics, however, disciplinary biases seem to account for the most significant divergences.

Starting with the economists, relative latecomers to the field, there is naturally a predisposition to emphasize the courts' economic role. More important still is

10. For a further discussion, see Shapiro's (1981) treatment of real judicial systems' divergences from the presumed fundamental characteristics of court operations.

their tendency to focus on dispute resolution and its impact on clarifying the rules of the game, alternatively called enhancing predictability, reinforcing juridical security, or reducing transaction costs. The underlying argument is that courts, by making decisions in accord with uniform, predictable criteria, signal to societal actors which rules will be enforced, how they will be further interpreted and applied, and the costs of noncompliance. This discourages rule violation, reduces conflicts, and contributes to societal well-being by allowing citizens to act and plan their future actions in a more certain environment. The model is not limited to economic transactions and can encompass all types of conflicts. It is clearly influenced by the economists' preference for market mechanisms and their belief in the market's ability to shape the behavior of large numbers of independent actors.

Most economists do not expect courts to operate like markets, but they do extrapolate from the market model in explaining their impacts.[11] This preference has caused them to focus largely on trial courts with considerably less attention to high courts, despite the latter's potential contribution to unifying standards. Probably this is because of a lesser faith in abstract orders from on high as opposed to the cumulate weight of the mass of individual rulings. Economic theorists have privileged speediness as well as uniformity and often suggest procedural simplification as a means of achieving both. Again drawing from the market model, they are usually proponents of simple changes to alter incentives, including those affecting judges' behavior.[12] These abstract arguments are increasingly accompanied by sophisticated quantitative analysis focusing on the relationships between economic growth and the speed of dispositions or procedural complexity.[13] The analysis does not test the signaling function itself—that is to say, whether the incidence of rule violation or court use is affected by parties' ability to predict outcomes. What support it provides for the model is largely inferential. Put in the disciplinary jargon, the economists' model of the judicial role emphasizes the public good (externality) of greater rule predictability deriving from the courts' provision of individualized private benefits via ordinary dispute resolution. They have been remarkably less attuned to the judiciary's political functions or its embeddedness in a broader power structure.

The political scientists entered earlier and have tended to focus on what the economists slight—the role of the courts in supporting an existing power structure

11. Their are exceptions—for example, an economist who made the mistake of suggesting court users choose their judges (so encouraging the most efficient) to a group of judicial reform experts. The latter responded by explaining the evils of judge shopping. Early reports from the World Bank's Doing Business group (Djankov et al. 2002), also recommended "deregulating justice," a term since dropped in favor of simplifying procedures.

12. Here, however, they might take a lesson from Scott's (1998) cautions on reductionist approaches to effecting institutional reform, as well as the arguments of behavioral economics about actors' real-life deviations from the rational choice model. See Sunstein 2000.

13. See Djankov et al. (2002), La Porta et al. (1998), Castelar (1998), and Castelar, ed. (2000).

and their potential use in reversing it. The first line of argument, also forwarded by critical sociologists and some academic lawyers, entered early and has exercised a diffuse influence to this day. Its proponents are among the strongest critics of reform practices, noting their tendency to overlook the role of "laws and legal institutions [in legitimating] hierarchies and hierarchic relationships."[14] Much of their work focuses on documenting these effects, with or without reform, and unlike that of the economists, looks at all court levels, the private bar, and various auxiliary institutions, but especially the police.[15] Their model and methodology are less elegant than those of the economists, relying largely on case studies and anecdotal evidence. This has not reduced their impact, which unfortunately does not extend to providing many clues as to how to escape the dilemma they depict. Still, both the early criminal justice reforms and the access approaches have used these arguments to develop their activities and their implicit theories concerning the judiciary's main functions.

The second half of the approach is more exclusive to political scientists, often of a more conservative bent than the first group. It is equally political but downplays the courts' dispute-resolution role in favor of their checks-and-balance function. Admittedly, the latter also involves dispute resolution, but of a more select type, involving alleged abuses perpetrated by government authorities. Some theorists prefer to term this the judiciary's role in enforcing horizontal accountability.[16] The accountability/checks and balances approach is in large part a prescriptive theory inasmuch as its proponents have few developing country examples of its working in practice. Moreover, as they sometimes fail to recognize, there are certain cultural and ideological obstacles to its universalization.[17] Nonetheless, it has gained ground in Latin America. Regardless of whether practitioners are familiar with the theoretical literature, similar ideas lie behind the emergence of public-interest law, constitutional changes to augment judicial independence and the judiciary's legal and constitutional review powers, and the creation of human rights ombudsmen and entities like Brazil's public ministry. Aside from promoting these changes, academics interested in the model have conducted research on the extent to which Latin American courts already play this role and the reasons for its emergence.[18]

14. Ee Dezalay and Garth (2002, 247).

15. See chapters in Méndez et al. (1999). Ungar (2002) and Popkin (2000), the former a political scientist and the latter a lawyer, are also relevant. Many works by NGOs feature this approach. See Spence et al. (1994) and Spence et al. (1995).

16. See Mainwaring (2003). The term "horizontal accountability" is usually attributed to Guillermo O'Donnell (1996, 1999), who has also written on the judiciary's role in supporting existing power structures. In some sense, the concept provides part of the missing answer as how to alter that effect.

17. Those with doubts are invited to discuss judicial independence with Chinese judges.

18. See Helmke (2005) and B. Magaloni (2003), for two slightly different explanations. Helmke focuses on the judges' own incentives. Magaloni emphasizes the reasons why political elites might allow these developments. Both use quantitative techniques as do many new scholars reviewing the emergence of

Possibly because of better access to data, their work and the school as a whole emphasize high-level courts. That focus, however, is also more congruent with the seeming assumption that political rather than ordinary dispute resolution is where the judiciary makes its greatest developmental impact and thus where reform should place most effort.

And what of the lawyers, the "owners" of the reforms? First, except as encompassed in the first two approaches, most of them have been less inclined to macrotheorizing about judicial reform's purposes. This may be a disciplinary bias or it may be that those closest to the reform movement have been too busy promoting the lower-level, practical changes they see as more critical to improving overall operations. Second, because of their proximity and their firsthand knowledge of how things really work, lawyers may be less inclined to the grandiose generalizations required by an overarching theory. Ask practicing attorneys about courts signaling to potential users, and they will counter with tales of clients hell-bent on bringing suit no matter what the odds, or the search for legal exceptions to the bright-line rule. Lawyers certainly recognize the functions privileged in the competing models described above, but are more inclined to see them as all having a role and as imperfectly realized in any event. In effect, although academic lawyers have produced many theories, the discipline does not appear to have a dominant theoretical model to bring to the reforms. The individual answers of lawyers involved in reform work are equally divided among the five partial strategies described in the first section of this volume. This is hardly surprising, because they have been the principal contributors to the strategies' evolution. Each partial strategy does have an implicit model underlying it, but these models focus more on what proponents believe unreformed courts are not doing well rather than on a macro vision of their overall functions.

This still leaves a smattering of minor disciplines (minor only in terms their contribution to the debate). There are, for example, legal anthropologists who emphasize the connections between dispute-resolution practices and cultural identity.[19] This might be considered a counter-reform model in that it questions the nearly universal assumption that the goal is to create a single national justice system. Another counter-reform example, discussed in chapter 4, comes out of the ADR movement and the arguments of some participants that the primary objective should be reducing conflict through the use of less legally centered types of dispute resolution, popular education in negotiation skills, and an emphasis on consensus building, especially at the community level. These individuals seem to

---

the courts' checks and balance powers in the region. See, for example, Taylor (2004), whose focus is less checks and balances than the use of the courts as an alternative forum for debates over public policy.

19. See, for example, Nader (1990) and Faundez (2005b). Although Faundez is a lawyer by training, he is also questioning of the wisdom of eliminating local practices, more for practical reasons (they work) than for a concern about cultural preservation.

discount efforts to strengthen courts as running contrary to their purpose, or at most as a minor part of the preferred strategy.[20]

As this digression should make clear, the major impediment to using overarching theory as a guide to future reforms is the considerable disagreement among the existing candidates for that role. A second, no-less-important obstacle is that what does exist is long on prescriptive goals and conspicuously short on practical advice as to how to advance them. Whether they recognize it (the political scientists) or not (the economists), present judicial operations rest on strong vested interests and so are unlikely to be changed by elegant models or statistical and other evidence. In the end, what courts do as well as how they do it are political choices. Theory can enrich our understanding of the alternatives and their likely consequences for societies adopting them, but it cannot impose the selection. At a lower level of theorizing and with much greater detail, that is also the aim of this volume. The next, and last, question addressed is thus how to ensure that this better understanding has a positive impact on reform efforts. In this the academic disciplines can make a further contribution, if one they may find less intrinsically interesting. It is to use their skills to assess and question ongoing programs, not against higher theory, but against what they claim to be doing. Macrotheory can have a place here in calling attention to what is overlooked, but its proponents' wish to impose their models, absent more agreement on their contents and far greater attention to their operationalization, is not likely to get far.

The Archimedes Principle

If judicial reform is to do more than enhance court budgets, add modern gadgets, and redraft laws, those entertaining doubts about its ability to improve judicial performance and contributions to broader political, social, and economic goals must find a way to introduce their reservations and positive suggestions into the current understanding of the purposes, potential, and actions embodied in reform programs. As their goal, we assume, is not to end the collective effort, but rather to improve and refocus its direction, they face the doubly difficult challenge of introducing criticisms while at the same time maintaining support for the overall undertaking. The earlier law and development movement is thus not the example to follow. Its internal and external critics succeeded in establishing the dubious track record of the programs, but only to the point of ending interest in maintaining them.[21] Law and development suffered an untimely demise and one that, in the eyes of later observers, was probably due to an exaggerated emphasis of its negative achievements and a failure to recognize both its accomplishments and potential for doing

20. See, for example, Golub (2003). Although a lawyer, Golub is a prominent critic of the court-centered approach to judicial reform.

21. See Gardner (1980), for one of the most influential insider's critiques.

still more. Much of the progress made in the current era can be attributed to the interest in judicial operations and in new ways of evaluating them introduced by law and development participants.[22] The agents, however, were so successful in documenting their shortcomings that the principals became convinced that withdrawing support was the most logical response.

Because the dissenters within the current programs are still a small minority, the region's judicial reforms do not yet appear threatened by a similar fate. The more likely scenario is a continuing expansion of objectives and activities, an increasing routinization of the reform recipe, and a constant level of investments in implementation until the impetus runs down (because there is no more room for additional funding) or the negative side-effects (court interference with high priority policy, uncurbed corruption, or escalating complaints about the same old problems, delay, and inefficiency) convince a majority of outsiders that the programs are not working. At that stage, more radical solutions—executive takeovers of reforms or the creation of special judicial or administrative tribunals for high-priority issues[23]—are one possible outcome. The other, more likely result is that things will be left as they stand. Judicial reform will stop, and judiciaries will continue to operate with both their old and new forms of poor performance. For those convinced that reform can serve a positive purpose, either outcome would be unfortunate. Thus, the challenge is how to prevent their occurring.

It would appear that the only way to reach this end is to convince political backers of the urgent need for improvements in the programs themselves. For this to happen, they must be made aware of the gaps between actual and potential achievements and of the importance and feasibility of closing it in a positive sense, that is to say, moving real achievements into the positive range. Just emphasizing the gaps is not enough. It would only lead to the law and development outcome, untimely termination of the entire effort. In terms of the second half of the equation, importance, and feasibility are equally significant. Backers must be shown that change is worthwhile and that it can be realized. Demonstrating importance without feasibility or feasibility without importance will not suffice.

To do this, the technical dissidents must themselves become political, thinking in terms of coalitions, stakeholders and political payoffs. Because they will never make their point solely on the correctness of their arguments, they must find a way to give those arguments political weight—to convince political leaders that they are not just a fringe group of resentful nonconformists, but rather a respectable and respected coalition of agenda setters. This is where the Archimedes principle

---

22. As anyone actively involved in reform programs can attest, many current reform proponents in Latin America were directly or indirectly influenced by the law and development programs.

23. Although "dejudicialization" and specialization are legitimate solutions for court congestion, the fear here is their use to favor certain, probably elite groups, or to give politicians more control over outcomes by sending disputes to forums they can manipulate more easily.

enters, because the position from which to leverage change and the way in which to turn expert knowledge into political pressure. That position probably is not located within a single assistance agency, national reform program, NGO, or research institution. Even where the dissenters are not in a minority, and they usually are, no single one of these entities is powerful enough to shift the content of reform discourse. Some come closer to that status. If the World Bank tomorrow announced its profound dissatisfaction with the state of all judicial reform programs and its resolve to work on the basis of accumulated knowledge and strategic planning, it might make an impact. It also might find it had far fewer reform projects to implement. Even if the bank's experts reached total agreement on that new direction, their internal constituencies, the country and sector directors responsible for making loans, would likely not endorse it because of the immediate impact on loan portfolios. This is highly hypothetical in any event, because even within the World Bank the likelihood of such a shift in expert views is minimal. The firemen's syndrome and the inverse principal-agent phenomenon have an overwhelming impact there as well. This kind of internal agreement is more likely within research institutions or NGOs. As we have seen, however, their impact on reform programming has so far been minimal. The same factors that might facilitate their agreement, their lack of a concrete stake in reforms, also impede their broader influence. Those who do not provide the funding will not have much effect on how it is used.

The solution would instead appear to be a cross-institutional coalition, conceivably supported by some external academic institution or NGO, but incorporating far more than its immediate members. The ultimate goal, developing a dynamic consensus on the objectives and the most likely means of improving the various aspects of judicial performance, a sort of applied discipline of judicial reform, would have to be sufficiently broadly based to encompass the variety of potential members but focused enough to encourage agreement on a set of common principles. There are a number of potential candidates for this role already. None has so far had much success in attracting outside participation or broader attention to their programs. That may well be because they still have too self-centered a focus, attempting to wield Archimedes' lever on the basis of their own internal strength and a handful of external allies.

The simple truth is that no existing organization has the self-contained legitimacy to play this role. If any of them is to make a dent in the problem, it will need to draw in a much wider community of experts, and especially those who are formally attached to other institutions. Five experts from Harvard, Yale, Stanford, or any independent NGO will not make an impact; a Harvard, Yale, Stanford, or NGO program that is backed by a community of the most prestigious experts from the donor community, various Latin American institutions, other universities, and other NGOs can begin to exercise influence—especially if its associated members can now call on the weight of collective opinion in challenging the received wisdom in their institutional homes. Because much of this received wisdom often constitutes little more than a sense that "we know what we are doing because we have been doing it for X years," part of the service may be in forcing the donors to analyze their own programs and proposals for internal consistency and to better articulate the knowledge base from which they believe they are working.

The proposal does not seek to impose a collective straightjacket. Fortunately, that would be very difficult, in light of the prevailing dispersion of energies and interests. Developing a broader consensus as to the feasible objectives of reform work, the most productive areas of activity, and the questions we have not yet answered, however, would be a decided step forward in improving ongoing programs and discouraging some of the less productive ventures. The goals is not to duplicate the increasingly discredited Washington Consensus. A more useful model would strive to approximate the situation in public health, education or post-Consensus development economics, where approaches can at least be divided into major schools and proposals can be and are debated within that context. Still, the parallels to the Washington Consensus are worth exploring inasmuch as in both cases, shared assumptions are now threatened and there is a need (admittedly less urgent in judicial reform) to revisit them and develop a new perspective. In the end, the problem faced by the reformers, those designing and implementing the programs, is much like that faced by the judiciaries and political leadership. It is a question of political will and a collective willingness to take risks that promise largely long-term payoffs and threaten some immediate discomforts. Presumably the reformers are better positioned to understand the trade-offs. The question is whether they will decide to use this privileged knowledge for the long-term, collective good, or continue to enlist it to further short-term private and mutual benefits.

REFERENCES

Abiad, Pablo, and Mariano Thieberger. 2005. *Justicia era Kirchner: La construcción de un poder a medida*. Buenos Aires: Marea.

Álvareaz, Gladys S., and Elena I. Highton. 2000. "Resolución alternativa de conflictos estado actual en el panorama latinoamericano." *California Western International Law Journal* 30 (2): 409–28.

Álvarez, José E. 1992. "Promoting the 'Rule of Law' in Latin America: Problems and Prospects." *George Washington Journal of International Law and Economics* 25 (2): 281–331.

Amaya Osorio, Carlos. 2005. "La Corte Constitucional 1992–2001: Diagnóstico estadístico de su gestión y propuesta de reforma a los recursos y acciones constitucionales." In *Hacia un Nuevo Derecho Constitucional*, ed. Daniel Bonilla and Maule A. Iturralde, 329–53. Bogotá: Facultad de Derecho, Universidad de los Andes.

Argentina, Ministerio de Justicia y Derechos Humanos, Secretaría de Justicia y Asuntos Legislativos. 2002. *Argentina: El sistema judicial, 2001/2002*.

Asheshov, Nicolas. 1988. "The 1987 Peruvian Bank Job." *Andean Report*, Lima, October: 233–77.

Aucoin, Louis M. 1992. "Judicial Review in France: Access of the Individual under French and European Law in the Aftermath of France's Rejection of Bicentennial Reform." *Boston College International and Comparative Law Review* 15 (2): 443–69.

Australian Law Reform Commission. 2000. *Managing Justice: Continuity and Change in the Federal Civil Justice System*. Sydney: Australian Law Reform Commission (www.alrc. gov.au/publications/finalreps.htm; July 2006).

Baldwin, John. 2000. "Access to Justice: The English Experience with Small Claims." *PREM Notes*, World Bank, May, no. 40.

Ballard, Megan J. 1999. "The Clash between Local Courts and Global Economics: The Politics of Judicial Reform in Brazil." *Berkeley Journal of International Law* 17 (2): 230–77.

Barker, Robert S. 2000. "Judicial Review in Costa Rica: Evolution and Recent Developments." *Southwestern Journal of Law and Trade in the Americas* 7 (2): 267–90.

Barr, Carl. 1999. "The Myth of Settlement." Paper presented at the annual meetings of the Law and Society Association, Chicago, May 28.

Barreto, Andrés, and Judd Kessler. 2004. "Latin Leaders' Legal Escape Hatch." *Washington Post*, May 23: B2.

Bastos Arantes, Rogelio. 1997. *Judiciário e política no Brasil*. São Paulo: Editora Sumaré.

———. 2002. *Ministério Público e política no Brasil*. São Paulo: Editora Sumaré.

Batista Cavalcanti, Rosangela. 1999. *Cidadania e acesso a justiça*. São Paulo: Editora Sumaré.

Baytelman, Andres. 2002. *Evaluación de la reforma procesal penal Chilena*. Santiago: Centro de Estudios de la Justicia, Escuela de Derecho, Universidad de Chile and Centro de Investigaciones Jurídicas, Facultad de Derecho, Universidad Diego Portales.

Bell, John, Sophie Boyron, and Simon Whittaker. 1998. *Principles of French Law*. London: Oxford University Press.

Beneti, Sidnei Agostinho. 2000. *Da conducta do juiz.* São Paulo: Editora Saraiva.

Berkowitz, Daniel, Katarina Pistor, and Jean-François Richard. 2001. "Economic Development, Legality, and the Transplant Effect." University of Michigan, William Davidson Institute Working Paper no. 410, September.

Bermudes, Sergio. 1999. "The Administration of Justice in Brazil." In *Civil Justice in Crisis: Comparative Perspectives of Civil Proceedings,* ed. Adrian Zuckerman, 347–62. Oxford: Oxford University Press.

Bernales Ballesteros, Enrique. 1996. *La constitución de 1993: Análisis comparado.* Lima: CIEDLA.

Biebesheimer, Christina. 2001. "Justice Reform in Latin America and the Caribbean: An IDB Perspective." In *Rule of Law in Latin America: The International Promotion of Judicial Reform,* ed. Pilar Domingo and Rachel Sieder, 99–141. London: Institute of Latin American Studies, University of London.

Biebesheimer, Christina, and Carlos Cordovez, eds. 1999. *La Justicia más allá de nuestras fronteras.* Washington, D.C.: Inter-American Development Bank.

Biebesheimer, Christina, and J. Mark Payne. 2001. *IDB Experience in Justice Reform: Lessons Learned and Elements for Policy Formulation.* Washington, D.C.: Inter-American Development Bank, Sustainable Development Department Technical Papers Series.

Bielsa, Rafael, and Eduardo Graña. 1996. *Justicia y estado: A propósito del Consejo de la Magistratura.* Buenos Aires: Fundación Centro de Estudios Políticos y Administrativos.

———. 1999. *Manual de la justicia nacional.* Buenos Aires: Ciencia y Cultura

Binder, Alberto. 2005. "El mercado de los servicios legales y la crisis de la abogacía." *Sistemas Judiciales* 5 (9): 61–65.

Binder, Alberto, and Jorge Obando. 2004. *De las "Repúblicas Aéreas" al Estado de Derecho.* Buenos Aires: Ad-Hoc.

Blair, Harry, and Gary Hansen. 1994. *Weighing in on the Scales of Justice.* Washington, D.C.: USAID.

Blank, Jos, Martin van der Ende, Bart van Hulst, and Rob Jagenberg. 2004. "Bench Marking in an International Perspective: An International Comparison of the Mechanisms and Performance of the Judiciary System." Netherlands Council for the Judiciary, May (www.logion.nl/publicaties/EE10407rap.pdf; August 2006).

Blankenburg, Erhard. 1994. "The Infrastructure for Avoiding Civil Litigation: Comparing Cultures of Legal Behavior in the Netherlands and West Germany." *Law and Society Review* 28 (4): 789–808.

———. 1996. "Political Regimes and the Law in Germany." In *Courts, Law, and Politics in Comparative Perspective,* ed. Herbert Jacob, Erhard Blankenburg, Herbert M. Kritzer, Doris Marie Province, and Joseph Sanders, 249–314. New Haven: Yale University Press.

———. 1999. "Civil Justice: Access, Cost, and Expedition: The Netherlands." In *Civil Justice in Crisis: Comparative Perspectives of Civil Procedure,* ed. Adrian Zuckerman, 442–63. Oxford: Oxford University Press.

———. 2000a. "A Flood of Litigation? Legal Cultures and Litigation Flows before European Courts in Historical and Comparative Perspective." Summary of *A Flood of Litigation* (Cologne: Budesanzieiger Verlag, 1990), prepared for the Role of Law Workshop: Legal and Judicary Reform in Developing Countries, Stanford Law School, 2001.

———. 2000b. "Indicators of Growth of the Systems of Justice in Europe of the 1990s: The Legal Profession, Court, Litigation, and Budgets." Prepared for the Role of Law Workshop: Legal and Judiciary Reform in Developing Countries, Stanford Law School, 2001

Boehmer, Martín. 2005. "Metas comunes: La enseñanza y la construcción del derecho en la Argentina." *Sistemas Judiciales* 5 (9): 26–38.

Brandt, Hans-Jürgen. 1987. *Justicia popular.* Lima: Fundación Friedrich Naumann.

———. 1990. *En nombre de la paz comunal.* Lima: Fundación Friedrich Naumann.

Brazil, Poder Judiciário, Tribunal de Justiça do Rio de Janeiro. 2004. "Perfil das maiores demandas judiciais do TJERJ. Draft document, Rio de Janeiro, August.

Brown, L. Neville, and John Bell. 1993. *French Administrative Law,* 4th ed. Oxford: Clarendon Press.

Burbank, Stephen, and Barry Friedman, eds. 2002. *Judicial Independence at the Crossroads: An Interdisciplinary Approach.* Thousand Oaks, Calif.: Sage.

Burki, Shahid Javed, and Guillermo Perry. 1998. *Beyond the Washington Consensus: Institutions Matter.* Washington, D.C.: World Bank.

Burridge, Roger. 2000. "Legal Education and Development: False Dawns, Fresh Breezes." In *Governance, Development, and Globalization,* ed. Julio Faundez, Mary E. Footer, and Joseph J. Norton, 105–21. London: Blackstone Press.

Buscalglia, Edgardo, and Maria Dakolias. 1999. *Comparative International Study of Court Performance Indicators: A Descriptive and Analytical Account.* Washington, D.C.: World Bank.

Buscaglia, Eduardo, and Thomas Ulen. 1996. "A Quantitative Assessment of the Judicial Sectors in Latin America." *International Review of Law and Economics* 17(2): 275–92.

Buscuñal V., Antonio, Carlos Cerda Fernández, Jorge Correa Sutil, and Manuel Gonzalez Vial. 1993. *Escuela judicial.* Santiago, Chile: Corporación Promoción Universitaria.

Cantuarias Salaverry, Fernando, ed. 2001. *¿Por qué hay que cambiar el codigo civil?* Lima: Universidad Peruana de Ciencias Aplicadas.

Carbonell, Miguel. n.d. "Poder judicial y reforma del Estado de México." Manuscript, Universidad Nacional Autónoma de México, Instituto de Investigaciones Jurídicas.

Carneiro, Luis Orlando. 2006. "Supremo proíbe nepotismo." *Jornal do Brasil,* February 17: A3.

Carothers, Thomas. 2003. *Promoting Rule of Law Abroad: The Problem of Knowledge.* Working Paper no. 34, Rule of Law Series. Washington, D.C.: Carnegie Endowment for International Peace.

Carranza, Elías, Mario Houed, Luís Paulino Mora, and Eugenio Raúl Zafaroni. 1988. *El preso sin condena en América Latina y el Caribe.* San José, Costa Rica: ILANUD.

Carrió, Alejandro. 1996. *La Corte Suprema y su independencia.* Buenos Aires: Abeledo-Perrot.

Carruthers, Bruce G., and Terrence C. Halliday. 1998. *Rescuing Business: The Making of Corporate Bankruptcy Law in England and the United States.* Oxford: Clarendon Press.

Castelar Pinheiro, Armando. 1998. "Credit Markets in Brazil: The Role of Judicial Enforcement and Other Institutions." Draft paper prepared for research project "Institutional Arrangements to Ensure Willingness to Pay in Financial Markets: A Comparative Analysis of Latin American and Europe, "Centro de Estudo de Reforma do Estado.

———. 2003. "Judiciário, reforma e economía: A visão dos magistrados." Discussion draft no. 966. Rio de Janeiro: IPEA.

———, organizer. 2000. *Judiciário e economía no Brasil.* São Paulo: Editora Sumaré

———, organizer. 2003. *Reforma do Judiciário: Problemas, desafios, perspectivas.* São Paulo: IDESP.

Cavalcanti Melo Filho, Hugo. 2003. "A reforma do Poder Judiciário brasileiro: Motivações, quadro actual e perspectiva." *Revista CEJ* (21): 79–86, Centro de Estudios Judiciários do Conselho da Justiça Federal, Brasilia.

Cazalet, Edgard. 2001. "Specialized Courts: Are They a Quick Fix or Long-Term Improvement in the Quality of Justice?" Paper prepared for the World Bank Second Global Conference on Legal and Judicial Reform, St. Petersburg, Russia, July 8–12.

CEBEPEJ. 2003. "O processo civil brasileiro." Unpublished research report prepared for the World Bank, June.

CEJA (Centro de Estudios de Justicia de las Américas). 2003. *Reporte sobre el estado de la justicia en las Américas, 2002–2003*. Santiago: CEJA.

———. 2005. *Reporte sobre el estado de la justicia en las Américas, 2004–2005*. Santiago: CEJA.

CELS (Centro de Estudios Legales y Sociales). 2004. *Política de seguridad ciudadana y justicia penal*. Buenos Aires. Siglo Veintiuno.

CEPEJ (European Commission for the Efficiency of Justice). 2002. *European Judicial Systems 2002*. Strasbourg: Council of Europe.

———. 2004. "Pilot-Scheme for Evaluating Judicial Systems." Strasbourg: Council of Europe.

Checchi and Company Consulting. 1991. "Final Implementation Unit Report: Improved Administration of Justice Project." USAID/Guatemala and the Judicial Branch of Guatemala, September. Unpublished manuscript, September.

Chemonics Internacional. 1996. *Informe del diagnóstico institucional y su entorno*. Report for Supreme Court of Bolivia, Proyecto de Reformas Judiciales. Draft report financed under a World Bank loan.

Chinchilla, Laura, and David Schodt. 1993. *The Administration of Justice in Ecuador*. Miami: Florida International University.

Ciudad, Tereza, and Alonso Zarzar. 1984. "El juez peruano en el banquillo." In *La administración de justicia en América Latina*, ed. Javier de Belaunde López de Romaña, 294–409. Lima: Consejo Latino Americano de Derecho y Desarrollo.

Cleaves, Peter, and Martín Scurrah. 1980. *Agriculture, Bureaucracy, and Military Government in Peru*. Ithaca: Cornell University Press.

Colombia, Comisión de Racionalización del Gasto y de las Finanzas Públicas. 1996. "El sistema judicial y el gasto público." Draft document, Santafé de Bogotá.

Concha Cantú, Hugo Alejandro, and José Antonio Caballero Juárez. 2001. *Diagnóstico sobre la administración de justicia en las entidades federativas: Un estudio institucional sobre la justicia local en México*. Mexico City: Universidad Autónoma de México, Instituto de Investigaciones Jurídicas, Serie Doctrina Jurídica, 61.

Contini, Francesco, ed. 2000. *European Data Base on Judicial Systems*. Bologna: Istituto di Ricerca sui Sisema Giudiziari, Consiglio Nazionale delle Ricerche.

Contreras, Carlos. 1991. "Conflictos intercomunales en la Sierra Central en los siglos XIX y XX." In *Los Andes en la encrucijada: Indios, comunidades y estado en el siglo XIX*, ed. Heraclio Bonilla, 199–219. Quito: Libri Mundi.

Cóppola, Patricia. 2002. *Informe de Córdoba, Argentina*. Proyecto de Seguimiento de los Procesos de Reforma Judicial en América Latina. Santiago: Centro de Estudios de Justicia de la Américas.

Corporación Excelencia en la Justicia. 2000. "Informe anual de la justicia 2000." Special edition of *Justicia y Desarrollo: Debates* 3: 14.

Correa Sutil, Jorge. 1990. "Formación de jueces para la democracia." *Revista de Ciencias Sociales* (Valparaíso, Chile), 34–35: 271–319.

———. 1994. "Capacitación y carrera judicial en Hispanoamérica." In *Justicia y Sociedad* Mexico City: Instituto de Investigaciones Jurídicas, Universidad Nacional Autónoma de México, 167–81.

———. 1999. "Judicial Reform in Latin America: Good News for the Underprivileged?" In *The (Un)Rule of Law and the Underprivileged in Latin America*, ed. Juan E. Méndez, Guillermo O'Donnell, and Paulo Sérgio Pinheiro, 255–77. South Bend, Ind.: Notre Dame University Press.

Correa Sutil, Jorge, Carlos Peña G., and Juan Enrique Vargas. 1999. "Poder judicial y mercado: ¿Quién debe pagar por la justicia?" Manuscript, Centro de Investigación, Facultad de Derecho, Universidad Diego Portales, Santiago, Chile.

Crohn, Madeleine, and William E. Davis, eds. 1996. *Lessons Learned*. Proceedings of the

Second Judicial Roundtable, May 19–22. Williamsburg, Va.: National Center for State Courts, USAID, and IDB.

Dainow, Joseph. 1967. "The Civil Law and the Common Law: Some Points of Comparison." *American Journal of Comparative Law* 15 (2): 419–35.

Dakolias, Maria. 1995. "A Strategy for Judicial Reform: The Experience in Latin America." *Virginia Journal of International Law* 36 (1): 167–231.

———. 1999. "Court Performance around the World: A Comparative Perspective." *Yale Human Rights and Development Law Journal* 2: 87–142.

———. 2001. "Legal and Judicial Reform: The Role of Civil Society in the Reform Process." In *Rule of Law in Latin America: The International Promotion of Judicial Reform*, ed. Pilar Domingo and Rachel Sieder, 142–63. London: Institute of Latin American Studies, University of London.

Damaska, Mirjan. 1997. *Evidence Law Adrift.* New Haven: Yale University Press.

Daniels, Stephen, and Joanne Martin. 1995. *Civil Juries and the Politics of Reform.* Evanston, Ill.: Northwestern University Press.

David, Rene, and Henry P. de Vries. 1958. *The French Legal System: An Introduction to Civil Law Systems.* New York: Oceana Publications.

Davis, William E., and Marco A. Lillo, eds. 1996. *La implementación de la reforma procesal oral.* Santiago: Centro de Desarrollo Jurídico Judicial.

De Belaunde, Javier. 1998. "Justice, Legality, and Judicial Reform." In *Fujimori's Peru: The Political Economy*, ed. John Crabtree and Jim Thomas, 173–91. London: Institute of Latin American Studies, University of London.

Dermizaky Peredo, Pablo. 1997. *Derecho Administrativo*, 3rd ed. Cochabamba: Editorial Serrano.

Devedjian, Patrick. 1996. *Le temps des juges.* Paris: Flammarion.

Dezalay, Yves, and Bryant G. Garth. 2002. *The Internationalization of Palace Wars: Lawyers, Economists, and the Contest to Transform Latin American States.* Chicago: University of Chicago Press.

Djankov, Simeon, Rafael La Porta, Forencio López-de-Silanes, and Andrei Schleifer. 2002. "Courts: The Lex Mundi Project." Draft report prepared for the World Bank, March.

Domingo, Pilar, and Rachel Sieder, eds. 2001. *Rule of Law in Latin America: The International Promotion of Judicial Reform.* London: Institute of Latin American Studies, University of London.

Doriat-Duban, Myriam. 2001. "Alternative Dispute Resolution in the French Legal System: An Empirical Study. " *Law and Economics in Civil Law Countries* 6: 183–97.

Douat, Étienne, director. 2001. *Les budgets de la justice en Europe.* Paris: La Documentation Française.

Duce, Mauricio. 1999. "Criminal Procedural Reform and the Ministerio Público: Toward the Construction of a New Criminal Justice System in Latin America." Master's thesis, Stanford University Law School.

Economist. 2004. "Economic Focus: Development Piecemeal," August 7: 63.

Eguiguren, Francisco J. 1998. "Poder judicial y Tribunal Constitucional en el Perú." In *Anuario de derecho constitucional Latinoamericano, edición 1998*, Centro Interdisciplinario de Estudios sobre el Desarrollo Latinoamericano (CIEDLA), 37–58. Buenos Aires: Konrad Adenauer-Stiftung and CIEDLA.

———, ed. 2002. *Gobierno y administración del Poder Judicial, organización de la función jurisdiccional y sistema de carrera judicial.* Lima: Pontificia Universidad Católica del Perú.

Epstein, Leo, and Gary King. 2001. "The Rules of Inference." *University of Chicago Law Review* 30 (1): 1–92.

Faundez, Julio. 2005a. "The Rule of Law Enterprise: Toward a Dialogue between Practitioners and Academics." *Democratization* 12 (4): 567–86.

———. 2005b. "Should Rule of Law Projects Take Community Justice Institutions Seriously? Perspectives from Latin America." Discussion notes prepared for World Bank Symposium, "Law, Equity, and Development," December 1–2.

Faundez, Julio, Mary E. Footer, and Joseph J. Norton, eds. 2000. *Governance, Development and Globalization.* London: Blackstone Press.

Feeley, Malcolm M. 1983. *Court Reform on Trial: Why Simple Solutions Fail.* New York: Basic Books.

Fennell, Phil, Christopher Harding, Nico Jörg, and Bert Swart, eds. 1995. *Criminal Justice in Europe.* Oxford: Oxford University Press.

FIAS (Foreign Investment Advisory Service of the International Finance Corporation and the World Bank). 2001. *Brazil: Legal, Policy, and Administrative Barriers to Investment in Brazil,* vol. 2. Washington, D.C.: World Bank and International Finance Corporation.

FIEL (Fundación de Investigaciones Económicas Latinoamericanas). 1996. *La reforma del poder judicial en la Argentina.* Buenos Aires: FIEL.

Finnegan, David Louis. 2001. "Observations on Tanzania's Commercial Court: A Case Study." Paper prepared for the World Bank Second Global Conference on Legal and Judicial Reform, St. Petersburg, Russia, July 8–12.

Fionda, Julia. 1995. *Public Prosecutors and Discretion: A Comparative Study.* Oxford: Clarendon Press.

Fix-Fierro, Héctor. 1995. *La eficiencia de la justicia.* Mexico: Universidad Autónoma de México.

———. 1999. "Poder Judicial." In *Transiciones y diseños institucionales,* ed. María del Refugio González and Sergio López-Ayllón, 167–221. Mexico: Universidad Nacional Autónoma de México.

Fix-Zamudio, Héctor. 1979. "A Brief Introduction to the Mexican Writ of Amparo." *California Western International Law Journal* 9: 306–48.

Florida International University. 1987. "La administración de justicia en Honduras." Report prepared for USAID Regional Administration of Justice Project, May.

Fox, Russell. 2000. *Justice in the Twenty-First Century.* London: Cavendish.

Freccero, Stephen P. 1994. "An Introduction to the New Italian Criminal Procedure." *American Journal of Criminal Law* 21 (3): 345–83.

Friedman, Lawrence M., and Rogelio Pérez-Perdomo, eds. 2003. *Legal Culture in the Age of Globalization: Latin America and Latin Europe.* Stanford: Stanford University Press.

Fruhling, Hugo. 1993. "Human Rights in Constitutional Order and in Political Practice in Latin America." In *Constitutional Democracy: Transitions in the Contemporary World,* ed. Douglas Greenberg, Stanley N. Katz, Melanie Beth Oliviero, and Steven C. Wheatley, 85–104. Oxford: Oxford University Press.

Frydman, Roman, Cheryl Gray, and Andrzej Rapaczynski, eds. 1996. *Corporate Governance in Central Europe and Russia,* vol. 2. Budapest: Central European University Press.

Fuentes, Alfredo. 2004. "La reforma en Colombia: tendencias recientes 1991–2003." In *En busca de una justicia distinta: Experiencias de reforma en América Latina,* ed. Luis Pásara, 141–93. Lima: Consorcio Justicia Viva.

Fuentes, Alfredo, and Carlos Amaya. 2001. "Demanda y oferta judicial: Dificultades de ajuste." Paper prepared for World Bank Conference, New Approaches to Meeting the Demand for Justice, Mexico City, May 11.

Galanter, Marc. 1974. "Why the 'Haves' Come Out Ahead: Speculations on the Limits of Legal Change." *Law and Society Review* 9: 95–160.

———. 1998. "An Oil Strike in Hell: Contemporary Legends about the Civil Justice System." *Arizona Law Review* 40: 717–52.

————. 2003. "Debased Informalism." In *Beyond Common Knowledge: Empirical Approaches to the Rule of Law*, ed. Erik Jensen and Thomas Heller, 96–141. Stanford: Stanford University Press.

Galindo, Pedro. 2003. "Indicadores subjectivos: Estudios, calificaciones de riesgo y encuestas de percepción pública sobre los sistemas de justicia. Resultados recientes para las Américas," *Sistemas Judiciales* 3 (6): 4–35.

Gamarra, Eduardo A. 1991. *The System of Justice in Bolivia: An Institutional Analysis*. Miami: Florida International University.

Garavano, German C., Héctor M. Chayer, Milena Ricci, and Carlos Alejandro Cambellotti. 2000. *Los usuarios del sistema de justicia en Argentina*. Final report for the World Bank, Foro de Estudios sobre Administración de Justicia (FORES), Buenos Aires, Argentina.

García Belaúnde, Domingo. 1979. *El hábeas corpus en el Perú*. Lima: Universidad Mayor de San Marcos.

García Rada, Domingo. 1978. *Memorias de un juez*. Lima: Editorial Andina.

García S., Fernando. 2002. *Formas indígenas de administrar justicia*. Quito: FLACSO.

García Villegas, Mauricio, Maria Isabel Borrero, Cristina Motta, Helena Olea, and Cesar Rodríguez. 1996. "Justicia constitucional y acción de tutela." Bogotá: Universidad de los Andes, Facultad de Derecho.

Gardner, James. 1980. *Legal Imperialism: American Lawyers and Foreign Aid in Latin America*. Madison: University of Wisconsin Press.

Genn Hazel. 1999. *Paths to Justice: What People Do and Think about Going to Law*. Oxford: Hard Publishing.

Germany, Bundestag. 2002. "Excerpts from the 'Explanatory Memorandum to the Draft of an Act to Reform the Law of Civil Procedure (Law of Civil Procedure Reform Act),'" Printed document 14/4722, Dundestagsdrucksache.

Geyh, Charles Gardner. 2002. "Customary Independence." In *Judicial Independence at the Crossroads: An Interdisciplinary Approach*, ed. Stephen Burbank and Barry Friedman, 160–87. Thousand Oaks, Calif.: Sage.

Girishanker, Navin. 2001. "Evaluating Public-Sector Reform: Guidelines for Assessing Country-Level Impact of Structural Reform and Capacity Building in the Public Sector." Operations Evaluation Department, Working Paper Series. Washington, D.C.: World Bank.

Goldman, Sheldon. 1991. "Federal Judicial Recruitment." In *The American Courts: A Critical Assessment*, ed. John B. Gates and Charles A. Johnson, 189–210. Washington, D.C.: Congressional Quarterly.

Goldstein, Leslie Friedman. 2004. "From Democracy to Juristocracy." *Law and Society Review* 38 (3): 611–29.

Golub, Stephen. 2003. *Beyond Rule of Law Orthodoxy: The Legal Empowerment Alternative*. Working Paper no. 41, Rule of Law Series, October. Washington, D.C.: Carnegie Endowment for International Peace.

Golub, Stephen, and Mary McClymont, eds. 2000. *Many Roads to Justice*. New York: Ford Foundation.

Gómez Albarello, Juan Gabriel. 1996. "Justicia y democracia en Colombia: En entredicho?" *Analisis Politico* 28: 42–64.

Gonzales Mantilla, Gorki, Jean Carlo Serván, Luciano López, and Hernando Burgos. 2002. "El sistema judicial en el Perú: Un enfoque analítico a partir de sus usos y de sus usuarios." Draft report prepared for the World Bank.

González Compeán, Miguel, and Peter Bauer, eds. 2002. *Jurisdicción y democracia: Los nuevos rumbos del Poder Judicial en México*. Mexico City: Ediciones Cal y Arena.

González Oropeza, Manuel. 1996. "The Administration of Justice and the Rule of Law in Mexico." In *Rebuilding the State: Mexico after Salinas*, ed. Monica Serrano and Victor

Bulmer-Thomas, 59–78. London: Institute of Latin American Studies, University of London.

Gregorio, Carlos 1995. "Investigación sobre demora en el proceso judicial." Buenos Aires: CEJURA.

———. 1996. "Case Management and Reform in the Administration of Justice In Latin America." In *Lessons Learned: Proceedings of the Second Judicial Roundtable*, May 19–22, Williamsburg, Va., ed. Madeleine Crohn and William E. Davis, 21–32. Williamsburg, Va.: National Center for State Courts, USAID, and IDB.

Grossman, Joel B., Herbert M. Kritzer, Kristin Bumiller, Austin Sarat, Stephen McDougal, and Richard Miller. 1982. "Dimensions of Institutional Participation: Who Uses the Courts and How?" *Journal of Politics* 44 (1): 86–114.

Guatemala, Supreme Court. 1994. *Seminario selección de los jueces, carrera e independencia judicial.* Guatemala.

Gupta, Poonam, Rachel Kleinfeld, and Gonzalo Salinas. 2002. "Legal and Judicial Reform in Europe and Central Asia." Washington, D.C.: World Bank Operations Evaluation Department, Working Paper Series.

Hadfield, Gillian. 2000. "The Price of Law: How the Market for Lawyers Distorts the Justice System." *Michigan Law Review* 98 (4): 953–1006.

Haeussler, Maria Josefina. 1993. *Experiencias comparadas de formacion judicial.* Santiago: Corporación de Promoción Universitaria.

Hammergren, Linn. 1998a. *Code Reform and Law Revision.* Washington, D.C.: USAID/Global Center for Democracy and Governance [G/DG].

———. 1998b. *Institutional Strengthening.* Washington, D.C.: USAID/G/DG.

———. 1998c. *Judicial Training and Judicial Reform.* Washington, D.C.: USAID/G/DG.

———. 1998d. *Political Will, Constituency Building, and Public Support in Justice Reform.* Washington, D.C.: USAID/G/DG.

———. 1998e. *The Politics of Justice and Justice Reform in Latin America: Peru in Comparative Perspective.* San Francisco: Westview.

———. 1999. "Diagnosing Judicial Performance: Toward a Tool to Help Guide Judicial Reform Programs." Paper prepared for Transparency International–USA, for presentation at the International Conference on Anti-Corruption, Durban, South Africa, October 10–15.

———. 2000a. "The Fujimori Judicial Reforms: Finally Cutting the Gordian Knot or Just Another Trojan Horse." Paper prepared for the 2000 Meetings of the Latin American Studies Association, Miami, March 16–18.

———. 2000b. "Law and Injustice in Latin America." *Journal of Democracy* 11 (3): 169–74.

———. 2002a. *Do Judicial Councils Further Judicial Reform? Lessons from Latin America.* Working Paper no. 26, Rule of Law Series. Washington, D.C.: Carnegie Endowment for International Peace.

———. 2002b. "Judicial Independence and Accountability." In USAID, *Guidance for Promoting Judicial Independence and Impartiality*, 149–57. Washington, D.C.: USAID Office of Democracy and Governance. Technical Publication PN-ACM-003, November.

———. 2003. "International Assistance to Latin American Justice Programs: Toward an Agenda for Reforming the Reformers." In *Beyond Common Knowledge: Empirical Approaches to the Rule of Law,* ed. Erik Jensen and Thomas Heller, 290–335. Stanford: Stanford University Press.

Helmke, Gretchen. 2005. *Courts under Constraints: Judges, Generals, and Presidents in Argentina.* Cambridge: Cambridge University Press.

Henderson, Keith, Angana Shah, Sandra Elena, and Violaine Autheman. 2004. *Regional Best Practices: Enforcement of Judgments: Lessons from Latin America.* Washington, D.C.: IFES Rule of Law Paper Series, April.

Hendley, Kathryn, Peter Murrell, and Randi Ryterman. 1999. "Law Works in Russia: The Role of Legal Institutions in the Transactions of Russian Enterprises." University of Wisconsin Law School, Legal Studies Research Paper Series.

Hensler, Deborah. 1994. "Does ADR Really Save Money? The Jury's Still Out." *National Law Review* 16: C-2.

Hernández Breña, Wilson. 2003. *Indicadores sobre administración de justicia: Mapa judicial, presupuesto y eficiencia en el desempeño judicial.* Lima: Justicia Viva.

Herrero, Alvaro. 2005. *Entre democracia, política, y justicia: Un análisis político institucional de la Suprema Corte de Justicia de la Provincia de Buenos Aires.* Buenos Aires: Fundación PENT.

Hewko, John. 2002. *Foreign Direct Investment: Does Rule of Law Matter?* Working Paper no. 26, Rule of Law Series. Washington, D.C.: Carnegie Endowment for International Peace.

Hidalgo López, Luis. 1996, *La responsabilidad civil de los empleados publicos: Las glosas de la Contraloría.* Quito: Pudeleco.

Highton, Elena I., Carlos G. Gregorio, and Gladys Álvarez. 2000. "Cuantificación de daños personales, publicidad de los precedentes y posiblidad de generar un baremos flexible a los fines de facilitar decisiones homogéneas y equilibradas." Unpublished paper, Buenos Aires, Argentina.

Hilbink, Lisa. 2003. "An Exception to Chilean Exceptionalism? The Historical Role of Chile's Judiciary." In *What Justice? Whose Justice? Fighting for Fairness in Latin America,* ed. Susan Eva Eckstein and Timothy P. Wickham-Crowley, 64–97. Berkeley and Los Angeles: University of California Press.

Hurtado Pozo, José. 1979. *La ley importada.* Lima: CEDYS.

Ibañez, Perfecto Andres. 1988. *Justicia/conflicto.* Madrid: Tecnos.

ILANUD. 1991. *Necesidades de capacitacion de los jueces en Ecuador.* San José, Costa Rica.

Infante, Edward A. 2002. "Judicial Case Management in the Federal Trial Courts of the United States of America." Draft paper prepared for World Bank.

Instituto de Defensa Legal. 1999. *La justicia de paz en debate.* Lima: Instituto de Defensa Legal.

Instituto Tecnológico Autónomo de México (ITAM) and Gaxiola Morailia y Asociados, S.C. 1999. "La administración de justicia de las entidades federativas mexicanas a partir del caso de la cartera bancaria." Draft document, October.

Inter-American Development Bank (IDB). 1993. *Justicia y desarrollo e América y el Caribe.* Washington, D.C.: IDB.

———. 1997. "Peru: Mejoramiento del acceso a la justicia. Project Document." Operation No. 1061/OC-PE, approved November 25.

Jacob, Herbert. 1955. *Debtors in Court: The Consumption of Government Services.* Chicago: Rand McNally.

———. 1984. *Justice in America: Courts, Lawyers, and the Judicial Process.* Boston: Little, Brown.

———. 1996. "Courts and Politics in the United States." In *Courts, Law, and Politics in Comparative Perspective,* ed. Herbert Jacob, Erhard Blankenburg, Herbert M. Kritzer, Doris Marie Province, and Joseph Sanders, 16–80. New Haven: Yale University Press.

Jacob, Herbert, Erhard Blankenburg, Herbert M. Kritzer, Doris Marie Province, and Joseph Sanders. 1996. *Courts, Law, and Politics in Comparative Perspective.* New Haven: Yale University Press.

Jarquin, Edmundo, and Fernando Carrillo. 1997. *La economía política de la reforma judicial.* Washington, D.C.: Inter-American Development Bank.

Jensen, Erik, and Thomas Heller, eds. 2003. *Beyond Common Knowledge: Empirical Approaches to the Rule of Law.* Stanford: Stanford University Press.

Jolowicz., J. A. 2000. *On Civil Procedure*. Cambridge: Cambridge University Press.

Jörg, Nico, Steward Field, and Christie Brants. 1995. "Are Inquisitorial and Adversarial Systems Converging?" In *Criminal Justice in Europe*, ed. Phil Fennell, Christopher Harding, Nico Jörg, and Bert Swart. Oxford: Oxford University Press.

Kagan, Robert A. 2001. *Adversarial Legalism: The American Way of Law*. Cambridge, Mass.: Harvard University Press.

Kaufmann, D., A. Kraay, and P. Zoido-Lobatón. 1999. *Governance Matters*. World Bank Policy Research Working Paper no. 2196. Washington, D.C.: World Bank.

———. 2002. *Governance Matters II*. World Bank Policy Research Working Paper no. 2772. Washington, D.C.: World Bank.

Khan, Mushtaq H. 2002. "Corruption and Governance in Early Capitalism: World Bank Strategies and Their Limitations." In *Reinventing the World Bank*, ed. Jonathan R. Pincus and Jeffrey A. Winters, 164–84. Ithaca: Cornell University Press.

Kleinfeld Belton, Rachel. 2005. *Competing Definitions of the Rule of Law: Implications for Practitioners*. Carnegie Papers, Rule of Law Series no. 55. Washington, D.C.: Carnegie Endowment for International Peace.

Komesar, Neil K. 1994. *Imperfect Alternatives: Choosing Institutions in Law, Economics, and Public Policy*. Chicago: University of Chicago Press.

Kritzer, Herbert. 1983. "The Civil Litigation Research Project: Lessons for Studying the Civil Justice System." In *Proceedings of the Second Workshop on Law and Justice Statistics*, U.S. Department of Justice, Bureau of Justice Statistics, 30–36.

———. 1986. "Adjudication to Settlement: Shading in the Gray." *Judicature* 70 (3): 161–65.

———. 1999. "Using Public Opinion to Evaluate Institutional Performance: The Experience with American Courts" (www1.worlbank.org/publicsector/legal/KritzerPremNote.doc; January 2006).

Kryshtalowych, Helen, and Greig Smith. 2000. "Ukraine's New Bankruptcy Law: The Demise of Dinosaurs?" *Law in Transition*, 56–60 (www.ebrd.com/pubs/legal/series/lit.htm; August 2006).

Langbroeck, Philip M. 2003. "Unity of Law as a Product of Coordinated Jurisprudence by Dutch Administrative Courts." Paper prepared for World Bank conference on administrative law, Washington, D.C., January.

Langer, Máximo. 2004. "From Legal Transplants to Legal Translations: The Globalization of Plea Bargaining and the Americanization Thesis in Criminal Procedure." *Harvard International Law Journal* 45 (1) (http://ssrn.com/abstract=707261; May 2006).

La Porta, Rafael, and Florencio López-de-Silanes.1998. "Capital Markets and Legal Institutions." In *Beyond the Washington Consensus: Institutions Matter*, ed. Shahid Javed Burki and Guillermo Perry, 67–86. Washington, D.C.: World Bank Latin American and Caribbean Region.

Lawyers Committee for Human Rights. 2000. "Building on Quicksand: The Collapse of the World Bank's Judicial Reform Project in Peru." New York: Lawyers Committee for Human Rights.

Lawyers Committee for Human Rights and the Venezuelan Program for Human Rights Education and Action. 1996. *Halfway to Reform: The World Bank and the Venezuelan Justice System*. New York: Lawyers Committee for Human Rights.

Ledesma Narvaez, Marianella. 1999. *Jueces y reforma judicial*. Lima: Gaceta Jurídica.

Leeth, Jon, Ana María Linares, Zenía de Moscote, and Robert Murphy. 1997. "Improved Administration of Justice Project Evaluation." Report for USAID/Panama.

León Pastor, Ricardo. 1996. *Diagnóstico de la cultura judicial peruana*. Lima: Academia de la Magistratura.

Leubsdorf, John. 1999. "The Myth of Civil Procedure Reform." In *Civil Justice in Crisis:*

Comparative Perspectives on Civil Procedure, ed. Adrian Zuckerman, 53–67. Oxford: Oxford University Press.

Llobet Rodríguéz, Javier. 1993. *La reforma procesal penal*. San José, Costa Rica: Corte Suprema de Justicia, Escuela Judicial.

Longley, Diane, and Horda James. 1999. *Administrative Justice: Central Issues in UK and European Administrative Law*. London: Cavendish.

López-Ayllón, Sergio, and Héctor Fix-Fierro. 2000. "'Faraway, So Close!' The Rule of Law and Legal Change in Mexico (1970–1999)." Stanford: Stanford University.

López Guerra, Luis. 2001. "Governing the Justice System: Spain's Judicial Council." *PREM Notes*, 54, June.

Lovatón Palacios, David, Jaime Márquez Calvo, Wilfredo Ardito Vega, and Iván Montoya Vivanco. 1999. *Justicia de paz: El otro poder judicial*. Lima: Instituto de Defensa Legal.

Magaloni, Ana Laura, and Layda Negrete. n.d. "El poder judicial federal y su política de decidir sin resolver." Manuscript, Centro de Investigación y Docencia Económicas, Mexico.

Maier, Julio, et al. 1993. *Reformas procesales en América Latina*. Santiago: Corporación de Promoción Universitaria.

Mainwaring, Scott. 2003. "Introduction: Democratic Accountability in Latin America." In *Democratic Accountability in Latin America*, ed. Scott Mainwaring and Christopher Welna, 3–33. Oxford: Oxford University Press.

Mainwaring, Scott, and Christopher Welna, eds. 2003. *Democratic Accountability in Latin America*. Oxford: Oxford University Press.

Malik, Waleed. 2002. "Judiciary-Led Reforms in Singapore: Framework, Strategies, and Lessons." Draft paper prepared for World Bank.

Marchal, Pierre. 2003. "Case Flow Management: The Identification of Certain Causes for the Overburdening of Courts." Paper presented at 11th International Judicial Conference, "Courts of Ultimate Appeal XI: Issues of Judicial Independence," Washington, D.C., May 21–23.

Marcus, Richard L. 1999. "Malaise of the Litigation Superpower." In *Civil Justice in Crisis: Comparative Perspectives of Civil Procedure*, ed. Adrian Zuckerman, 71–116. Oxford: Oxford University Press.

Marks, Robert. 2002. "Costs of Change." In *Justice in the Twenty-First Century*, ed. Russell Fox, 227–35. London: Cavendish.

Martínez Neira, Nestor Humberto. 1997. "Estado de derecho y eficiencia económica." In *La economía política de la reforma judicial*, ed. Edmundo Jarquín and Fernando Carrillo, 17–29. Washington, D.C.: Inter-American Development Bank.

———. 1999. "De los diez pecados de la reforma judicial y algunos anatemas." In *Estado y economía en America Latina*, ed. Rolf Luders and Luís Rubio, 375–423. Mexico: CIDAC.

Matus, Alejandra. 1999. El *libro negro de la justicia chilena*. Buenos Aires: Editorial Planeta; Santiago: Editorial Sudamericana.

McArthur, John Burritt. 2000. "Lessons for Judges from the Civil Justice Reform Act." *Judicature* 83 (5): 222–23.

McKie, Craig, and Paul Reed. 1979. "A Statistical Study of Canadian Civil Justice." *Canadian Statistical Review*, August, vi–xii.

Méndez, Juan E., Guillermo O'Donnell, and Paulo Sergio Pinheiro, eds. 1999. *The (Un)Rule of Law and the Underprivileged in Latin America*. South Bend, Ind.: University of Notre Dame Press.

Merry, Sally Engle. 1993. "Sorting Out Popular Justice." In *The Possibility of Popular Justice: A Case Study of Community Mediation in the United States*, ed. Sally Engle Merry and Neal Milner, 31–66. Ann Arbor: University of Michigan Press.

Merryman, John Henry. 1985. *The Civil Law Tradition: An Introduction to the Legal Systems of Western Europe and Latin America,* 2nd ed. Stanford: Stanford University Press.

———. 1996. "The French Deviation." *American Journal of Comparative Law* 44 (1): 109–19.

Mexico, Primer Congreso Nacional de Mediación. 2001. "Pronunciamentos." Draft statement, Hermosillo, Sonora, November 10.

Moody's Investors Service, Global Credit Research. 2002. "Calificaciones de ejecutabilidad de contratos mercantiles e hipotecarios," April.

Mora Mora, Luis Paulino. 2001. "El acceso a la justicia en Costa Rica." Paper prepared for World Bank Regional Conference on "New Trends in Justice Reform," Mexico City, May 11.

Motta, Cristina. 2001. "Esquema general del derecho a la información como mecanismo de control a la corrupción en Argentina." Background paper prepared for World Bank, *Anti-corruption Diagnostic for Argentina: An Overview of Three Reports and Recommendations,* Report No. 20133-AR. Washington, D.C.: World Bank.

Mudge, Arthur. 1997. "Justice Sector Reform Support Project Midterm Evaluation." Report prepared for USAID/Guatemala, May.

Mudge, Arthur, Ricardo Córdoba, Luis Alonso Reyes, Tirsa Rivera, and Mary Said. 1996. "Judicial Reform II Evaluation." Draft report prepared for USAID/El Salvador, Management Sciences International, December.

Mudge, Arthur, Steve Flanders, Miguel Sanchez, Adolfo Suarez, and Gilberto Trujillo. 1988. "Evaluation of the Judicial Reform Project No. 519-0296." Draft report prepared for USAID/El Salvador, March.

Nader, Laura. 1990. *Harmony Ideology: Justice and Control in a Mountain Zapotec Village.* Stanford: Stanford University Press.

Nemoga Soto, Ricardo. 1988. *El estado y la administración de justicia en Colombia.* Bogotá: Ministry of Justice.

Neubauer, David W., Marcia J. Lipetz, Mary Lee Luskin, and John Paul Ryan. 1981. *Managing the Pace of Justice: An Evaluation of LEAA's Court Delay-Reduction Programs: Executive Summary.* U.S. Department of Justice: National Institute of Justice.

North, Douglass. 1990. *Institutions, Institutional Change, and Economic Performance.* Cambridge: Cambridge University Press.

O'Donnell, Guillermo. 1996. "Illusions about Consolidation." *Journal of Democracy* 7 (2): 34–51.

———. 1999. "Horizontal Accountability in New Democracies." In *The Self-Restraining State: Power and Accountability n New Democracies,* ed. Andreas Schedler, Larry Diamond, and Mark F. Plattner, 29–52. Boulder, Colo.: Lynne Rienner.

Oliva, Roberto, José María Méndez, and Mario Antonio Solano, *Reformas constitucionales del órgano judicial.* San Salvador, El Salvador: CENITEC.

Ontario Law Reform Commission. 1998. *Rethinking Civil Justice: Research Studies for the Civil Justice Review.* Ontario: Canada.

Pásara Luis. 1982. *Jueces, justicia, y poder en el Peru.* Lima: CEDYS.

———. 1984. "Peru: Administración de justicia?" In Consejo Latinoamericano de Derecho y Desarrollo, *La administración de justicia en América Latina.* 194–278. Lima.

———. 2004. "Lecciones ¿aprendidas o por aprender?" In *En busca de una justicia distinta: Experiencias de reforma en América Latina,* ed. Luis Pásara, 515–70. Lima: Consorcio Justicia Viva.

———. 2005a. "La enseñanza del derecho en Perú: Su estado crítico." *Sistemas Judiciales* 5 (9):15–25.

———. 2005b. *Los abogados de Lima en la administración de justicia: Una aproximación preliminar.* Lima: Justicia Viva.

Pásara, Luis, ed. 2004. *En busca de una justicia distinta: Experiencias de reforma en América Latina*. Lima: Consorcio Justicia Viva.

Pastor Prieto, Santos 1993. *Ah de la justicia! Política judicial y economía*. Madrid: Editorial Cívitas.

Pastor Prieto, Santos, and Carmen Vargas. 2000a. "La justicia civil en la República Dominicana," Unpublished report for the World Bank.

———. 2000b. "Un análisis empírico de la justicia en República Dominicana: La jurisdicción laboral." Unpublished report for the World Bank.

Pérez Perdomo, Rogelio. 1993. "La justicia en tiempos de globalización: Demandas y perspectivas de cambio." In Inter-American Development Bank, *Justicia y desarrollo e América y el Caribe*, 137–52, Washington, D.C.: Inter-American Development Bank.

———. 2005. "Educación jurídica, abogados y globalización en América Latina." *Sistemas Judiciales* 5 (9): 4–14.

Peru, Defensoría del Pueblo. 1999. *Debido proceso y administración estatal*. Lima.

Peru, Poder Judicial. 2000. "Proyecto modernización de la justicia." Draft report.

Piaggi de Vanossi, Ana I., ed. 2000. *Poder judicial, desarrollo económico y competitividad en la Argentina*, vol. 1. Buenos Aires: De Palma.

Piano, Aili, and Arch Puddington. 2005. "The 2005 Freedom House Survey: Progress in the Middle East." *Journal of Democracy* 17 (1): 119–24.

Pinheiro Carneiro, Paulo Cezar. 2000. *Acesso a justica: Juizados especiais civeis e ação civil pública*. 2nd ed. São Paulo: Editora Forense.

Pistor, Katarina. 1995. "Law Meets the Market: Matches and Mismatches in Transition Economies." Background paper prepared for the *World Development Report*, World Bank, 1996.

Popkin, Margaret. 2000. *Peace Without Justice: Obstacles to Building the Rule of Law in El Salvador*. University Park: Pennsylvania State University Press.

Posner, Richard A. 1998. "Creating a Legal Framework for Economic Development." *Research Observer* 13:1–11.

———. 2001. *Frontiers of Legal Theory*. Cambridge, Mass.: Harvard University Press.

President's National Bipartisan Commission on Central America. 1984. *Report*. New York: Macmillan.

Prillaman, William C. 2000. *The Judiciary and Democratic Decay in Latin America*. Westport, Conn.: Praeger.

Provine, Doris Marie. 1996. "Courts in the Political Process in France." In *Courts, Law, and Politics in Comparative Perspective*, ed. Herbert Jacob, Erhard Blankenburg, Herbert Kritzer, Doris Marie Provine, and Joseph Sanders, 176–248. New Haven: Yale University Press.

Rabasca, Michael H. 1984. "Data Analysis Problems at the State Level: Data Problems and Data Collection." In *Proceedings of the Second Workshop on Law and Justice Statistics*, U.S. Department of Justice, Bureau of Justice Statistics, 46–49.

Ramasastry, Anita, Stefka Slavova, and Lieve Vandenhoeck. 2000. "EBRD Legal Indicator Survey: Assessing Solvency Laws after Ten Years of Transition." In *Law in Transition*, 34–43.

RAND Institute for Civil Justice. 1996. *Just, Speedy, and Inexpensive? An Evaluation of Judicial Case Management under the Civil Justice Reform Act*. Santa Monica, Calif.: RAND.

Renoux, Thierry S., ed. 1999. *Les conseils supérieurs de la magistrature en Europe*. Paris: La Documentation Française.

Rico, José María. 1993. *Los consejos de la magistratura: Análisis crítico y perspectivas para América Latina*. Miami: Center for Administration of Justice, Florida International University.

Riego, Cristián. 2002. *Informe comparativo*. Proyecto de Seguimiento de los Procesos de Reforma Judicial en América Latina. Santiago: Centro de Estudios de Justicia de la Américas.

Rivas, María Victoria. 2002. *Informe de Paraguay*. Proyecto de Seguimiento de los Procesos de Reforma Judicial en América Latina. Santiago: Centro de Estudios de Justicia de la Américas.

Rodycz, Wilson Carlos. 2001. "El juzgado especial y de pequeñas causas en la solución del problema del acceso a la justicia en el Brasil." Paper prepared for World Bank Conference, "New Approaches to Meeting the Demand for Justice," Mexico, May 11.

Rosenn, Keith S. 1998. "Judicial Reform in Brazil." NAFTA: *Law and Business Review of the Americas* 4 (2): 19–37.

Rubio, Luis, Beatriz Magaloni, Edna Jaime, and Hector Fix-Fierro, eds. 1994. *A la puerta de la ley*. Mexico City: Cal y Arena.

Rubio Correa, Marcial, and Enrique Bernales. 1988. *Constitución y sociedad política*. Lima: Mesa Redonda Editores.

Sachs, Jeffrey, and Katarina Pistor. 1997. *The Rule of Law and Economic Reform in Russia*. Cambridge, Mass.: Harvard University Press.

Sadek, Maria Tereza. 1995. "Institutional Fragility and Judicial Problems in Brazil." In *Growth and Development in Brazil: Cardoso's Real Challenge*, ed. Maria D'Alva Kinzo and Victor Bulmer-Thomas: 159–70. London: Institute of Latin American Studies, University of London.

———. 2004. "El poder judicial brasileiro." In *En busca de una justicia distinta: Experiencias de reforma en América Latina*, ed. Luís Pasara, 89–140. Lima: Consorcio Justicia Viva.

Sadek, Maria Tereza, org. 1995a. *Uma introdução ao estudo da justiça*. São Paulo: Editoria Sumaré.

———. 1995b. *O Judiciário em debate*. São Paulo: Editoria Sumaré.

———. 2000. *Justiça e cidadania no Brasil*. São Paulo: Editora Sumaré.

———. 2001a. *Acesso a justiça*. São Paulo: Konrad Adenauer Shiftung.

———. 2001b. *Reforma do Judiciário*. São Paulo: Konrad Adenauer Stiftung.

Sadek, Maria Tereza, Rogerio Bastos Arantes, and Armando Castelar Pinheiro. 2001. *Os juices e a reforma do Judiciario*. São Paulo: CETAC.

Sadek, Maria Tereza, and Rosângela Batista Calvalcanti. 2003. "The New Brazilian Public Prosecutor." In *Democratic Accountability in Latin America*, ed. Scott Mainwaring and Christopher Welna, 201–27. Oxford: Oxford University Press.

Saez Garcia, Felipe. 1998. "The Nature of Judicial Reform in Latin America and Some Strategic Considerations." *American University International Law Review* 13 (5): 1267–325.

———. 2002. "The Judiciary." In *Colombia: The Economic Foundation of Peace*, ed. Marcelo M. Giugale, Olivier Lafouracade, and Connie Luff, 897–930. Washington, D.C.: World Bank.

Sajó, András, ed. 2004. *Judicial Integrity*. Leiden: Martines Nijhoff.

Salas, Luis. 2001. "From Law and Development to Rule of Law: New and Old Issues in Justice Reform in Latin America." In *Rule of Law in Latin America: The International Promotion of Judicial Reform*, ed. Pilar Domingo and Rachel Sieder, 17–46. London: Institute of Latin American Studies, University of London.

Santiago H., Alfonso. 2003. *Grandezas y miserias en la vida judicial: El mal desempeño como causal de remoción de los magistrados judiciales*. Buenos Aires: El Derecho.

Santiso, Carlos. 2001. "Democratic Governance and Second Generation Economic Reforms in Latin America." *Revista Instituciones y Desarrollo* 8 (9): 325–66.

———. 2003. "Economic Reform and Judicial Governance in Brazil: Balancing Independence with Accountability." *Democratization* 10 (4): 161–80.

Santofimio G., Jaime Orlando. 1996. *Tratado de Derecho Administrativo.* Bogotá: Universidad Externado de Colombia.

Schwartz, Herman. 2000. *The Struggle for Constitutional Justice in Post-Communist Europe.* Chicago: University of Chicago Press.

Scott, James C. 1998. *Seeing Like a State: How Certain Schemes to Improve the Human Condition Have Failed.* New Haven: Yale University Press.

Shapiro, Martin. 1981. *Courts: A Comparative and Political Analysis.* Chicago: University of Chicago Press.

Shavell, Steven. 1997. "The Fundamental Divergence between the Private and the Social Motive to Use the Legal System." *Journal of Legal Studies* 26 (2): 575–61.

Sheldon, Charles H., and Nicholas P. Lovrich Jr. 1991. "State Judicial Recruitment." In *The American Courts: A Critical Assessment,* ed. John B. Gates and Charles A. Johnson, 161–88. Washington, D.C.: Congressional Quarterly.

Sherwood, Robert M., Geoffrey Shepherd, and Celso Marcos de Souza. 1994. "Judicial Systems and Economic Performance." *Quarterly Review of Economics and Finance* 34 (special issue): 101–16.

Shihata, I. F. I. 1991. "Issues of 'Governance' in Borrowing Members: The Extent of Their Relevance under the Bank's Articles of Agreement," February 5.

Siebrasse, Norman. 1997. *A Review of Secured Lending Theory.* Washington, D.C.: World Bank, PRMPS.

Sieder, Rachel. 2002. "Recognizing Indigenous Law and the Politics of State Formation in Mesoamerica." In *Multiculturalism in Latin America: Indigenous Rights, Diversity, and Democracy,* ed. Rachel Sieder, 184–207. London: Institute of Latin American Studies, University of London.

Sierra, Maria Teresa. 1995. "Indian Rights and Customary Law in Mexico: A Study of the Najas in the Sierra of Puebla." *Law and Society* 29 (2): 227–54.

Simon, Farith, Jacqueline Vásquez, Jorge Arroba, Fabián Múñoz, Javier Andrade, and Lorena Cascante. 2002. *Informe final de la investigación sobre el uso de la justicia civil en el Ecuador.* Quito: Fundación Esquel. Report prepared for the World Bank, December 9.

Smith, Gordon B. 1996. *Reforming the Russian Legal System.* Cambridge: Cambridge University Press.

Solomon, Maureen, and Douglas K. Somerlot. 1987. *Caseflow Management in the Trial Court: Now and for the Future.* Chicago: American Bar Association.

Solomon, Peter H. 2004. "Judicial Power in Russia: Through the Prism of Administrative Justice." *Law and Society Review* 38 (3): 549–82.

Sousa Santos, Boaventura de, Maria Manuel Leitão Marques, João Pedroso, and Pedro Lopes Ferreira. 1996. *Os Tribunais nas sociedades contemporâneas: O caso português.* Lisbon: Edições Alfrontamento.

Sousa Santos, Boaventura de, and Maurico García Villegas, ed. 2001. *El caleidoscopio de las justicias en Colombia: Análisis socio-jurídico.* Bogotá: Siglo de Hombre Editores and Universidad de los Andes.

Spain, Consejo General del Poder Judicial. 1999. *Memoria.* Madrid.

Special Commission on the Administration of Justice in Cook County. 1998. *Final Report.* September. Chicago: Circuit Court of Cook County.

Spence, Jack, and George Vickers. 1994. *A Negotiated Revolution? A Two-Year Progress Report on the Salvadoran Peace Accords.* Cambridge, Mass.: Hemispheric Initiatives.

Spence, Jack, George Vickers, and David Dye. 1995. *The Salvadoran Peace Accords and Democratization: A Three-Year Progress Report and Recommendations.* Cambridge, Mass.: Hemispheric Initiatives.

Stand Lund, Eilert. 2003. "Access to Justice: Case Flow Management." Paper presented at

11th International Judicial Conference, "Courts of Ultimate Appeal XI: Issues of Judicial Independence," Washington, D.C., May 21–23.

Stanga, Silvana. 1996. *El saber de la justicia.* Buenos Aires: Fundación de la Ley.

Stavenhagen, Rodolfo. 2002. "Indigenous Peoples and the State in Latin America." In *Multiculturalism in Latin America: Indigenous Rights, Diversity, and Democracy,* ed. Rachel Sieder, 24–44. London: Institute of Latin American Studies, University of London.

Stepán, Jan. 1994. "Possible Lessons from Continental Criminal Procedure." In *The Economics of Crime and Punishment.* Washington, D.C.: American Enterprise Institute.

Stone, Andrew, Brian Levy, and Ricardo Paredes. 1996. "Public Institutions and Private Transactions: A Comparative Analysis of the Legal and Regulatory Environment for Business Transactions in Brazil and Chile." In *Empirical Studies in Institutional Change,* ed. Lee J. Alston, Thrainn Eggertsson, and Douglass North, 95–128. Cambridge: Cambridge University Press.

Strier, Franklin. 1996. *Restructuring Justice: An Agenda for Trial Court Reform.* Chicago: University of Chicago Press.

Sunstein, Cass, ed. 2000. *Behavioral Law and Economics.* Cambridge: Cambridge University Press.

Sunstein, Cass, Reid Hastie, John W. Payne, David A. Schkade, and W. Kip Viscusi. 2002. *Punitive Damages: How Juries Decide.* Chicago: University of Chicago Press.

Tate, C. Neal, and Torbjorn Vallinder, eds. 1995. *The Global Expansion of Judicial Power.* New York: New York University Press.

Taylor, Matthew. 2004. "Activating Judges: Courts, Institutional Structure, and the Judicialization of Policy Reform in Brazil, 1988–2002." Ph.D. dissertation, Georgetown University.

Thome, Joseph. 1992. "Administration of Justice in Latin America: A Survey of AID Funded Programs in Argentina and Uruguay." Arlington, Va.: Development Associates.

———. 1998. "Searching for Democracy: The Rule of Law and the Process of Legal Reform in Latin America." Unpublished paper prepared for Workshop on "Reforma judicial, motivaciones, proyectos, caminos recorridos, caminos por recorrer," Instituto Internacional de Sociología Jurídica, Oñati, Gipuzkoa, Spain, April 6–7 (http://darkwing. uoregon.edu/caguirre/lawandsociety.htm; April 2002).

Tobin, Robert W. 1999. *Creating the Judicial Branch: The Unfinished Reform.* Williamsburg, Va.: National Center for State Courts.

Toharia, José Juan. 1999. "La independencia judicial y la buena justicia." Manuscript based on a paper presented at the Workshop, "El juez ante el siglo XXI: Etica y función judicial," Spanish Judicial School, May 18–21.

———. 2003. "Assessing a Judiciary's Performance through Public Opinion." In *Beyond Common Knowledge: Empirical Approaches to the Rule of Law,* ed. Erik Jensen and Thomas Heller, 21–62. Stanford: Stanford University Press.

Trochev, Alexi. 2004. "Less Democracy, More Courts: A Puzzle of Judicial Review in Russia." *Law and Society Review* 38 (3): 513–48.

Tshuma, Lawrence. 2000. "The Political Economy of the World Bank's Legal Framework." In *Governance, Development, and Globalization,* ed. Julio Faundez, Mary E. Footer, and Joseph J. Norton, 7–27. London: Blackstone Press.

Turcey, Valery. 1997. *Le prince et ses juges.* Paris: Plon.

Twohig, John, Carl Baar, Anna Myers, and Anne Marie Predko. 1998. "Empirical Analyses of Civil Cases Commenced and Cases Tried in Toronto, 1973–1994." In *Rethinking Civil Justice: Research Studies for the Civil Justice Review,* Ontario Law Reform Commission, 77–181. Ontario, Canada.

Ungar, Mark. 2002. *Elusive Reform: Democracy and the Rule of Law in Latin America.* Boulder, Colo.: Lynne Reinner.

United Nations, Economic and Social Council, Commission on Human Rights. 2002. "Civil and Political Rights, Including Questions of: Independence of the Judiciary, Administration of Justice, Impunity." Report of the Special Rapporteur on the independence of judges and lawyers, Dato'Param Cumaraswamy, Addendum: Report on the mission to Mexico. E/CN 4/2002/7 2/Add1, January 24.

United States General Accounting/Accountability Office (GAO). 1992. "Foreign Assistance: Police Training and Assistance." (GAO/NSIAD-92-118).

———. 1993. "Foreign Assistance: Promoting Judicial Reform to Strengthen Democracies." (GAO/NSIAD-93-194).

———. 1997. "Foreign Assistance: Harvard Institute for International Development's Work in Russia and Ukraine." (GAO/NSIAD-97-27).

———. 2000. "Foreign Assistance: Any Further Aid to Haitian Justice System Should Be Linked to Performance-Related Conditions." (GAO-01-24).

United States Agency for International Development (USAID). 1998. *Handbook of Democracy and Governance Program Indicators.* Washington, D.C., USAID Center for Democracy and Governance.

———. 2000. *Foreign Aid in the National Interest: Promoting Freedom, Security, and Opportunity.* Washington, D.C.: USAID.

———. 2001. *Case Tracking and Management Guide.* Washington, D.C.: USAID Center for Democracy and Governance, Technical Publication Series.

———. 2002a. *Achievements in Building and Maintaining the Rule of Law: MSI's Studies in LAC, E and E, AFR, and ANE.* Washington, D.C.: USAID Office of Democracy and Governance, Occasional Papers Series, no. PN-ACR-220, November.

———. 2002b. *Guidance for Promoting Judicial Independence and Impartiality.* Washington, D.C.: USAID Office of Democracy and Governance, Technical Publication PN-ACM-003, November.

Uprimny, Rodrigo. n.d. "Legitimidad y conveniencia del control constitucional a la economía." *Revista de Derecho Público* (Universidad de los Andes, Bogotá) 12: 145–83.

Valenzuela, Eugenio S., ed. 1991. *Proposiciones para la reforma judicial.* Santiago: Centro de Estudios Publicos.

Van Cott, Dona Lee. 2002. "Constitutional Reform in the Andes: Redefining Indigenous-State Relations. In *Multiculturalism in Latin America: Indigenous Rights, Diversity, and Democracy,* ed. Rachel Sieder, 24–44. London: Institute of Latin American Studies, University of London.

Varela, David, and Veena Mayani (2000), "The Dominican Republic: A First Statistical Analysis of the Justice Sector." Working paper. Washington, D.C.: World Bank.

Vargas, Adrián. 2005. "La pesificación, sin definer." *La Nación* (Buenos Aires), December 12: 10.

Vargas, Juan Enrique. 1999. *Recursos destinados a la justicia en Chile: Análisis de su evolución y productividad.* Chile: Centro de Investigaciones Jurídicas, Facultad de Derecho, Universidad Diego Portales, Informes de Investigación, 3 (1), July.

———. 2003. "Eficiencia en la justicia." *Sistemas Judiciales* 3 (6): 68–92.

———, ed. 2005. *Reformas procesales penales en América Latina: Resultados del proyecto de seguimiento.* Santiago: CEJA.

Vargas, Juan Enrique, and Jorge Correa. 1995. *Diagnóstico del sistema judicial Chileno.* Santiago, Centro de Desarrollo Jurídico Judicial. Corporación de Promoción Universitaria.

Vargas, Juan Enrique, Jorge Correa, and Carlos Pena. 1998. *Poder judicial, acción de los privados y de las agencias públicas, informe final.* Santiago: Universidad Diego Portales.

———. 2001. "El rol del estado y el mercado en la justicia." Santiago: Universidad Diego Portales, *Cuadernos de Análisis Jurídico,* no. 42.

Verbitsky, Horacio. 1993. *Hacer la corte: La construcción de un poder absoluto sin justicia ni control*. Buenos Aires: Planeta.

Walsh, Catherine. 1997. *Secured Credit: A Review of Selected Foreign and Comparative Law Sources*. Washington, D.C.: World Bank, PRMPS.

Washington Office on Latin America (WOLA). 1990. "The Administration of Justice Program in Latin America." Washington, D.C.: WOLA.

Watanabe, Kazuo, org. 1986. *Juizado especial de pequenas causas*. São Paulo: Editora Revista dos Tribunais.

Webb, Douglas. 1996. "Legal System Reform and Private Sector Development in Developing Countries." In *Economic Development, Foreign Investment, and the Law*, ed. Robert Pritchard, 45–65. Boston: Cluwer Law International.

Weber, Daniel. 2006. "Quase ninguém perde o emprego," *O Globo* (Rio de Janeiro), February 16: 3.

Werneck Viana Luiz, org. 2002. *A democracia e os três poderes no Brasil*. Belo Horizonte and Rio de Janeiro: Editora UFMG and IUPERJ/FAPERJ.

West, Andrew, Yvon Desdevise, Alain Fenet, and Marie C. Heussaff. 1992. *The French Legal System*. London: Todley.

Wildavsky, Aaron, and Jeffrey Pressman. 1973. *Implementation*. Berkeley and Los Angeles: University of California Press.

Williams, Jackson. 2002. "What the Growing Use of Pre-dispute Binding Arbitration Means for the Judiciary," *Judicature* 85 (6): 266–67.

Wilson, Bruce M., Juan Carlos Rodríguez Cordero, and Roger Handberg. 2004. "The Best Laid Schemes . . . Gang Aft A-gley: Judicial Reform in Latin America: Evidence from Costa Rica." *Journal of Latin American Studies* 36 (3): 507–32.

Wollschlager, Christian J. 1990. "Civil Litigation and Modernization: The Work of the Municipal Courts of Bremen, Germany, in Five Centuries, 1540–1984," *Law and Society Review* 24 (2): 261–81.

———. 1998. "Historical Civil Litigation Rates: An International Perspective." In *Examining the Work of State Courts, 1996: A National Perspective from the Court Statistics Project*, ed. Brian J. Ostrom and Neal B. Kauder, 15–17. Williamsburg, Va.: National Institute for State Courts.

Woodson, Roderic L. 1998. Memorandum to Richard Messick, World Bank, on Techniques of Judicial Evaluation.

Woolf, The Right Honourable Lord. 1996. *Access to Justice: Final Report to the Lord Chancellor's Office on the Civil Justice System in England and Wales*. London: Her Majesty's Stationery Office.

World Bank. 2001a. *Anti-Corruption Diagnostic for Argentina: An Overview of Three Reports and Recommendations*, Report no. 20133-AR. Washington, D.C.: World Bank.

———. 2001b. *Bolivia: From Patronage to a Professional State. Bolivia Institutional and Governance Review*, Report no. 20115-B, vol. 2. Washington, D.C.: World Bank.

———. 2002a. "Brazil: Insolvency and Creditor Rights Systems." Final report on the Observance of Standards and Codes (ROSC). November. Manuscript.

———. 2002b. *The Juicio Ejecutivo Mercantil in the Federal District Courts of Mexico: A Study of the Uses and Users of Justice and Their Implications for Judicial Reform*, Report no. 22635-ME. Washington, D.C.: World Bank.

———. 2003a. *An Analysis of Court Users and Uses in Two Latin American Countries*, Report no. 26966. Washington, D.C.: World Bank.

———. 2003b. *Brazil: Judicial Performance and Private Sector Impacts*, Report no. 26261-BR. Washington, D.C.: World Bank.

————. 2004. *Brazil: Access to Financial Services*, Report no. 27773-BR. Washington, D.C.: World Bank.

————. 2005a. *Breaking with Tradition: Overcoming Institutional Impediments to Improve Public Sector Performance*, Report no. 31763-PY. Washington, D.C.: World Bank.

————. 2005b. *Doing Business in 2005: Removing Obstacles to Growth*. Washington, D.C.: World Bank, International Finance Corporation, and Oxford University Press.

————. 2005c. *Making Justice Count: Measuring and Improving Judicial Performance in Brazil*, Report no. 32789-BR. Washington, D.C.: World Bank.

World Bank, Legal Vice Presidency. 2002. *Legal and Judicial Reform: Observations, Experiences, and Approach of the Legal Vice Presidency*. Washington, D.C.: World Bank.

————. 2003a. *Ecuador Judicial Assessment*. Washington, D.C.: World Bank.

————.2003b. *Impact of Legal Aid: Ecuador*. Washington, D.C.: World Bank.

World Bank, World Bank Institute. 1997. *World Development Report 1997: The State in a Changing World*. Washington, D.C.: World Bank.

————. 2002. *World Development Report 2002: Building Institutions for the Market*. Washington, D.C.: World Bank.

Younes Moreno, Diego, and María Aurora Mejía Novoa. 2003. "Descongestión de la jurisdicción contencioso administrativa y, en particular en el Consejo de Estado." Bogotá: Proyecto Colombo-Alemán de Cooperación Técnica, GTZ, Reformas en la Rama Judicial. Manuscript.

Yrigoyen Fajardo, Raquel. 2002. "Peru: Pluralist Constitution, Monist Judiciary: A Post-Reform Assessment." In *Multiculturalism in Latin America: Indigenous Rights, Diversity, and Democracy*, ed. Rachel Sieder, 208–26. London: Institute of Latin American Studies, University of London.

Zepeda, Guillermo. 2000. *Transformación agraria: Los derechos de propiedad en el campo mexicano bajo el nuevo marco institucional*. Mexico City: CIDAC.

Zuckerman, Adrian, ed. 1999. *Civil Justice in Crisis: Comparative Perspectives of Civil Procedure*. Oxford: Oxford Unversity Press.

INDEX